James K. Polk
1845-1849

Zachary Taylor
1849-1850

Millard Fillmore
1850-1853

Franklin Pierce
1853-1857

James Buchanan
1857-1861

Abraham Lincoln
1861-1865

Andrew Johnson
1865-1869

Ulysses S. Grant
1869-1877

Rutherford B. Hayes
1877-1881

James A. Garfield
1881

DATE			

THE
• PUGNACIOUS
• • PRESIDENTS

THE
• PUGNACIOUS
• • PRESIDENTS

White House Warriors on Parade

by
Thomas A. Bailey

THE FREE PRESS
A Division of Macmillan Publishing Co., Inc.
NEW YORK
Collier Macmillan Publishers
LONDON

The Free Press
A Division of Macmillan Publishing Co., Inc.
866 Third Avenue, New York, N. Y. 10022

Collier Macmillan Canada, Ltd.

Library of Congress Catalog Card Number: 80-1646

Printed in the United States of America

printing number
1 2 3 4 5 6 7 8 9 10

Library of Congress Cataloging in Publication Data

Bailey, Thomas Andrew
The Pugnacious Presidents.

Bibliography: p.
Includes index.
1. Presidents—United States. 2. United States—History, Military. I. Title.
E176.1.B175 973'.009'92 80-1646
ISBN 0-02-901220-1

CONTENTS

PREFACE

In the folklore of politics, we often hear that the Democrats are the party of war and the Republicans are the party of depression. But because wars and depressions have come unwanted under both parties, the conclusion seems tenable that circumstances over which the incumbent President had little or no control have contributed largely to these disagreeable intrusions. I have therefore undertaken a President-by-President analysis of each incumbent's militancy or combativeness and have permitted the evidence to point to my conclusions.

For more than a century, the inexorable operation of the business cycle has brought a major panic about every twenty years, bedeviling, for example, the Democratic Cleveland in 1893–1897 and the Republican Hoover in 1929–1933. The Spanish-American War came under the Republican McKinley in 1898, and World War I under the Democratic Woodrow Wilson in 1917. Ironically, the bloodiest war in American experience, costing about as many lives as all of the rest combined, flared forth in 1861 under a kindly Republican, Abraham Lincoln. The evidence herein presented will surprise many, distress some, and gratify still others.

For a critical reading of the manuscript, I am indebted to my esteemed colleague, Professor Don E. Fehrenbacher, and to Captain Paul B. Ryan, my collaborator on *The Lusitania Disaster* (1975) and *Hitler vs. Roosevelt* (1979).

Thomas A. Bailey
Stanford University
Stanford, California

tary despot. In his youthful days he had been "charmed" by the whistle of bullets, but he got over that delusion during Braddock's defeat in 1755, when four bullets passed harmlessly through his coat and others killed two horses under him. His frustrating experiences as Commmander-in-Chief during the War of Independence, especially with poorly trained and deserting troops, were enough to make him preeminently a man of peace.

Yet Washington did not spend the rest of his life, as he had hoped, in the peace and quiet of Mount Vernon. He viewed with alarm the disorders that erupted in the wake of the American revolution, notably Captain Daniel Shays's armed rebellion in 1786 against injustices in Massachusetts. Perhaps the big revolution would break up into a batch of smaller ones, like some giant monster coming apart in its death agonies.

Washington played an active role in the move to strengthen the feeble government under the Articles of Confederation and served as a member of the Virginia delegation to the immortal constitutional convention that met in Philadelphia to draw up the present long-lived Constitution. He was overwhelmingly named presiding officer of that conclave, and his very presence enlisted support for the new charter among nervous citizens who had feared the creation of a monarchy or a dictatorship.

Washington remembered his frustrating experiences with the old Continental Congress, and he must have been pleased with those provisions of the new constitution that strengthened the hands of the Chief Executive. He was to be Commander-in-Chief of the armed forces of the United States, and the Congress was empowered "to raise and support armies," "to provide and maintain a navy," and to call forth "the militia to execute the laws of the union, suppress insurrections, and repel invasions." Gone were the days when Washington in the field had to plead in vain with an inept Congress to keep his men armed, fed, clothed, shod, and paid.

Red Men and Red Tomahawks

When Washington was inaugurated President in 1789, the Indians were continuing to ravage the frontier, most bloodily northwest of the Ohio River, in present Ohio and Indiana. The red men had fought on the side of the British during the Revolutionary War, most conspicuously against George Rogers Clark in his memorable campaign in the Old Northwest. The Indians had also taken to the warpath in the Southwest, notably west of settled Georgia. Here the Creeks and the Cherokees were most actively involved, supplied as they were with firearms and firewater by the Spaniards in Florida or in the Louisiana area.

From one point of view, Washington's campaigns against the Indians were a kind of civil war and not foreign wars in the conventional sense. But this notion can be overstressed. Until 1871 the United States government, regarding the Indians as independent entities, negotiated and duly ratified scores of treaties with them as foreign nations, with the advice and consent of the Senate. The natives involved were technically transformed into foreigners within their own country. In frequent messages to Congress, President Washington referred to the Indian "nations" and specifically to the "Six Nations" of the Iroquois tribes. To the dismay of the red men, many of these treaties were ultimately violated by the grasping white men, and to some extent by the natives themselves.

There was another reason why the Indian campaigns of Washington in the Northwest were foreign. First, these warring

President-elect Washington, en route to New York to be inaugurated, honored in New Jersey. Library of Congress.

Indians had been allies of the British Redcoats during the War of Independence, during which the red warriors had ravaged the frontier, particularly that of Kentucky, and they continued on the warpath as surrogates of the British. For them the peace treaty of 1783 bound only the signatories, Great Britain and the United States. To the British themselves the pact meant little more than parchment. The London government, alleging that the United States had not carried out the terms of the treaty, announced an unwillingness to honor its commitment until the Americans honored theirs.

The British were quite correct in charging that the Americans had not observed the letter and spirit of the peace treaty of 1783. The ex-colonials had failed to pay off the prewar debts owing British merchants, and had not ended persecutions of the Loyalists who had remained faithful to George III. The British had a valid grievance here, but to many Americans these complaints seemed more like pretexts than reasons.

In retaliation for noncompliance, the British continued to occupy a string of seven fortified trading posts on American soil, ranging from north of Lake Champlain (Dutchman's Point) on the east to Michilimackinac (in present Michigan), on the west. In between were such well-known outposts as Niagara and Detroit. Through these bustling centers the lucrative fur trade of the Indians was funneled to shipping points in Canada, notably Montreal, and British merchants naturally wanted to retain this business there as long as possible.

Yet the Indian problem probably concerned British officialdom more than the fur trade. The blunt truth is that the hard-pressed British had been so eager to negotiate a peace treaty with the United States at Paris in 1783 that they had overlooked the interests of their painted allies. Perhaps in revenge the luckless Indians would attack the British outposts, in the manner of Pontiac's rebellion in 1763–1764. Still, these red allies might be used to check or contain the explosive expansion of the westward-moving American pioneers. In this way the Canadian frontier could be safeguarded for years to come.

So it was that the British held on to the seven American posts on American soil, flying the Union Jack in the American breeze over American terrain. All the while these intruders were encouraging the red men to believe that the Great White Father with a red coat in London would return if they only stood their ground. Along with such incitement, and in exchange for furs, the British provided generous supplies of firearms, firewater, gunpowder, and scalping knives.

Thus the British would use their allies of the recent war to continue fighting the Americans during the nominal peace. Perhaps an Indian buffer state, designed to protect semi-defenseless Canada from the grasping Yankees, would one day be formed. This, in fact, was a concept that London continued to entertain seriously for about twenty years. When President George Washington took office, the British made no official announcement of their support of these Indian allies, but the repeated burnings, killings, and scalpings on the frontier spoke louder than words.

Also ominously, the informal British–Indian alliance in the Northwest was paralleled by the informal Spanish–Indian alliance in the Southwest. Spain had fought in the coalition against Britain while the United States was fighting the British for independence, but the Spaniards were never formal allies of the Americans. Among other obstacles, an independent and democratic United States might set a dangerous example for the restive inhabitants of Spain's vast Latin American empire, as indeed proved to be the case. If the British were worried about ax-wielding American pioneers moving in on Canada, the Spaniards were even more worried about long-rifled American frontiersmen swarming across the Mississippi into Spain's enormous Louisiana area. They might even turn south toward Spanish Florida or, worst of all, New Orleans, which commanded the mouth of the mighty Mississippi.

Thus, like the British to the north, the Spaniards were trying to stem the westward-flooding American pioneers by enlisting the tomahawks of the Indians, in this case the Indians of the Southwest. Conspicuous among the tribes cooperating with Spain were the Creeks, generously supplied with arms and other necessities from Spanish Florida and New Orleans. Through Indian surrogates, the British and Spaniards between them thus exercised some control over much of the American territory beyond the Alleghenies. This expanse involved roughly half of the territory claimed by the United States under the Treaty of 1783 with Britain. As a consequence, the sprawling but weak new nation could not exercise full sovereignty over the bulk of its trans-Allegheny birthright.

Battling Britain's Indian Allies

After the "New Roof" constitution was duly ratified by the required nine states, Washington was elected President by unanimous vote of the Electoral College in 1789. He proved to be the first, last, and only Chief Executive to be so honored. In truth, the Constitution might have been rejected if the assumption had not been widespread that Washington would consent to serve as the first President. That document conferred enormous powers on one man, who might turn out to have dictatorial ambitions. But George Washington could be trusted, for he had already spurned a dictatorship.

If Washington had looked forward with some satisfaction to being Commander-in-Chief of adequate armed forces, he must have been grievously disappointed. His three-man Cabinet comprised Alexander Hamilton (Treasury), Thomas Jefferson (State), and the corpulent Secretary of War Henry Knox, who had inherited a minuscule army of 672 officers and men. Knox was also entrusted with management of the navy, but there had not been a single warship under the new American flag since 1785. If Washington had been determined to make war, he would have had to improvise the weapons with which to wage it.

America's glaring military and naval weakness under the old Articles of Confederation (1781–1789) had been one of the major reasons for hammering out a new government that could uphold the dignity and honor of the United States. Without a navy Washington could do nothing about the depredations of the Barbary pirates in the Mediterranean; he could only continue to pay protection money and ranson American seamen and others thrown into vile dungeons. But with the Northwest Indians he could do something—and did. Lest one conclude that he was athirst for war, one should remember that Washington inherited this death struggle on the frontier; it had been going on bloodily for a dozen years before he became the presidential Commander-in-Chief. In a sense, the War of Independence from Britain had really never ended.

President Washington had no particular fondness for the Indians. In his early years he had fought them, and he recognized that a continuing clash between the land-hungry whites and the landholding Indians was inevitable, North, South, and West. He also knew that in many instances lawless whites had started the butchering on all fronts. On December 15, 1792, he issued a presidential proclamation offering a reward of $500 for the arrest and conviction of any of the "lawless and wicked persons" in the Georgia area who had burned and destroyed a town of "the Cherokee Nation" while killing several Indians "in amity with the United States."

The Northwest Indian "nations" presented a more pressing problem, for there the British were dishonoring the Treaty of 1783 by lingering at their fortified posts and encouraging the red men to butcher the intruding American pioneers. The hand that dispensed the firewater indeed ruled the tomahawk. Washington had taken a constitutional oath to "preserve, protect, and defend" the Constitution, including its citizens, and this Western area legally belonged to the United States. Washington, the slaveholder, was ever a slave to duty.

Washington entrusted General Josiah Harmar with the first punitive expedition. With a small army of regulars and ill-trained militia, totaling about 1,500 men, the general set off full of hope in the autumn of 1790. The militia proceeded to fall into a bloody ambush and were forced to retreat, leaving the Ohio frontier open to Indian torches and scalping knives.

The second expedition, commanded by General St. Clair, numbered about 3,000 men, mostly militia. Also poorly trained, this army was surprised in November 1791, losing about one-third of its number in killed and wounded before the survivors fled to safety. It was the bloodiest rout at the hands of the Indians since Braddock's defeat in 1755. Washington was greatly upset, while the British and confederated Indians gained renewed faith in the likelihood of an Indian buffer state to hold back the westward-flowing tide of pioneers. The British were so greatly heartened that they erected a new log fort, Fort Miami, some sixty miles southwest of Detroit. Detroit was already on American soil, and this new invasion with armed forces of sovereign American territory was plainly an act of war by Great Britain.

Washington had no choice but to fight back a third time. With some misgivings he entrusted command of the new army to General Anthony Wayne, popularly known as "Mad Anthony" for his daring exploits during the Revolutionary War. Belying his nickname, Wayne trained his force with extreme care, advanced with all necessary precautions, and in 1794 crushed the Indians at Fallen Timbers, a tangled mass of trees laid low by a tornado. Victorious American troops chased their red foes to the walls of Fort Miami, from which had come some thirty white Canadian volunteers to join in the battle. (The bodies of three of them were found on the tangled battlefield.) The British had lighted the matches with which to discharge their cannon, but fortunately for peace no shooting occurred, and the elated Americans withdrew. Seldom in history had a possible shooting war been averted by so narrow a margin.

This single victory by a "mad" general had a widespread ripple effect. The beaten Indians buried the tomahawk and signed the Treaty of Greenville (at Fort Greenville), thus formally yielding about 25,000 square miles of the Ohio country. The British in Canada temporarily abandoned their dream of the Indian buffer state and further acknowledged the unreality of this scheme by evacuating the seven American posts, pursuant to the terms of John Jay's treaty. This epochal pact had been negotiated in London in 1795, while "Mad Anthony" Wayne was pushing toward the battlefield of Fallen Timbers.

The Whiskey War

While General Wayne was routing the Northwest Indians, Washington became personally involved in a decisive campaign employing a much larger army, this time against the whiskey rebels of western Pennsylvania.

An excise tax, favored by Secretary of the Treasury Alexander Hamilton, had been enacted in 1791 by the new federal Congress. Although affecting in some way various parts of the country, it seemed outrageously inequitable to the distillers of western Pennsylvania. To transport their bulky grain on horseback over the mountains was far less profitable than condensing it into whiskey, which was swilled on the Western frontier. As a result, the "Whiskey Boys" terrorized federal officials, robbed the mail, and closed the courts. The question was basically one of law and order: Should the mob rule or the duly constituted new federal government?

Secretary Hamilton was eager to teach these mutinous moonshiners a harsh lesson, and Washington's Cabinet voted to crack down on the dissenting distillers. State militia to the number of about 15,000 men were summoned from Virginia, Maryland, and Pennsylvania, roughly six times the force being led by

General Wayne against the Indians. Washington, as chief commander, rode in the presidential coach with this formidable force a part of the way. When the invading troops arrived in distillery country, the resistance had evaporated. A score or so of the "Whiskey Boys" were seized, and two small-fry culprits were tried and found guilty of high treason. They were pardoned by President Washington, who felt that they had learned their bitter lesson without the need for hanging.

George Washington was not a dictator or even a militarist, and he could not have enjoyed this extravagant parade of power. But the very foundations of the new government were being shaken, and he had felt duty bound to overawe the rebels. He would thus discourage future outbursts, while demonstrating that the new government was not yielding to mob rule. And he succeeded completely by resorting to overkill.

Washington's employment of the militia against the Whiskey rebels focuses attention on his attitude toward these new troops. When he called upon the states for assistance, he had reason to fear that there would be a dismaying response, especially from Pennsylvania, whose citizens presumably would not relish shooting fellow citizens in revolt against high taxes. He was agreeably surprised by the large turnout. If only a few hundred militia had marched into western Pennsylvania, they would probably have encountered considerable resistance, especially of the guerrilla variety. But if 15,000 armed men marched, the populace would be intimidated, and there would be no resistance. This is precisely what happened.

Washington could not have particularly admired the militiamen or have preferred them to disciplined regulars. His private correspondence during the Revolutionary War abounds with references to the unreliability of the militia—their indiscipline, cowardice, and lack of patriotism. But he also was well aware of the strong opposition that had been voiced against the creation of a standing army during the recent struggle over the new constitution. The prospect of such a body of troops rekindled popular resentment against the Redcoats and British tyranny, as well as fears of the dictatorial man on horseback. In his various messages to Congress, Washington had not urged the creation of a large standing army, or even a small standing army, but had sought the improvement of the militia, who "may be trained to a degree of energy equal to every military exigency of the United States."

The Pro-French Frenzy

While President Washington was still involved with the Indians and British in the Northwest, the French Revolution erupted with the fall of the Bastille on July 14, 1789, two and one half months after his inauguration. Many American citizens still felt gratitude for French support during the recent War for Independence, and they applauded the gains for republicanism that were expected to flow from this second chapter of America's own war against tyranny. Not only is imitation the sincerest form of flattery, but also the French were still nominal allies of the United States under the lifesaving alliance of 1778.

But the revolution took an ugly turn early in 1793, when Louis XVI was guillotined and France declared war on Great Britain and Holland on February 1. The First Coalition against France was formed on February 13, consisting of Britain, Austria, Prussia, Holland, Spain, and Sardinia. The Reign of Terror quickly followed in France, as monarchical heads, including the head of the Queen, rolled monotonously into the executioners' baskets. In America the Democratic-Republicans, with Thomas Jefferson their stellar leader, rejoiced over these epochal gains for liberty and democracy. The Federalists, with Alexander Hamilton their ablest champion, deplored the grievous setback for law and order. For them one revolution in a generation—their own—was quite enough.

The ominous news of the French declaration of war on Britain arrived on American shores early in April 1793. Washington consulted his three-man Cabinet, particularly Jefferson and Hamilton. Though in disagreement on many other issues, the two rivals finally agreed that a proclamation of neutrality was the wisest possible course. Washington duly issued the memorable document that enjoined all loyal and law-abiding American citizens to remain on the sidelines in the developing conflict.

Such a declaration of neutrality clashed head on with the existing Franco-American treaty of alliance of 1778, which the Americans had initially been most eager to sign. By its specific terms the United States was to help France defend her sugar-rich West Indian islands, not for a term of years but "forever." Now that America had gained what she wanted from the alliance, namely her independence, the French compact was a dead albatross hung around her neck. But the question of dishonoring or honoring it disappeared when the Paris government did not demand compliance. In this case weakness was a virtue, for the United States had no navy with which to defend the French islands. But she did have a merchant fleet with which to feed them by running a British blockade. From the point of view of the French, the Americans were more valuable as fattening feeders than as futile fighters.

As luck would have it, Citizen Edmond Genêt arrived as the first Minister from the new French republic on April 8, 1793, two weeks before Washington issued his timely Neutrality Proclamation. The Frenchman landed at Charleston, South Carolina, and promptly engaged in fitting out French privateers, an act objectionable to the British. His leisurely journey up the coast was such a triumphal procession that it completely turned his head, a giddy head to begin with. He gained the impression that the pro-French American people did not approve of Washington's Neutrality Proclamation but were on fire to plunge into the war on the side of their beloved French ally.

After arriving in Washington, Genêt busied himself with fitting out privateers in American ports, as he supposed he was entitled to do under the treaty of alliance. But he was notified that the obligations of neutrality prevented him from sheltering French privateers in American waters or permitting them to send their prizes to American ports. He entered into schemes for enlisting the aid of disaffected American frontiersmen, including George Rogers Clark, for attacks on British outposts and also southward attacks against Spanish territory, including New Orleans. Spain, as we have noted, was then enrolled in the ranks of France's enemies.

Citizen Genêt, misled by the plaudits of the Jeffersonian Republicans, bent the bow too far when he threatened to appeal over the head of "old Washington" to the sovereign masses. The President forthrightly demanded the recall of the bungling diplomat but did not deport him to France for possible execution. Genêt faded from history when he wooed and won the daughter of the Governor of New York, with whom he faced the altar instead of the guillotine.

The Jay Treaty Uproar

In June and November of 1793, overlapping Genêt's strange doings, the London government ordered the seizure of neutral ships transporting provisions to France or produce from the French West Indies. Some of this commerce was carried on under color of the British-spawned Rule of 1756 (Seven Years' War); it stipulated that trade closed to foreign nations in time of peace, such as that with the French colonies, could not be thrown open to them in time of war. Under such sanction, British warships seized about 250 American merchant ships, mostly involved in trade with France or the French West Indies. At the same time a number of American seamen were imprisoned or impressed into service with the British Navy, under circumstances that seemed to many Americans, especially Jeffersonian Republicans, to be intolerable acts of war. An outcry arose for fighting the old enemy, Britain, on the side of the old friend, France.

Amid this uproar, Washington kept his head and reached the eminently wise decision to try to patch up peace. Secretary Hamilton's elaborate financial structure might not be able to withstand the shock of a war with Britain. So the President dispatched John Jay to London, there to hammer out a commercial treaty with the British that would avert hositilities.

Jay, backed by a tiny army and no navy whatever, simply could not wring many concessions from the British. But he did persuade them to evacuate the seven border posts (which they had already agreed to abandon in the peace treaty of 1783). Also, trade with the British West Indies was to be opened on a limited basis, and other disputes were to be referred to joint arbitral commissions. These arbitrations involved such problems as compensation for the recent illegal maritime seizures in the West Indies and the referral to arbitration of pre-Revolutionary debts owed British merchants. But nothing whatever was said in this treaty about other running sores between the two nations—Indian agressions in the Northwest, impressment of sailors, the Loyalists' claims or the dispute over slaves removed by the British at the end of the Revolutionary War. Yet one should also note that the referral of disputes to arbitral commissions was a landmark in the revival of the modern concept of arbitration, and as such it proved to be an enormous gain for peace. Moreover, this was the first commercial treaty that the British had condescended to make with their rebellious offspring.

President Washington was sorely disappointed that Jay had not wrested greater concessions from the British. The Jeffersonian Republicans were outraged that the American negotiator had made commercial concessions to Great Britain that seemed to undercut the Franco-American Alliance of 1778. The partisan outcry from the Jeffersonians was almost overwhelming. But a level-headed Washington perceived that the hard choices were this treaty or none at all, with rejection almost certain to bring war with Britain. Indeed, any kind of commercial treaty with the former foe was a victory of sorts. In one of the most courageous acts of a courageous career, Washington threw his great influence behind the pact, which scraped over the Senate reef, with one article eliminated, by the narrowest of margins.

Some critics have concluded that Jay's treaty was less important for what it did than for what it caused to be done. Like olives pouring out of a bottle once the first one is dislodged, a series of peace-sustaining treaties followed the approval of Jay's handiwork by the Senate on June 24, 1795.

On August 3, 1795, as earlier noted, the Northwest Indians concluded the treaty of Greenville with the victorious General Wayne. Deserted by their unreliable British friends at the seven posts, the feathered red men had no choice but to knuckle under.

On September 5, 1795, the United States concluded a treaty of peace and amity with the piratical Mediterranean state of Algiers. The terms provided for the annual payment of tribute, which could not have been pleasing to President Washington. But he had no navy, and the only alternatives were continued seizures, imprisonments, and deaths for the captured American seamen. Sensibly, Washington chose to buy peace rather than fight in vain for it.

The following month, on October 27, 1795, Thomas Pinckney, the American envoy to Spain, signed at San Lorenzo the epochal Pinckney treaty. The Spaniards, deserted by their British allies in Jay's treaty, abandoned their efforts to hold back the westward-pushing American pioneers by encouragement of the Indians. In the Pinckney treaty the Spaniards yielded thousands of square miles when they agreed to reduce their boundry north of East and West Florida southward to the thirty-first parallel. At the same time they conceded the right of American frontiersmen to navigate the Mississippi River to its mouth and then to deposit their river-borne produce at New Orleans over a period of three years. These surprising concessions helped set in motion the events that enabled the United States in 1803 to acquire the magnificent Louisiana Purchase.

The next year, on June 29, 1796, the United States concluded a treaty with the Creek nation of Georgia. It clarified the rights of these Indians to a reduced amount of land and brought an end to their Spanish-encouraged depredations.

Some three months later, on October 2, 1796, the British, pursuant to Jay's treaty, evacuated the last of the seven American outposts, that at Michilimackinac. For the first time the Union Jack ceased to fly over soil legitimately claimed by the United States.

The following month, November 4, 1796, the American envoy signed a treaty with the predatory state of Tripoli for the protection of American shipping and seamen. This concession, as the pact stated, was made in return for "the money and presents demanded by the Bey of Tripoli." In short, protection money. This concession must have gone hard with Washington, but what else could he do for American lives and property without a chastising navy?

But a navy was being born, and the corsairs of Algiers served as unwitting midwives. In response to their depredations, Congress on March 27, 1794, had authorized the building of six frigates, but with the stipulation that work on them should cease if a peace-ransom treaty should be concluded with Algiers. The pact in question was in fact signed on September 5, 1795, and President Washington was required by law to end the construction. Reluctant to do so, he tossed the issue back into the lap of Congress, which compromised by authorizing the construction of three of the six frigates. They were completed in 1797, under President John Adams, and the Navy Department was formally created the following year. At long last the United States under the Constitution had a tiny navy of three first-class frigates, which Washington had helped to father.

Washington's Farewell Forewarnings

Washington could have had a third term if he had only said the word. But he was physically tired and emotionally weary of the partisan abuse being showered on him by the pro-French Jeffersonian Republicans for having kept the nation out of war at the time of the fight over Jay's treaty. He had seen enough of armed conflict, and he longed for the quiet of Mount Vernon. His last major contribution to peace was his Farewell Address. Released to the press on September 17, 1796, it was designed in part to influence the presidential election of that year. Critics called it a campaign document tailored to ensure the election of the anti-French Federalist candidate, John Adams.

Most of the Farewell Address related to purely domestic affairs, especially recent pro-French politics. But Washington went out of his way to offer some fatherly advice concerning foreign affairs, especially as they related to recent friction with France and Great Britain.

Ever just, Washington counseled, "Observe good faith and justice toward all nations. Cultivate peace and harmony with all." Yet "inveterate antipathies against particular nations and passionate attachments for others should be excluded." For that "nation which indulges toward another an habitual hatred [Britain] or an habitual fondness [France] is in some degree a slave." It becomes "a slave to its animosity or to its affection, either of which is sufficient to lead it astray from its duty and its interest." Indeed, "an attachment of a small or weak toward a great and powerful nation dooms the former [America] to be the satellite of the latter [France]." In short, countries that seek protectors will not lack masters.

Europe, Washington continued, had a set of "primary interests" little related to those of the New World. If the republic remained united under "an efficient government," the belligerent nations of Europe would respect American neutrality. The nation's "true policy" was "to steer clear of permanent alliances with any portion of the foreign world." If the Americans made themselves militarily respectable, "they may safely trust to temporary alliances for extraordinary emergencies."

In dealing with other nations, Washington concluded, the United States should pursue "good faith and justice." And Americans should remember that "it is folly in one nation to look for disinterested favors from another; that it must pay with a portion of its independence for whatever it may accept under that character. . . . There can be no greater error than to expect or calculate upon real favors from nation [France] to nation [America]."

Washington's farewell formula for peace proved to be a sound one for a weak and still disunited nation. He did not warn against *all* alliances, only "permanent" ones, like the current encumbrance with France. A superpower inherits responsibilities that do not burden mini-nations or developing nations.

In grading Washington as a peace President, the historian cannot avoid giving him high marks. He provoked no war, he fought only in self-defense on the frontier, and he opted for peace with Great Britain when he backed Jay's unpopular treaty. This act of courage came at a time when extremists were clamoring for a war that could only have been disastrous for the United States. Washington adamantly refused to be stampeded into a conflict with France following French reprisals against American commerce after Jay's pro-British treaty. He may not have been first as a military genius, and he was clearly not first in the hearts of many partisan countrymen, but his record as President reveals that in truth he was "first in peace."

Washington believed in peace through preparedness, not peace through submission, and he deeply resented having to pay ransom to the Barbary pirates. Lacking complete confidence in ill-trained militiamen, he recommended to Congress the establishment of a national "military academy" of the kind that was finally established at West Point in 1802. As he declared in his first annual address to Congress in January 1790, "To be prepared for war is one of the most effectual means of preserving peace."

CHAPTER 2

JOHN ADAMS: THE UNDECLARED WARRIOR

An efficient preparation for war can alone insure peace.

President John Adams,
message to Congress,
December 8, 1798

An Inherited Fracas with France

John Adams, of Braintree, Massachusetts ("The Duke of Braintree") was born in 1735 and died at age ninety-one on the Fourth of July 1826, the oldest ex-President in American history. He graduated from Harvard College, became a lawyer, and then as the "Colossus of Independence" took his place in the Continental Congress and in diplomatic negotiations abroad, including negotiations with France, Holland, and Britain. As a Founding Father, he was unquestionably one of the giants, although a portly five feet, seven inches ("His Rotundity").

Adams never served in armed forces—he was past forty years of age when independence was declared—but he did defend in court British soldiers involved in the so-called Boston Massacre of 1770. With the town aroused to a fever pitch, this action required both moral and physical courage. Much later, under the new Constitution, Adams put in eight frustrating years (1789–1797) as Vice-President under the great George Washington—an office that he regarded as far beneath him. In 1796 he was elected President in his own right over Jefferson by a margin of three electoral votes, and this narrow victory also hurt his pride, which was considerable.

As a pro-British and anti-French Federalist, President Adams inherited a nasty quarrel with France from his distinguished predecessor. It had grown largely out of Jay's treaty of 1795, which had granted the British the right to seize American merchant ships carrying noncontraband cargoes to France. In French eyes the ungrateful American ally had joined hands with the British, the ancient enemy, against France, America's benefactor and friend.

James Monroe, the future President and then the passionately pro-French Minister to France, was left dangling in an impossible position. He had assured his hosts that John Jay would never negotiate a treaty resolving current British-American controversies, and certainly not a pact at the expense of France. The angered Paris government retaliated by issuing a decree, on July 2, 1796, declaring that France would treat neutrals as they allowed Britain to treat them. This meant that French warships would seize scores of American merchant ships bound for British ports with noncontraband. A crestfallen Monroe, his usefulness ruined, was recalled the next month by the administration of George Washington, and the French government retaliated by recalling its Minister in protest against Jay's treaty.

The bungling Monroe was replaced by Charles C. Pinckney, a South Carolina Federalist whose enthusiasm for the French Revolution had cooled. But the new Paris government, under the corrupt five-headed Directory, flatly refused to receive him as Minister. Pinckney lingered from December 1796 until February 1797, when the police notified him that unless he received a permit he would be liable to arrest. Gravely affronted, he left French soil for Holland. This rebuff in itself was hardly a valid excuse for armed hostilities, for nations often declare envoys unacceptable (*persona non grata*) in advance of their coming.

The blunt truth is that the French, by repeated seizures, had already been making a war of sorts on United States shipping before Adams became President, and they continued to do so relentlessly. In June 1797 Adams's Secretary of State Pickering reported that the staggering total of 316 American merchant ships had been captured by armed French vessels in the preceding eleven months. Often the crews were imprisoned and barbarously ill treated. The principal difference between this situation and conventional warfare was that the United States was not fighting back.

John Adams not only inherited a war with France but unwisely permitted himself to inherit Washington's Cabinet. The three most influential of the four members were undoubtedly loyal, but not to their new chief. Former Secretary of the Treasury Alexander Hamilton, now a lawyer in private life, played the underhanded role of power behind the throne, for he had Adams's Cabinet in his pocket. Like Adams, he was a strongly pro-British Federalist, but unlike Adams he craved military glory.

Adams's handling of the French crisis was complicated by other distressing circumstances. His Vice-President, Thomas Jefferson, headed the Democratic-Republican party, which was fanatically pro-French. In addition, Adams absented himself from Philadelphia, the temporary capital for many months, much of the while when his wife, remaining in Massachusetts, was critically ill, as were America's foreign affairs. All told, Adams was absent from the helm of the ship of state for more than one year out of his stormy four. He claimed that he could conduct official business adequately from Massachusetts, but dispatches drawn or carried by horses were slow in arriving. If he had been minding the store during these many anxious months, he might have perceived earlier how Hamilton was manipulating his Cabinet behind his back. A final complication was that round-trip communications between America and Paris could consume several months, at best. There was then no Atlantic cable, and contrary winds often proved uncooperative with sailing ships.

The XYZ Affair

At the call of President Adams, Congress met in special session on May, 1797, to consider the ruptured state of relations with

Paris. Adams formally reported the expulsion of Charles C. Pinckney as Minister to France, assured Congress that he would endeavor to reopen negotiations, and urged the adoption of defensive measures, particularly naval preparedness.

About two weeks later Adams submitted the names of three men as a commission to reopen negotiations with Paris, and they were duly confirmed by the Senate. Among them was the Federalist Minister who had been expelled from France, Charles C. Pinckney, who was still lingering in Holland. He was to be joined by John Marshall of Virginia, a dyed-in-the-wool Federalist and a future Chief Justice of the United States. The third envoy was Elbridge Gerry, a signer of the Declaration of Independence and a future Governor of Massachusetts, after whom the political tactic of "gerrymander" was to be named. His Federalism was so lukewarm that he was suspected of having pro-French leanings.

When the American trio finally reached Paris, in October 1797, they received the cold-shoulder treatment. Between maddening delays they were approached by secret agents (X, Y, and Z) of the French Foreign Minister, the crafty and unscrupulous Talleyrand, a turncoat bishop. Also involved was a beautiful and seductive woman, Madame Violette, then a charming widow of thirty-two. She was the niece and adopted daughter of the freethinking Voltaire, but the tongue of scandal suggested a greater intimacy. She greatly impressed bachelor John Marshall, the future legal giant, who once broke an engagement with his colleague, Charles C. Pinckney, to escort her to the theater.

Agents X, Y, and Z laid down certain conditions before official negotiations could begin. Included was the demand for an apology for certain critical references to France in a recent message to Congress by President Adams. In addition to this self-abasement, Talleyrand's agents presented two monetary demands. First was a "gift" (bribe) of approximately $250,000 in American money for the grasping Talleyrand. Second was a loan of about $10 million, which in these circumstances would be largely or wholly a gift from a financially shaky United States.

When one go-between agent made brutally clear that the French wanted a great deal of money, one of the American trio replied heatedly, "No, no, not a sixpence." They had no option but to take this course, since they had no large sum of money with them, and their instructions, which they were obligated to follow, made no provision for such. Even if they had been budgeted for bribery, the sums involved were too much for a pinched Treasury to pay for the mere privilege of talking with Talleyrand, with no assurances whatever of tangible results. Certainly, the granting of a loan as large as $10,000,000 could be interpreted by the British as an unneutral act in the Anglo-French war then being waged. The backlash from such an act could conceivably trigger the hostilities with England that Jay's recent treaty had sidetracked. The French, of course, would have been delighted to see their archfoe, Britain, weaken herself in a full-fledged war with her rebellious American offspring.

The American trio were not so naive as not to know that bribes and petticoats were standard fare in Old World diplomacy. But the bribe, the loan, and the demand for an apology added up to an assault on the nation's honor. When the President of the United States delivers a message to Congress (and the American people), he is not speaking to a foreign nation but to his fellow citizens. Foreigners may take offense, but forcing the President to eat his words is not normally their prerogative, except, that is, at the cannon's mouth. And in matters of national pride young nations on the make are apt to be more sensitive than older ones.

Fed up with French greed and lack of respect for American honor, two of the indignant trio, Pinckney and Marshall, concluded that further talk would be fruitless and consequently left for home in a huff. Talleyrand, who did not desire either a rupture of relations or a war with the United States, now realized that he might have outsmarted himself in dealing with agents whom he regarded as country bumpkins from backwoods America. Accordingly, he persuaded the supposedly pro-French Elbridge Gerry to linger in France, much to the annoyance of President Adams, who would have preferred the strength of a united front and who finally recalled Gerry. But this envoy's defection turned out to have the great merit of keeping open vital lines of communication with Talleyrand.

Adams the War Hawk

When the full force of Talleyrand's insolence reached America, there followed an outburst of indignation the like of which the young republic had not yet seen. "Millions for defense but not one cent for tribute" overnight became the slogan of the hour, as the newly launched "Hail Columbia" was sung to the tune of "President's March," and "Adams and Liberty" was bawled by thousands of throats.

The President was outraged. As a conservative Federalist, he naturally harbored a bias against revolutionary France and a corresponding partiality for Great Britain. On March 5, 1798, he informed Congress in a brief message that the first dispatches of the three envoys in Paris had reached the Department of State. He further reported that the documents in question were all in code and that they would require "some days to be deciphered."

Two weeks later Adams, after shelving a more bellicose draft, presented another brief message to Congress declaring that the dispatches in question had all been "examined and maturely considered." His conclusion was that no ground existed for believing that the three envoys could accomplish "the objects of their mission" in a manner "compatible with the safety, the honor, or the essential interests of the nation." Yet for "the preservation of peace" he had done everything possible consistent with "our national sovereignty." In concluding this short but militant message, President Adams urged Congress to pass with "promptitude" all necessary warlike measures for the protection of "our seafaring and commercial citizens" and for the defense of all exposed territory.

These resolute reactions by Adams do not clothe him in the feathers of a cooing dove. He was saying in effect that he would not demean the nation by making another try at diplomacy but instead would prepare the country for the war that France was forcing on it. The honor and pride of the youthful United States had been so deeply wounded that he could not or would not turn the other cheek. At this stage Adams evidently wanted a formal declaration of war, but he refrained from saying so, because the pro-French Republicans in Congress might unite to defeat it, with humiliating loss of face for Adams. He much preferred to have the French declare hostilities first.

The President's reference to the deciphered dispatches, included in his message of March 19, 1798, had been enough to arouse the country further and inflame public prejudices. Unbelieving, the Republican-dominated House of Representatives passed a resolution requesting copies of the instructions given to the three American envoys, plus the ciphered dispatches sent back by them.

Adams willingly obliged on April 3, 1798. He added that he was "omitting only some names and a few expressions descriptive of the persons." Instead, he substituted the letters X, Y, and Z for three of the shadowy go-betweens, presumably to spare them and Talleyrand further embarrassment. Adams's only request was that these confidential communications be withheld from publication until the members of Congress had an opportunity to study them fully and digest their import. The anti-French Federalists were delighted with what they found; the pro-French Republicans were crestfallen.

Publication of the damning dispatches soon began, thanks to Federalist pressures in Congress, and in short order some 10,000 copies were distributed, all to the acute embarrassment of the pro-French Republicans. The public was already in an uproar, and these cloak-and-dagger doings only added fuel to the roaring flames. Much of the clamor involved politics, and in playing this game Adams himself was no babe in the woods.

The stereotype of John Adams as a man of peace during these weeks of frenzy against France is seriously undermined by his conduct. He was not required to tell Congress formally that he would not continue his effort to patch up differences through diplomacy but instead would turn to preparing for war. His inflammatory message played directly into the hands of the anti-French Federalist warmongers, conspicuous among whom was former Secretary of the Treasury Hamilton, now a private citizen. Like Adams, he wanted a declaration of war, but like Adams he perceived the wisdom of having France declare it first.

Admirers of Adams have ignored the further fact that he was not required to submit the confidential XYZ dispatches to Congress, except perhaps to spur war preparations. He could have withheld these explosive documents, as other Presidents have done, on grounds of executive privilege or confidentiality. He could hardly have been unaware of the precedent, already established by George Washington himself, when Adams was Vice-President. The skeptical House of Representatives had passed a resolution, in March 1796, requesting confidential papers relating to the negotiation of Jay's treaty. Obviously the Jeffersonian Republicans would have made much political profit with these documents. But Washington had flatly declined to deliver the papers for fear of creating, as he said, "a dangerous precedent." Moreover, under the Constitution the Senate, not the House, normally makes or breaks treaties.

In brief, Adams's priorities were such that he was prepared to let a shooting war come rather than compromise the honor and dignity of the United States. On June 21, 1798, Adams informed Congress that Gerry, still lingering, was "to consent to no loans, and therefore the negotiation may be considered at an end." With ringing words, Adams concluded his announcement: "I will never send another minister to France without assurances that he will be received, respected, and honored as the representative of a great, free, powerful, and independent nation."

Rebirth of the Navy

A nondescript United States naval force had been improvised during the Revolutionary War, with John Paul Jones the stellar commander, but when peace came the navy was allowed to die. President George Washington had no navy at all, and this obvious weakness forced him to pay humiliating tribute to the Barbary pirates rather than try to chastise them.

When the XYZ crisis convulsed the country early in 1798, President Adams had no navy either, unless one counts a few small revenue cutters, each manned by six men. The three stout frigates, finally authorized under Washington in response to the Barbary corsairs, would not be ready until many months had passed, and then they rendered yeoman service.

Throughout the quarrel with France and the following undeclared war, President Adams kept prodding Congress to strengthen the nation at sea. Unlike Washington, who was basically land-minded, Adams preached that a small but strong navy, quickly expandable, was the true first line of defense. Once created, it could remain in existence, always usable if kept in a state of readiness. The navy could also be employed to escort American shipping (mostly Federalist) in time of war, and it could fight the enemy off the coast instead of on American soil. Here Adams unwittingly anticipated the later teachings of Admiral Alfred T. Mahan. Such a navy could also destroy enemy shipping, enemy military supplies on neutral ships, and enemy transports carrying invading armies. Additionally, naval strength would be less costly to maintain in time of war or peace than large standing armies, which were then regarded in America as a standing invitation to a potential dictator on horseback.

In response to the President's pleas for naval muscle after the XYZ insults, Congress took such vigorous action that Adams was properly dubbed "Father of the American Navy." Pro-French Jeffersonian Republicans, however, were prone to jeer at the seamen as "John Adams's Jackasses."

In April 1798 Congress authorized the creation of the Navy Department, independent of the War Department, under whose jurisdiction naval affairs had formerly been lodged. The next month Adams was clothed with authority to order commanders of United States warships to seize any French-armed vessel attacking American merchantmen. (Simultaneously, the President was authorized to raise an army of 10,000 volunteers for three years.) In June of the same year the Congress suspended all commerce with France and her dependencies. In July Congress abrogated all treaties with France, thus at one stroke unilaterally ending the Alliance of 1778 with the French, although Paris did not accept the abrogation. Finally, in July 1798 Congress established the Marine Corps, which fought bravely in this undeclared war and which has continued its leather-neck tradition to the present.

Fighting with France lasted two and one-half years. It was confined to the sea, especially the West Indies, although invasion by a French army was greatly feared at one stage. The small but efficient American navy, increased from three frigates to fifty-five improvised vessels and supported by privately owned warships (privateers), captured some eighty armed French vessels. United States national warships were under strict orders to spare the relatively few French merchant vessels that were armed, thus adding further limitations to the limited war. All told, the Americans lost several hundred merchant ships in this falling-out with France, either abroad or in North American waters, where enemy privateers swarmed.

Aside from privateers, about nine encounters occurred between warships of the French navy and armed vessels of the American navy. With superfrigates like the *Constellation* (thirty-eight guns), the United States won all of those engagements, except for one in which the schooner *Retaliation* (fourteen guns) fell prey to two French frigates (total, eighty guns). Luckily for the Americans, the powerful British navy pinned down the big French ships of the line (about seventy-four guns) in European waters, especially after Admiral Nelson wiped out Napoleon's fleet at the Battle of the Nile in 1798.

Virtually unnoticed in this war were the exploits of Captain Edward Preble with his frigate, the *Essex*. To protect American merchant ships against French privateers in the Far East, including the China trade, he had set out for the Indian Ocean in January 1800, by way of the Cape of Good Hope. Cruising for two months near the straits of Sundra (south of Singapore), he provided needed protection for American commerce against French privateers and national warships. He returned to New York late in November 1800, escorting an impressive convoy of fourteen merchant ships. One is surprised to find so much Asiatic trade with Americans at this early date, and also to note that the United States, regarded in Europe as a feeble nation, was deploying naval strength effectively in a hemisphere so remote from home.

Nor was the quasi-war with France fought entirely at sea. The new Marine Corps assisted Toussaint L'Ouverture and his blacks, then fighting against French rule, on the island of Hispaniola (Haiti and Santo Domingo). The U.S. Marines distinguished themselves by landing at Puerto Plata, in the present Dominican Republic, where they helped to capture a French privateer under the guns of the fort. The Americans made no effort to conquer the French islands in the Caribbean, but in September 1800 Captain Henry Geddes, with the good ship *Patapsco* and twenty Marines, dislodged the French forces that had taken over a part of the Dutch island of Curaçao.

British Cooperation and Coercion

As the old saying goes, the enemy of my enemy is my friend. Great Britain was delighted to see her former colonials busily fighting the common French foe, albeit on an undeclared basis. The British and Americans, both threatened with invasion, were actually drawn more closely together than they were to be for about a century. The Mother Country provided the United States with substantial supplies of cannon and other war material; the British also shared their naval signals so as not to interfere with the operations of their American offspring. The pro-British Federalists, led by pro-British John Adams, were riding high and could confidently expect to win the presidency again for him in

1800. The Jeffersonian Republicans had to grit their teeth and endure the disgraceful conduct of their fine-feathered French friends.

Yet a number of highhanded incidents occurred to mar friendly relations with the British, who might have had a war with America on their hands if the French had not been guilty of even greater offenses. Notorious was the fate of the *U.S.S. Baltimore*, a sloop of twenty guns recently acquired by the United States. Stopped by a stronger British warship near Havana, Cuba, in November 1798, the American vessel was robbed of fifty-five crewmen by heavy-handed impressment gangs. But all except five seamen were returned after Captain Isaac Phillips protested that he could not sail his ship safely without them.

This outrageous affair was an intolerable stain on the nation's flag, for it involved a ship of the United States navy, not an ordinary merchant vessel. The incident generated great bitterness in America and helped build up the impressment pressures that ultimately led to the War of 1812. Captain Phillips was dismissed in disgrace from the service, and orders were issued to all commanders of United States warships to fight back, even against overwhelming force, before honorably surrendering their bloodied and battered hulks. Such instructions were issued at the command of President Adams himself, who was then much concerned with the larger dishonor of the XYZ affair. His pugnacity pressure had risen to a high pitch.

The army of 10,000 men authorized by Congress was only partially and clumsily brought up to about 3,000 ill-trained recruits. General George Washington, the weary warrior, was called upon to head this force but stipulated that he would not take command until it was ready for action. In the meantime he insisted that Alexander Hamilton, a frustrated Napoleon, be named second in command. President Adams consented to this arrangement with great reluctance, for he was jealous of Hamilton, now commissioned a major general, and justifiably suspicious of this egoist's military ambitions.

We now know that the passionately pro-British Hamilton, who expected full cooperation from the British navy, dreamed dreams of glory. Spain had allied herself with France in 1796, and Hamilton would bring plaudits to himself and prestige to his country by despoiling the Spaniards of the Floridas, Louisiana, and points south, including some of South America.

Adams Opts for Peace

Frosty old John Adams, who had never before enjoyed great popular acclaim, evidently savored the public applause that sprang from the XYZ affair and his bellicose response to it. But his pride, which was inflated, appears to have been unduly sensitive on points of prestige and honor. He recognized that the war with France was getting nowhere, for neither nation could deploy enough naval power to threaten seriously the home soil of the other. The new American navy, though of superior quality, was of unimpressive quantity, and additionally had to rely on the British fleet to blockade French ports. George Washington's policy during the Jay treaty turmoil had been to avoid war like the plague while the nation was militarily weak and thinly peopled. Time was on the side of the procreative and expansive Americans, and if they did not squander their strength in war they would one day be strong enough to command respect. As Washington's Vice-President, Adams could hardly have been unaware of this sage counsel.

The attitude of Talleyrand, now belatedly conciliatory, apparently impressed Adams. The much-too-clever Frenchman was now the laughingstock of Europe, having been outwitted by the three country bumpkins from the New World. Through various channels, official and unofficial, he let it be known that he was prepared to enter into negotiations for peace if the United States would only make the next official move. He went so far as to inform the American Minister in the Netherlands, William Vans Murray, that he would respectfully receive an envoy or envoys representing the United States.

With these beckoning signals coming from Talleyrand, Adams's Puritanical conscience probably told him that he should not continue to fight a war when all he had to do was to accept these overtures for peace. Yet continuing hostilities would certainly sustain his new personal popularity, strengthen his Federalist party, split the Jeffersonian Republican party, and probably ensure Adams's reelection in 1800. On the other hand, the ambitious Alexander Hamilton might elbow Adams aside as President, especially after a laurel-laden military campaign against the Spaniards in Florida, Louisiana, and Mexico. The time had clearly come for Adams to put the welfare of the country above that of his party and his own ambitions for reelection.

In making this crucial decision, Adams did not consult his Federalist Cabinet. Containing holdovers from Washington's administration, it was as much a cabal as a Cabinet. Behind the scenes the two-faced Hamilton was working hand-in-glove with its members. Then, to the consternation of the Federalists in the Senate, Adams unexpectedly submitted to that body, on February 18, 1799, the nomination of William Vans Murray, then in Holland, as the new Minister to France.

The astounded Federalists, about to be deprived of their politically rewarding war with France, reacted with fury to this unexpected preference for peace. The only concession that Adams would make after month-long arguments was to expand the one-man envoy into a commission of three, all reliable Federalists. The Federalist party was hoping that this expansion would make for delays, as it certainly did. After more than eight months of dillydallying, Adams sternly ordered the three appointees on their way. Many of the moderate Federalists, to their credit, glumly accepted this last-chance gamble for peace.

Between the nomination of the three envoys to France and their sailing, Adams had resolutely quelled the Fries rebellion in eastern Pennsylvania in March 1799. New federal taxes, made necessary by the current war preparations against France, had been imposed on land and houses. In eastern Pennsylvania, the people, led by a popular auctioneer named John Fries, rose in arms and resisted the taxing authorities, who were mistakenly believed to be measuring windows for the purpose of imposing a hated window tax.

President Adams, proclaiming that more than one hundred armed men were treasonably levying war against the United States, sent in an overpowering force of federal troops. There was no bloody confrontation, but Fries was captured, found guilty of treason, and sentenced to be hanged. Adams, following the compassionate example of President Washington in the Whiskey Rebellion, pardoned this leader. Although the Fries rebellion was only a police action, Adams was not at all squeamish about discharging his duties under the Constitution with an iron fist. Oddly enough, during the undeclared war with France the only armed confrontation on United States soil took place in eastern Pennsylvania against fellow Americans.

As luck would have it, these maddening delays worked to the advantage of the United States, even though the quasi-war continued relentlessly. The corrupt five-man Directory of XYZ days was gone; the ambitious Napoleon Bonaparte was in the saddle as First Consul and disposed to patch up peace with America. He had no desire to force the United States into the war as an ally of England, partly because he had grandiose plans for taking over the vast expanse of Louisiana (nominally achieved three years later). Continued hostilities or a widened war with America could disrupt his schemes. Against this background the three American negotiators slowly hammered out the Convention of 1800, also known as the Treaty of Mortfontaine, signed on September 30 after seven months of wearisome negotiations.

The three American envoys had sought major concessions from France. First was a formal release from the two Franco-American treaties of 1778, especially the bothersome treaty of alliance. Second was the payment of about $20 million for the allegedly illegal seizure of American merchant ships since the war began with Britain several years earlier. After prolonged haggling, a swap was finally arranged. As the treaty was modified by the United States Senate, the Americans would give up their demand for the money, while the French would consent to the termination of the two treaties. Such was the alimony paid for ending what turned out to be a painful marriage of inconvenience. And thus formally ended America's first entangling alliance—one that really had entangled. As a bonus, unforeseen by Adams, the Treaty of Mortfontaine (Convention of 1800) set up conditions that made possible the breathtaking Louisiana Purchase of 1803.

Adams the Hawklike Dove

The historian cannot give John Adams high marks as a man of peace. The French did not want an undeclared war with the United States following the XYZ affair, and conceivably an informal clash could have been avoided under different leadership in America. But Adams was a vain man with an inferiority complex, not helped by his years in the shadow of the great Washington. His pride in himself and his nation combined with politics to bring about the protracted breach with France. In 1780, some seventeen years earlier, he had haughtily informed the French Foreign Minister while an envoy in France: "The United States are a great and powerful people, whatever European statesmen may think of them." This rejoinder had come when the badly divided thirteen colonies were still fighting for their independence.

There was a high degree of inconsistency in Adams's battling for the nation's honor. The affront of the XYZ affair was so great that the country rang with the slogan "Millions for defense but not one cent for tribute." Yet during the Adams administration the United States, thanks to treaties negotiated under Washington and Adams, was continuing to send tribute (protection money) to the Barbary pirates in large amounts. In January 1798, a few weeks before the first XYZ dispatches reached the United States, a ship left for Algiers with twenty-six barrels of "blackmail" American dollars.

In the autumn of 1800, while the three American envoys were still negotiating in France, an American warship of twenty-four guns, curiously misnamed *George Washington*, arrived in Algiers with the annual tribute. The Dey of Algiers not only accepted this blackmail but forced the American commander, under threat of a declaration of war, to hoist the Algerian flag and carry presents to the Turkish overlords in Constantinople. Adams seems to have swallowed his pride, for he sent no message to Congress detailing this outrageous stain on American honor. Possibly he partially salved his conscience with the knowledge that the treaty with Algiers had been concluded in 1795 under the incomparable George Washington.

As for the French crisis, the unflattering truth seems to be that Adams chose the road to nominal peace in part because of his jealousy of Hamilton and his fear that this rival would oust him as leader of the Federalist party. "Honest John" Adams at length acted in the national interest, evidently for considerations that were not as worthy as one would expect to find in a statesman of his caliber.

CHAPTER 3

THOMAS JEFFERSON: THE PEACEFUL WARRIOR

Peace is our passion.

Jefferson to John Sinclair,
June 30, 1803

Jefferson: A Bundle of Contradictions

Red haired and lanky Thomas ("Long Tom") Jefferson, towering six feet, two and one-half inches, was a revolutionist and an ardent foe of injustice, but not a warrior. A Virginia aristocrat, he attended the College of William and Mary, from which he graduated in two years, and then became a practicing lawyer. Highly critical of haughty British overlordship he sat as a delegate in the Continental Congress in 1775 and the next year drafted and signed the immortal Declaration of Independence, thereby virtually putting his neck in the hangman's noose. He did not volunteer for the fighting front but served locally in the state legislature and as governor of Virginia (1779–1781), at which time he narrowly escaped capture when British cavalry raided his beautiful Monticello estate.

As Secretary of State under President Washington, "The Sage of Monticello" favored the French over the British in their struggle for liberty, and finally resigned from the Cabinet in 1793. As Vice President under Adams, Jefferson parted company with the President over his bellicose handling of the XYZ affair and the creation of a standing army. Then, in 1800, Jefferson defeated Adams for the presidency, after having established himself as preeminently a man of peace. His correspondence and public papers abound in expressions of his detestation of war and all that it entailed.

Jefferson's classic inaugural address of March 1801 gave ample evidence of his pacific leanings. As for the recent electoral struggle between the Hamiltonian Federalists and the Jeffersonian Republicans, he attempted to lull the Federalist opposition by saying, "We are all Republicans, we are all Federalists." As for international relations, he called for "peace, commerce, and honest friendship with all nations, entangling alliances with none." As regards defense, "a well-disciplined militia" was "our best reliance in peace and for the first moments of war, till regulars may relieve them." We should also observe that Jefferson, who had little love for the Federalist navy of John Adams, did not mention the navy at all.

The Tussle with Tripoli

The Tripolitan war was not of Jefferson's seeking or making. The Bashaw of Tripoli, unhappy with the amount of blackmail apportioned to him under the treaty of 1796, declared war on the United States when he issued orders to cut down the American flag at the consulate in the city of Tripoli in May 1801. Jefferson could either knuckle under or respond with naval action. He opted to react. As he wrote privately the next year, peace was "the most important of all things for us, except the preserving an erect and independent attitude."

Though a man of peace, Jefferson did not agonize unduly over the decision for war with Tripoli. While earlier serving as Minister to France (1785–1789), he had been authorized to ransom captured American sailors from the dungeons of the Barbary "hellhounds." Deeply touched by the moans and groans of

"The Providential Detection." The American Eagle snatches the Constitution from Jefferson, who is about to burn it on the altar to French revolutionary despotism. Massachusetts Historical Society.

his fellow citizens, he had then vainly proposed that the powers of Europe join forces and wipe out these "pyrates."

Responding to Tripoli's challenge in 1801, Jefferson first sent naval vessels to the Mediterranean Sea to protect American commerce against the corsairs. Interpreting his constitutional powers narrowly, he did not authorize the navy to conduct offensive operations against Tripoli itself until Congress had formally clothed him with the requisite power. That august body responded on February 6, 1802, with a counter declaration of war.

The Tripolitan conflict dragged on from 1801 to 1805. The war was almost exclusively a naval one, which meant essentially a blockade of the coastal waters of Tripoli. Attention focused on the city and harbor of Tripoli, defended by small warships and solid forts with about 115 cannon. American warships bombarded this key area repeatedly without serious effect, largely because cannon on floating wooden decks must necessarily fight at a disadvantage. At the peak of this war the United States assembled a fleet of about ten well-armed ships, including superfrigates, supported by many lighter craft, especially small gunboats with one or two large guns.

In 1803 the frigate *Philadelphia* had the misfortune to run onto a reef in the harbor of Tripoli. The crew of about three hundred officers and men were captured and imprisoned, and then the ship was refloated, thus giving the captors a formidable warship that could be turned against their foes. The Americans eliminated this menace by a daring night raid with almost sixty men, under war hero Stephen Decatur. They burned the *Philadelphia*, despite heavy fire, and providentially escaped with only one man wounded. Subsequently the American fleet, by a naval demonstration off the city of Tangier, forced the Emperor of Morocco to make amends for treaty violations. The remaining Barbary states were thus kept in line.

The tedium of the prolonged naval blockade was relieved by an incredible overland expedition from Egypt. William Eaton, a former captain in the United States army and recently consul in Tripoli, decided to help fight the war on his own. Evidently exceeding his instructions from Commodore Barron, Eaton took up the cause of the exiled older brother of the Bashaw of Tripoli, and located him in Egypt. There and along the way Eaton raised a motley army of some five hundred or six hundred ill-assorted Arabs, Greeks, Italians, and others, all spearheaded by an American midshipman, a noncommissioned officer, and eight U.S. Marines. By exercising his iron will, "General" Eaton led this ragtag force, critically short of essential water and food, across some 500 miles of the burning desert to attack the important Tripolitan city of Derna. With the cooperation of three American warships offshore, he captured this place by assault and was preparing to march on to the city of Tripoli, which lay some 600 miles to the west.

At this point, with complete victory for the United States in sight, a treaty with Tripoli was announced that brought the war to a close. Owing in part to slow communication with Washington, its terms, to "General" Eaton's acute distress, did not reflect the improved American position. The pact did abolish all annual payments, while granting more favorable commercial terms than those yet secured by any other nation. But the United States, though now winning the war, agreed to pay $60,000 in ransom for the three hundred or so American officers and men captured from the *Philadelphia*. Payment of this large sum was infuriating to many Americans, but the prisoners had already suffered nineteen months of degrading maltreatment, and for them every day of delay was an eternity. In this case America secured peace with a taint of dishonor. But the other Barbary states received a thorough chastisement from Stephen Decatur's naval operations after the War of 1812, and all blackmail payments ceased as far as the United States was concerned. By this time the European nations were more willing to join in wiping out these piratical lairs.

Jefferson gleaned some definite advantages from the prolonged war with Tripoli, with small cost in blood but considerable financial cost in maintaining a fleet on prolonged active duty some 3,000 miles from home, along a coastline that stretched for hundreds of miles. He certainly accomplished more in this area than either President Washington or Adams, but neither of Jefferson's predecessors had the naval strength at hand to do the job.

Ironically, the Navy reaped these laurels under the supreme command of a President who disliked costly navies. A number of the officers gained valuable experience that they would put to excellent use in the forthcoming War of 1812. Admiral Nelson, the British hero then blockading Toulon in Southern France, graciously praised the burning of the *Philadelphia* as "the most bold and daring act of the age."

Certainly the American exhibition of naval might made something of an impression in Europe and heralded the beginning of the end of all Barbary blackmail. Those who think that the United States was unable to deploy naval strength to other continents until it acquired the Philippines in 1899 would do well to ask a simple question: What other powers in the world, including Europe, would have been able or willing to maintain a dozen or so sizable warships in combat 3,000 miles away to root out piracy in the American Caribbean? None but a great naval power like Britain or France would have had the strength, the financial resources, or even the will to do so. Certainly the major nations of the Old World had tolerated the Barbary pirates for many years, and these corsairs lurked in Europe's front yard. Under authority from Congress, Jefferson did what he could do and what he felt he had to do.

From this experience with the Barbary corsairs Jefferson drew one misleading lesson. During inshore operations the U.S. Navy had employed a few tiny gunboats to operate over reefs against small Tripolitan craft. The penny-pinching President gladly embraced the idea that these cheap, one-gun gunboats could be used with comparable effectiveness to protect the lengthy American coasts. Accordingly, he undertook to lay up the big frigates and concentrate on building a swarm of the smaller craft—what his Federalist opponents jeeringly dubbed the "Mosquito Fleet." Responding to his recommendations, Congress authorized a total of 278, of which 176 were finally constructed. They were relatively inexpensive to build and could save money by being pulled up on shore under sheds when not in use.

Actually these tiny gunboats were so topheavy as often to be more of a menace to their small crews than to the British enemy whom they later fought futilely. After the War of 1812 erupted, President Madison would probably have been fortunate if he could have traded the entire lot for one forty-four-gun frigate of the *Constitution* ("Old Ironsides") class.

The Louisiana Windfall

Napoleon is often quoted as having remarked that he preferred generals who were lucky to those who were brilliant. Jefferson's acquisition of Louisiana—some 828,000 square miles of virtually virgin land at three cents an acre—was primarily an incredible stroke of good luck. Although the area was secured peacefully, it provides a revealing test of how close Jefferson was willing to court war rather than lose the mouth of the Mississippi River, the great "Father of Waters."

The story in brief is this. In 1800, by secret treaty, Spain ceded to France the immense expanse west of the Mississippi known as Louisiana. Napoleon, dreaming of empire, planned to use this acquisition as a granary to supply foodstuffs for France's Caribbean colonies. In 1802, before the transfer could be completed, Spain in effect closed the mouth of the Mississippi to downriver American flatboatmen. A tremendous outcry promptly arose from these doughty Westerners, especially those in Kentucky and Tennessee. They talked loudly and wildly of descending on New Orleans, long rifles in hand, thus precipitating war with Spain and perhaps with France as well. The West in its anger might even have broken off from the United States, in which case Jefferson would have had the first War of Secession on his hands. Moreover, the Westerners were generally Jeffersonian Republicans, and he would do well politically to keep them in his camp and continue to weaken the Federalists.

Jefferson had been willing to tolerate Spain's occupancy of Louisiana, for her decaying empire was weak and growing weaker by the year. The American frontiersmen could move in whenever enough of them chose to do so. But France, headed by the military genius Napoleon, was a menace of a different color. She was too strong militarily for the United States alone to dislodge, and consequently Jefferson would be forced to seek an alliance, which he dreaded, with the lordly British, whom he despised. Although an inveterate foe of "entangling alliances," Jefferson wrote privately, in April 1802, that from the moment France took over New Orleans "we must marry ourselves to the British fleet and nation."

A worried Jefferson dispatched James Monroe to Paris early in 1802, there to continue negotiations with Minister Livingston for New Orleans and as much to the *east* in West Florida as could be obtained. The diplomatic duo were to offer a maximum of $10 million, and if France proposed to close the Mississippi entirely or seemed "to meditate hostilities," the two envoys were to proceed to England, there to enter upon negotiations looking toward, of all things, an entangling treaty of alliance.

Through other diplomatic channels Jefferson did his bit toward urging the French to grant an outlet at New Orleans, at the very least. But the decision to sell rested primarily on Napoleon's caprice rather than on the nudges of Jefferson. Napoleon had looked upon Louisiana as a future granary for Santo Domingo, but he was unable to reconquer the island from the revolting blacks, led by the gifted Toussaint L'Ouverture, "Bonaparte of the Antilles." So what need had he for the granary? Napoleon knew that war was going to be renewed with England, because he planned to start it anew, as in fact he did in May 1803. Then why make New Orleans and all Louisiana a gift to the hated British navy? Why not sell the area for $15 million to the Americans, avoid war with them, bolster them against the hated British, and use the money to build up his invasion fleet (as he did) for the projected attack on England (never attempted).

So it was that out of a clear sky, in April 1803, Napoleon offered to dump the coveted territory, all of it, into the laps of the Americans for $15 million. In flagrant disregard of instructions to pay only $10 million for New Orleans and territory to the east, Livingston and Monroe signed treaties to purchase all the land to the west for $15 million.

Jefferson, a strict constructionist of the Constitution, was initially disturbed by what his emissaries had signed. There was nothing in that beloved charter that specifically authorized the Chief Executive to purchase enormous areas, especially those inhabited by thousands of Spaniards, French, Indians, and others. America was not then in pressing need of more land, for Jefferson had said in his inaugural address that there was already "room enough for our descendants to the thousandth and thousandth generation." But the acquisition of Louisiana was so overwhelmingly in the national interest that Jefferson swallowed his scruples and completed the transaction in accord with his treaty-making power under the Constitution. Among other drawbacks, the French title to the new acquisition was highly questionable, so much so that Jefferson has been called a receiver of stolen goods or the "accomplice" of the great highwayman, Napoleon Bonaparte.

The acquisition of Louisiana, to Jefferson's credit, was an enormous gain for peace. It may well have averted potential armed conflicts with the Western American pioneers, the Spaniards, and the French. In addition, the necessity of making a war-breeding alliance with Great Britain evaporated. A scheming Napoleon remained purposely vague about the boundaries of the purchase, for he was not at all averse to involving the United States in war with Spain and especially Great Britain. Squabbles did result with the British in the north and the Spaniards in the south, but these differences were all adjusted ultimately without resort to shooting.

America's appetite thus whetted by the Louisiana purchase, Jefferson continued to cast longing eyes on West Florida, particularly that portion of present Mississippi and Alabama fronting the Gulf of Mexico and embracing the Mobile area. He knew perfectly well that this territory was not included in the Louisiana windfall, but his wishful thinking told him otherwise.

Jefferson first used the quiet channels of diplomacy, and then, surprisingly for so peaceful a man, tried bluster. In his annual message of December 1805, he referred in a belligerent tone to relations with Spain and suggested the necessity of raising 300,000 soldiers for defense and offense. But Jefferson succeeded only in arousing the combined suspicions of the French, the Spaniards, and the British. On the eve of leaving the presidency in 1809 he was heard to say, "We must have the Floridas and Cuba."

In retrospect, a lucky Jefferson deserves praise for promoting peace through the Louisiana Purchase, but he must share the credit with others. A critic cannot overlook the impotence of Spain, the impatience of Bonaparte, the resistance in Haiti of Toussaint L'Ouverture and his fellow blacks, and the naval might of Great Britain.

Maritime Manhandling

It is an arresting fact that every time there has been a major war involving control of the high seas, particularly in the Atlantic Ocean, the American people have been sucked into the fray. The combined conflicts attending the French Revolution, 1793–1802, involved President Adams in the quasi-war with France of 1798–1800. The Napoleonic wars of 1803–1815 enmeshed the United States in the War of 1812, when President Madison held office. Jefferson, for reasons that will become evident, kept the nation out of a European war, although there was some minor bloodshed. But all this was in addition to his economic warfare of embargoes and nonintercourse.

In May 1803, about two weeks after signing away the vastnesses of Louisiana, France (Napoleon) declared war on Great Britian. The conflict was destined to run its bloody course for twelve years until 1815, when Napoleon met his Waterloo and was exiled to the south Atlantic island of St. Helena.

Incredible though it may seem, American shippers flourished as neutral carriers during the first two or three years of the renewed war, 1803–1805. Interruptions of this commerce by the sea-dominating British were annoying but profitably tolerable, for such trade involved principally the French and Spanish West Indies. Ultimately, British warships began to seize scores of American merchant vessels, chiefly those engaged in the West

Indian trade. Pained cries of protest rose in mounting volume from American commercial centers, especially in New England.

A related grievance against the British was the impressment of American citizens from American merchant ships on the high seas. This centuries-old practice was a crude form of conscription and was the only method the British had been able to devise that would keep the "floating hells" of their chronically short-handed navy properly manned. Yet Great Britain set limits to this disageeable practice. Invoking the principle "once an Englishman, always an Englishman," the London government claimed the right to seize any able-bodied seaman on British soil or on merchant ships, British or otherwise, sailing the high seas.

Burning grievances were thus generated on both sides of the impressment controversy. No one could tell by merely looking at a sailor of British parentage whether or not he had been born in America or England. His Majesty's press gangs, when in doubt, would claim the victim as one of their own, especially if their ship was dangerously short-handed. They would brush aside naturalization papers or birth certificates, partly because fraudulent papers were notoriously being bought by British deserters for trifling sums. The net result was that, especially during the Napoleonic wars, the British impressed perhaps as many as several thousand bona fide American citizens. Many of them were shot or drowned in action, while the bitterness of their relatives mounted and the honor of the nation was besmirched.

In May 1806, as the nation's anger was rising dangerously against Great Britain, Jefferson, the ardent lover of peace, made a special effort to iron out friction over current ship seizures and impressments. He sent William Pinkney, a Baltimore attorney, to London, there to assist James Monroe, the regular Minister, in pressing for an accommodation. The British, for understandable reasons, refused to renounce impressment in a formal treaty. But they would supplement such a pact with an informal pledge to exercise "the greatest caution" in judging the nationality of prospective victims.

Jefferson refused to submit this treaty to the Senate, for he was dissatisfied with such informal handling of impressment, as well as with some other aspects. Instead, he advised the two negotiators to reopen negotiations in conformity with their original instructions. Jefferson's unwillingness to accept a half-loaf solution does not reflect his avowed "passion for peace." The British had previously found ample excuses for violating the Anglo-

American peace treaty of 1783, and if they were going to ignore restrictions on impressment they would evidently continue to do so, whether the assurances were formal or informal. With an eye to their own aroused public opinion, the London officials probably preferred to keep any concessions on impressment to a gentleman's agreement, which probably would have had more of an appeal to the British sense of honor.

As an anti-warship man, Jefferson probably never fully realized how desperately the British navy lacked men or how necessary their stout wooden walls were to them if they hoped to keep Napoleon at bay. Nor does Jefferson seem to have been fully aware of the stubborn fact that the British would fight before they would abandon impressment. Actually they fought the United States in the War of 1812, after which they continued to claim the right to impress for many years.

Bloodied Decks

Closely related to impressment, and sometimes involving it, was the British practice of hovering. Most obnoxiously, the Royal Navy stationed warships off the three-mile line of the port of New York, where they "hovered" in such force as virtually to establish a blockade. Here, usually on the high seas, they exercised the undoubted right of a belligerent to visit and search a neutral vessel so as to establish its national identity and ascertain the nature of its cargo. If even suspected of irregularities, the neutral ship could be taken for further examination to faraway Halifax, Nova Scotia, where at best the victim would suffer costly inconvenience and delay. The cargo might even be confiscated, in whole or in part.

On April 25, 1806, off New York harbor, one of these hovering British men-of-war, the *Leander*, fired a solid shot across the bow of a ship as the conventional signal to heave to for visit and search. Unfortunately, the cannonball continued its flight and killed one John Pierce, a United States citizen on an American merchant ship some distance beyond, allegedly in the territorial waters of the United States. His mangled body, when exhibited, triggered mob demonstrations on shore. Angered countrymen intercepted supplies for the British squadron and compelled the few British officers on shore to hide. Pierce's funeral turned into a mass protest, and the captain of the offending British warship was indicted for murder. The Mayor of New York sent on to Washington the necessary affidavits, on which Jefferson could base such action as he deemed fit.

A conventional diplomatic protest was clearly in order for this accidental killing, but Jefferson went much beyond such a formality and displayed a degree of bellicosity that did not square with his alleged "passion for peace." Evidently his patience with the three principal British blockading ships was exhausted, for he named not only them but also their captains in his special proclamation dated May 3, 1806. He declared that Captain Henry Whitby of the *Leander*, if apprehended, was to be brought to trial for murder. The three British ships and their captains were to leave American waters forthwith, and any other vessels that any of these three men should ever command were "forever" to be interdicted. All Americans who provided these three ships with supplies or other succor, except to speed their departure, would be prosecuted under the law. As time passed, the excitement gradually died down, but the memory lingered and festered.

The impressment issue came to a furious boil a little more than a year later, on June 22, 1807, in the tragic case of the *Chesapeake*, a frigate of the United States Navy, bound for the Mediterranean. It encountered a British frigate, the *Leopard*, about ten miles off the coast of Virginia. The *Chesapeake* had enrolled in her crew four men (two blacks and two whites) who had deserted from the British navy several months earlier. Three of the quartet were Americans who allegedly had been impressed earlier by the British.

The captain of the British frigate approached, evidently on a friendly mission of some sort, but he then requested the surrender of the four men. Though totally surprised and unprepared to resist attack, the American commander refused to submit, whereupon the British frigate poured in three broadsides at short range, thus killing three men and wounding eighteen others. The Americans finally fired one shot with a live coal in honor of the flag. The defenseless *Chesapeake* then surrendered, and a British boarding party retrieved the four alleged deserters, leaving the bloodied and battered ship to limp back to Norfolk. As if to turn the knife in the wound, the *Leopard* returned to her anchorage in American waters.

We must note that this outrageous incident was not technically a case of impressment but of the recovery of four deserters.

The British party that boarded the *Chesapeake* spotted a number of seamen whom they might have impressed as resembling British subjects, but the boarders strictly followed orders that had issued from Halifax. Moreover, the British had never claimed the right to board and search a neutral warship for any purpose, and in so doing they were clearly in the wrong, as the London government conceded. (Warships might shoot back.) The British were willing to make the necessary amends but, strangely enough, were delayed by the pacifistic Jefferson.

Red-blooded Americans found this outrage simply intolerable, and an unthinking cry for war rocked the entire country, even Federalist New England. An enraged mob at Norfolk destroyed the water casks of the British fleet, and British officers on shore leave fled to their ships. With the benefit of hindsight, we can see that if the Americans were going to fight England, just as they did five years later, they could have fought better, but perhaps as futilely, at that time, when the country was united. Evidently all Jefferson had to do was send a war message to Congress and the War of 1812 would be known today as the War of 1807.

But Jefferson shrank from hostilities. Not until ten days after the outrage did he issue a proclamation ordering all British warships out of American territorial waters, while denying their officers and crews succor of any kind. At the end of this document Jefferson softened the blow considerably by granting a temporary exception to British ships in distress, whether from storms, need of repairs, or other necessities.

Jefferson continued his evident determination to permit passions to cool off, for he waited five weeks after the assault on the American frigate to summon Congress into extraordinary session. Even then he set the date for convening at October 26, 1807, or nearly four months after the *Chesapeake* "enormity." Clearly in no mood to rush into war, he would leave any belligerent action up to a cooled-off Congress.

In this instance Jefferson's "passion" for peace seems to have been deepened by several considerations. For one thing, he realized that American shipping the world over, completely unwarned of a war with Britain, would be sitting ducks for British warships and privateers. The fate of thousands of inocent seamen, not to mention their ships, was at stake. Moreover, Jefferson seems to have thought that he could use Britain's admitted blunder as a club with which to force her to abandon the impressment of American citizens, especially those on unprotected

American ships. As he said, "Now then is the time to settle the old and the new."

Jefferson also realized that the United States could not hope to defeat Britain in a formal war, and here he was probably right. If the Americans could not do so in 1812, when they were stonger by five years, there was not much hope for them in 1807. Few thoughts can promote a pacific disposition quicker than a realization that one's nation probably will suffer defeat. Then why not find a substitute for a shooting war in economic warfare? This idea Jefferson had long toyed with philosophically, and it found realization in the self-crucifying embargo of 1807 to 1809.

The *Chesapeake* atrocity thus left a five-year running sore that oozed into President Madison's administration. The British finally and formally disavowed this outrage in 1811 and returned two surviving American deserters. The bona fide British deserter had been hanged, and one of the three Americans had died in captivity. But by this time the American people were preoccupied with seizing British soil, and the slogan of the hour was not "Remember the *Chesapeake*" but "On to Canada."

Jefferson's "Dambargo"

In 1806, the year before the *Chesapeake* indignity, the war in Europe took on a different and uglier face. The change came following the titanic naval battle at Trafalgar in 1805, which the British won overwhelmingly, plus the land battle of Austerlitz, where Napoleon crushed the Austrian and Russian armies. Apprehensive neutral nations now witnessed a classic confrontation between the tiger and the shark. Britannia was supreme on the sea; Napoleon was supreme on the land. The nutcrackered neutrals, notably the maritime United States, were squeezed in the middle and bound to suffer indignities from both sides.

Beginning in May 1806 the British government issued an epochal Order in Council proclaiming a blockade of the European coast from Brest, in France, to the Elbe River, in present West Germany. Napoleon countered with a decree proclaiming a blockade of the British Isles. Then followed reciprocal British Orders in Council and French decrees; in effect they enabled the belligerents to seize any American vessel entering European waters.

Caught between the hammer and the anvil, American shippers lost scores of ships to the belligerents. But if one vessel in three got through the blockades, the owners could still net a profit. Both camps of belligerents were violating American rights wholesale and continuing to show scant respect for them. After all, the clashing nations were making war; the Yankees were making money. The Americans had ample grounds for declaring war on either Britain or France, or even both. But because the United States was not strong enough to bring either power to terms, it would have to swallow its pride and scrape together what profits it could, or find some retaliatory substitute for a shooting war.

At this point President Jefferson came up with what a later generation would call "economic sanctions." He had long toyed with this idea, and remembered that the First Continental Congress in 1774 had adopted the famous Association. Through it the members had pledged themselves to refrain from importing, exporting, or consuming British goods. The plan achieved considerable success, for this was a time when patriotism had risen to a high level and self-abnegation brought satisfaction.

Forced by the iron hand of necessity to strike back—or so it seemed—Jefferson engineered the passing of the Embargo Act by Congress in December 1807, some six months after the *Chesapeake* unpleasantness. This onerous new law, strengthened with the iron teeth of supplementary legislation, virtually prohibited the export of any goods from the United States by sea or by land. The President's theory was that the belligerents, desperately in need of American foodstuffs and other necessities, would be forced to come around, hat in hand, and promise to respect American rights. In short, Jefferson rather naively reasoned that by waging economic warfare on the belligerents he would bring them to accept the kind of terms that victors dictate from the battlefield.

Jefferson's ill-fated embargo achieved several spectacular results—largely of a negative nature. It dealt a body blow to the American shipping industry, as forests of dead masts sprang up in (Federalist) New England, with consequent unemployment and hunger. Wholesale smuggling mushroomed, for Americans have ever been prone to make a fast dollar, especially in defiance of unpopular laws. Profitable activity, even if illegal, is better for a nation's morale than quiet starvation. On Lake Champlain huge produce-laden rafts, protected by scores of armed men, openly defied federal revenue officers and state militia as they headed for the Canadian border. Jefferson was forced to issue a proclamation (April 19, 1808) commanding the authorities to arrest all insurrectionists who would not "instantly" retire to "their respective abodes."

Law and order had clearly broken down, and there was wild talk of secession, especially in New England. Jefferson himself later wrote that he felt "the foundation of government shaken under my feet by the New England townships." Critics of the Embargo Act declared that it was like cutting one's throat to cure the nosebleed, and cynics transposed letters in the hated word to read "Go Bar 'Em," "O-grab me," and "Mob-rage," which seemed imminent.

In a sense, Jefferson was warring against his own people more than against the offending powers. Ironically, his hatred of war was focused on its fostering of corruption and its restrictions on liberties—and the embargo begat both. But at the same time it reduced impressment by grounding many American seamen.

Jefferson's determination to find a peaceful substitute for war—a noble experiment indeed—has usually been written off as an abject failure. Jefferson himself later admitted that it was three times more costly than actual war. In the closing days of his second term Congress, conceding failure, repealed the embargo and substituted nonintercourse with Britain and France. Jefferson signed this watered-down bill, as well he might have, for these two belligerents were more important to the United States than all of the neutral world put together. In short, Jefferson's successor, President Madison, was committed to carrying on his predecessor's policy of peaceful but war-breeding economic sanctions. As we shall note later, Jefferson's modified policy of economic sanctions came much closer to achieving ultimate success than is commonly supposed. Failure or not, the embargo proved to be what he called a "candid and liberal experiment" and what historians have hailed as his most original and daring act of statesmanship.

Any evaluation of Jefferson as a warrior must result in high marks for his lifelong devotion to peace. He led the United States into no major foreign war, although he probably could have secured from Congress a formal declaration of war against Britain after the outrageous *Chesapeake* affair. He did not take the United States into the Tripolitan war; Tripoli declared it first and Jefferson refused to respond aggressively until Congress had passed a counter-declaration. Then he prosecuted the conflict with considerable credit to American arms and wound up with a reasonable satisfactory peace treaty.

As for Jefferson's Louisiana Purchase, by promoting and then accepting this spectacular windfall, he avoided war with France. By resorting to the self-crucifying embargo, he may have averted a larger shooting war with Britain or France or even both. His embargo was a daring stroke for peace that pinched both Britain and France, but it fell short of hoped-for success primarily because a hostile public opinion, chiefly Federalist, would not permit it to be rigidly enforced. Like the prohibition of alcohol in the 1920s, the prohibition on foreign commerce was never fully tried.

CHAPTER 4

JAMES MADISON: THE SCHOLARLY WARRIOR

Anxious to abridge the evils from which a state of war can not be exempt, I lost no time after it was declared in conveying to the British Government the terms on which its progress might be arrested. . . .

President Madison, Fourth
Annual Message to Congress,
November 4, 1812.

Madisonian Muddlings

Virginia-born President Madison, though a giant intellectually, was a near-dwarf physically. Weighing a scant 100 pounds, and standing only five feet, four inches, he was the shortest of all the Presidents of the United States. His unimpressive physique, combined with a baldish head, blond hair, blue eyes, and a weak speaking voice, did not radiate bellicosity or even aggressiveness. Nicknames attached to him were "Little Jemmy" or "Master Jemmy." The famed contemporary writer, Washington Irving, called him a "withered little applejohn."

Like Jefferson and John Adams before him, and Woodrow Wilson long after, Madison was regarded as a "scholar in politics." A graduate of what is now Princeton and a lawyer, he was never a soldier, although he did serve in the Continental Congress for three years during the Revolution, 1780–1783. Famous as a thinker, a writer, and a constitutionalist, he had played a key role among the Founding Fathers at the Philadelphia Convention of 1787, from which he emerged as "The Father of the Constitution."

As a philosophical man of peace, Madison came to the presidency in 1809 ill equipped to grapple with the problem of restraining the two fearsome giants, Britain and France. Both were thrashing around in a death struggle with scant regard for the rights and physical well being of commercially oriented neutrals, notably the United States. And although Madison had served competently as Secretary of State under Jefferson, and hence had some idea of what he was getting into, he was not equipped to ride the whirlwind and direct the storm. No American was. As events proved, the United States was too weak to fight a great power successfully but too strong to endure insult interminably.

Madison, a dyed-in-the-wool Jeffersonian Republican, was heavily committed to the policies of his predecessor. Like Jefferson, he was forced to place heavy reliance on the unreliable militia and the mothballed seagoing navy, while relying on the tiny gunboats to protect American shores against an enemy's two-decked frigates and three-decked ships of the line. Like Jefferson, Madison was weary of being kicked around by the belligerents and, like him, chose economic reprisals—embargoes instead of bullets—as the only feasible alternative. This was the policy that he had consistently followed while Secretary of State.

We recall that Jefferson's commercial embargo against all nations was repealed on March 1, 1809, three days before Madison took the presidential oath. At the same time, Congress provided a limited substitute. Nonintercourse was to be continued against only Britain and France, the two most important powers, until they agreed to respect American maritime rights.

David M. Erskine, the British Minister in Washington, now appeared on the stage of history. Unwisely exceeding his instructions from London, Erskine negotiated an agreement that bound Britain to end her restrictions on American shipping, in return for a repeal of America's nonintercourse against the British and its enforcement against the French.

The ordinarily cautious Madison, gripped by Jeffersonian passion for peace, now blundered badly. Naively assuming that

London would honor the agreement negotiated by Erskine, Madison forthwith proclaimed a renewal of intercourse with Britain while retaining nonintercourse against France, effective June 10, 1809. When the British Foreign Office discovered that its Minister in Washington had grossly exceeded his instructions, his commitments were disavowed and Erskine was recalled. A crestfallen Madison was forced to renew nonintercourse against Britain, on August 9, 1809. Having thrown himself into the arms of the Mother Country, he had been flung back again, this time onto the road toward war.

Not content with being duped by the British Minister in Washington, a naive Madison permitted himself to be duped by Napoleon. The villain in this episode was Macon's Bill No. 2, passed by Congress and approved on May 1, 1810, as a substitute for nonintercourse. It provided that if either France or England repealed its offensive maritime restrictions, the United States would invoke nonimportation against the nonrepealing power.

This was a situation made to order for the double-dealing Napoleon. In an ambiguous statement, he ostensibly lifted his offensive maritime decrees (while seizing American ships) and called on the United States to reimpose nonintercourse against Britain. The angered British stood firm, and on March 2, 1811, the Congress officially renewed nonimportation against Great Britain, thus further arousing British resentment against the "money-grabbing Yankees."

Drifting Toward War

In the summer of 1811, while maritime grievances against both Britain and France continued to fester, a new British Minister arrived in Washington with instructions to salve the running sore of the *Chesapeake* affair, now four years old. He was astonished to find interest in that outrage eclipsed by excitement over the *Little Belt* affair. This British corvette, mounting twenty guns and thought to be harassing American commerce off the New York coast, encountered in the gathering dusk a powerful United States frigate, the forty-four-gun *President*. Which ship fired the first shot is still a mystery, but in the ensuing mismatch the British ship suffered thirty-two killed and wounded. As the American frigate lost no life, the enemy sacrificed four killed for every one earlier killed on the ill-fated *Chesapeake*.

To many Americans, sweet but belated vengeance had been achieved. Nevertheless, the new British Minister, as instructed, formally disavowed the *Chesapeake* incident, more than four years after the tragedy. He agreed to return the two surviving Americans to her decks and also to provide appropriate monetary compensation for the victims or their families. On November 13, 1811, President Madison communicated his acceptance of these terms to Congress. Such salve came much too late to do much soothing. This tardy apology almost certainly would have come several years earlier if Jefferson had not so stubbornly tried to couple reparation with a renunciation of the brutal but centuries-old practice of impressment.

Late in 1810, while slithering into a showdown with Great Britain, the peace-loving Madison acquired a substantial chunk of West Florida from Spain by what the Spaniards regarded as an act of war. The sprawling Louisiana Purchase did not cover this area, although Jefferson had done his best to make it stretch. If Madison did not actually involve his country in war to get this morsel of West Florida, he and his government evidently connived at theft to get it, in a manner worthy of Napoleon and not conforming to the highest ethical standards.

In brief, the story is that American settlers had moved into West Florida and, as they were later to do in Texas, they chafed under this foreign yoke. The epidemic of revolutions in Latin America against Spanish rule appears to have spread its contagion to the shores of West Florida. In September 1810 the American settlers there, encouraged by the Madison administration, if not assisted by it, rose in revolt. They stormed the Spanish fort at Baton Rouge, on the east bank of the Mississippi, and killed the Spanish commander. On September 26, 1810, the victors proclaimed the "Republic of West Florida," somewhat after the manner of later American settlers in Texas and California.

President Madison, though usually regarded as a quiet closet philosopher, grabbed for the Florida fruit. He issued a proclamation on October 27, 1810, extending United States jurisdiction over the area of West Florida that stretched all the way to the Perdido River. Actually, the land claimed by the rebels extended only to the Pearl River, about one hundred miles to the west. The President also had Congress pass a resolution in secret session, January 15, 1811, asserting jurisdiction over this coveted territory to the Perdido.

Madison justified this Florida seizure by noting that the area in question had been embraced in the Louisiana Purchase, and hence belonged to the United States anyhow. But he knew better, and a troubled conscience was probably what led him to falsify the dates on certain important documents, evidently to deceive posterity. The American Minister to Russia undertook, with some embarrassment, to explain to the Czar how the land-rich United States had acquired Spain's semi-defenseless territory. His Majesty, thinking of Napoleon's reshaping of the map of Europe, replied amiably, "Everyone grows a little in this world."

Spain protested heatedly but vainly against this West Florida grab, but she was too deeply involved in her desperate war with Napoleon to do much. The British were likewise aroused by this latest exhibition of Yankee greed, and His Majesty's Minister in Washington condemned the occupation of West Florida as "contrary to every principle of public justice, faith, and national honor."

The British then had their hands full with Napoleon, but they did not forget. During the War of 1812, the embittered *Times* of London declared that "Mr. Madison's dirty, swindling manoeuvers in respect to Louisiana and the Floridas remain to be punished." Madison may have been a man of peace, but he was not unaffected by the virus of imperialism or by what a later generation would call Manifest Destiny.

Madison Yields to the War Hawks

While American maritime rights were being flouted wholesale by Britain and France alike, another burning grievance against Great Britain came to an explosive head on the battlefield of Tippecanoe, in present Indiana, on November 7, 1811.

Increasing encroachments by the whites on lands north of the Ohio River were forcing the Indians into a far-flung confederation, organized under the gifted Tecumseh and his one-eyed brother, The Prophet. The red men were receiving generous supplies of arms and ammunition from their friends in red coats on the Canadian side of the boundary line. There can be little doubt that the British, with firearms and firewater, were secretly encouraging the Indians to resist and thus protecting Canada from Yankee invasion. Such instigation was probably not so serious as painted, but the rumor was rife on the frontier that "British hairbuyers" were offering bounties of six dollars for each white scalp.

General William H. Harrison, commanding some one thousand men, many of them regulars, advanced cautiously toward the Indian encampment near Tippecanoe. A bloodly engagement ensued, during which about two hundred combatants were killed or wounded on each side. General Harrison hastily withdrew to safe terrain, leaving the Indians free to butcher the exposed frontiersmen in their cabins, but the farther he got away from Tippecanoe the more glorious the victory loomed. Freshly marked British arms, obviously imported by way of Canada, were found on the battlefield, and they gave further impetus to the cry of the Westerners, "On to Canada!"

On November 4, 1811, three days before the Tippecanoe clash, the newly elected Twelfth Congress assembled in Washington. About one-half of the membership of the House had been purged of "submission men," and many of the newcomers were "War Hawks," on fire to settle old scores with England. Some of their leaders hailed from the South and West. Although remote from the sea, they greatly resented impressment as a stain on American honor, and as growers of agricultural produce they suffered in the pocket nerve from wholesale British and French seizures of American shipping.

The principal foes of the War Hawks were the Federalists, notably in New England, who still cherished their sentimental attachment to the Mother Country, as well as their antipathy to the ideals unleashed by the French Revolution. These English-speaking Yankees recoiled from the treachery of stabbing Britain in the back—a nation that then represented the last real bulwark of constitutional government in the Old World. Such Federalists deplored the cry of the War Hawks, "On to Canada," and accordingly gave blunt notice that they would drag their feet if the Madison administration pushed the country over the precipice into war.

After President Madison was safely renominated in 1812 by the Congressional caucus of his Republican party, he submitted his memorable war message to a confused and contentious Congress on June 1, 1812. He did not, as commonly supposed, flatly ask that divided body to declare war on Britain or any other nation. He issued no ringing call to battle. He realized perfectly well that only Congress could declare war, and that there was a separation of powers among the three branches of government, as established by the Constitution that he had helped to draft.

What Madison did in his historic "war message" was to list at length the major grievances of the United States against Great Britain. Chief among these were the brutal impressments of countless American citizens; the virtual blockade of American coasts by "hovering" British warships; the "pretended blockades" of areas under the control of France; the forgeries and perjuries with which Britain carried on commerce with her European enemy to the exclusion of American shipping; and the British-inspired attacks by the Indians, who "spare neither age nor sex." At this point Madison put his finger on a great truth: "We behold, in fine, on the side of Great Britain a state of war against the United States, and on the side of the United States a state of peace toward Great Britain."

Yet Madison, as President, did not urge Congress to fight back. This was "a solemn question which the Constitution wisely confides to the legislative department of the Government." But he was "happy in the assurance that the decision will be worthy [of] the enlightened and patriotic councils of a virtuous, a free, and a powerful nation." Here Madison more than hinted that the declaration of war he favored would be the outcome if Congress should prove true to itself.

As if to balance the scales, President Madison paid his disrespects to France in the closing paragraph of this message, in which he suggested that a declaration of war against France also would be in order. Her decrees had violated neutral rights; her seizures of American shipping by the illegal operations of privateers and national warships had been notorious; and she had not pledged or paid any indemnity for the extensive spoliations of American commerce under arbitrary Napoleonic decrees. But Madison recommended no "definitive measures" against France, because the results of ongoing negotiations in Paris might yet enable Congress to act more wisely in regard "to the rights, the interests, and the honor of our country."

Unlike the Congressional War Hawks, Madison at no point in his war message of June 1, 1812, indicated a hunger for neighboring Canada. But it is hardly conceivable that he did not have his neighbor's vast territory in view, because it was the only place where he could attack the British by land. He may have had no intention of retaining any Canadian soil, but it might prove useful during peace negotiations as a prize that could be swapped for American territory seized by the British.

On June 4, 1812, only three days after Madison's "war message," the House of Representatives, the nest of the War Hawks, responded by passing a war resolution directed at Britain, 79 to 49. Most of the support came from the thinly populated West, from the agricultural areas (especially in the South), and from other bastions of the Madisonian Republicans. Politics made possible this divisive little war.

The Senate presented a different complexion, for it harbored conservative oldsters, predominantly Federalists. These men usually hailed from the shipping and commercial areas of the East and Northeast, especially those of the New England Federalists. During the Senate debate attempts were made to retreat from outright war by simply authorizing the cheap and profitable use of privateers against both England and France, and then against England alone. All such diversionary efforts failed, partly because the conquest of Canada seemed easy, and on June 17, 1812, after a delay of sixteen days, the Senate narrowly voted for war against Great Britain, 19 to 13. A shift of only a few votes would have deadlocked the decision, leaving the tie-breaking vote to the presiding officer. A vote for war in either house of Congress by this narrow a margin is a sure guarantee of disunity and probable disaster, as the ensuing conflict abundantly demonstrated.

The Unwisdom of War

Madison, we recall, had suggested in his war message the possibility of fighting the French in the event of the failure of negotiations then under way in Paris. Yet a proposal to include France with Britain in the declaration of war was defeated in the Senate by the narrow vote of 18 to 14. A switch of only three votes would have carried the day. Most of the eighteen opponents were pro-French Republicans who remembered that during the American Revolution France had been the welcome ally and Britain the relentless foe. The pro-British Federalists, on the other hand, believed that the Mother Country, combating French revolutionary ideals, should not be stabbed in the back, as indeed she was, while fighting the despotic enemies of constitutional government.

France, no less than Great Britain, was then making war on the United States, and had been for years. The responsibility of Congress was to recognize these hostilities, as many Federalists argued, by a counter-declaration of war against the dictatorial Napoleon. During the five-year period prior to 1812 the French had confiscated 558 American ships; in the same period Britain had seized 389, although her total bag since 1803 had been 917 Yankee craft. Napoleon had impressed few Americans, not needing them for his navy, now blasted and blockaded by the British. Yet he had imprisoned the crews of confiscated American merchant ships and treated then inhumanely. Even so, the abuse of fellow citizens some 3,000 miles away in France seemed much less offensive than the impressment of seamen from merchant ships within sight of the American coast.

As between Napoleon and Britain, the War Hawks reached the more realistic decision. There was no way to strike directly at France except with privateers, which the British were already using effectively. But British Canada, a rich hostage, lay next door for the taking, as advertised by the popular slogan "On to Canada." Such an invasion would be a "mere matter of marching," observed the retired Jefferson; the militia of Kentucky alone could do it, cried the chief War Hawk, Henry Clay, "The Cock of Kentucky." At the same time the American invaders would wipe out the Indian supply base, while annexing all or large parts of the snow-shrouded neighbor to the north. The Americans would thus stab the Mother Country in the back while she was desperately locked in deadly combat with Napoleon, the antichrist of the age.

The War Hawks, for all their boasting, were realistic enough to choose the one foe that would be easiest to strike and that would presumably yield richer rewards. In so doing the Americans became virtual allies of the treacherous Bonaparte, the "Corsican butcher," who was the bloodiest ruler of his era. His victories in Europe were acclaimed joyously by the Madisonian Republicans; his defeats were celebrated hilariously, especially in New England, by the Federalists. Many Federalists likewise rejoiced over American defeats in the various attempts to invade Canada, mostly with frustrating or disgraceful results.

The American people, ignoring George Washington's solemn warning in his farewell address, split disastrously in their support of the two major powers. One of them, Britain, was an open enemy; the other, France, was an unofficial enemy. Bitterly divided and weak nations usually do not win military contests with undivided and powerful ones. The War of 1812 was no exception. In later years Madison told the historian George Bancroft that he was aware "of the unprepared state of the country, but he esteemed it necessary to throw forward the flag of the country, sure that the people would press forward and defend it." Many of them, conspicuously the New England Federalists, were content to let the Stars and Stripes lie in the mud.

The multipronged American invasions of Canada all failed, some disastrously, in 1812 and again in 1813. In 1814 the United States was desperately fending off invasions by the British redcoats, who sacked and burned the chief public buildings of Washington, including the White House. Madison and his entourage were chased out into the woods of Virginia like frightened rabbits. By this time Napoleon had been marooned on isolated St. Helena, and thousands of veteran British soldiers had been released for duty in the United States. America's stab in Britain's back had failed, and the Yankees would have to face British wrath alone. Early in 1815 an army of about 7,500 crack British soldiers were preparing to seize New Orleans and presumably to detach huge strategic areas of the United States, at least temporarily.

On the high seas the final story was dismal. The few American superfrigates and sloops of war won most of their single-ship duels with the British, but gradually the tiny American navy was virtually wiped out, leaving Britain where she had been, undisputed mistress of the seas.

The Battle of the Peace Table

One of the most curious ironies of the War of 1812 is that it was totally unnecessary, but America was not patient enough to reap the rewards of long-term suffering. On June 16, 1812, two days before President Madison signed the fateful war resolution, Foreign Secretary Castlereagh announced to the House of Commons that the odious maritime decrees called Orders in Council, so galling to American shippers, would be immediately suspended. This was a momentous concession to the Yankees. If there had then been a transatlantic cable, President Madison might not have signed the war resolution, and hostilities would have been averted. But the dogs of war were now unleashed.

In past wars the combatants ordinarily had met on the field of battle, and one side or the other had triumphed or fought to a stalemate. Then, after some delay, peace terms were dictated or negotiated and a treaty of peace was signed. But in the case of the War of 1812 both combatants, in a figurative sense, fought with the sword in one hand and an olive branch in the other.

Despite his somewhat ambiguous war message to Congress, President Madison did not really want war and forthwith took steps to bring it to an honorable end. As his Secretary of State wrote to Jonathan Russell, the American chargé d'affaires in London, "At the moment of the declaration of war the President, regretting the necessity which produced it, looked to its termination, and provided for it." Accordingly, Russell was authorized by his instructions, dated about a week after America's formal declaration of war, to agree on an armistice designed to obtain peace, but on two conditions. One was the revocation of the ship-seizing Orders in Council (already essentially renounced); the other was the abandonment of man-snatching impressment so odious to Americans.

On August 29, 1812, Lord Castlereagh rejected the armistice proposed by Madison. He pointed out that Britain had already conceded the point regarding Orders in Council, but he would not give up impressment. Britain's existence as a dominant power depended on her navy, and life on the tempestuous waves was so harsh and hazardous that the fleet simply could not be properly manned without impressment. The London government had already made its stand clear to Jefferson at the time of the *Chesapeake* incident and the ill-fated Monroe-Pinkney negotiations of 1806. Why President Madison, then Secretary of State under Jefferson, had not yet grasped this stubborn truth remains something of a mystery.

Strangely enough, the next major move toward peace came on September 13, 1812, from the Czar of Russia, who was then desperately fighting off Napoleon's massive but ill-fated invasion. Britain was allied with Russia against France, and evidently the Czar did not want to see the British waste their strength in America when he desperately needed all the support he could muster in Europe. In any event, his intercession set in motion a series of events that brought to the quaint Flemish town of Ghent five able American negotiators, including John Quincy Adams, Henry Clay, and Albert Gallatin. For its part, the London Foreign Office unwisely sent two nonentities, who met more than their match in these American notables.

The peace negotiations at Ghent were influenced by news constantly flowing in from the battle front in North America. At the outset, the United States agents insisted on the abandonment of impressment and the granting of other concessions. The British, for their part, stood fast on impressment and demanded huge expanses of territory from the United States, because at that stage of the war in America Great Britain plainly had the upper hand. But when news reached Ghent that a formidable force of about 10,000 crack redcoats had been forced to retreat from the Lake Champlain area, the British withdrew or modified their demands. The Americans, on the other side of the table, gave up their insistence on the cessation of impressment. One reason for so doing was that the conclusion of the war in Europe had ended the necessity of impressment and the obnoxious Orders in Council.

Because neither side could or would impose its will on the other by force of arms, the Peace of Ghent was essentially a temporary suspension of hostilities—a restoration of the *status quo ante bellum*. Both combatants simply agreed to stop fighting and hand back the territory that they had wrested from their foe, with the British restoring far more acreage than the Americans. Of signal importance in the history of arbitration (and peace), the Treaty of Ghent also set up several mixed arbitral tribunals to settle boundary disputes along the Canadian-United States border. All this was a large plus for Madison as a man of peace.

A Frustrating Conflict

By coincidence, the last battle and the most smashing victory of the War of 1812 was won at New Orleans against some 7,500 British veterans. The Americans were commanded by General Andrew Jackson, on January 8, 1815, two weeks *after* the signing of the peace treaty of Ghent, December 24 (Christmas Eve), 1814. The British unwisely launched a frontal attack on Jackson's prepared positions, which were manned by local militia, Kentucky and Tennessee riflemen, blacks, pirates, and a few regulars, all told numbering six thousand to seven thousand troops. The attackers lost some two thousand men killed or wounded, while the Americans lost about seventy, of whom only thirteen were killed.

The tremendous victory at New Orleans over the conquerors of Napoleon had no bearing whatever on the Treaty of Ghent. If the British had won, they might or might not have carried through formal ratification. But this is all useless speculation, because the British suffered a defeat. The glorious news from New Orleans reached Washington early in February 1815; about ten days later the newly signed treaty arrived from Ghent. Wild was the rejoicing, because many Americans had fully expected to lose substantial amounts of territory. The slogan of the hour now became "Not One Inch of Territory Ceded or Lost," quite in contrast with the earlier "On to Canada.

But the sequence of events was grossly misleading. First came the victory at New Orleans, and then the treaty. Many unthinking Americans leaped to the false conclusion that the beaten British, humiliated at New Orleans and elsewhere, had come down off their high horse and hastened to beg for peace. If a nation is able to win only one sensational victory in a poorly fought war, a better taste is left in the mouth if that triumph comes at the end. Thus was born the myth that the United States whipped the British "twict," first in the Revolutionary War and then in the War of 1812.

Actually, neither combatant won the War of 1812. Both sides racked up victories on land and sea. The individual ship duels were overwhelmingly won by the Americans, but in the end the British sea power destroyed the American navy or bottled up what little was left of it. On land neither nation imposed its will on the other, and in this sense both lost.

The opposition Federalists branded this futile little conflict "Mr. Madison's War." It was that, in the sense that the President in effect had asked Congress for it and then had signed the war resolution. This document formally recognized that in effect Britain for years had been making war on the United States. Although a man of peace, the scholarly Madison stepped out of character by becoming a man of war in 1812. He stubbornly believed, despite overwhelming evidence to the contrary, that he could force the dogged and desperate British to give up impressment.

As a war leader, Madison proved singularly inept, as could have been expected, for he was anything but a martial figure or mentality. He knew that the country was dangerously divided between Federalist doves and Republican hawks; he also knew that the nation was wretchedly unprepared. He wound up with his

White House burned, his navy virtually destroyed, his treasury bankrupt, and the New England Federalists, not content with aiding the enemy, seriously preaching or plotting secession. When the British invaders struck at Washington, Madison did what no President in his right mind should do, not even a martial one—he risked capture or death by rushing to the front lines on horseback, and then fleeing to the outskirts of the city to watch the billowing smoke from the Virginia woods. The War Department was kept too long in the clumsy hands of John Armstrong, who came close to matching Madison himself in ineptitude. But in the end, trial-and-error generals had emerged, and the regular soldiers were becoming battle-singed veterans.

Peace, rather incidentally, provided a welcome bonus for the Americans on the northern frontier. The Indian tribes, some already badly mauled, made what treaties they could with the Great White Father in Washington. The luckless red men, forsaken by their British allies at Ghent, had no alternative.

Paradoxically, the Treaty of Ghent derived virtues from its defects, and in this way it unintentionally contributed to an enduring Madisonian peace. It was not a victor's vengeance, which would have made necessary another war to rewrite its terms. No territory was wrested away, so none had to be reconquered. Both sides saved face, and each grudgingly gained a new respect for the other. No longer did British editors sneer at the few "fir-built frigates," manned by "bastards and outlaws," and flying "striped bunting."

The Push Toward Florida

Several rather minor episodes or sideshows during these years throw additional light on the warlike inclinations of President Madison. He had gulped down his first chunk of West Florida with such ease in 1810 that he was tempted to take an additional bite of Spanish East Florida, specifically the area on the Atlantic Coast stretching about sixty miles south of the Georgia border. This territory, though nominally held by Spain, sheltered lawless and otherwise undesirable elements, including British smugglers flouting America's commercial nonintercourse policies.

In January 1811 Congress authorized Madison to take temporary possession of East Florida. He was to act either by agreement with the local authorities or if a foreign power (presumably

Britain) threatened to take possession. When the local Spanish officials proved unwilling to vacate, General George Mathews, a semiliterate former Governor of Georgia, was presumably authorized to encourage a local rebellion in the northeast corner of East Florida. The rebels, supported by American recruits and warships, captured Ferdinanda (on Amelia Island) and undertook to besiege St. Augustine, in June 1812, after turning over captured objectives to United States troops.

These prizes quickly became too hot to handle after formal protests were lodged by both Britain and Spain. Secretary of State Monroe was forced to disavow an embittered Mathews, who felt that he had been exploited and misled by the authorities in Washington. He vowed that he would "be dam'd if he did not blow them all up," but fortunately for Madison's schemings Mathews died suddenly. Spain did not fully reestablish her authority in East Florida until after American troops had left in May 1813. From a strictly ethical standpoint, Madison does not appear in a favorable light during the dubious doings in East Florida.

One of the great ironies of the War of 1812 is that after all the outcry about "On to Canada," the only permanent territorial acquisition by the United States was the Mobile area of West Florida. At the time of the uprising against the Spaniards at Baton Rouge, President Madison had annexed the area eastward up to the Pearl River, in response to an act of Congress passed in January 1811. At that time he had authorized the occupation of West Florida as far east as the Perdido River, where Mobile is located. In April 1813, General Wilkinson, acting under these orders, forced the Spanish garrison at Mobile to surrender. In this way he bloodlessly gained formal possession of the area as far east as the Perdido River.

The Indians of the South, notably Creeks, took to the warpath during the War of 1812. Abundantly supplied with British arms, they massacred more than five hundred whites at Fort Mims, Alabama, on August 30, 1813. General Andrew Jackson, in a rugged campaign that earned him the sobriquet "Old Hickory," inflicted a crushing defeat on the red men at Horseshoe Bend. Pushing on to defend New Orleans, he flouted his orders and attacked Pensacola, east of the Mobile area, and forced the Spanish garrison there to surrender. A British force blew up a nearby fort and departed. But the United States did not then retain Pensacola; it was to be included in the Florida annexation treaty with Spain in 1819, five years later.

Humbling the Barbary Cutthroats

A gratifying postscript to the War of 1812 for Madison involved a thorough chastisement of the piratical Barbary states of North Africa, and here again the President did not shrink from using the sword of righteousness. Tripoli had already been beaten into line in 1805, after the capture of Derna by Eaton's nondescript army. American "protection" payments to the other three states had continued. But during the absence of American warships from the Mediterranean in the War of 1812, Algiers seized American merchant vessels and demanded heavy ransom.

On February 23, 1815, President Madison "recommended" to Congress the declaration of a "state of war" between the United States and Algiers. We should note that he was more insistent on a specific course of action than he had been in his memorable war message against Britain of June 1, 1812. About a week later Congress formally authorized the use of force against the Dey of Algiers for the protection of American commerce. Madison and Congress alike preferred war to tribute.

On May 20, 1815, three months after the Treaty of Ghent was ratified, Commodore Decatur, the hero of the *Philadalphia* burning (1804) in Tripoli harbor, left New York with ten warships of assorted sizes, including three stout frigates. In a running fight in the Mediterranean, Decatur captured the flagship of Algiers and extorted a treaty as humiliating to the proud ruler of Algiers as it was satisfying to the Americans. Among various stipulations, there were to be no future payments of protection money, restorations of all American property, and ten thousand dollars as compensation for merchant ships recently seized.

Not content with this blow for humanity and a free sea, the American squadron forced Tunis and Tripoli to agree to equally harsh terms. A strong naval force remained in the Mediterranean under the Stars and Stripes, thus ensuring the safety of American commerce in the future—"peace without tribute," as Madison wished. In his seventh annual message to Congress (December 5, 1815), Madison referred with satisfaction to the "successful termination" of the Algerian war. He believed that the "subsequent transactions" with Tunis and Tripoli would provide for the "future security" of American commerce in the Mediterranean.

A French philospher once observed that a certain animal was extremely wicked: If one poked him with a sharp stick he fought back. The scholarly Madison got into war with the Creek Indians, the Barbary pirates, and Great Britain because these assorted foes had all engaged in repeated warlike acts against American citizens. He showed great patience, but finally chose to fight Great Britain to uphold the rights and honor of the United States. He was not by nature combative, but he had taken a presidential oath to use his constitutional powers to "provide for the common defense" and "secure the blessings of liberty to ourselves and our posterity."

Less defensible was Madison's acquisition of East Florida from the semi-defenseless Spaniards, and particularly his machinations to secure a part of East Florida through the backfiring intervention of General Mathews. To Madison's credit, he did not rush into any of his wars, particularly the War of 1812. But there is a limit to what a proud and virile people will endure, especially if there is a good chance of winning the war and gathering in a prize as rich as Canada to boot.

President James Monroe, Madison's successor, did not become involved in a European conflict, because there was no general war involving a contest for control for the seas until 1914—a century after Napoleon met his Waterloo in 1815. Monroe was lucky; his immediate predecessors had been less favored.

CHAPTER 5

JAMES MONROE: THE GOOD FEELINGS PRESIDENT

It has been the invariable object of this Government to cherish the most friendly relations with every power, and on principles and conditions which might make them permanent.

James Monroe, Eighth Annual
Message to Congress,
December 7, 1824

A Warrior in the White House

President James Monroe, the last of the so-called Virginia dynasty of Washington, Jefferson, Madison, and Monroe, was an impressive figure of a man. Six feet tall, broad-shouldered, and large of features, he made friends easily with his agreeable smile and approachable manner. He was inferior as a political philosopher to Jefferson and Madison, but those two predecessors respected him for his abilities. Like George Washington, whom he resembled physically, Monroe was somewhat slow in thought but generally sound in judgment. Before winning the White House he had served in the Virginia legislature, the Continental Congress, the Constitutional Convention, the United States Senate, and as a Governor of Virginia, to say nothing of diplomatic missions abroad.

The Jeffersonian Republicans elevated Monroe to the presidency in 1816 by an electoral count of 183 to 34 over the dying Federalists. He was reelected in 1820 with only one dissenting vote, a record topped only by the unanimity for Washington in his two elections. The contemporary accolade, "The Era of Good Feelings," has been attached imperishably to his eight years in the rebuilt White House, although the domestic feelings were not conspicuously good.

As a patriot during the War for Independence, Monroe had left the Virginia College of William and Mary to volunteer for military service from 1776 to 1780, and had risen from the rank of cadet to that of lieutenant and then lieutenant colonel. He experienced action in a half-dozen or so important battles and was severely wounded at Trenton, where he suffered a severed artery and was lucky to come out alive. General Washington promoted him to the rank of captain for "bravery under fire." Monroe appears to have been the only one of the Founding Fathers to suffer serious bloodshed on the battlefield. Better than most men, he discovered at first hand what war entailed, and he was wise enough and fortunate enough to stay out of armed hostilities during his eight years of "Good Feelings."

Monroe's understanding of what war involved, already extensive, was sharpened during the War of 1812. When it erupted, he was serving President Madison as Secretary of State. After two successive Secretaries of War had amply demonstrated their incompetence, Monroe was called upon to straighten out the mess, though continuing with his labors as Secretary of State. This double duty descended on him only six days after the British had burned the main public buildings in Washington.

As will become evident, President Monroe was not only lucky enough to avoid a full-dress war but fortunate enough to enlist as his Secretary of State the redoubtable John Quincy Adams. Already experienced as a Minister to the Netherlands, Prussia, Russia, and Great Britain, Adams worked smoothly and successfully in harness with President Monroe to achieve several peaceful settlements of disputes that redounded greatly to the advantage of the United States.

The Canadian Compromises

The War of 1812 had demonstrated beyond doubt that naval control of the Great Lakes was essential for another American invasion of Canada or for the defense of the United States in any future conflict. The Canadians, who had fought well in the recent struggle, were fearful that the frustrated Yankees would come again. After the war ended in 1815, both the Americans and the British were maintaining or building large wooden warships on the northern lakes, all designed for offensive-defensive operations in the troubled future. The stage was set for a highly expensive and mutually burdensome naval race, with all the dangers of possible collisions with competing ships.

Reciprocal disarmament on the Great Lakes was by no means a new idea. When the Madison administration formally proposed it to the British Foreign Office in November 1815, Foreign Secretary Castlereagh showed little enthusiasm. He was concerned about the backlash at home and in Canada that would come, and did come, from leaving the Canadians naked in the face of their vengeful Yankee neighbors. But Castlereagh gradually saw the light, especially when he perceived that costly warships constructed on an escalating scale would be of no use whatever to the salt-water British Navy on the high seas in other wars.

Negotiations for a disarmament agreement on the lakes were next shifted from London to Washington, where Charles Bagot represented Great Britain. Unlike some of his undiplomatic predecessors, he concealed his distaste for the Yankees while plying them with flattery. Finally, an exchange of notes between him and the Acting Secretary of State, Richard Rush, constituted the memorable Rush-Bagot arms limitation agreement for the lakes.

Minister Bagot, wanting the pact to be more binding, suggested that the document be submitted to the Senate for approval, thus giving it the status of a treaty. This was done. The Senate advised ratification on April 16, 1818, and two days later the agreement was formally proclaimed by President Monroe.

Contrary to a common misconception, the Rush-Bagot agreement did not provide for complete disarmament on the lakes. In the interest of proper policing of these waters, both sides were limited to the same number and size of patrol craft to apprehend smugglers and other lawbreakers. Specifically, on

Lake Ontario there was to be one vessel not exceeding 100 tons burden and armed with a single eighteen-pound cannon; on the other Great Lakes there could be a total of two such vessels for each side; and on Lake Champlain, one such vessel for each side. Both parties to the pact agreed that "all other armed Vessels on these Lakes shall be forthwith dismantled, and that no other vessels of war shall be there built or armed." Finally, each party to the agreement could give formal notice of annulment, effective after the expiration of six months.

The Rush-Bagot agreement, though a landmark in naval disarmament, has been much overpraised. For many years the two former enemies kept their dismantled warships and naval stations in mothball readiness. From time to time both sides technically violated the letter of the agreement, and during the American Civil War Secretary of State Seward gave six months' notice of abrogation but withdrew it before the stipulated time had elapsed. During World War I and World War II, when Canada and the United States were both fighting Germany, the pact was reinterpreted to permit American naval construction, naval training, and related activities on the relatively quiet waters of the Great Lakes.

Nor did the Rush-Bagot agreement apply immediately to land armaments. The Canadians did not feel sufficiently secure until 1871, after the Treaty of Washington had dispelled the war clouds, to allow their border fortifications to rot away. But thanks in large part to the war-born Rush-Bagot agreement, the United States and Canada do today present the heartening example of two friendly nations with a completely unarmed border 5,527 miles in length. It is the longest unfortified boundary in the world, and President Monroe deserves much of the credit for it.

By contrast, the much-underrated Convention of 1818 with Britain was in effect a supplement to the somewhat disappointing Treaty of Ghent of 1815. Like the Rush-Bagot disarmament agreement of 1817, this new pact took care of some important loose ends left at the peace table in 1815.

Specifically, the Convention of 1818 formally renewed the coveted commercial treaty with Great Britain that had been negotiated in 1815. The pact of 1818 also dealt, on a temporary basis at least, with the question of the northern boundary line, as well as fishing privileges on Canadian waters for American fishermen. British cruisers had been provoking much ill will by seizing American vessels in areas where they had formerly been allowed to fish. The new Convention of 1818 narrowed somewhat the liberties granted to these fishermen but left them enough leeway so that they could continue their operations profitably.

Of extreme importance for the future was the arrangement decided upon in this Convention of 1818 regarding the Canadian-American boundary. The northern demarcation of the Louisiana purchase was established by a line running westerly along the 49th parallel from the Lake of the Woods to the Rocky Mountains. From that point to the Pacific Ocean stretched what was known as the vast Oregon country, in which British and Americans alike could now reside on a "free and open" basis for ten years, without "prejudice" to the claims of either side. This arrangement was inaccurately but understandably called "joint occupation." It had the effect of postponing the fate of the Oregon country and of making possible the final acceptance in 1846 of the 49th parallel as the boundary of the enormous wilderness north of California and south of Alaska. The agreement of 1818 substantially achieved for some years its "only object," which was "to prevent disputes and differences" between the "contracting parties."

Time was on the side of the United States, which was growing spectacularly in population and wealth. The importance of the Convention of 1818 is that it postponed for nearly thirty years a final peaceful decision that was probably more advantageous to the United States than it otherwise would have been. The pact was one more unobtrusive feather in President Monroe's peace hat.

The Florida Fruit

One of the greatest strokes for peace in the administration of Monroe and his Secretary of State, John Quincy Adams, was the acquisition, by peaceful means, of the strategic area of East Florida, thrust like a gigantic thumb into the Gulf of Mexico. The problem was extremely complex, and the two statesmen revealed both the pacific and the belligerent sides of their natures in working out an amicable settlement with Madrid.

The problem confronting the American negotiators was to pressure Spain into ceding Florida peacefully, rather than provoke her into clinging to it forcibly. An immensely complicating factor was the series of revolutions in South America, beginning in 1809 and 1810, against Spanish overlordship. American sympathies naturally went out to the rebels, who seemed to be doing what the United States itself had done during the War of Independence in resisting the tyranny of an overseas despot.

Many Americans, emotionally involved in this fight for independence and democracy, sought to assist the South American rebels. Small filibustering expeditions were dispatched, and at least two American ports became notorious bases for privateers that were attacking Spanish shipping.

A watchful Congress, fully aware that Spain must not be provoked unduly if East Florida was to be obtained by peaceful means, passed a new and comprehensive neutrality act in 1818. But it was ineffectual in stopping unneutral aid to the Spanish-Americans. The American people, at least from the days of the Stamp Tax of 1765 onward, have repeatedly demonstrated that when public opinion, or a substantial part of it, resents restrictive legislation, that law will be flouted.

The policy of avoiding offense to Spain was further undercut by the popular demand for extending formal recognition to the revolting Spanish-American colonies. The leading spokesman for the rebels in Congress was the eloquent Henry Clay, the onetime War Hawk from Kentucky, who hailed "the glorious spectacle of eighteen millions of people, struggling to burst their chains and be free."

Secretary of State Adams was caught in a painful dilemma. If the Washington government waited too long before extending formal recognition to the South American rebels, the United States would incur their ill will and probably a loss of markets to British rivals. If the Monroe administration acted too soon, the powerful European monarchs might conceivably come to the aid of the faltering King of Spain, with a consequent crushing of the Hispanic rebels. Worst of all, premature recognition would probably be so offensive to Madrid as to kill all prospects of securing the rich plum of East Florida by peaceful means.

The delicacy of the dilemma was such that the Monroe-Adams administration was forced to dampen whatever enthusiasm it may have harbored for the South American rebels. Secretary Adams not only discouraged popular enthusiasm for these fighting patriots but also gave the cold shoulder to Latin American agents in Washington. He further made an important contribution to the recognition policy of the United States when he perfected the formula that formal recognition should be withheld until the prospects of recovery by the mother country were "utterly desperate." Because the chances of reconquest were not yet that bleak, a recognition resolution before the House of Representatives lost by a margin of more than two to one in March 1818.

For some little time before the spring of 1818 Secretary Adams had been sounding out the Spanish Minister in Washington for the transfer of Florida, as well as for the solution of other pressing problems. These conversations had been making rather promising progress when General Andrew Jackson, a veritable bull in the china closet, threatened to end not only the negotiations for Florida but also all diplomatic relations with Spain.

Law and order had suffered in East Florida after Spain had withdrawn most of her troops to fight the South American revolutionists. In 1816 United States forces destroyed a stronghold known as Negro Fort, which had harbored white renegades and other outcasts of various kinds who had repeatedly raided across the border. Amelia Island, just across the Georgia line in Florida, was such a haven for buccaneers and others. In 1817, under orders from President Monroe, United States forces landed and expelled this nestful of smugglers, adventurers, and freebooters.

Most troublesome of all were the elusive Seminole Indians of Florida. Joined by runaway black slaves, white renegades, and other outcasts, they repeatedly sallied across the Georgia border to despoil and kill the American settlers. Many of these outcasts harbored genuine grievances against the Americans, but the sheltering of such bands of cutthroats by the Spanish government was a clear violation of the good-neighbor pledges embodied in the Pinckney treaty of 1795. Yet Spain, having denuded Florida of troops to fight the South American rebels, was admittedly unable to restrain these lawless marauders.

Jackson's Florida Foray

The simmering situation in Florida came to a boil early in 1818, when Andrew Jackson, the hero of the West and the chastiser of Indians, burst upon the scene. Late in 1817 he had been commissioned by the Monroe government to smite the Seminoles. He was authorized to pursue the Indians across the Spanish border into Florida, if necessary, but he was "to respect the Spanish authority wherever it is maintained." He later claimed, although

Monroe convincingly denied the charge, that the President had sent additional instructions to seize Spanish towns. Whatever the truth, Jackson acted as though he felt he had received such orders.

With all the fury of an avenging angel, General Jackson descended on Spanish Florida in April 1818, occupied the military post of St. Marks, and raised the Stars and Stripes over Spanish soil. He seized two Indian chiefs and hanged them like horse thieves, without benefit of trial. He also captured two British subjects who were alleged to be inciting the Indians against the American whites. After a hasty court martial, Jackson had one shot and the other hanged. Upon hearing that some Indians had fled westward to Pensacola, the chastising general made haste to seize this old Spanish town, which he had once before captured from the British late in 1814.

A vengeful Jackson had indeed thrown the fat into the fire. In a few short weeks in the spring of 1818, he had defeated the Indians, occupied two important Spanish outposts, seized the royal archives, removed the Spanish governor, named an American instead, executed two British subjects, and established the revenue laws of the United States. The pugnacious Jackson, whom we shall meet again as President, saw what he conceived to be his duty—and overdid it.

The British were outraged by Jackson's "murder" of two British subjects, both of whom had a better right to be in Florida than he. But Lord Castlereagh appears to have exaggerated when he later remarked that war might have erupted "if the ministry had but held up a finger." Castlereagh himself came to the conclusion that the two luckless British subjects had been engaging in such lawless activity by inciting the Indians as to have deprived themselves "of any claim on their government for interference."

More than ever the Hero of New Orleans, General Jackson received popular acclaim, especially in the West, where little sympathy was wasted on hostile Indians, conniving British agents, and indifferent Spanish dons. But Jackson's political enemies attempted to pass four resolutions of condemnation in Congress, only to have these proposals lose by substantial majorities. So great was Jackson's popularity that politicians did not relish the prospect of tangling with the "Old Hero."

The first reaction of official Washington was that the "madman" Jackson had about ruined all hope of a negotiated acquisition of Florida. Monroe's entire Cabinet, with the sole exception of Secretary of State Adams, agreed that the unbridled Jackson had been guilty of an unauthorized and indefensible act of war against Spain. But the canny Secretary Adams believed that he could ride out the storm and use the Jackson foray as a lever for the United States in the Florida negotiations.

So Monroe, a good politician, was persuaded not to discipline Jackson, the hotheaded but immensely popular hero. The President appeased Spain by returning the posts that "Old Hickory" had captured, and hence avoided a clash with Jackson. Monroe even went so far as to falsify certain documents so as to cause the impetuous troublemaker to appear in a more favorable light.

Secretary Adams, brushing aside heated protests from the Spanish Minister in Washington, sternly rejected all demands for punishing Jackson and paying an indemnity for the losses inflicted. In response, Adams justified the Jacksonian incursion on the simple grounds of self-defense. If, he said in effect, Spain could not or would not restrain her Indian marauders, as bound to by the treaty of 1795, the United States Army would. This, he could have added, was common sense rather than international law. For good measure, Adams defended the summary execution of the two British troublemakers, for he bluntly concluded that Jackson would have been completely justified in hanging both adventurers without even a court martial.

Not content with defending Jackson, Secretary Adams took the offensive and bluntly accused the Spanish officials of having sheltered the renegade Indians and then having encouraged them to launch their bloody incursions. He even demanded the punishment of the offending Spanish officials, as well as an indemnity from Spain for the expenses involved in chastising the Indians. If, he declared no less bluntly, this public nuisance was not eliminated by Spain, American forces might have to invade again, and in this case "another unconditional restoration . . . must not be expected." Spain had already confessed her inability to control the Indians, and consequently, in Adams's view, her only alternative was to cede Florida to the United States. To him Florida was a dangerous derelict on the international sea that must be towed into the haven of the United States.

In reflecting on Jackson's bull-in-the-china-shop foray, we should note that President Monroe first opted for handling Spain with kid gloves. Secretary of State Adams was the pugnacious one, even threatening Spain with an official invasion of Florida—in short, formal warfare. In several other instances, as we shall observe, Adams, the future President, was to be much more aggressive, even belligerent, than his chief.

The Transcontinental Treaty with Spain

All the while that Jackson had been upsetting the diplomatic applecart in Florida, Adams had been pursuing his negotiations with the Spanish Minister in Washington, Luis de Onís, for the peaceful acquisition of Florida and a clear definition of the western boundary of the United States. This area had been only vaguely delineated by the Louisiana Purchase.

Oddly enough, the outrageous behavior of Jackson, though temporarily disrupting negotiations with Madrid over Florida, finally resulted in a treaty that provided for the peaceful transfer of Florida. Adams was clever enough to press his advantage mercilessly, for Spain was beset with domestic difficulties at home, revolution in South America, and nonsupport by Great Britain. Florida was obviously destined by geography to fall to the pushful Yankees sooner or later, perhaps after a bloody, expensive, and losing war. Why not save face by disposing of so costly a liability gracefully for valuable considerations while there was yet time? Why fight the inevitable?

The epochal Adams-Onís treaty with Spain was finally signed in Washington in February 1819. By its terms the United States received the Floridas, East and West. (In this way the two seizures of West Florida in 1810 and 1813 were fully legitimized.) In addition, the United States received a precise delineation of the western boundary of the Louisiana Purchase. The line was to run from the mouth of the Sabine River (the present eastern boundary of Texas) northwesterly to the forty-second parallel (the present northern boundary of California), and thence due west to the Pacific Ocean.

In return for these sweeping concessions, the United States yielded its shadowy title to Texas, a claim that had grown out of a grasping interpretation of the Louisiana Purchase. Further, the federal government assumed the damage claims against Spain by its own citizens in the sum of $5 million, which was small change indeed when compared with the value of the territory transferred.

The Adams–Onís treaty was signed in February 1819, but the formal exchange of ratifications did not occur until February 1821, some two years later. We now know that the Spanish officials deliberately dragged their feet, partly out of fear that the United States would promptly recognize the revolted republics of South America as soon as Florida was officially transferred. The delay was hard on the nerves of the Washington government, and President Monroe, ordinarily more circumspect, asked Congress on December 7, 1819, to consider acting as though the treaty had been ratified—in short, a forcible occupation of Florida.

Fortunately for Spanish pride and American honor, Madrid yielded, and the Adams–Onís treaty was officially proclaimed on February 22 (Washington's birthday), 1821. The next year, pursuant to Monroe's recommendation, Congress took the necessary steps to implement diplomatic recognition of the Latin American rebels. This step promoted peace in the Americas.

In negotiating with Spain for Florida, the tactics of the Monroe–Adams tandem were not above question. The invasion in peacetime by General Jackson, whether formally sanctioned or not, went far beyond a simple pursuit of fugitives from justice. On the other hand, Spain was weak, dilatory, and irresponsible in permitting a public nuisance to develop. Yet the Monroe administration, provoked into acting in self-defense, was rough, highhanded, and even arrogant. The methods used may not have been conspicuously peaceful, but in the long run the results made for peace as the United States took a giant stride toward fulfilling its "physiographical destiny."

The Menace of Monarchy

While the attention of the United States was being focused on Spain's Florida and her rebellious South American colonies, concern for the emerging new Hispanic republics deepened for other and more alarming reasons. Following the Napoleonic upheaval and the return of much-traveled monarchs to their battered thrones, the rulers of Europe joined hands in a concert to turn back the clock to the good old days before the French Revolution in 1789. This Quadruple Alliance, including the despotic Czar of All the Russias, also embraced Austria, Prussia, and England; it later added France to form the Quintuple Alliance.

The potent new four-power compact was popularly confused with the Holy Alliance, which did not include Britain but did avow Christian principles. The Quadruple (Quintuple) Alliance, a kind of monarchal protective association, was dedicated to the unholy objective of preserving the prerevolutionary social and political order with a mailed fist.

The haunting fears of the rethroned monarchs were abundantly justified. From 1820 to 1823 a rash of revolutions broke out in Portugal, Naples, Greece, and Spain. The alarmed monarchs responded with ferocity and dispatch. Especially brutal was the crushing of a Spanish uprising by French troops in the spring of 1823, followed by the restoration of the ruthless Ferdinand VII to the vacated throne of his ancestors. The reactionary powers then considered plans for a congress in Paris, which, rumor had it, would authorize a potent French force to stamp out the current crop of infant Hispanic-American republics—a prospect that struck fear into the hearts of democracy-loving Americans.

In the face of these severe repressions, Great Britain became an unhappy member of the expanded Quintuple Alliance. For one thing, the European balance of power was being disturbed by the French forces in Spain. For another thing, Britain lived by trade, and the now juicy Latin American markets, once tightly reserved for Spain under the old regime, would again be closed by a monarchal restoration. This ugly eventuality was something that the powerful commercial classes of Great Britain simply could not permit to happen, whatever the cost.

Anxiety in the United States deepened for other and more alarming reasons. If the powers of Europe should stamp out the flames of revolution in South America, would they be content to stop there? Using nearby bases, would they not turn against the United States, the real hotbed of revolution and democracy in the Americas? Rumor had it in the spring of 1823 that France would receive Cuba as her reward for helping Spain to regain ancient colonies.

Historians now know what Monroe, Adams, and others did not know, namely that the powers of Europe had worked out no definite plans for restoring Latin America to the stubborn Ferdinand VII. Yet Secretary of State Adams wrote privately that the French invasion of Spain had left Secretary of War Calhoun "perfectly moonstruck"; that President Monroe was alarmed "far beyond anything I could have conceived possible"; and that Adams himself found the challenge "a fearful question."

The diplomatic chessboard, already cluttered, was complicated for the United States by the presence in Alaska of a scattering of Russian colonists, traders, and shippers. Annoyed by intruders who traded illegally with the natives, the Czar had issued a disturbing imperial edict in September 1821. It forbade foreign ships to venture within 100 miles of the coast of Alaska north of the fifty-first parallel. This vast expanse was far in excess of the 3-mile limit then sanctioned by international law, and hence an outrageous claim to sovereignty over the high seas.

In 1812 the Russian fur traders had already established a trading post and well-defended bastion at Fort Ross, a relatively short distance north of San Francisco Bay and the mouth of the Russian River. The Czar's edict seemed to be strong evidence that Russia was preparing to push her southern boundary of Alaska deep into the Oregon country, which the British and Americans had already agreed to share jointly under the Convention of 1818.

Monroe's Memorable Message

With foreign affairs generally in this crisis stage, the British Foreign Secretary, George Canning, unveiled one of the most amazing propositions in the annals of American diplomacy. In August 1823 he proposed to Richard Rush, the American Minister in London, that the United States join hands with Great Britain in a common front to head off possible intervention by the European powers in revolutionary Spanish America. Canning's obvious purpose was to keep open those coveted South American markets for British traders. But why clasp hands with the militarily weak Americans when the British navy alone could provide more than adequate protection? Canning's motives remain unclear, but he seems to have had partly in mind preventing his grasping Yankee partners from annexing Cuba or some other Spanish area to the south.

Minister Richard Rush was totally without authority to accept a quasi-alliance with Britain, the traditional enemy, so he sent the Canning proposal home to Washington. At first sight President Monroe was rather inclined to accept it, but before making so momentous a decision he decided to consult his two elderly predecessors. Jefferson, the old foe of "entangling alliances," surprisingly counseled cooperation, and Madison, whose White House had been burned by the British, did likewise. But Secretary of State Adams, the lone-wolf supporter of Jackson's foray into Florida, favored a completely independent course.

Why, in rejecting the Canning proposal, did Adams again favor a more aggressive stance than his chief? First of all, he was a sterling patriot who believed that it would dampen the dignity of the United States to come trailing along "as a cock-boat in the wake of the British man-of-war." He also suspected that the British wanted to join hands with the Americans so as to keep American hands off Spanish territory to the south. This kind of self-denial was definitely not in harmony with America's expansionist character.

As for restraining the European allies from stamping out the South American revolutions, Adams was perceptive enough to recognize a basic truth. Whatever the United States did or did not do, the formidable British navy would not permit France or any other power or combination of powers to restore the Spanish king and choke off the lush commercial prizes recently thrown open to British merchants. It was perfectly safe for the United States, which at this time had only one warship the size of a frigate operational in the Atlantic Ocean, to act or not to act, just as it chose. Behind the stout oaken walls of the British navy, Uncle Sam could sound a republican blast of defiance at the ermined monarchs of Europe. And they were powerless to do anything about it, except to voice their resentment.

The nationalistic Secretary Adams rather easily persuaded his colleagues to support a go-it-alone course. But he encountered resistance when he proposed to announce his views to the powers of Europe (including Britain) in sharp diplomatic notes. Instead, Monroe hit on the idea of proclaiming America's defiant policy, rather incidentally, in a routine annual Message to Congress. His judgment was that the European powers would be less likely to take offense if notified generally rather than individually in offensive diplomatic notes. As events turned out, the public warning probably aroused more resentment than a series of quiet and confidential protests would have done.

In a sense, the Monroe Doctrine was co-authored by Secretary Adams and President Monroe. Adams was largely responsible for the lone-wolf feature. At the same time, he helped persuade Monroe to refrain from championing the Greeks in their current armed struggle against Turkish overlords. Adams also induced Monroe to proclaim in rough form the doctrine of the two hemispheres: America would stay on her side of the water and expect the European powers to stay on theirs.

When the private arguments had ended, what is now known as the Monroe Doctrine was embedded in the President's lengthy annual message of December 2, 1823. Rather unobtrusively, it consisted of several widely separated passages. Evidently referring to the current discussions with Russia over the Alaska dispute, Monroe served notice that "the American continents" were "henceforth not to be considered as subjects for future colonization by any European powers." Thus emerged the doctrine of the two hemispheres.

Then came an intermission of seven printed pages, followed by a blunt and provocative warning obviously inspired by rumors that the combined monarchs of Europe were about to reimpose their "political system" on the emerging democracies of Spanish America. Monroe declared bluntly that the United States would "consider any attempt" on the part of the powers "to extend their system to any portion of this hemisphere as dangerous to our peace and safety." He went on to say, "With existing colonies or dependencies of any European power we have not interfered [Florida?] and shall not interfere." But if the European concert of powers should attempt to impose monarchy in independent republics in the Western Hemisphere, the United States would regard such intervention as "the manifestation of an unfriendly disposition toward the United States." In the understated language of diplomacy, this warning in effect referred to an act of war.

As a final refinement of the doctrine of the "two hemispheres," Monroe stated that the United States would continue its policy of keeping out "of the wars that have so long agitated" Europe. In this instance, he was referring to the Greek war for independence, in which a considerable number of American patriots were clamoring for involvement. In short, Europe must stay out of the Americas and the United States would stay out of Europe. Superficailly, the tradeoff looked like fifty-fifty. Actually there was scant prospect of effective interference in Greece by the United States, while there was a menacing prospect of intervention by Europe in the Americas.

The monarchs of Europe, seeing through the President's thin deplomatic language, were infuriated by the bumptious, even bellicose, challenge of the Monroe Doctrine. Their anger was heightened by the knowledge that they were powerless to chastise the insolent Yankees because the fearsome British navy lay in the way. The monarchs had evidently worked out no effective plan for intervention, but if Britain had not stood in the way they might well have come up with one.

The Monroe Aftermath

The Monroe Doctrine (or doctrines) was greeted in America with what one newspaper called a "universal burst of applause." But there were a few dissenting voices, especially among critical politicians. One Congressman found Monroe's message "rash and inconsiderate," while another branded it "an unauthorized, unmeaning, and empty menace, well calculated to excite the angry passions and embroil us with foreign nations."

In England the influential London *Times*, no friend of America, praised the "resolute policy" proclaimed by Monroe, and cheered the notice served on the European powers that intervention would be "a just cause of war." Obviously the mercantile elements in Britain were delighted to have this additional insurance that the valuable new markets of Spanish America would be kept open. But Foreign Secretary Canning was less happy. A wary Monroe had spurned his invitation to join Britain in a hands-off declaration. The hands of the Yankees were still free to seize Cuba and grab a large chunk of Mexico. Worse yet, the United States could forbid the British, as well as the Continental powers, to take any more of the Americas than they already had.

Intimately related to the Monroe Doctrine was the treaty that Secretary Adams negotiated with Russia the next year, 1824. By its terms the Czar agreed to retreat up the northwest coast from 51° in the Oregon country to 54°40', the present southern tip of the Alaska panhandle. This significant concession seems to have been more the fruit of Adams's aggressive diplomacy than of Monroe's menacing message. The Russian government, preoccupied in Europe and overextended in Asia, followed a predetermined policy rather than punish Monroe for what Europeans regarded as insolent Yankee pretensions disproportionate to America's actual power. All informed observers recognized that the Monroe Doctrine in 1823 was a barefaced bluff, actually no stronger than the British navy.

President Monroe, the man of peace, was fortunate enough to keep out of foreign conflicts, primarily because there was no major war then being waged that could drag in the United States. His administration is properly credited with the Rush-Bagot agreement to limit armaments on the Great Lakes. The Convention of 1818 preserved peace on the Canadian frontier and helped to cement America's claim to a substantial share of the Oregon country.

Monroe had a precedent for ordering American troops under Andrew Jackson into Florida in a justifiable police action, but he certainly did not instruct Jackson to flout Spanish sovereignty or execute British subjects. He went along with Secretary Adams, who was usually more aggressive than he, in pushing helpless Spain into ceding Florida and defining the western boundary of the Louisiana Purchase.

The Monroe Doctrine, obviously a colossal bluff backed unwittingly by the British navy, was in considerable part the work of the aggressive Adams. This pronouncement came close to being bellicose, but only in words, and its ultimate effect was to promote peace in the Americas. Monroe was lucky enough to earn—and deserve—good marks as a peace President.

One should note in passing that Monroe, on a small scale, engaged in police actions, like those of Jefferson and Madison against the Barbary pirates, in the interests of safeguarding peaceful commerce and protecting American lives. Aside from the occupation of Amelia Island and Jackson's punitive incursion into Florida, American naval units, from 1820 to 1823, partially suppressed the slave trade on the African coast, pursuant to an act of Congress in 1819. In 1822 United States naval forces landed on the northwest coast of Spain's Cuba and burned a pirate station. The next year five brief interventions again occurred on that island in pursuit of pirates. In 1824 the *U.S.S. Porpoise* landed bluejackets in Cuba while engaged in a similar mission. In the same year Commodore David Porter invaded Spain's Puerto Rico with two hundred men and attacked a town that had sheltered pirates and insulted American naval officers. He secured an apology.

These were all minor police actions and of no real importance. The tradition of protecting American lives and property, not by ransom but by force of arms, was thus being carried forward since the days of Jefferson. Such landings were not started in the big-stick days of Theodore Roosevelt. In American eyes, Spain's inability to cope with lawlessness, whether in Florida, Cuba, or Puerto Rico, conferred on the United States the right to intervene in her stead. At least this was the position usually taken by the United States in later years in smaller countries where it was feasible to deploy ships and land Marines.

CHAPTER 6

JOHN QUINCY ADAMS: THE "CORRUPT BARGAIN" PRESIDENT

Less possessed of your confidence in advance than any of my predecessors, I am deeply conscious of the prospect that I shall stand more and oftener in need of your indulgence.

President John Quincy Adams, Inaugural Address, March 4, 1825

The Advent of Adams

John Quincy Adams, who had served so ably as President Monroe's Secretary of State, was elevated to the White House in 1825. His credentials in law, diplomacy, and statecraft were impressive to a high degree. Educated in France, in Holland, and at Harvard, he had served at various times as United States Minister to Holland, Portugal, Prussia, and England. He had also been one of the five American negotiators during the six-month negotiations at Ghent in 1814, and had followed this triumphant ordeal with eight years of brilliant service as Secretary of State under President Monroe. An able lawyer like his father, John Quincy Adams is generally ranked as one of the nation's greatest Secretaries of State but one of its least successful Presidents. His main initiatives toward peace generally encountered frustration and failure. Why?

Heredity evidently gave Adams a brilliant mind at the expense of an attractive personality, for he was a veritable chip off the old family glacier. He said it best himself when he wrote in his dreary diary in June 1819, "I am a man of reserved, cold, austere, and forbidding manners: my political adversaries say, a gloomy misanthropist, and my personal enemies, an unsocial savage." His father, John Adams, could have written just about the same introspective analysis of himself.

Like John Adams of Quincy, Massachusetts, John Quincy Adams was five feet, seven inches in height and rotund of body. Observers noted his shiny bald head (like his father's), abundant white sideburns, and watery eyes that were a constant annoyance. For some reason or reasons he did not care much for spectacles. He was the only President whose father had been President, and like his father he was not reelected to a second term, although the margin of defeat in both cases was quite respectable. As Chief Executives, both statesmen came under heavy fire, partisan and nonpartisan, for their handling or mishandling of foreign affairs, although both had stockpiled rich experience in the diplomatic service of their country.

John Quincy Adams was an unlucky President, just as Monroe had been a lucky one. Monroe had not created the Era of Good Feelings; he had merely presided over and encouraged the serene atmosphere. He had come into office in the afterglow of Jackson's smashing victory at New Orleans and in an era when nationalism, not sectionalism, was the guiding spirit. By the time John Quincy Adams moved into the White House the impulse toward nationalism was fading, and the North, South, East, and West were sinking deeper into the bog of sectional disputes.

The Federalist party of George Washington and John Adams had essentially died following the disgraceful conduct of many partisans during the War of 1812. At the same time, the Democratic-Republican party of Thomas Jefferson was splintering into factionism. In the hotly contested presidential contest of 1824 the four leading candidates were all from the same party, but they represented different facets of it. "Old Hickory" Jackson finished first with 99 electoral votes; Adams second with 84; Crawford third with 41; and Henry Clay, the "gallant Harry of the West," fourth with 37, and hence was completely eliminated. Because no candidate received a majority, the decision among the top three had to be left up to the House of Representatives, as required by the Constitution.

The stage was all set for a backstairs political deal. Henry Clay was the influential speaker of the House, and hence in a position to throw his powerful support effectively behind either Adams or Jackson. Clay coveted the position of Secretary of State, which had been the runway to the presidency for three of the preceding Presidents. Accordingly, the ambitious Kentuckian met privately with Adams and later threw his decisive influence in the House behind the second-place candidate, John Quincy Adams, who was then triumphantly elected. A few days later the winner announced that Henry Clay would be the new Secretary of State.

Jackson's supporters, thus robbed of the presidency, raised the angry and anguished cry of "Corrupt Bargain." The circumstantial evidence is strong that some kind of arrangement was privately reached, but today it would be called a "political deal," such as contributed to the presidential nomination of Abraham Lincoln in 1860. What evidently bothered the Jacksonites most was that the Adamsites had got to Clay and Jackson had not. In any event, the cry of corruption was raised from the day of Adams's election and sustained for the four years of the Adams interregnum. This clamor created an atmosphere in which this gifted and highly experienced diplomatist could encounter mainly frustration. Moreover, he was the nation's first minority President, but by no means the last; fewer than one-third of the electorate had voted for him.

Adams multiplied his difficulties in both domestic and foreign affairs by refusing to use the spoils of office to promote his own political fortunes. This course may have been in part Puritanical highmindedness to offset the "corrupt bargain," but the new President removed only twelve officeholders, thus alienating his supporters, many of whom were more concerned with the spoils of office than the toils of office.

A dyed-in-the-wool nationalist, Adams did not recognize clearly that the country was veering away from post-Ghent nationalism to sectionalism and states' rights. In his first annual message to Congress he recommended a national university, and even urged the "erection of an astronomical observatory" that would emulate Europe's 130 or so "light-houses of the skies." To stump-grubbing American pioneers all this would be a scandalous waste of taxpayers' money.

Adams also attempted to deal fairly with the Cherokee Indians of Georgia, who had few white friends, especially in the West. The Governor of the state threatened to resist federal meddling with arms, and the President was forced to back off. This affair was one of the early conspicuous instances of a state's defying and hence nullifying federal authority.

Foreign Frustrations

One would think that a stellar Secretary of State, with a free hand as President, would rack up an outstanding record in dealing with the nation's foreign affairs. But such was not to be the outcome, for obvious reasons. There were no great wars being waged in Europe, and the major powers were showing no eagerness to challenge Monroe's doctrine of America for the Americans, backed though it was by the hollow threat of armed interference by the Yankees.

Potential trouble with the two most bothersome European neighbors, Britain and Spain, had been removed, or at least postponed. To the north, a settlement of the boundary with Canada had been accomplished or deferred by the Convention of 1818, which Secretary John Quincy Adams had himself engineered. The joint-occupation arrangement of 1818 for ten years was renewed indefinitely by the Convention of 1827.

To the south and west there was no serious trouble. All of Florida, East and West, had been brought legally under the American flag by the treaty of 1819 with Spain, belatedly ratified in 1821. At the same time the western boundary of the United States had been clearly established by the same pact, which was one of the brilliant achievements of Secretary John Quincy Adams. The independence of Mexico had been duly recognized by Spain in 1821, as it had been by the United States in the same year (also under Secretary Adams). In addition, the United States had extended formal recognition to the leading Spanish republics of Latin America. In short, the magician Secretary Adams had run out of diplomatic rabbits to pull out of his hat by the time he became President. He had little or no opportunity to use the threat of war as an instrument of national policy, as he had earlier.

A final roadblock to diplomatic triumphs was the formidable antipathy of Britain's Foreign Secretary Canning. He could not forget that the United States had spurned his invitation to join hands against the Continental powers in 1823. Monroe and Adams had also reversed the tables against Britain herself in the high-and-mighty pronouncement of Monroe. With the whole world as witnesses, the Yankees had thus challenged Great Britain's determination to gain the upper hand in the Latin American markets.

Canning's position was much strengthened in 1824, when he won the British government over to his scheme of recognizing the newly born Spanish-American republics. As he gloated, "The deed is done; the nail is driven; Spanish America is free; and if we do not mismanage our affairs badly, *she is English*." He did not mismanage. Protective as he was of British markets and fearful of possible Yankee domination, he blocked President Adams wherever Britain's interests dictated. When Canning died in 1827, Adams noted the event in his diary with ghoulish satisfaction.

The Panama Congress, an idea developed by the South American revolution hero, Símon Bolívar, took more concrete form in 1825, when the United States was invited to send delegates to this gathering. The objective was to discuss problems common to the recently formed Spanish-American republics or, as Adams put it, "objects of peculiar concernment to this hemisphere." Secretary of State Henry Clay, "the corrupt bargainer" and the leading enthusiast for cooperation with these newly hatched nations, induced President Adams to cooperate.

Acceptance of the Pan-American invitation seemed both neighborly and an important step toward peace. Unity under the banner of the Monroe Doctrine would obviously generate greater strength to resist European intervention in the uncertain future. But President Adams at the outset made what turned out to be an unnecessary mistake. He sought approval by the Senate of his two appointees, plus an appropriation from both houses of Congress for their expenses.

President Adams was evidently a stickler for the Constitution, which requires the advice and consent of the Senate for the appointment of "ambassadors, other public ministers, and consuls." Yet these two delegates to a short-term conference were not "ministers and consuls" accredited to any nation in the conventional sense, and since that day the President has sent appointees to numerous international conferences without seeking or needing the approval of the Senate. As for their expenses, these probably could have been squeezed out of contingency funds available to the Department of State.

At all events, President Adams mistakenly turned to Congress, which promptly became deadlocked in a bitter debate. Much of the opposition sprang from the desire of the Jacksonites to embarrass the administration, for they could never forget the "corrupt bargain" and their desire for revenge at the next presidential election. Some Congressmen were genuinely worried about becoming involved in foreign entanglements, against which Washington and Jefferson had warned. Southerners were deeply concerned that slavery would be discussed at a Panama conference in which there would be some blacks "putting on airs." On the other hand, there was strong support in the North for the Panama Congress, which presumably would gain some advantages for American merchants over rival Britons.

At long last the three-month debate in the House ended, and the two delegates were formally though grudgingly approved. One of the duo died en route; the other started so late that he failed to reach the conference. The luckless Adams, having stirred up all this political venom, had nothing whatever to show for his efforts except bruised feelings.

In the short run, the absence of two delegates from the United States made no difference. The Panama conferees were almost drowned in a sea of high-flown rhetoric. None of the formal recommendations was ever adopted; none of the proposed conferences was ever held. If the two delegates had arrived in time, they would have run into the British delegate, whom Canning had sent to undercut Yankee influence and strengthen that of Great Britain in Latin America.

In the absence of representatives from the United States, incomparably the most powerful American nation of all, there could have been no real Pan-American conference. The first genuine one was finally assembled in Washington in 1889, sixty-four years later. It in turn accomplished little, other than to give some life to a movement that in time was to achieve significance. President Adams may have missed the boat in 1826, but it is impossible to demonstrate that this failure meaningfully altered the course of history.

Adams's Fumbling Diplomacy

Persistent friction with Great Britain over American trade with the British West Indies presented President Adams with a problem that would test both his diplomatic skill and his ability to work out some kind of compromise that would ensure more peaceful relations with the Mother Country.

During colonial days American shippers, particularly those from New England, had enjoyed a lucrative trade with Britain's Caribbean islands, such as Jamaica and Barbados. Much of this traffic was in sugar, which New Englanders distilled into rum. In turn this fiery beverage was traded for African slaves, who were then enchained and transported in slavers to the New World. The British naturally had reserved this coveted commerce with the Caribbean islands for their loyal subjects, and when the thirteen colonies withdrew in 1776–1783 the rebels lost this profitable trade.

The old privileges for the Americans had never been completely restored, although in emergencies sometimes partially lifted. In 1822, in the days of President Monroe, Parliament went so far as to open limited West Indian trade to the Americans but on conditions that provided a constant irritant.

Such was the diplomatic Gordian knot presented to President Adams when this master of diplomacy took over the White House in March 1825. Some four months later Parliament passed another act that opened this controversial commerce, but again under restrictions that were distasteful to the Americans. They wanted a larger share of the profits that also went into British pockets.

In the light of hindsight, which is obviously more reliable than foresight, President Adams fumbled away this opportunity. Instead of accepting the West Indian half-loaf with gratitude, he dallied a year before acting. He then sent to London the veteran Albert Gallatin, his gifted former colleague at the Ghent peace table in 1814, who carried with him instructions to secure more favorable terms. The old aggressiveness of Adams again showed through when he took the inflexible stance that trade with the British West Indies should be demanded as a right and not requested as a privilege. George Canning, Adams's old adversary, who had been Prime Minister in 1827, told Gallatin bluntly that what Great Britain did with the trade of her colonies was nobody's business but her own. Gallatin arrived too late, for the concessions that Parliament had offered about a year earlier had been completely withdrawn.

There were plenty of Jacksonians and other political foes of Adams eager to denounce the doughty New Englander. A Virginia newspaper assailed "the clumsy and mischievous manner" in which these trade benefits had "been lost by the Administration." Indeed, this setback for Adams's "diplomatized Administration" was one of his most serious handicaps when he ran unsuccessfully against Jackson for reelection in 1828.

It is easy to second-guess Adams, but this West Indian episode does not reveal him at his best. He gambled on getting better terms, and lost. Yet knowing that he might lose, he was no doubt aware that this dispute was not serious enough to produce a war, at least not at this stage. The issue was not one of war or peace, as it had been in the days of impressment. At stake was only an improved relationship.

President Adams suffered yet another setback in his diplomacy involving Texas. We recall that, as Secretary of State, he had acquired Florida in the transcontinental treaty of 1819 by yielding America's shadowy claim to Texas. The elastic blanket of the Louisiana Purchase simply could not be stretched that far west. Besides, far-off Texas would keep until such time as enough Western pioneers, carrying their long rifles, were on hand to absorb it. Yet the surrender of Texas for nearby Florida outraged many Westerners, who felt that their interests had been thoughtlessly sacrificed.

Upon becoming President in 1825, Adams remembered the Western outcry against his "surrender," and he undertook to extend the American claim to Texas all the way from the Sabine River to the Rio Grande. Secretary of State Clay was instructed to open negotiations looking toward a peaceful purchase of this vast region. Among various arguments that he used with the Mexicans was the absurd one that if the Mexicans were to sell Texas, their capital city would be situated nearer the center of their own country.

The proud Mexicans did not want to sell, and in 1827 President Adams tried again. He authorized the American Minister in Mexico to offer $1 million as inducement to the Mexicans to move their boundary line from the Sabine River, the present eastern boundary of Texas, to the Rio Grande, the present western boundary. Again the sensitive Mexicans flatly refused to sell, and there was nothing that Adams could do about it, unless he used the armed forces.

But Adams was essentially a man of peace. Although lawless and predatory men had gathered at present Galveston, Texas, as they had in Florida's Amelia Island, this situation was different. Florida was relatively close to the populated areas of the United States, and Texas was not. Adams would not find it easy to assemble a formidable army to invade Texas. The Mexicans might put up a prolonged and even successful resistance, including guerrilla warfare. The part of wisdom was to wait and let the expanding pioneer population determine whether Americans or Mexicans would retain Texas. Adams consequently backed off and chose the peaceful route of waiting for time and the prolific American pioneers to solve the problem—as they did.

The Passing of a Peaceful President

Adams's troubled administration also carried forward the now well-established tradition of overriding local sovereignty and protecting American lives and property wherever imperative and feasible. In March 1825 American and British forces, acting in cooperation, landed in Spain's Cuba at Sagua La Grande to root out pirates. In October and November 1827 American landing parties, reacting to the lawlessness created by the protracted Greek revolution against the "terrible Turks," hunted down pirates on three Grecian islands. The United States, though not generally regarded as a world power at this time, was certainly throwing its weight around in a far-off corner of the world. But such interventions did not yet involve remaining as invaders for protracted periods and operating the governments of the involuntary hosts. President John Quincy Adams referred approvingly to these interventionists episodes in his various messages to Congress, and in so doing reflected the support he had given as Secretary of State to Jackson's wild foray into Florida in 1818. In short, weak nations that will not or cannot police their own criminals must not be surprised if the offended nation takes punitive action itself. At least this appears to have been Adams's philosophy.

Before becoming President, John Quincy Adams had been an aggressive, almost bellicose, Secretary of State. While in the

White House he was oddly restrained, perhaps in part as a result of the shadow cast by his tainted election through the "corrupt bargain." After leaving the presidency he did not regard it as beneath his dignity to serve in Congress, and this he did in the House of Representatives from 1831 to 1848, dying in the harness in 1848. During these seventeen years his latent pugnacity flowered fully under the warm sun of the burning slavery issue. "The Old Man Eloquent" made himself famous and notorious by the ferocity with which he fought the black curse and particularly the "gag resolution" to table without debate any discussion in Congress of antislavery petitions. For whatever reason, Congressman Adams proved to be far more pugnacious than President Adams.

CHAPTER 7

ANDREW JACKSON: THE PEOPLE'S PRESIDENT

Collision with France is the more to be regretted on account of the position she occupies in Europe in relation to liberal institutions, but in maintaining our national rights and honor all governments are alike to us.

President Andrew Jackson,
Sixth Annual Message,
December 1, 1834

"Old Hickory" in the White House

On the basis of his previous record, Andrew Jackson was unquestionably the most pugnacious man ever to enter the White House. Born near the border between North and South Carolina, and orphaned at age fourteen, he fought the British as a mere boy of thirteen in the Revolutionary War. Captured by the Redcoats, he was slashed across the face with a sword when he refused to clean an officer's boots. This white scar he carried with him to his grave.

Lacking parental guidance, young Jackson had misspent his youth. He was more interested in cockfighting, horse racing, and brawling than in reading and writing, and his spelling throughout his adult life continued to be atrocious. Yet he moved "up west" to Tennessee, where a fighting man was more highly esteemed than a writing man, and there read enough law to be made an honorable but unlearned judge. By exercising common sense, he did tolerably well on the bench, became active in politics, and twice was sent by the people of Tennessee to Congress for brief terms. Thomas Jefferson, then Vice-President and presiding officer of the Senate, remembered that in debate Jackson would become so choked with rage that he could not speak coherently. John Quincy Adams referred privately to "that brawler from Tennessee." Indeed, Jackson's physical altercations with clubs, knives, and pistols seem to have run into the dozens.

Jackson gradually outgrew the roughneck reputation of his youth and became a frontier aristocrat in Tennessee, where he owned a large plantation with a high-columned, palatial home, The Hermitage. His most famous duel, involving a point of personal honor, was fought in 1806 with the pistols of a gentleman, not the knives of a thug. Jackson suffered a shattering wound in the shoulder but held his fire and then deliberately and fatally shot down his opponent, a crack marksman. During much of his adult life Jackson carried about in his body two bullets, which probably caused some lead poisoning.

Six feet, one inch tall, and weighing a scant 140 pounds, "Old Hickory" took to his grave a gaunt, hawklike face, crowned by bushy gray-white hair. As President, his manners were generally dignified and courtly, and the derisive nickname "King Andrew the First" was not altogether unfitting. Although he lived to be seventy-eight, his ill health probably contributed substantially to his cantankerousness, shortness of temper, and determination to have his own way.

In assessing "Old Hickory's" pugnacity level, we must remember that he was a professional military man and an iron disciplinarian who had authorized hanging six Tennessee militiamen for alleged mutiny. Entering politics, he had been named a major general of the militia in 1801, and in 1814 he rose to the rank of major general in the United States Army. He fought a brilliant campaign against the Creek Indians, culminating in the remarkable victory at Horseshoe Bend in 1814.

General Jackson was more lucky than brilliant when he repulsed the British bloodily at New Orleans in 1815. He prepared his defenses belatedly, and when the British rashly launched a frontal attack on his prepared positions, an awful slaughter of the Redcoats was inevitable. If the enemy had only sent a powerful force to Jackson's rear across the river, instead of a small one, there would have been no "Hero of New Orleans" to become President of the United States—or much of anything else.

We have already noted Major General Jackson's punitive pursuit of the Seminole Indians into Florida in 1818, together with the execution of two British subjects after hasty courts martial. This clearly was a case of overkill, but Secretary of State Adams used an instance of what appeared to be insubordination to negotiate with Madrid the peaceful acquisition of Florida and to settle the western boundary of the United States. Jackson's martial exploits undoubtedly propelled him into the White House, despite the four-year sidetracking engineered by John Quincy Adams and Henry Clay in the alleged "corrupt bargain" of 1824-1825.

The presidency of the hotheaded Jackson was not tranquil, but the big battles were virtually all waged on the domestic front. He fought "Old Nick" Biddle and the Bank of the United States, both of which he crushed without resort to arms. The closest call involved the nullifiers of South Carolina, and in this instance, Jackson seemed determined, if necessary, to employ what army there was against the Palmetto State and its stubborn leader, John C. Calhoun.

In 1832 the state of South Carolina formally nullified the relatively high tariff passed by Congress in that year. The chief complaint was that it conferred favors on Northern manufacturers to the detriment of Southern agriculturists, including cotton producers. In line with the state's defiance of the federal government, the rebellious South Carolinians began to gather arms and make other military preparations for their defense.

"Old Hickory" Jackson, his fighting instincts aroused, reacted predictably. In private, he threatened to invade the wayward state in forty days with a large (nonexistent) army of 50,000 men—and another 50,000 in forty more days. In public, Jackson appeared much more moderate. Unobtrusively, he transferred

Andrew Jackson tramples on the Constitution. Cartoon used in the campaign of 1832.

several dozen more soldiers to Charleston Harbor; he also dispatched seven revenue cutters and a warship with orders to be ready for action at a moment's notice. Publicly Jackson's biggest blast was a belligerent proclamation (ghost-written) declaring: "Disunion by armed force is *treason*."

The Civil War might have erupted in 1833 if Senator Henry Clay had not stepped forward with a compromise tariff bill that was enacted by Congress. Reluctantly accepted by Calhoun and other South Carolinians, it would gradually reduce the high tariff act of 1832 to a mildly protective level. Ironically, Henry Clay, the great compromiser whom Jackson hated, helped to bail the President out of this ugly dilemma.

The Soldier Becomes a Diplomat

We are more concerned with manifestations of Jackson's pugnacity in dealing with foreign nations, and here the record is dramatic indeed. In 1818 President Monroe had asked Jefferson for his reactions to sending Jackson on a diplomatic mission to Russia. "Good God," was the reply. "He would breed you a quarrel before he had been there a month!"

"Old Hickory" inherited the sticky problem, already clumsily handled by President John Quincy Adams, of reopening trade on an unrestricted basis with the British West Indies. An observer would not expect much success in dealing with this perennial problem from a hotheaded man who harbored so little love for the British. Every time he looked in the mirror he could see the boyhood scar on his face left by a British sword. But Jackson hated both John Quincy Adams and his Secretary of State, Henry Clay, and he may have had a strong desire to make them look less statesmanlike. In any event, he reversed President Adams's tough stance and requested participation in trade with the British West Indies as a privilege rather than a right.

The British, probably expecting hot words, were pleasantly surprised by this diplomatic approach from a fiery leader who, they had every reason to fear, would be violently anti-British. In 1830, the year after Jackson's inauguration, London unexpectedly consented to a compromise. The terms provided that direct commerce with the British West Indies would be thrown open to the United States, subject to reasonable duties. But the trade *was* opened.

Jackson's admirers loudly proclaimed that their champion had shown up the "blundering diplomacy" of the diplomatized administration of President Adams. But in fairness we should note that Prime Minister George Canning, Adams's resentful rival, was now dead and that British faith in the hoary navigation laws was weakening under the more tractable Foreign Secretary, Lord Aberdeen. Besides, trade restrictions are often two-edged, and the West Indies needed imports of American foodstuffs and lumber. Lady Luck often plays a crucial role in diplomacy.

If Jackson surprised the British by his sweet reasonableness, he angered the French in 1834–1835 by acting as an undiplomatic bill collector. The background is complicated, but in simple terms the Paris government had signed a treaty in 1831 agreeing to pay a bill of 25 million francs for spoliations of American commerce growing out of the European war that had begun in 1793. There were to have been six annual installments. In 1834, after delaying a year, the French Chambers flatly refused to make the first payment. Jackson's fighting spirit was now thoroughly aroused. Reportedly he shouted, "I know them French. They won't pay unless they're made to!" He laid the issue before Congress in his annual message of December 1, 1834, by which time two unpaid payments were overdue.

Jackson explained to Congress (and France) that American institutions were "essentially pacific." "Peace and friendly intercourse" were desired by the American government and people alike. But such goals were not to be obtained "by surrendering the rights of our citizens or permitting solemn treaties . . . to be abrogated or set aside." One retaliatory weapon available to the United States was to ban trade with France, but such a backfiring blunderbuss would hurt Americans also. As Jackson declared, it would weaken sentiment for "the rights and honor of the nation which must now pervade every bosom."

The "Old Hero" went on to advise Congress that if "prompt execution of the treaty" should be further delayed, then the Americans should "take redress into their hands." A quarter of a century had elapsed since the treaty had been finally signed, and another wasted "quarter of a century" was not to be "tolerated." The principle was established in international law, avowed Jackson, that in these circumstances "the aggravated party may seize on the property of the other, its citizens or subjects, sufficient to pay the debt without giving just cause for war."

Jackson ringingly added that if the French Chambers did not pay their debt at the next session, "every day's delay on our part will be a stain upon our national honor, as well as a denial of justice to our injured citizens." He therefore recommended that Congress pass a law "authorizing reprisals upon French property" in the event that the scheduled payments were not sanctioned at the next session of the French Chambers.

The President concluded by asserting that a "collision" with this debtor "was to be regretted," but the nation's "rights and honor" were involved. If a clash should take place with a France that was "clearly in the wrong," the responsibility for the result would "rest on her own head."

The French Furor

These were fighting words, just as Jackson evidently intended them to be. A tale going the rounds in Washington was that when his advisers tried to soften the harsh language behind his back, they were treated to an outburst of sulfurous profanity. Fellow Democrats generally applauded the "Old Hero's" resolute words, but the Whigs, especially those living in commercial centers being hurt by rumors of war, condemned the President's "coarse and offensive language" as proposing "legalized piracy." A hostile Henry Clay, the prominent Whig leader, joined Jackson's senatorial foes in denouncing the President's message as further evidence of his unfitness for his high office.

But Gallic pride, notoriously sensitive, was deeply hurt. The French Minister in Washington revealed his government's pique by demanding his passports and leaving the legation to a *chargé d'affaires*, Alphonse Pageot. The French Chambers were stirred into passing the belated appropriation but stipulated that the money not be disbursed until Jackson had satisfactorily explained the harsh words of his message. He reportedly burst out, "Apologize! I'd see the whole race roasting in hell first!" The popular slogans of the hour were "Hurrah for Jackson!" "No Explanations!" and "No Apologies!"

The deadlock drifted from bad to worse. The Ministers on both sides had gone home, and then the chargés, American and French, returned to their respective homelands. Diplomatic relations were now completely severed—a normal prelude to warfare. Belatedly naval preparations were stepped up in the United States, while the Paris government dispatched a special squadron for the defense of its valuable French West Indies.

Confronted with this ugly crisis, and exercising untypical restraint, the normally hot-tempered Jackson undertook to make explanations without apologies in his annual message to Congress of December 7, 1835. He declared that his duty required him to protect the honor of the United States and uphold the right of its citizens to secure just compensation from France. He insisted that a communication from the President to Congress was meant for the eyes of Congress alone and not some foreign power. He reminded this body that the French had earlier taken deep offense at certain communications of President Washington and President Adams, as indeed they had. He denied that he had intended to "intimidate by menace," although that was what he clearly had been trying to do.

Surely Jackson could not have been so naive as to suppose that the French would not read his vigorous message to Congress and react angrily. The nearest that Jackson would come to an apology was a complicated explanation. Lest this veiled disclaimer be regarded as an actual backdown by the French, Jackson later added in the same message to Congress: "The honor of my country shall never be stained by an apology from me for the statement of truth and the performance of my duty; nor can I give any explanation of my official acts except such as is due to integrity and justice and consistent with the principles on which our institutions have been framed."

As time passed, the passions generated on each side substantially cooled. Both France and the United States were obviously prepared to retreat somewhat, provided that they could do so without undue loss of face. The angry deadlock was partially broken in January 1836 by the timely mediation of Great Britain, now an ally of France. The British did not relish the prospect of seeing their neighbor waste her strength in a foolish and fruitless war with the Yankees. The French, under nudging from London, discovered that their wounded honor had been salved by Jackson's "explanatory messages" and that both adversaries could withdraw gracefully from their high ground. The resourceful French were now able to find sufficient apology in the messages to Congress of Jackson, who continued to deny that he had in fact apologized. France next arranged to pay the delinquent funds, and normal diplomatic relations were restored between the two former allies.

At no time during this comic-opera controversy did a full-dress war seem probable, although a kind of quasi-war, like the prolonged clash with France in 1798–1800, was conceivable. "The Hero of New Orleans" was just an impatient and outraged bill collector, and there was no rankling grievance of a fundamental nature between the two former allies. Even so, where sensitive national honor is involved, there is inevitably some loose talk of fighting back. At the height of the crisis John Quincy Adams, the experienced diplomat and bitter political rival of Jackson, concluded that "if the two countries be saved from war, it seems as if it could only be by a special interposition of Providence." Pessimists in Paris and London expressed similar views.

Even giving Jackson the benefit of doubts, the irascible "Old Hero" in the White House seems to have been more provocative than necessary. He had never been abroad, and he evidently did not realize fully that the Ministry in Paris could not yield supinely to the Jacksonian threat of seizing French property.

The best that can be said of Jackson's bullying methods is that he had strong provocation and that he got positive results. He whipped up the support of public opinion at home over an issue that had long simmered; he brought to a peaceful conclusion a grievance that might ultimately have caused a violent collision. He also created in the chancelleries of Europe a new respect for an up-and-coming transatlantic republic.

Turbulent Texas

As previously noted, President John Quincy Adams had made a serious effort to purchase Texas from Mexico but found the proud Mexicans unwilling to sell. In August 1829, some six months after entering the White House, President Jackson attempted to reopen negotiations for Texas but ran into a stone wall. Unfortunately for his plans the United States Minister in Mexico City, the unscrupulous Anthony Butler, turned out to be what Jackson finally called a "scamp." Butler surmised that the sum of $500,000, "judiciously applied," would secure Texas. But the Mexican officials finally found his maneuverings so offensive that they handed him his passports.

Such clumsy efforts by Jackson to buy Texas merely deepened Mexican suspicions, and no government in Mexico City was willing to incur the wrath of the masses by selling. Too proud to barter and too weak to fight was the judgment finally passed on the luckless Mexicans. God was high in the sky and the "gringos" were pouring in as settlers from the nearby United States.

In 1835 the American newcomers in Texas, claiming that their local rights were being swept away, rose in revolt. Following the massacre at the Alamo in 1836, with Davy Crockett and Jim Bowie among the nearly two hundred defenders, sentiment in the United States went out strongly to the Texas Americans. Hundreds of supporters from the United States flocked to the rescue, and without them independence probably could not have been won.

Jackson cherished no love for the Mexicans but felt a strong comradely attachment to some of the Americans fighting in Texas, notably his esteemed old friend, Sam Houston. Publicly, Jackson maintained a strict neutrality during the darkest days of this revolution. But after the resounding victory at San Jacinto in 1836, Jackson privately contributed some money to the rebellious Texans, although he tried to maintain a public neutrality by attempting to enforce the inadequate neutrality law of 1818. But such legislation could not have been satisfactorily upheld in the teeth of so much popular support for the Texans, whose cry "Remember the Alamo" tugged at American hearts.

The breach of official neutrality that most angered the Mexican government came in 1836, when General Edmund P. Gaines, under discretionary orders from President Jackson, occupied the Texan town of Nacodoches from July to December. The Mexicans were allegedly attempting to enlist the Indians of east Texas on their side, and Jackson evidently feared that these ravaging red allies would burst across the border into the United States. The Mexican Minister in Washington, interpreting General Gaines's invasion of Texan (Mexican) soil as intolerable aid and comfort to the rebels, left the United States in a huff. The American Minister in Mexico City in turn withdrew from his post.

Texas won her independence in 1836, although it was not then recognized by Mexico, and sought shelter under the familiar folds of the Stars and Stripes. Under ordinary circumstances Jackson would have rolled out the welcome mat. But the Texans had black slaves, and annexation would further stir up heated agitation against slavery in the North, as indeed it had done already.

Jackson, despite his personal sympathies for the Texans, backed off from annexation. He was fearful of disrupting the Union over the slavery issue; he recoiled from goading Mexico into war; he suspected that he might split his own Democratic party so badly as to make impossible the choice of his handpicked successor, Martin Van Buren.

Early in July 1836 both houses of Congress approved resolutions favoring the recognition of Texas as an independent nation, but still Jackson held off. Not until the last day of his administration, and after "Matty" Van Buren was safely elected, did Jackson formally recognize the independence of Texas. His wait of some eight months after Sam Houston's smashing victory at San Jacinto was far less hasty than some presidential recognitions have been since then. Besides, recognition was not annexation.

From Red Indians to East Indians

The only serious warfare during Jackson's eight years in the White House involved the various Indian tribes of the Southeast. These outbreaks resulted from the massive Indian removal policy, favored and implemented but not originated by the famed Indian fighter himself. The red men rather respected him, for they called him "Big Knife," "Sharp Knife," and "Pointed Arrow."

Legend to the contrary, Jackson evidently harbored no burning hatred for peaceful Indians; those whom he had fought had been killing encroaching whites. The outworn policy of having the Indians, with their alien culture, live side by side with a mushrooming white population simply had not worked amicably, to the lasting hurt of both races. There is reason to suppose that Jackson sincerely believed or hoped that this assisted uprooting would bring peace.

The westward transplanting of some sixty thousand reluctant Indians involved enormous hardships and much loss of life on the "Trail of Tears." About one-quarter of the Cherokee tribe perished. There were only two major areas of armed resistance. The Sauk and Fox Indians, in the Illinois and Wisconsin country, unwilling to pull up stakes on the treaty terms offered by the palefaces, took to the warpath in 1832. They were crushed with heavy losses by regulars and the militia, notably at the Bad Axe Massacre, where scores of the remaining red men were butchered. Among the militiamen called to arms was a young volunteer captain by the name of Abraham Lincoln, the future leader of the Union against the Confederacy. He served for eighty days in the Black Hawk War, during which most of his fighting, as he later confessed, consisted of "many bloody struggles with the mosquitoes."

The Seminoles of Florida also resisted removal in what is known as the Second Seminole War, which dragged on from 1835 to 1842, a total of seven years. The whites campaigned at a disadvantage in the swampy Everglades of this alligator-infested region: altogether they lost about 3,500 killed, including two "massacres" of about one hundred whites each. The most prominent Seminole leader, Osceola, was treacherously seized under a flag of truce, and substantial resistance finally ended, after a cost of some 1,500 soldiers and more than $40 million. Most of the embattled Seminoles finally consented to be moved to present Oklahoma, although about 1,200 of the descendants of fugitives may be found in Florida today.

So Jackson had to fight two local wars with Indian tribes, technically foreign nations with which removal treaties had been concluded. The clash with the Seminoles did not come to a partially successful conclusion until 1842, five years after Jackson had left the White House. This was yet another war that the United States did not fight through to complete victory.

As for more remote corners of the globe, in 1831-1832 United States naval forces operated on or near the Falkland Islands, off the coast of southern Argentina. These units were under orders to investigate the capture of three American sealing vessels and to protect American interests. Jackson took particular note of this intervention in his annual message of December 6, 1831, and expressed the hope that Congress could provide for a force that would ensure "complete protection of our fellow-citizens fishing and trading in those seas."

In this same message Jackson noted that a "daring outrage" had been committed in the Dutch East Indies "by the plunder of one of our merchantmen" involved in trading for pepper in a port of Sumatra. Because the murderous attackers were not under the authority of a civilized government, Jackson had "forthwith dispatched a frigate with orders to require immediate satisfaction for the injury and indemnity to the sufferers."

The sequel came in Jackson's annual message of the next year, 1832. He reported that he had instructed the commander of the frigate *Potomac* to proceed to Sumatra and determine first if the "atrocious piracy" had been committed by a regular government or by "lawless pirates," as he supposed. In the latter case the commander of the frigate should "inflict such a chastisement as would deter them and others from like aggressions."

This he had done, "and the effect has been an increased respect for our flag in those distant seas and additional security for our commerce." So much for American naval power in far off Sumatra in the 1830s.

Odds and Ends

During October 31 to November 15, 1833, an American force was sent ashore at Buenos Aires, Argentina, to safeguard American lives and property, as well as the interests of other countries, during an insurrection. In December 1835 and January 1836, and also from August to December 1836, U.S. Marines protected American interests in the cities of Callao and Lima, Peru, during an attempted revolution.

Lest one think that "Old Hickory" had gone completely soft in regard to Mexico, we should note a belligerent message that he sent to both houses of Congress on February 6, 1837, less than a month before he completed his two terms. The subject matter was the long-time grievance that the United States had against Mexico for damages to American lives and property. Many of these disorders had grown out of the fighting attendant upon Mexico's revolutionary war against Spain, beginning in 1810 and not formally ending until 1821, though internal conflicts continued for many years. These bills for damages had gone unacknowledged and unpaid by Mexico City. Also, the losses to American property had increased during the futile attempt by Mexico to crush the Texas uprising in 1836. Not surprisingly, Americans had not been popular in any part of Mexico (including Texas) during this bitter struggle.

Jackson then got to the point in his message to Congress of February 6, 1837. He declared: "The length of time since some of the injuries have been committed, the repeated and unavailing applications for redress, the wanton character of some of the outrages upon the property and person of our citizens, upon the officers and flag of the United States, independent of recent insults to this Government and people by the late extraordinary Mexican minister, would justify in the eyes of all nations immediate war."

At this point in his message Jackson retreated somewhat when he conceded that "immediate war" should not be used by "just and generous nations," if such a remedy "can be honorably avoided." He had concluded that because Mexico was then suffering from an "embarrassed condition," the part of "wisdom and moderation" would be to give "Mexico one more opportunity to atone for the past before we take redress into our own hands." But to protect America's "national character from reproach" and to avoid "misconception on the part of Mexico," this last opportunity should be given with the clear intention of taking "immediate satisfaction" if not complied with.

Jackson therefore recommended that Congress pass an act "authorizing reprisals and the use of a naval force" if the Mexican government refused to "come to an amicable adjustment." Should the Congress conclude that there were "well-grounded reasons" for hoping that an adjustment of the dispute could be achieved without such strong measures, then Jackson would cooperate in "any other course that shall be deemed honorable and proper." In short, the President would abide by the wishes of Congress in milder remedies to secure redress, and to this extent he retreated from recommending extreme measures. As we shall see later, President Polk embraced them in 1846.

In brief, Jackson's bark was sometimes more fearsome than his bite. While talking tough on several occasions, notably against France and Mexico, he passed on to Congress the responsibility for actually taking warlike measures. Despite his notorious pugnacity, he managed to avoid armed hostilities with domestic and foreign adversaries alike.

CHAPTER 8

MARTIN VAN BUREN: THE LITTLE MAGICIAN

Bound by no entangling alliances, yet linked by a common nature and interest with the other nations of mankind, our aspirations are for the preservation of peace. . . .

Martin Van Buren, Annual
Message to Congress
December 5, 1840.

Van Buren's Beginnings

President Martin Van Buren, descended from colonial Dutch stock, was born in Kinderhook, New York, and there he died at age seventy-nine. His birth occurred in 1782, during the closing months of the War of Independence, and hence he was the first President, although the eighth to occupy the post, to be born an American citizen, not a British subject.

Van Buren was not impressive physically. Only five feet, six inches in height, slender, erect and fair-complexioned, "Little Van" dressed fashionably. Close observers took note of his bald head, high and protruding forehead, small but brilliant blue eyes, and curly red sideburns ("Sweet Sandy Whiskers").

Like Washington and Jackson before him, the Sage of Kinderhook never attended college. More than ordinarily intelligent, he read law, became a first-rate lawyer and ultimately the Attorney General of the state of New York. He also gained fame as organizer of the Albany Regency, one of the nation's first major political machines. It flourished in the spoils-system democracy that reached flood tide in the heyday of the "reign" of "King Andrew" Jackson.

Van Buren's fame as a wire-puller led to such sobriquets as "The Wizard of Albany," "The Red Fox," "The Little Magician," and "The American Talleyrand." As John Randolph said, "He rowed to his object with muffled oars." Certainly Van Buren was smooth as silk, polished, courteous, self-assured, and urbane. He was the prototype of the new professional politician who could cater to the people and implement the desires of the now new democracy through the agency of political parties. Though something of an aristocrat, he helped substantially in making the new democracy work.

Van Buren's pre-presidential experience in high political position, both state and national, was greater and more varied than that of many of his predecessors and successors. He served for seven years in the Senate of New York State, and then for seven years in the Senate of the United States. After several

Jackson leads a reluctant Van Buren away from Kinderhook toward the White House. Campaign cartoon. Library of Congress.

months as Governor of New York, he resigned to become Secretary of State for two years under President Jackson. Appointed Minister to England, he served for about half a year and then came home when the Senate, on political grounds, rejected his nomination. His next post was Vice-President of the United States for four years under tough old President Jackson, cynically called "King Andrew the First," who anointed "King Martin" his legitimate successor.

As Chief Executive, Van Buren suffered from handicaps that cast a permanent pall over his four long years in the White House. First of all, as Jackson's fair-haired boy and as an improbable "Young Hickory," he inherited Jackson's numerous enemies without also inheriting "Old Hickory's" war-born popularity. (The dandified Van Buren had never served in the armed forces.) "Little Van" was also so unlucky as to suffer from a withering depression that was known as the Panic of 1837, probably triggered in part by Jackson's bull-in-the-china-closet concepts of finance. Martin Van Buren was soon dubbed "Martin Van Ruin."

A bothersome hangover from the Jackson administration that did Van Buren's fortunes no good was the proposed annexation of Texas, recognized by President Jackson in March 1837 as an independent republic. In August 1837 the newly spawned republic formally petitioned the Washington government for both annexation and admission to the Union. The swelling throng of antislaveryites, particularly in the North, reacted with alarm. They deluged both houses of Congress with scores of petitions bearing thousands of signatures protesting against annexation in the strongest terms.

What other great nation in the imperialistic nineteenth century would have spurned the free offer of so vast and rich an expanse as Texas? But Van Buren, to his credit, rejected annexation. Mexico had not yet come to terms with Texas, and "Little Van," the man of peace, had no desire to annex a war, as President Tyler subsequently did in 1845. Moreover, at heart Van Buren was opposed to extending the curse of black slavery, which was now firmly established in Texas. To what extent he was influenced by the inpouring of petitions from the antislavery zealots cannot be determined, but it seems clear that his own instincts coincided with these pressures. In any event, Texas was left for seven years as a kind of dangerous derelict on the international sea.

The Canadian Insurrection

The depressing Panic of 1837 was President Van Buren's most vexatious problem on the domestic front, but the uprisings of that year in Canada provided a series of real war scares. How the President handled these outbreaks proved to be an exacting test of his desire for peace.

Relations between the United States and Canada had long been uneasy, at times critical. The thirteen revolting colonies in 1775 had been eager to have French-inhabited Canada join hands with them as the fourteenth colony, but unwisely the rebels tried military conquest. Two invading American armies were driven back from the walls of Quebec on a snowy December 31, 1775, and the ambitious invasion ended in retreat.

During and after the United States War of Independence, an estimated sixty thousand or so American Loyalists fled for sanctuary to British Canada, thus giving this spacious land its first large influx of English blood as an offset to the conquered French inhabitants (*habitants*) already there. These newcomers formed themselves into the organization known as the United Empire Loyalists (UEL), who clung with almost fanatical allegiance to the British crown.

During the war of 1812, American forces repeatedly attempted to invade and embrace Canada, but they were driven back, leaving behind many ugly memories. Conspicuous among the defenders, fighting side by side with British Redcoats, were the ex-Loyalists. Having once lost their homes and lands in the United States to the Yankees, they were most reluctant to see them lost again. When peace finally came in 1815, these resolute United Empire Loyalists were greatly distressed to discover that the Mother Country was not making what they regarded as adequate provisions for their defense against another attempt at seizure.

During much of the nineteenth century, when serious friction developed between Britain and the United States, one of the first thoughts that crossed American minds was the old war cry, "On to Canada." Throughout most of this troubled era, the Canadians must have had the feeling that they were living on the slopes of a volcano about to erupt.

In 1836–1837 William Lyon Mackenzie seized center stage in Canada. A fiery Scotsman and journalist, he spoke out vigorously against the governing British–Canadian clique. Although five times expelled illegally from the Legislative Assembly of Upper Canada for alleged libel, he was as many times reelected by his stubborn constituency. With a group of insurrectionists he tried to seize Toronto in Upper Canada in 1837, but his following was so weak militarily that the initial uprising was quickly crushed, as was a parallel outbreak in the French-speaking province of Quebec. Mackenzie fled to hospitable American soil with some of his followers but was ultimately arrested and imprisoned for more than a year by the United States authorities for violating neutrality statutes.

At the outset of these two outbursts in Canada, large numbers of Americans, especially in states strung along the northern border, cheered loudly. They assumed—incorrectly—that the uprising was an attempt by the formerly spineless Canadians to throw off the tyrannical yoke of overseas Britain. Heirs of the American Revolution, the Yankees generally supported antimonarchial uprisings anywhere. They were flattered to view these minor uprisings in Canada as but another chapter in the great book of revolution begun by them in 1775–1776. (Some critic has said that the Americans in the nineteenth century applauded every rebellion against authority regarded as oppressive, except their own sanguinary Civil War.)

Along the American side of the northern border in 1837 dwelt a considerable contingent of New England Puritans who felt impelled by a strong missionary urge to bring the blessings of liberty to their "benighted" and royalist Canadian neighbors. If these newly spawned rebels had only had real "Yankee gumption," it was believed, they would have risen up long ago and thrown off the yoke of the British crown. But American interest in Mackenzie's ill-starred Canadian rebellion was by no means completely unselfish. With a helping hand from America's freedom-loving patriots, the insurgent Canadians might win their independence. In this event, what would then be more logical and inevitable than the union of the two English-speaking republics (including French-speaking Canadians) under the Stars and Stripes?

British military forces and the Canadian militia, with little effort, were able to crush and disperse Mackenzie's tiny bands of rebels in both Montreal and Quebec. Many of the fugitives fled to sanctuary in the United States. Mackenzie himself found refuge in Buffalo, New York, where, from his new headquarters at the Eagle Tavern, he tauntingly flung his insurgent flag to the breeze. Such a flagrant action by the exiled rebel-in-chief was naturally infuriating to loyal Canadians and Britons alike. One can well imagine what the feeling would have been in the United States if a comparable band of defeated American rebels had fled to Canada. Indeed, during the Civil War of 1861–1865 Confederate agents and soldiers did stir up great bitterness by operating on occasion from Canadian soil against the United States.

In 1837 the atmosphere along the Canadian border was charged with trouble. An ingrained Anglophobia was heightened by a natural sympathy for the underdog Canadian rebels, by the presence of many of the revolutionists as fugitives, and by exaggerated rumors of the severity of their punishment. In addition the prostrating panic of 1837 had left many Americans jobless, especially along the waterfront of the Great Lakes, where hard-fisted characters were both desperate and irresponsible. Many of them flocked to the rebel banner, lured on by glowing promises of land, ranging in expanse from 160 to 320 acres.

This open aid and comfort to the Canadian rebels, many of them now fugitives in the United States, ran counter to the neutrality laws already passed by Congress. Such assistance certainly contravened the spirit of the neutrality proclamation of George Washington in 1793. Yet defiant American citizens, singing the "Marseillaise," openly enlisted in the forces of the insurrectionists on United States soil. Uncontrollable mobs also looted several American arsenals and turned the weapons over to the Canadian rebels.

The ultimate outcome, perhaps inevitable, was a minor undeclared war between the British authorities in Canada and unauthorized American volunteers in the United States. On the American side of the border, the sympathizers with the rebels were so numerous and the authorities so few that the neutrality laws of the United States could not be adequately enforced, no matter how zealous the officials. From the days of Jefferson's self-crucifying embargo to the present, the American people have been notorious for flouting and negating restrictions of which they generally disapprove.

The *Caroline* Crisis and After

A dangerous embroilment with Britain was precipitated late in December 1837. With American help, the Canadian rebel Mackenzie had attained a precarious new foothold on a small island on the British side of the Niagara River, just above the famous falls. A tiny steamer, the *Caroline*, was then hired to carry rebel supplies to him from the New York side—a grossly unneutral act. The vessel had made only three trips in a single afternoon when she was set upon in American waters by a raiding party of British-Canadian volunteers that had daringly rowed across the swift current. One American was killed in the melee, and the *Caroline* was turned adrift without occupants and sank before reaching the Niagara Falls.

This raid was a counterviolation of neutrality with a vengeance. It brought to the fore the "international derelict" argument that Secretary Adams had used so effectively in supporting Jackson's unrestrained foray into Florida. In short, if a nation cannot enforce its own neutrality statutes, it must not complain if the aggrieved party takes the law into its own hands. Canadian loyalists and the British, at home and in Canada, applauded the heroic destruction of the *Caroline*. The London government, after concluding that justified self-defense was involved, fended off the demands of Washington for apology and reparation. Not until 1842, six years later, did a representative of the British government express modified regrets, cleverly using the word "apology" without actually apologizing. But by then the passage of time had allowed passions to cool.

The immediate response in America to the *Caroline* counter-outrage was a loud demand, especially along the northern frontier, for retribution in blood. The national honor, many sterling patriots felt, had been sullied by that ancient foe, the bullying British. But the farther one traveled from the border the less enthusiasm one found for warlike measures. Much of the appeal of Canada lay in its being so near—yet so far.

President Van Buren's response to the "dangerous excitement" provoked by the *Caroline* reprisal was to issue a neutrality proclamation dated January 5, 1838. At the outset he reported that he had already given special instructions regarding enforcement to United States officials on the Canadian frontier. He had also called upon the governors of the adjoining states to prevent unlawful interference in the current insurrection. The chief magistrates of New York and Vermont had issued appropriate proclamations, but the wholesale violation of neutral duties and obligations was still going on, including the enlistment of American volunteers on American soil and the procurement of arms.

In ending his proclamation, Van Buren earnestly exhorted the law violators to return "peaceably to their homes." Those who did not heed his warning would be liable to "arrest and punishment." They could also expect no protection from the federal government if charged with "the violation of the laws of their country and the territory of a neighboring and friendly nation."

President Van Buren followed up his proclamation by specifically requesting the governors of New York and Vermont to call their militia into service. He also sent General Winfield Scott, a hero of the War of 1812 and a future hero of the Mexican War, to the northern border, where he and his small band of regulars did outstanding work as dampeners of inflamed feelings. All told, Scott traveled up and down some 800 miles of the frontier.

Tensions along the northern border eased markedly early in 1838 with the almost complete stamping out of the hapless and hopeless Canadian insurrection. But during the ensuing months several alarming incidents occurred, conspicuously the total destruction of a Canadian vessel, the *Sir Robert Peel*, which was operating within American jurisdiction on the St. Lawrence River in May 1838. A band of disguised Americans boarded, looted, and then burned the ship. They shouted to the half-dressed passengers set ashore, "Remember the *Caroline*." In short, a steamboat for a steamboat.

Despite Van Buren's earnest efforts, the undeclared war on the border was kept alive by the organization of secret Hunters' Lodges from Vermont to Michigan. Their membership was swollen by many thousands of men—estimates ran from 15,000 to an extravagant 200,000—who took a solemn oath "to emancipate the British Colonies from British Thraldom." Actually, only about one thousand of the Hunters were even armed for invasion. They evidently expected that the royalty-ridden Canadians would rise and greet them as democratic deliverers. Several small armed bands did push northward across the border in November and December of 1838 ("Battle of the Windmill"). They were easily crushed, and some of the prisoners were either executed or shipped off to the penal colony in what is now Tasmania, south of Australia.

The incursions of the Hunters into Canada, in conjunction with Canadian rebels, prompted President Van Buren to issue a second and more blistering proclamation enjoining neutrality, that of November 21, 1838. He found the invaders "in perfect disregard of their obligations as American citizens and of the obligations of the Government of their country to foreign nations." He therefore called upon his "misguided or deluded" fellow citizens to maintain the nation's precarious neutrality and thus preserve "the honor and good faith" of their government. The lawbreakers who had "nefariously invaded Canada" were again warned that they could not expect interference "in any form on their behalf" from the government of their own country.

Canadians in particular have criticized Van Buren harshly for having failed to halt the vast amount of hostile activity along the common boundary. They were put to great trouble and expense to restore calm. But Van Buren deserves full credit for a sincere and vigorous attempt to enforce the neutrality laws. His task was complicated by the hundreds of miles of border, the inflamation of public opinion, the tiny number of federal officials, and the inadequacy of existing neutrality legislation.

Aside from the federal precautions previously enumerated, Van Buren directed vigorous legal actions against violators of the neutrality laws. One of the American ringleaders, the immensely popular General Rensselaer Van Rensselaer, was convicted by an American jury and sentenced to prison for one year. President Van Buren was subjected to immense pressure to pardon him by some 300,000 petitioners. He showed rare political courage when he deferred taking such action until after his campaign for reelection in 1840, when he was defeated by "Old Tippecanoe" Harrison. One cannot doubt that Van Buren's faithful discharge of his duties hurt him politically, for "Woe to Martin Van Buren" was the campaign cry of the Hunters and other Canada sympathizers.

The Aroostook War

Hardly had the rebel-Hunters' invasions of Canada passed the crisis stage, late in 1838, when another undeclared conflict broke out on the Maine border in February 1839. Called the "Aroostook War" after a river in a part of the area in disupte, the clash fortunately involved no bloodshed, except for a few bloody noses and cracked heads.

The prolonged dispute over the location of the boundary between Maine and Canada dated far back to the ambiguous provisions of the Treaty of 1783, which had officially ended America's War of Independence with Great Britain. To the credit of both the stormy Jackson administration and the London government, the two nations agreed in 1827 to submit the question at issue to arbitration by the King of the Netherlands. In 1831 the royal arbitrator handed down a compromise decision. Unable to locate the precise boundary from the confusing language of the Treaty of 1783, he realistically undertook a rough splitting of the difference. The United States Senate rejected this decision.

The Maine boundary issue came to life again in 1837-1838, the years of the ill-starred Canadian insurrection. During these grave disorders, as during the War of 1812, the British had found their movement of troops hampered by the annual freezing over of the St. Lawrence River. The most practicable alternative would be a military road stretching from St. John and Halifax, Nova Scotia, to Quebec and Montreal. Such a route would have to run through a part of the large Maine salient, claimed by the Americans, north of the St. John River.

A crisis developed in February 1839, when a party of heavy-fisted Canadian lumberjacks moved into this forested area and began to chop down the virgin timber on the Aroostook River, well within the disputed area. Upon being warned to depart, the intruders seized the United States agent and stood fast.

The response to this invasion was predictable. Rival American lumberjacks, also handy with their fists, moved in. Maine called out her militia; the Canadians of New Brusnwick did likewise. The legislature of Nova Scotia, amid singing of "God Save the Queen," voted money for additional arms. In Washington, Congress appropriated $10 million and authorized President Van Buren to summon fifty thousand volunteers.

Fortunately for sanity, the "Aroostook War" proved to be a war in name only. There were no armed clashes between official forces of the antagonists. Van Buren dispatched to the danger zone his gifted peacemaker, war hero General Winfield Scott. He arrived in Augusta, Maine, early in March 1839, and before the month was out he had managed to work out a truce during which the two antagonists could cling fast to their respective claims. Three years later a compromise boundary line was agreed upon in the delicate negotiations conducted by Secretary of State Daniel Webster with Lord Ashburton in 1842.

Throughout the Aroostook War, President Van Buren, as during the Canadian insurrection, proved to be a model of fairness, justice, reason, restraint, and moderation, including his dealings with Congress. He recognized his duty to protect the valid interests of Maine, to uphold the rights and honor of the United States, and to avoid the abyss of a shooting war. In all three areas he succeeded admirably in pursuing what he called "a just spirit of conciliation and forbearance."

Uprooting the Red Men

Van Buren appears in a less pacific light in connection with the policy of Indian removal to the west, particularly as he commented on it in successive messages to Congress. From the outset he strongly defended this large-scale uprooting, for he was faithful to the policy being implemented by his predecessor, President Jackson. He routinely reported that the process of making treaties with the Indians had been going forward successfully, and that this transplanting was clearly the only solution for the whites and red people alike. He did concede that there had been some cheating and other mistreatment of the Indians, but such unethical schemes had not been a part of government policy. Unscrupulous outsiders had all too often taken advantage of the red men to feather their own nests.

In the case of the reluctant Seminole Indians of Florida, the President was obliged to make an exception to this "near approach to a happy and certain consummation." As he related in his second annual message to Congress (December 3, 1838), about four hundred Seminoles had emigrated in 1836 and 1,500 in 1837 and 1838, leaving behind an estimated two thousand. Those remaining had continued their "treacherous conduct" by "butchering whole families of the settlers of the [Florida] Territory without distinction of age or sex." The embittered Seminoles had ventured into "the very center and heart of the country" with their butcheries. They had attacked the lighthouses along the "dangerous coast," with the result that they had been able to lure and murder the passengers and crews of ships wrecked on the reefs and keys. Such inhumane conduct left the Washington government, concluded Van Buren, with "no alternative but to continue military operations against them [Seminoles] until they are totally expelled from Florida." These treacherous Indians, he declared, had signed treaties with the federal government to move west, as had the other tribes, and to permit the Seminoles to flout their obligation would be "of evil example in our intercourse with other tribes."

The war would have to go on, Van Buren concluded, despite the swamps, marshes, and extreme summer heat ("sickly season"), so as to ensure more efficient protection of the Floridans from this "inhuman warfare." Van Buren, be it noted, had not willed all this bloodshed, and it had been started under his "illustrious predecessor." Yet he favored the policy that had provoked it, although as a choice of evils, and clearly believed that not to fight the conflict through to the bitter end would be breaking faith with the tribes that had, with great reluctance, already honored their treaty obligations. Before the Seminole War erupted, representatives of the Seminoles had actually gone west and approved the site selected for their new homes.

American Rights on Foreign Shores

If Van Buren was determined to protect the rights of Canadians from unneutral activity on the American side of the border, he was no less vigilant in protecting the rights of Americans in remote places. During Jackson's incumbency the Navy had already taken punitive action against the natives of the town of Quallah Battoo, on the East Indian island of Sumatra, in February 1832. But the strong medicine administered by American naval forces did not have a lasting effect. In the days of President Van Buren, from December 1838 to January 1839, the American chastisers were forced to come again. They severely punished the natives of the towns of Quallah Battoo and Muckie (Mukki), Sumatra, for depredations on American shipping.

In his third annual message to Congress (December 2, 1839), Van Buren referred to this incident by saying, "The Navy has been usefully and honorably employed in protecting the rights and property of our citizens wherever the condition of affairs seems to require its presence."

The U.S. Navy, Van Buren could also announce, had been employed in the Fiji Islands, east of Australia (July 1840) to punish certain natives for attacking American parties of explorers and surveyors. A related action had occurred in 1841 on Drummond Island, Kingsmill Group, to avenge the murder of a seaman by certain natives. Likewise in 1841, an American naval force had been utilized to avenge the murder of an American seaman on Upolu Island, Samoa. During these same years American warships were also deployed against slavers off the coast of Africa "to prevent a fraudulent use of our flag by foreigners."

In December 1840, three months before bowing out, President Van Buren incorporated a classic statement of his general approach to foreign affairs in his fourth annual message to Congress. He declared that a "rigid and perservering abstinence from all interference with the domestic and political relations of other States" had been his lodestar. He had faithfully observed "the practice of speaking plainly, dealing justly, and requiring truth and justice in return" as being "the best conservatives of the peace of nations." The result had been "honorable peace" with "all the powers of the world. Although the nation's "aspirations are for the preservation of peace," the United States could maintain its "independent rights" only by "a resolute bearing" and clothing itself "with defensive armor."

President Van Buren deserves commendation for having preserved the peace and for having upheld American rights and honor. Aside from some necessary but minor police actions in distant seas, and apart from his having to prosecute the Seminole war that had broken out under his predecessor, the record is remarkably pacific. His most strenuous efforts were directed at restraining his countrymen from precipitating another war with Great Britain during the insurrection in Canada. Here he succeeded in the teeth of grave difficulties.

Yet critics have been unkind to Van Buren. He came to the presidency better prepared for that burdensome post—in intellect, temperament, and experience—than the great majority of his predecessors. Andrew Jackson's act was a hard one to follow, filled as it was with clatter, head-cracking, and controversy. Van Buren did not provide fireworks, so the people felt let down. He was sneered and jeered at, then and later, as a "first-class second-rate man."

The "Tippecanoe and Tyler Too" campaign of 1840, with its populist hoopla for log cabins and hard cider, undid Van Buren. The opposition Whigs pictured him as a dandified fop, who lolled about in the White House ("President's Palace"), eating fancy French food with a golden spoon, from a silver plate. A political battle cry, "Van, Van, Is a Used Up Man," became self-fulfilling because an ignorant and vocal electorate deluded itself into believing campaign propaganda.

Actually, Van Buren was as level-headed a statesman as he was a skilled politician. He had the misfortune to lose the presidency in 1840 as the result of outrageous campaign smears. His political enemies in the South harped on his antislavery rejection of Texas and in the North on his "pro-British" neutrality during the Canadian insurrections of 1837–1838. Defeated for reelection by "Old Tippecanoe" Harrison, Van Buren polled nearly 47 percent of the popular vote, which was actually a larger percentage than that garnered in the winning campaigns of a number of his successors, including Abraham Lincoln, Woodrow Wilson, and Richard Nixon in his first successful presidential election.

CHAPTER 9

WILLIAM H. HARRISON: THE HERO OF TIPPECANOE

Long the defender of my country's rights in the field, I trust that my fellow citizens will not see in my earnest desire to preserve peace with foreign powers any indication that their rights will ever be sacrificed....

President Harrison, Inaugural
Address, March 4, 1841

William Henry Harrison, "The Log Cabin President" for only thirty-two days in 1841, could claim a number of distinctions. Scion of an authentic FFV (First Family of Virginia), he was the son of a signer of the Declaration of Independence. He entered Hampton-Sidney College in Virginia when only fourteen years of age, and thus could claim some college education, which Van Buren and Jackson, his two predecessors, could not do. "Old Tippecanoe" Harrison was a professional military man of martial bearing (five feet, eight inches) who had risen to the rank of major general. He was also an inveterate officeholder. He had ranged from membership in Congress, both House and Senate, to the governorship of Indiana Territory.

"Old Tip" was additionally an authentic war hero, having defeated (but not too convincingly) the Indians at Tippecanoe, Indiana. He gained greater fame in the War of 1812, for he had led the army that defeated the British and Indians at the Battle of the Thames in Canada in 1813. Here Tecumseh was killed, the spirit of the Indians was broken, and General Harrison was awarded a gold medal by Congress.

The ablest and most prominent Whigs finally backed Harrison for the presidency because they concluded, after witnessing the successive electoral triumphs of General Jackson, that another war hero from the West would at last bring victory to the Whigs. The result was the empty-headed hoopla campaign for "Tippecanoe and Tyler Too," with false emphasis on "poor man" Harrison's supposed occupancy of log cabins and quaffing of hard cider. Unadulterated froth and buncombe won out over sober issues, and Harrison was figuratively swept into office on a tidal wave of hard cider (the poor man's champagne).

Old General Harrison, at sixty-eight the most elderly man ever elected to the Presidency thus far, delivered by far the longest and deadliest inaugural address yet presented by any man entering the White House. It ran over 8,570 words and required one hour and forty-five minutes for delivery, in cold and stormy weather. Shortly thereafter Harrison died of pneumonia, after holding office for about a month, by far the shortest term in American presidential history.

How militant Harrison would have been, had he lived out his four years, is a matter of pure speculation. His having been an experienced general offers no reliable clue, for several of the most distinguished military men, from Washington to Eisenhower, have been cautious enough or lucky enough to escape a real war.

A possible hint of a pacific course may be found in a single paragraph near the end of Harrison's long-winded inaugural address. He declared that it was his "intention to use every means in my power to preserve the friendly intercourse which now so happily subsists with every foreign nation." Harrison evidently ignored the acute disharmony existing with Mexico over the prospective annexation of Texas, as well as the difficulties with England over the friction that had sprouted from the insurrections in Canada and the Aroostook War in Maine.

Harrison concluded the portion of his address devoted to foreign affairs by assuring his listeners that the current "friendly intercourse" was such that he could not foresee the advancement of "any claim or pretension" by foreign nations to which "our honor would not permit us to yield." Long a defender of his "country's rights in the field," he would never sacrifice the "rights" or tarnish the "honor" of the nation. As for the Indians ("aboriginal neighbors"), he could be counted on to follow the course of "liberality and justice" established by his two "illustrious predecessors." This statement seemed to mean that this old Indian fighter and land-grabber would continue the existing policy of transplanting the Indians and bringing the protracted Seminole War to a victorious end.

CHAPTER 10

JOHN TYLER: THE FIRST ACCIDENTAL PRESIDENT

We can never be too tardy to begin the work of blood.... It is a bad mode of settling disputes to make soldiers your ambassadors, and to point to the halter and the gallows as your ultimatum.

President Tyler, printed
letter, August 24, 1841

The Canadian Aftershocks

President Tyler was the first man to reach the White House as a result of the death of the incumbent Chief Executive. Six feet tall, Tyler had long limbs, a narrow chest, light brown hair, and blue eyes. He looked every inch the Virginia gentleman that he was.

On paper, Tyler had many of the qualifications that one would like to find in a potential Chief Executive. He had been born in Virginia, "The Mother of Presidents," like five of his nine predecessors. At age twelve he had entered the College of

William and Mary, Thomas Jefferson's alma mater, was graduated in 1807, and was admitted to the bar in 1809. In 1813, while the War of 1812 was in progress, Tyler served for a time as a captain of the volunteers defending Richmond. But the enemy did not descend, and Tyler's military service was evidently bloodless. Still, it *was* military service.

During the 1820s and 1830s Tyler gained wide experience as a member of the House of Representatives from Virginia, Rector of the College of William and Mary, Governor of Virginia, United States Senator from Virginia, and member of the Virginia House of Delegates. In 1840 Tyler, the Virginia aristocrat, was tapped as a vice-presidential running mate with "Old Tippecanoe" Harrison. The scheme was to "balance the ticket" by appealing to the South and also to the states' rights wing of the Whig party, to which Tyler, a former Jackson Democrat, now belonged.

Henry Clay, Daniel Webster, and other leaders of the nationalist wing of the Whig party clearly did not expect Harrison to die in office. Tyler, the new "Accidental President," subsequently and stubbornly wielded his veto pen to block their nationalistic plans, notably a new Bank of the United States and a highly protective tariff. As a result, "Traitor Tyler" was formally read out of the party in September 1841. His entire inherited Cabinet resigned in a body, except Secretary of State Daniel Webster, who was then in the midst of delicate negotiations with the British envoy to settle explosive disputes between the two countries. This bitter intraparty infighting must be kept in mind as we consider what was happening on the diplomatic front.

From the outset Tyler's "accidental" administration had to cope with the continuing aftershocks of the Canadian insurrections that had broken out in 1837. Excitement and anger over the spectacular destruction of the "pirate ship" *Caroline* had largely subsided when flames flared anew over an incendiary aftermath.

In November 1840 a Canadian by the name of Alexander McLeod was arrested on the soil of New York State after he had allegedly boasted of participation in the *Caroline* raid. One American had been killed in this affair, and the New York authorities placed the talkative Canadian under arrest, charging him with murder and arson.

An indignant London government protested against the arrest in strong terms, War is legalized murder, and the British took the position that McLeod, even if a member of the attacking party, was acting under military orders and hence immune from prosecution. The Foreign Office "formally demanded" the release of the prisoner and also made clear that a refusal would result in the most serious consequences. This was a delicate way of saying the ugly word "war."

But the lordly British were not fully aware of the peculiarities of the American judicial system. The sovereign State of New York had complete jurisdiction over the unfortunate McLeod in a case of murder, and President Tyler was legally powerless to fend off the hand of justice. Yet the Washington government did bring strong pressure to bear on the state to transfer the case to a federal court—without success. Passions still ran so high along the northern border that New York stood defiantly on its legal rights, regardless of the consequences. In England there were undisguised threats of war over McLeod's "judicial lynching."

The legal machinery of New York ground on inexorably as McLeod went before a jury in Utica. The town teemed with strangers, among whom there was some loose talk of lynching. Fortunately for the defendant, the prosecution was weak, and McLeod, who claimed that he had been five or six miles away at the time of the *Caroline* raid, presented a convincing alibi. It must have been air-tight, because the New York jury, obviously not prejudiced in his favor, returned a verdict of "not guilty" after only twenty minutes of deliberation.

If McLeod had been found guilty and war seemed imminent, his counsel could have tried remaining legal expedients. Governor Seward of New York, aware of his grave responsibility, probably would have pardoned the unhappy Canadian—at least he so informed Secretary of State Daniel Webster. The British Minister in Washington had instructions to leave Washington if McLeod should be executed. President Tyler took the unusual step of informing the envoy that his passports would not be handed to him, and that he would be detained until the London government had ample time to reflect on its warlike course.

President Tyler, the experienced lawyer, noted with satisfaction the fortunate outcome of the McLeod trial. He had not been able to intervene directly to save the accused man, but in his first annual message to Congress (December 7, 1841) he suggested that appropriate legislative action be taken to prevent one state from provoking a war that all the others would have to fight. Specifically, he proposed that the legislators take proper steps to transfer such cases "from the state to the federal judiciary." Such a step, he predicted, would promote "the maintenance of peace and the preservation of amicable relations with the nations of the earth." Congress failed to comply with Tyler's request.

The Webster–Ashburton Diplomatic Duel

By the spring of 1842 a large number of grievances on both sides brought Anglo-American relations dangerously close to the boiling point again. The British had not offered reparation or even regret for the rankling *Caroline* affair. The Maine boundary dispute, which had sounded a temporary alarm in the Arrostook War, could explode into violence at any moment. The rising demand from the west for a clear title to the Oregon country, jointly occupied by treaty with Great Britain, was growing more clamorous. On the high seas the British navy was searching slave ships illegally flying the American flag, thus reviving ugly memories of the hated visit-and-search procedures of the days preceding the War of 1812.

In the hope of solving or at least salving some of these problems, the British Foreign Office dispatched to Washington a special envoy in the person of Lord Ashburton. A tactful and gracious man, although not a career diplomat, he had achieved distinction in both the political and financial worlds. After opening conversations with Secretary of State Webster in June 1842, Ashburton found in his able adversary something of a kindred spirit. On the whole, negotiations went off more smoothly than the poisoned atmosphere portended.

As for the Maine-Canadian boundary, the documentary evidence was so contradictory and confusing that the two negotiators finally decided on a rough splitting of the difference. The disputed line was finally drawn in such a way as to permit Canada to retain about 5,000 of the 12,000 square miles of the Maine land in dispute. The British could then build their cherished military road through the area they had long claimed. Lord Ashburton also consented to a minor adjustment of the boundary in Upper New York and Vermont, and the concession to the United States of a line between Lake Superior and the Lake of the Woods. Here the United States unwittingly received the priceless

Messabi iron deposits, which were not discovered until 1866, twenty-four years later.

The issue of searching of slave ships (slavers) came near wrecking the Webster-Ashburton negotiations. Great Britain had already abolished slavery in her colonies, and in a burst of humanitarianism was now taking energetic steps to wipe out the African slave trade. The greatest obstacle proved to be the American flag. In time of war a belligerent nation has a right to search neutral ships on the high seas for contraband of war. But such a privilege does not exist in time of peace, unless specifically granted by the nation whose vessel is involved. Such a concession had been made through treaties with a number of nations, thus giving the British a free hand to search their ships for suspected slave cargoes.

The United States, in which slavery had not yet been abolished, refused to grant the British visitation privileges. Patriotic Americans had too keen a memory of the practice of visit and search, plus the impressment of seamen, that had preceded the War of 1812. So it was that the glorious Stars and Stripes waved ingloriously over every wretched slave ship bold enough to raise American colors. Some of these floating hells thus protected were so filthy that, with the wind blowing from the right direction, they actually could be smelled before being seen coming over the horizon.

Humanitarian Britons were outraged by this flagrant abuse and misuse of American colors. Forced to concede that there was no right of search in time of peace, the British tried to establish the right to visit a suspected ship to ascertain its true status. But even a fool could see that the right to visit would be the entering wedge for the right to search; there would be no point in boarding if the intruders did not keep their eyes and nostrils open. Some patriotic Americans even feared that British press gangs might even start impressing seamen again. As Tyler told Congress in his first annual message, he denied "the right" of such peacetime visit and search "by any one or all of the nations of the earth without our consent." Yet he continued to affirm his abhorrence of the slave trade.

After a prolonged argument in Washington, Webster and Ashburton hammered out a compromise. Both America and Britain agreed to keep naval patrols of no fewer than eighty guns off the slave-trading African coast. Each of the two nations would enforce its own laws on its own ships, and both would act in concert when the need arose. This scheme did not work out satisfactorily, primarily because the United States failed to go to the trouble and expense of providing its full quota of ships. But at least the right to visit in time of peace became less of a burning issue.

Salving Secondary Irritants

Several pressing problems of the second degree were taken care of by the all-embracing Webster-Ashburton negotiations. The recent and prolonged disturbances along the border with Canada provided a painful reminder that the extradition provisions of the Jay Treaty had expired. The negotiators agreed to include in the new treaty such nonpolitical offenses as "the crime of murder, or assault with intent to commit murder, or piracy, or arson, or robbery, or forgery, or the utterance of forged paper." Embezzlement of funds was not on the list; hence "Gone to Canada" for many years told the story of absconding American bank clerks.

The planters of the slaveholding South had been greatly aroused in November 1841 by the explosive *Creole* affair. This vessel was an American brig sailing from Hampton Roads, Virginia, to New Orleans with a valuable shipment of slaves. En route the officers were overpowered by the rebellious cargo, and the white owner was killed. The mutinous blacks then found refuge at Nassau, a port in the British Bahamas. Despite the demands of the owners and loud protests from numerous Southerners, the British authorities flatly refused to turn the cargo of "black ivory" over to the American authorities. But the ex-slaves charged with murder were held for their crime.

The *Creole* affair was so complicated legally as to jeopardize the whole Webster-Ashburton negotiation. The British envoy was entirely without instructions to handle the problem, but Webster persuaded him to make a substantial concession. Ashburton finally promised in a note (not in the text of the treaty) that the governors in the British colonies would be instructed to avoid "officious interference" with ships driven by stress of weather or by violence into their jurisdiction. Webster was then content to let the issue drop, for the slaveholding South was bound to derive some satisfaction, as it did, from such a concession. Even greater satisfaction was obtained when the Anglo-American mixed claims commission ultimately (1853) awarded $110,330 to the United States to idemnify the slaveowners for their valuable lost property.

The spectacular *Caroline* affair, still a rankling grievance for more than four years, was settled on a less satisfactory basis. Try as Webster would, he could do no more than induce a reluctant Ashburton to express his "regret" that the incident "should have disturbed the harmony" existing between Great Britain and America. To this the Briton added: "Looking back to what passed at this distance of time, what is, perhaps, most to be regretted is, that some explanation and apology for this occurrence was not immediately made." A careful reading of this "apology" will reveal that Ashburton did not apologize at all. But he did employ the word "apology," and the resourceful Webster made the most of it. He issued a reply, clearly for home consumption, which made it appear that Ashburton had conceded more than he had actually yielded.

Ashburton had secured authorization from London to work out a fair division of the Oregon country with the Americans. But the two negotiators preferred to let well enough alone. As President Tyler explained in his second annual message to Congress, the Oregon question might have led to a prolonged discussion that "might embrace in its failure other more pressing matters." He added that even though the Oregon dispute might not for "several years to come involve the peace of the two countries," he would not delay urging on Britain the importance of an "early settlement."

The historian finds it difficult to point to any single negotiation in the history of American foreign affairs that either settled or swept under the rug more issues of major importance, practically all of them fraught with the dangers of war. A great clearing of the air resulted. Tyler, often labeled a flat failure, had a large hand in this bold and comprehensive stroke for peace. Although he did not interefere officiously in the delicate Webster–Ashburton negotiations, he cordially supported his Secretary of State and helped where he could. Specifically, he played an important role in the negotiations with Maine and Massachusetts, both of which were induced to abandon their claims by a reimbursement of $150,000 each.

President Tyler submitted the Webster–Ashburton treaty to the Senate with his approval as a document that represented the best terms available. He noted that the article on extradition excluded "all political offenses or criminal charges arising from wars or intestine commotions." Thus, he said, "Treason, misprision of treason, libels, desertion from military service, and other offenses of similar character are excluded."

The Webster-Ashburton diplomatic notes relating to the *Creole* and the *Caroline* were in themselves adjuncts to the treaty, and President Tyler also described them to Congress as satisfactory. He even found Lord Ashburton's watered-down apology regarding the *Caroline* to be so acceptable as "to warrant forbearance from any further remonstrance against what took place as an aggression on the soil and territory of the country." As a strong nationalist, Tyler did not add that the *Caroline* had been intruding upon the soil and territory of Canada by carrying supplies to the Canadian rebels on Navy Island.

White and Red Rebels

In the spring of 1842, while the Webster-Ashburton negotiations were getting under way, the Dorr rebellion in Rhode Island presented President Tyler with an excellent but unusual opportunity to employ military force. A struggle had developed between the conservatives and the liberals, led by reformer Thomas W. Dorr. At issue was the proposed substitution of a liberal, manhood-suffrage constitution for the existing illiberal colonial charter of 1663. When the rebels took to arms, the Governor of Rhode Island appealed to Tyler for federal aid, as did Dorr.

The President recognized his constitutional right to protect each state against "domestic violence and foreign invasion" but judged that the revolt had not yet reached alarming proportions. He declined to intervene and urged the disputants to work out their differences without federal intercession.

Tyler was a zealous states righter, and his convictions probably helped to hold him back, even though he privately sided with the conservatives. In any event, he left the contesting parties to work out the problem peacefully in their own way. The result was a more liberal constitution that the yellowing colonial charter.

In a special message to the House of Representatives, April 9, 1844, Tyler patted himself on the back with these words: "The desire of the Executive was from the beginning to bring the dispute to a termination without the interposition of the military power of the United States, and it will continue to be a subject of self-congratulation that this leading object of policy was finally accomplished." In this instance, Tyler did not sound like Jackson lashing out at the State of South Carolina, which had defied federal authority. But in Tyler's case the two parties were asking for federal intervention, not condemning it.

In assessing Tyler's level of pugnacity we must note that in his administration and on his orders the Seminole War officially ended on August 14, 1842, by proclamation. It had been waged intermittently since 1837, thus becoming the longest, most grueling and costly Indian war in the long and bloody roll of Indian wars.

In his message of May 10, 1842, to Congress, Tyler painted a bleak picture. The Seminole population of Florida, once numbering several thousand, was now driven into almost impenetrable swamps. It was believed to have dropped to some 240 persons, of whom about 80 warriors or males were capable of fighting. Their very fewness was a source of strength, because they obviously could not be fought by masses of armed men. Like frightened animals, they could not even be presented with overtures for peace. Tyler had therefore instructed the colonel in command, as soon as he had deemed it expedient, "to declare that hostilities against the Indians have ceased."

Winning a war usually means achieving one's avowed objectives. In this case the Jackson administration had undertaken to move the Seminoles to an area west of the Mississippi, and after several years of fighting, the government had to concede that a complete removal, if possible, was not worth the cost. Thus the United States, with all its might, lacked the capacity or the will to move all of the Seminoles and left behind some several hundred of them. Today there are about 1,200 Seminoles in Florida, the descendants of those who fled to impenetrable swampy areas.

Although most of these Seminole Indians had been moved to Oklahoma, where about three thousand of their descendants live today, a minority were not. In this sense they won the war. During the frustrating conflict in Vietnam in the 1970s, the suggestion was made that the United States, after winning most of the pitched battles, declare that it had won the war and come home. This is essentially what was done with the Seminole remnant in 1842.

Tyler was a realist in dealing with the Indians. He openly deplored the enormous amount of cheating and grafting by the whites, much at government expense, that had accompanied the removal of "the children of the forest." Yet he favored giving protection and assistance to white settlers moving onto the Florida frontier. He was a stubborn man but not one to continue butting his head indefinitely against a stone wall.

The Texas Derelict

The annexation of Texas as the twenty-eighth state in the Union was achieved in 1845 under the aggressive leadership of President Tyler, the converted Whig now without a party. In achieving this goal Tyler used harsh, even truculent, language toward Mexico, which in turn had been threatening war on the United States. The eleventh-hour annexation of Texas led inexorably to war with Mexico in 1846 under President Polk and left much of the responsibility for the clash of arms at Tyler's door.

We recall that lone-star Texas had won her independence of Mexico in 1836 but that President Jackson, despite his personal sympathies for the Texans, shunned annexation and even deferred recognition until the next to his last day in office. Jackson was no coward on the military battlefield, but in the political arena he feared stirring up the passions of the antislavery agitators and ruining his plans for passing the presidency on to his hand-picked Martin Van Buren. The black blot of slavery had been transplanted to Texas from the Southern part of the United States.

As Tyler told Congress in a special message on December 18, 1844, he was not recommending well-deserved reprisals against Mexico to vindicate the "national honor," for he had a "sincere desire to preserve the general peace." But he did favor annexation by joint resolution. "By adopting that measure the United States will be in the exercise of an undoubted right; and if Mexico, not regarding their forbearance, shall aggravate the injustice of her conduct by a declaration of war against them, upon her head will rest all the responsibility."

As President Tyler's stormy administration neared its end, he had few qualms about antagonizing the antislavery zealots. He had deserted the Democratic party to join the Whig party, which by now had formally washed its hands of him. He was going nowhere except into retirement at his restful Virginia estate. "His Accidency" was now completely free to do what he thought was best in the national interest, without regard to possible election "in his own right."

In successive messages to Congress, Tyler vigorously marshaled the arguments for annexing Texas. Reaching far back, he claimed that this vast area had actually (though dubiously) been included in the Louisiana Purchase of 1803 and had been unwisely abandoned by (the Yankee) Secretary Adams in the so-called Florida treaty with Spain in 1819. Texas, so Tyler claimed, was obviously desirable in her own right. Her agriculture and commerce would add immeasurably to the wealth and prosperity of the United States. What nation in its right mind would reject so fair and fruitful a windfall?

Texas, so Tyler further asserted, was perfectly free to dispose of herself as she saw fit. She had been independent for eight long years and was growing stronger by the day. Unwilling to face facts, Mexico still claimed Texas and repeatedly asserted that she was going to reconquer her wayward territory. But she had made only two feeble attempts to invade the area, or rather raid it, and that was two years earlier, in 1842.

Not only was Texas independent, Tyler believed, but she had been formally recognized as such by Britain and France. Mexico should face realities and not take offense at the acquisitive interest of the United States, much less declare, as President Santa Anna had done on August 23, 1843, that the annexation of Texas by the Yankees would be equivalent to a declaration of war. Surely a wait of eight or nine years from the beginning of the courtship to the consummation of the marriage would be a decent wait.

President Tyler, we should particularly note, regarded the annexation of Texas as a giant step toward peace, not war, and here he employed strong arguments. He asserted that a weak Texas, more or less a derelict adrift on the international sea, was a menace to navigating the American ship of state (as Spanish Florida had been). Britain and France in particular were supporting Texan independence with considerable vigilance and vigor. British abolitionists regarded this weak new country as a fertile field for their endeavors, much to the alarm of the slaveholding Southern states. British and French diplomatists also perceived in an independent Texas a valuable source of a needed cotton, as well as a commercial bonanza for a foreign manufactured goods that would be free of the onerous protective tariffs of the United States.

Even more alarming to President Tyler was the evident determination of Britain and France to create a satellite state that would enable them to play the hoary diplomatic and military game of divide and conquer in the New World. An independent Texas could serve as a strong barrier to the southward expansion of the grasping Yankees. Perhaps Texas could expand in its own right (as it actually tried to do in the Santa Fe expedition of 1841), and one day might fight the insolent Yankees over California, much as the South was to fight the North in the upcoming Civil War. In short, Texas might well become a makeweight in a European-controlled balance of power, and America might be Balkanized by fragmented and quarreling American states, with consequent militarization and arms races.

There can be little doubt that President Tyler was gravely concerned over British and French machinations in Texas, and that he sincerely believed that bringing the Lone Star Republic into the American fold would promote international peace, even though it probably would lead to domestic discord over slavery.

The ticklish issue of taking Texas into the fold, plus wresting all of Oregon from the British, was tossed into the noisy arena of the presidential campaign of 1844. The expansionist Democratic candidate, James K. Polk, narrowly triumphed over the less expansionist candidate, the perennial Henry Clay.

President Tyler, now a lame duck, informed Congress that a mandate had been given by the voters in this recent close election to take Texas forthwith. Actually, there were so many confusing issues that no clear mandate could possibly have been given on any one of them. In June 1844, before the recent Polk-Clay election, a treaty to annex Texas had been defeated by a wide margin in the Senate. Shortly after the balloting, Tyler so despaired of success in the Senate that he formally recommended to Congress annexation by joint resolution. It would require only a simple majority in both houses of Congress, rather than the requisite two-thirds majority in the Senate alone. Such a measure was triumphantly passed three days before Tyler left the White House for good.

It is reasonable to conclude that Tyler, whatever his shortcomings, was not playing politics when he opted for annexing Texas by a joint resolution of Congress. A renegade Democrat who had been read out of his Whig party, "Traitor Tyler" had no place to go except home to Virginia. Texas could not help him materially as far as national eminence was concerned, especially among the antislaveryites. As a dedicated states righter, Tyler was an inflexible man of principle. In 1836, while a member of the Senate, he had resigned, although he did not have to, rather than follow instructions voted by the legislature of his state. He assuredly was not one to put politics above principle. So little was he concerned about his political image, and so devoted was he to states' rights, that he took a conspicuous part in the secession movement of 1860–1861, and in 1861 was elected to the first Confederate Congress. Tyler seems to have taken Texas, which brought on a war with Mexico, largely to head off future crises manipulated by designing European powers. But basically he probably wanted it primarily to aggrandize the United States.

Eastward Entanglements

Elsewhere, in the area of peaceful commercial intercourse, the Tyler administration planted seeds in Hawaii and China that were to bear highly significant fruit in later years.

Earlier in the nineteenth century, American whalers and other ships had found the Hawaiian islands useful as both a base and a rendezvous. By 1842 five-sixths of all ships calling at these idyllic islands flew the Stars and Stripes. In that year Secretary Webster and President Tyler declared that although the United States had no intention of annexing the islands, it could not view with indifference their acquisition by any other foreign power. The next year the British and French bound themselves not to acquire Hawaii, but the United States, true to its policy of nonentanglements, declined to join these two powers in any such joint agreement. The door was thus left wide open for the American annexation that finally came in 1898, during the Spanish–American war.

The Tyler administration also opened important peaceful intercourse through the silken curtain of China. Pursuant to a recommendation by the President, Congress voted funds for a special mission that would be concerned primarily with improved commercial relations. The famed Cushing mission of four warships, laden with specimens of Western wonders and other gifts, arrived in China in 1844. This impressive demonstration—warships for peace—resulted in the epochal Treaty of

Wanghia, by which concessions recently granted to other powers were put on a formal basis with the United States.

In Africa the United States likewise made its presence felt. Pursuant to its anti-slave-trade commitment under the Webster-Ashburton Treaty of 1842, the United States Navy engaged in extensive operations off the slave-center coast of Africa in November and December 1843. Four American vessels not only demonstrated but landed various armed parties, one of them consisting of some two hundred Marines and sailors. The objective was to discourage piracy and slave trade, particularly along the Ivory Coast, and to punish attacks by natives on American seamen and shipping.

On balance, the maverick President Tyler deserves commendation as an apostle of peace and a preventer of war. The sweeping Webster-Ashburton negotiations alone were an achievement, the like of which any administration could be proud to claim for itself.

CHAPTER 11

JAMES KNOX POLK: SERVANT OF MANIFEST DESTINY

The (Mexican) war will continue to be prosecuted with vigor as the best means of securing peace.

President Polk, Second
Annual Message,
December 8, 1846

Polk the Pugnacious

President Polk, by using war or threats of war, brought under the Stars and Stripes more territory than anyone else in the nation's history, not even excluding Thomas Jefferson with his magnificent Louisiana Purchase. By preaching peace while waging war, Polk raised grave doubts as to his candor—or what a later generation would call "credibility." Some critics have called him "Polk the Mendacious," a delicate way of saying "Polk the

Liar." But whatever the means, Polk got results; what he went for, observers remarked, "he fetched."

Polk was not a commanding figure of a man, and in this respect the office brought him the distinction that his person did not. Five feet, eight inches tall, he was of slight build and wore clothes that seemed too large for his frame. He took life seriously, as one would judge from his cold gray eyes and his firmly set mouth, as though holding onto something with a bulldog grip. He was grimly determined, purposeful, even bellicose, and by fair means or foul carried through a sweeping political, military, and economic program with spectacular success but with some tragic consequences.

Like Jackson, Polk was born in one of the Carolinas, and like Jackson he moved to Tennessee, where he became a protégé of "Old Hickory." Rather unconvincingly, he was accorded the nicknames "Young Hickory" and "Little Hickory." Unlike Jackson, he was a college graduate, in his case from the University of North Carolina, and he became a well-trained lawyer who, unlike Jackson, could write with exceptional skill and clarity. Also unlike "The Hero of New Orleans," he had no war record whatever.

Polk entered politics and became an effective campaigner, as evidenced by the sobriquet "Napoleon of the Stump." He advanced by gradations from two years in the Tennessee House of Representatives, fourteen years in the national House of Representatives (including four years as Speaker of the House), and two years as Governor of Tennessee. In 1841 and 1843 he was twice defeated for reelection and was widely regarded by many voters as a dead duck. He evidently lacked presidential charisma.

When Polk's fellow Democrats met in their Baltimore convention in 1844, Polk was not even considered as a presidential nominee. His name was not mentioned on the first seven ballots, during which a deadlock developed between the two leading candidates. On the next two ballots the convention unaccountably stampeded to Polk, the first really "dark horse" candidate of a major American political party. Polk was undeniably a "dark horse," yet this designation does not mean that he was an unknown horse. As Congressman and Speaker of the House of Representatives, he knew the Washington scene intimately. The position of Speaker of the House, which he had held for four years, carried with it even more prestige and power than it does now. He was the first and last Speaker ever to reach the White House.

As President, Polk evidently worked himself into an early grave. With prematurely white hair worn long, he was at forty-nine the youngest man then to have been elected President. So determined was he to achieve his announced objectives that he was reluctant to delegate responsibility. He may have become a "workaholic" as a result of his determination to prove to doubters that he deserved to be regarded as a front runner rather than a late-entry dark horse, with dubious credentials as a statesman. He risked war with Great Britain over Oregon and invited war with Mexico to uphold the honor and interests of the United States. And in both cases he attained his goals.

The Oregon Fever

The campaign that swept Polk into the White House fully reflected the expansionist fever of the 1840s known as Manifest Destiny. Included in the last paragraph of the Democratic platform was a passage that screamed defiance at both Great Britain and Mexico. It declared that America's "title to the whole of the Territory of Oregon is clear and unquestionable" and that "the re-occupation of Oregon and the re-annexation of Texas" as soon as "practicable" were urgently recommended.

The extravagant Democratic pronouncement asserted specifically that the United States was claiming Oregon all the way to the line of 54°40′, the southern tip of the present Alaska panhandle. As for "re-occupation" of the area, the reference was to America's temporary loss of Oregon to British fur traders and naval power during the War of 1812. As for "re-annexation," the implication was that the United States had enjoyed a valid claim to all of Texas to the Rio Grande, but that Secretary Adams unwisely bartered it away in 1819 in order to engineer a swap with Spain for Florida. The southern wing of the Democratic party, with slaveholders dominant, favored reannexing Texas, while the Northern wing clamored for Oregon as a potential haven for free-soil settlers.

In the heated race for the White House, Polk, the Tennessee slaveholder, defeated glamorous Henry Clay, the Whig candidate, by the narrowest margins. In view of the closeness of the contest and other factors, Polk's Democratic party did not receive a mandate to do much of anything. Yet President Tyler himself interpreted his election as a mandate to take Texas. As a result, the Lone Star Republic was formally annexed by a joint resolution of Congress, which President Tyler had recommended as he was about to pass the torch on to President Polk. As events turned out, Polk inherited both Texas and a war with Mexico.

Polk's inaugural address, March 4, 1845, was bellicose in tone, probably more so than any previous or succeeding one. Normally, such presentations are deadened by platitudes, with specifics reserved for individual messages to Congress. But Polk promptly got down to cases, and then pulled no punches. He declared that it was his duty "to assert and maintain by all constitutional means the right of the United States" to its territory "beyond the Rocky Mountains." America's title to the country of the Oregon was "clear and unquestionable," and settlers were even then "preparing to perfect that title by occupying it with their wives and children."

It is true that Polk's Democratic platform did assert that "our title to the whole of the Territory of Oregon is clear and unquestionable." But this was a purely partisan pronouncement designed to win the election for the Democrats; such rhetoric had no place in an inaugural address, even if a statement of fact, as it was not. Polk knew perfectly well that Oregon was being jointly occupied by the Americans and British under the ten-year agreement set forth in the treaty of 1818. This pact had been renewed in 1827, with the proviso that either party could give a year's notice of termination. The very existence of joint occupation was a confession by the Americans and the British alike that neither had a "clear and unquestionable" title to all of the Oregon country up to 54°40′. In his inaugural address Polk was being recklessly irresponsible.

The British were outraged by Polk's bellicosity, and naval preparations were ominously increased. Foreign Secretary Aberdeen declared in the House of Lords that Britain possessed rights that "were clear and unquestionable," and that they would be maintained. The London *Times* proclaimed that Oregon would never be "wrested from the British Crown" except "by WAR." In the United States, Democratic journals tended to support Polk's extreme claim, but the critical editor of one organ declared that war over Oregon would be one of "the most reckless and insane exhibitions that the civilized world has ever witnessed."

Polk puts his head in the mouth of the British lion. London Punch, *1846.*

At the outset of his term Polk did not take such a belligerent stance on Oregon as his inaugural address portended. Evidently he felt committed to some extent by the previous split-the-difference offers of his predecessors. In July 1845 Secretary of State Buchanan was authorized to inform the British Minister in Washington that the United States was prepared to divide the Oregon country by the forty-ninth parallel—the present Canadian-United States boundary line. Her Majesty's envoy committed a major diplomatic blunder when he flatly rejected the American offer without first consulting London.

Polk was apparently angered by this blunt refusal, all the more so because he perceived that his tactical position was strong. He had backed down from his extreme campaign pledges so far as to propose the familiar forty-ninth parallel, but the offer had been thrown back into his face. He now felt justified in withdrawing his latest offer and reasserting the claim of the United States to the extreme line of 54°40′. As he privately insisted, "if we do have war it will not be our fault."

This rejection of Polk's overture by the British Minister in Washington was promptly disavowed by London, and the chastened envoy hastened to make two new offers of arbitration during the following weeks. But Polk, his back up, insisted that Britain's turn had come to make some substantial concession. In his diary he recorded a conversation with a timid Congressman. "I remarked to him," wrote Polk, "that the only way to treat John Bull was to look him straight in the eye." Polk regarded "a bold and firm course on our part the pacific one." If Congress faltered or hesitated, "John Bull would immediately become arrogant and more grasping in his demands."

In the public eye Polk showed that he was as uncompromising as he was in private, for he laid down the law in his annual message to Congress of December 1845. After reviewing the history of the Oregon dispute, he belligerently declared that the United States was now prepared to reassert its claim to the whole Oregon area. As a preliminary step, he recommended serving notice on Great Britain that the one-year notice of terminating joint occupation be given. He could have taken this step himself, as other Presidents have done, but he evidently wanted to shunt the onus onto Congress. His awareness of the joint-occupation treaty seems to be proof of his awareness that America's title to all of the Oregon country was not "clear and unquestionable."

Polk went on to tell Congress that after due notice of termination had been given, "we shall have reached a period when the national rights in Oregon must either be abandoned or firmly maintained." That they cannot be "abandoned without sacrifice of both national honor and interest is too clear to admit of doubt." This was arrant nonsense. The British were not claiming any of the Oregon country south of the Columbia River all the way to the northern border of California at forty-two degrees. The Yankees might be shouting "Fifty-four forty or fight," but the British were not responding with "Forty-two or to Hell with You."

At this point in his annual message to Congress of December 1845, Polk moved on to a reaffirmation of President Monroe's virtually forgotten Monroe Doctrine. Polk asserted unequivocally and defiantly, as Monroe had done, that "no future European colony or dominion shall with our consent be planted or established on any part of the North American continent." Polk did not refer specifically to Oregon, but in this context he could have been saying that the British were not free to establish their dominion over any of the Oregon country south of 54°40′. The evidence is strong that Polk also had in mind warning the British to keep their grasping hands off California, for the activity of their agents in that sun-blessed land threatened to undercut Polk's own expansionist plans.

The President's surprising invocation of the Monroe Doctrine did not evoke nearly so much excitement as his extravagant claims to all of the Oregon country. In fact the Monroe Doctrine did not scare the British, for they had accepted and supported it in 1823. But we should note that the tough-talking Polk actively resurrected the moribund doctrine of the aggressive Monroe. From then on it became an American shibboleth, which thousands of Americans were prepared to die for without knowing precisely what it meant.

Some two years later, on April 29, 1848, Polk reaffirmed to Congress his earlier endorsement of the Monroe Doctrine. He served blunt notice on Britain and France that the Mexican peninsula of Yucatan, the scene of grave local disorders, could in "no event" be "permitted" to become "a colony of any European power."

The Partitioning of Oregon

Polk's audacious annual message to Congress aroused many of his fellow Democrats to a fighting pitch, although the opposition Whigs were generally more restrained. The windy debate in Congress over ending joint occupation dragged on throughout four months. In England preparations for war continued unabated, as Polk well knew, and many patriotic Britons, including government leaders, were in a mood to fight the "insolent" Yankees again.

Fortunately for peace, sobering forces were at work in England. A political overturn had brought to power a new ministry that was disposed to be conciliatory. Under the best of circumstances Oregon would be difficult to defend against the thousands of American pioneers pouring in over the Oregon trail. War with America would also bring commercial dislocations, and the "Little Englanders" were concluding that Britain already had imperial headaches enough. The crux of the dispute was the triangle in the present State of Washington formed by the forty-ninth parallel on the north and the Columbia River, which the Hudson's Bay Company had wanted for its fur trade. Yet recently the company, having "furred out" this area, had moved north from the Columbia River to Vancouver Island, in present Canada. Why fight for an unpopular company that had voluntarily abandoned an outpost that was supposed to be worth fighting for?

At this auspicious time word came to London from Washington that the United States had recently given courteous notice of the termination of joint occupation. The British government chose to regard this gesture as a reopening of negotiations by Polk, and hence revived his compromise offer of the forty-ninth parallel. The belligerently patriotic President was now "certain" that it ought to be rejected, for the proposal in its final form guaranteed to British subjects (including the Hudson's Bay Company) the same rights as Americans to navigate the Columbia River. But a majority of Polk's Cabinet believed that the pact should be submitted to the Senate for *previous* advice—a most unusual procedure not required by the Constitution. If the Senate advised ratification, the opprobrium for retreating from 54° 40′ would, as partisans pointed out, fall on the Democratic-Whig Senate. Indicative of Polk's militancy is the fact that he apparently consented to this buck-passing stratagem for peace with considerable reluctance.

After only two days of debate the Senate advised acceptance of the Oregon compromise treaty. On June 15, 1846, the new pact was signed without a single alteration and approved by the Senate three days later. The pro-Texas people had already "re-annexed" Texas and were satisfied with the Oregon treaty, but in the Senate fourteen "fifty-four forties" voted vainly with the opposition. Most of these legislators hailed from the expansionist North and Northwest, where many citizens suspected that Polk was a braggart who had sounded his horn for 54° 40′ and then had beaten a cowardly retreat back to the forty-ninth parallel.

A fairer assessment would be that Polk was a compulsive saber-rattler without much of a saber to rattle. More than that, he was a desperate gambler who chould have lost his breathtaking gains in Oregon, California, and Mexico by forcing a war at the same time with the naval might of Great Britain. The victorious conquest of Mexico by way of Vera Cruz and Mexico City could never have been launched in the teeth of the British navy. The same could probably be said of the conquest of the Oregon country north of the Columbia River.

The Mexican War actually began on April 25, 1845, when Mexican troops attacked and bloodied a detachment of General

Taylor's army in southeastern Texas. Congress formally declared war on May 13, 1845. On June 3, with the United States more than a month deep in war with Mexico, the final compromise offer on Oregon arrived from London—basically Polk's initial proposal, which he was now reluctant to accept. The British had dispatched this final offer only ten days before news reached England by ship of the outbreak of hostilities between the United States and Mexico. If this headline news had come two weeks sooner, would the British officials have taken advantage of the Mexican War to yield to their own jingos and not sent their compromise offer? Would Britain have gone to war with the United States, thus denying Polk both Oregon and California? We can only speculate on the outcome. With the stakes so high, we can begin to wonder about Polk's sanity as well as his pugnacity.

The Texas Dispute

While Oregon was being "reoccupied" under the treaty with Great Britain of June 15, 1846, the Lone Star Republic of Texas was being "reannexed" as a state on terms of equality with her sister states on December 29, 1845.

The backlash from Mexico was predictable. The Mexican Minister in Washington lodged a stern protest and demanded his passports on March 6, 1845. Similarly, the United States Minister in Mexico City was notified three weeks later that diplomatic relations between the two countries were severed. These, of course, were the usual preliminaries in that day to a declaration of war. In mid-June 1845, the American Secretary of State assured Texas of American protection if the Texans would consent to the proposed terms of annexation, as the people of this thinly populated republic soon did. Thus, by annexing Texas, the United States under Polk annexed a war. The Mexicans had never conquered Texas, although claiming that they would *mañana*; technically they were still at war with the Texans, although making no progress whatever in subduing their rebels. Yet Mexican officials and nonofficials openly threatened that they would fight the United States if Texas were brought into the American fold.

Polk naturally felt an obligation, or so he told Congress, to extend protection to the annexed Texans. He therefore issued orders on June 15, 1845, to General Zachary Taylor to move into

Texas with a small army, which stationed itself at Corpus Christi, Texas, just south of the mouth of the Nueces River. This muddy stream had long been regarded as the southwestern border of Texas, although the large-minded Texans claimed all the land to the Rio Grande, about 150 miles beyond.

An enlarged Texas sprawling south of the Nueces River had never been a part of Spanish or Mexican Texas, and the claim to this larger area by the Texans was not as ironclad as they could have wished. The captured Santa Anna, after his defeat by the Texans at San Jacinto in 1836, had signed two treaties conceding the extravagant Texan claim, as Polk pointed out in a message to Congress. But as an experienced lawyer he could have added, but did not, that agreements signed under duress do not have a legal leg to stand on. Yet Polk argued that he had an obligation not only to defend an annexed Texas but also to defend her in her boundary claims, extravagant though they might be.

To his credit, Polk was determined to make one last-chance effort to reopen diplomatic negotiations with Mexico before sending General Taylor's army from the Nueces River southward to the Rio Grande, where these troops could easily provoke an armed clash. The President negotiated through the American consul remaining in Mexico City, and thus received word from the Mexican Foreign Minister that the Mexicans would receive a *commissioner* from the United States to discuss only the status of the boundary. To the mortification of the Mexican government Polk dispatched a full-fledged Minister Plenipotentiary, not a mere commissioner, in the person of John Slidell, from slave-holding Louisiana. The new envoy was empowered to discuss, not solely the Texas boundary, as stipulated, but also the unpaid claims against Mexico and the acquisition of California by purchase.

As for the disputed boundary, Polk stoutly upheld the claim of Texas to the Rio Grande as far west as El Paso, that is, south of present New Mexico. But he did concede that the title of Texas to the New Mexico area was open to negotiation. For their part, the Mexicans were obviously unable to pay the defaulted damage claim to the United States—more than $2,000,000—so Slidell was authorized to assume the payment of the claims against Mexico if the Mexicans would agree to the Rio Grande as the western boundary of Texas. Slidell was further instructed to propose an extra $5 million for all of New Mexico. He was also to offer $25 million, as well as to assume the defaulted claims, for Upper California and the connecting terrain.

News of Slidell's secret mission quickly leaked out in Mexico City and caused an angry outcry. The government refused to receive the envoy lest it be overthrown (it was anyhow), for it had agreed to receive only a lowly commissioner to discuss the problem of the Texas boundary. Polk then instructed Slidell to approach the new government anyhow, but it would have none of him. He wrote to the President that "nothing is to be done with these people until they shall have been chastised."

So on January 13, 1846, the day after learning of Slidell's final rejection, Polk ordered General Taylor to move southward the 150 miles from the Nueces River to the Rio Grande, where he established himself provocatively with about three thousand troops. He hastily built a fort, Fort Brown, on the left bank of the Rio Grande, with his guns commanding the Mexican town of Matamoros on the other side of the river. He also blocked the mouth of the Rio Grande a few miles below at Port Isabel, his base for water-borne supplies. There he was able to deny to the Mexican armed forces such control of the river as was necessary to bring up their needed provisions. The Mexicans, defenseless and facing starvation, regarded these activities, including the invasion, as acts of war. Indeed they were, from the Mexican point of view.

During the many weeks that General Taylor had been stationed near the mouth of the Nueces River, the Mexican armed forces had not attacked him. They regarded all of Texas, stretching to the boundary of the State of Louisiana, as still theirs, and they resented the invasion of their territory by a foreign army. Even so, they might have tolerated Taylor's presence indefinitely if Polk had not pushed the dispute to a showdown, as he did on January 13, 1846, the day he issued orders to Taylor to proceed to the Rio Grande.

Did President Polk expect war? As one reads through his intimate diary entries for these anxious weeks one finds ample evidence that Polk, with an ear cocked to the border, expected the Mexicans to attack Taylor's army. More than that, he apparently hoped that such an incident would occur, and he was evidently keenly disappointed that it had not. How else was he to acquire California and force a recognition of Texas with maximum boundaries if the Mexicans would not even negotiate? If the prospective seller has something valuable that he will not sell or even talk about selling, the buyer will have to back off or grab what he covets, thus precipitating war.

Giving up was not in Polk's character, and in addition some other nation might acquire California in defiance of the Monroe Doctrine. Actually, British agents were notoriously active in Upper California, although the London government was not seriously interested. Yet Polk could judge only from outward appearances, and they were scary.

His patience exhausted, Polk met his Cabinet on May 9, 1846, the day after the spurned John Slidell returned from his fruitless trip to Mexico City. The President stated that he had ample reasons for sending a war message to Congress, including the Slidell rejection, the unpaid claims, the refusal to sell California, and the unwillingness of Mexico to make other territorial adjustments. Yet the Mexican government had never agreed to receive a full-fledged Minister. Moreover, defaulting on claims was something that the Americans had done to the British after the War of Independence and that the Spanish and French had done to the United States before 1846, all without a declaration of war on either side.

We recall that in the Louisiana Purchase of 1803 the United States agreed to pay France $15 million for Louisiana, $3,750,000 of which was to go to American citizens for French spoliations of American commerce. Partly because some of these claims were padded, as usually is the case, not all of the claimants received payment in full. On August 8, 1846, while deep in the Mexican War, President Polk, whose heart bled for the American claimants against Mexico, vetoed a bill for discharging in full the constitutional obligation of the United States to its own citizens growing out of the ancient French claims. Ironically, he justified his veto in part with the same argument that the Mexicans had used for default: The United States treasury was in the red owing to war preparations. Was "Polk the Mendacious" also "Polk the Hypocritical"?

Provoking War with Mexico

After Polk had proposed sending a war message to Congress at his crucial Cabinet meeting of May 9, 1846, two key members demurred. Secretary of the Navy Bancroft stated that if the Mexicans should commit an act of armed aggression, he would favor a declaration of war. Secretary of State Buchanan (the future President) was willing to vote for hostilities, but his conscience would rest easier if Mexican troops first attacked the Americans. Still determined to fight, Polk ended this remarkable meeting by offering to prepare a war message anyhow and submit it for later discussion.

That very evening there occurred one of the strangest coincidences in history. Dispatches arrived from General Taylor reporting that Mexican forces had crossed the Rio Grande on April 25, 1846, attacking his men and killing or wounding sixteen of them. This was the Pearl Harbor that Polk, the devout Presbyterian, had been hoping for and possibly praying for. The misgivings of his advisors evaporated, and the country could rally around the flag with high enthusiasm.

Polk presented his war message to Congress on May 11, 1846, and in it he gave further color to his reputation as "Polk the Mendacious." He outlined in grim detail the accumulated grievances against Mexico that had exhausted "the cup of forbearance." Now the Mexicans had crossed "the boundary of the United States" and "shed American blood upon the American soil." Polk went on to proclaim that "war exists, and notwithstanding all our efforts to avoid it, exists by the act of Mexico itself."

Congress responded to Polk's appeal for a war declaration with patriotic enthusiasm, Democrats and Whigs alike. The vote was 40 to 2 in the Senate, 174 to 14 in the House, thanks in large measure to clever Democratic stampeding. But the Whigs soon found their voices, particularly when they became fully aware that potential slave territory would bring in more "slave pens." About a year and a half later, the "Spotty" Abraham Lincoln, a freshman Whig Congressman from Illinois, made himself both conspicuous and obnoxious with his famous but futile "spot resolutions." They demanded to know at what spot on "American soil" American blood had been actually shed.

Polk's truthfulness was certainly open to question. He could have said that American blood had been shed on disputed soil that the Mexicans with good reason claimed as their own. He could have said that he had first tried the slow processes of diplomacy and then had deliberately provoked a border clash. In subsequent messages to Congress relating to the war he tiresomely repeated the formula that Mexico had provoked hostilities. One has the impression that a guilty Presbyterian conscience was causing him to protest too much and too often. He even said on one occasion that this war "has not been waged with a view to conquest," although we now know that he had California high on his "must list." In fact, he was careful not to mention California at all in these earlier messages to Congress, possibly in an effort to conceal his real aims.

Did Polk really want war? Probably not, but he did want California, and Mexico would not sell this favored land to the hated Yankees at any price. Because war was the only viable alternative, Polk cleverly arranged to goad Mexico into appearing as the aggressor. After the shooting started, he tried to buy the kind of peace that he wanted by a rather discreditable arrangement. Word came to Polk that Santa Anna, the fallen dictator then exiled in Cuba, wanted to return to power in Mexico, where he would sell to the Yankees the territory they wanted. At Polk's direction, orders were issued to the American blockading fleet to let Santa Anna slip through. This was done, but the restored ruler double-crossed the double-dealing Polk by arousing his people against the Yankee invader. A purchased peace seemed as far away as ever.

The Mexican War and After

Polk's next attempt at strategy was to "conquer a peace," that is, invade Mexican territory, hold it, and then pay the Mexicans what the United States was prepared to offer. The subsequent conquest of New Mexico and California was absurdly easy. Indeed, the American settlers in California anticipated the intervention of United States naval forces, earlier sent by Polk, by setting up the short-lived Bear Flag Republic. In doing so, they demonstrated that in time the Californians probably would have joined the Union by the Texas route, though with fewer complications. This strong probability suggests that Polk should have been more patient, although the strategic value of the area and the presence of British agents imposed a strain on his nerves.

The principal campaign of the Mexican War, with essential naval support, was the conquest in 1847 of Mexico City, by way of the mountainous route up from Vera Cruz on the coast. This was a brilliant achievement by General Winfield Scott in the teeth of strong Mexican resistance and numerous natural and man-made obstacles. President Polk, still desirous of purchasing peace, took the extraordinary step of sending along with General Scott the Chief Clerk of the State Department, Nicholas Trist—a classic case of fighting with the olive branch in one hand and the sword in the other.

Dissatisfied with the bungling negotiations of Nicholas Trist, Polk summarily recalled him. The envoy's very presence had created the impression among Mexican defenders that the United States was desperately anxious for peace. But Trist suddenly glimpsed an opportunity to negotiate a treaty while there was a government still in power willing to incur the opprobrium of taking such a craven step. Because communications with Washington were slow and the existing opportunity might not arise again, Trist decided to disregard his recall and negotiate terms that substantially followed his original instructions.

Polk was furious, and his first impulse was to repudiate the insolence of this "impudent and unqualified scoundrel." But the President perceived that Trist had got essentially what he had been sent for, and that anarchy might leave Mexico with no government at all to conclude a treaty. Moreover, an all-of-Mexico movement was developing, largely in response to the spirit of Manifest Destiny, with all that complete annexation implied in subject peoples and endless guerrilla warfare. So Polk reluctantly submitted the treaty of Guadalupe Hidalgo to the Senate, which approved it by a comfortable margin of 38 to 14 on March 10, 1848.

Trist's treaty ceded New Mexico (including present Arizona) and California to the United States. Additionally, the pact finally confirmed America's title to Texas as far as the Rio Grande, thus ending the dispute over the boundary, at least as far as Mexico was concerned. The total areas ceded, including Texas, amounted to roughly one-half of Mexico. For its part, the United States agreed to pay $15 million and to assume the long-deferred claims of its own citizens in the amount of $3,250,000.

The payment of so large a sum of money by the victor was surprising and certainly unconventional. Polk regarded the territory involved as an indemnity exacted from the Mexicans for having provoked the war. If so, why should the victor pay an indemnity, rather than the vanquished? Having conquered the territory at heavy expense, why should Polk pay out money for a "purchased peace?" Was not the the conquered land recompense enough, especially after gold was discovered in California in

1848, nine days before the signing of the treaty but without the knowledge of the negotiators. Some critics have argued that Polk was bothered by a guilty conscience, which may or may not be true. Others have said that the monetary concessions were characteristic of "American generosity and fair play."

As for assuming the $3,250,000 for American claimants, it is evident that this was done so that these injured parties would secure long-deferred recompense while they were still living. To judge from Polk's lurid and lengthy recitations to Congress of the wrongs inflicted on these people, he felt deeply on this subject. If the bankrupt Mexican government could not pay its claims to foreigners before the costly Mexican War, it was not likely to do so at any time in the predictable future.

"Dark Horse" James Knox Polk, though something of a bluffer and buck-passer, must take high rank as one of the most warlike of the American Presidents, if not the most warlike. He deliberately provoked hostilities with Mexico that lasted more than half of his four years in office. He gambled recklessly and dangerously, with both Mexico and Britain, but he was lucky enough to win and then rake in enormous territorial chips. Before his administration began, the United States was regarded as just another second-rate Atlantic power. When Polk left the White House in 1849, the expanding republic was a Pacific power as well. It boasted more than 1,300 miles of ocean frontage facing the Orient and ranging from the Canadian border to Mexico.

Europe, the home of the self-anointed world powers, was deeply impressed. Foreign military experts had placed little confidence in the ability of the American clodhoppers and shopkeepers to invade successfully an immense and rugged land, especially after the glaring ineptitudes and failures of the War of 1812 in Canada. Anyone wanting to know when the United States became a world power, rather than just another minor-league power in the world, could well take another hard look at the United States as it existed when Polk left the White House.

As Polk declared in his final and self-congratulatory annual message to Congress, the war with Mexico had "undeceived" the skeptical European powers. He went on to boast that the recent territorial gains (including Oregon) had given the United States "nearly as great an extent of territory as the whole of Europe, Russia only excepted." As the current phrase went, America had become "some pumpkins."

In this fourth and final annual message of December 1848, Polk did not boast of his recent backfiring attempt to buy Cuba. As the willing servant of the South, of slavocracy, and of Manifest Destiny, he had authorized the United States Minister in Madrid (June 1848) to offer as much as $100 million for this island gem, the Pearl of the Antilles. News of this secretive approach leaked out, causing a public uproar and evoking from the Spanish Ministry a declaration that Spain would rather see the island "sunk in the ocean" than transferred to any other power. Further designs on Cuba were to come later under Polk's successors.

As for the Mexican War, aside from the cost in lives and money, it left at least two ugly scars. Latin American distrust of the Colossus of the North deepened, and the era of the Bad Neighbor policy was well on its way. The Mexicans, in particular, have never forgotten or forgiven the Yankees for having torn away about half of their country. Included were such treasures as timber, minerals, and oil. Now that the Mexicans have discovered vast new reserves of petroleum in their own country, they are prepared to sell to the Yankees only what they choose—and at their price.

The second ugly scar was the black blemish of bondage, especially as it related to annexed Texas. Polk's fruits of victory rearoused the snarling dog of the slavery controversy. The monster did not cease yelping until drowned in the blood of some 600,000 American soldiers, North and South. The Civil War, followed in the next century by the successful invasion of millions of illegal Mexican immigrants, may properly be called Santa Anna's revenge.

CHAPTER 12

ZACHARY TAYLOR: THE HERO OF BUENA VISTA

It is to be hoped that no international question can now arise which a government confident in its own strength and resolved to protect its own rights may not settle by wise negotiation....

Zachary Taylor,
Inaugural Address,
March 4, 1849

The Rise of Zachary Taylor

President Taylor still merits the distinction of being the only military man to have spent his entire adult life in the army, for a total of forty years, before being elected to the White House. After brief service as a volunteer in 1806, he was commissioned a first lieutenant at about age twenty-two in 1808. He rose to the rank of general while serving with distinction in a series of conflicts, beginning with the War of 1812, the Black Hawk War, and the prolonged Seminole War. He commanded the small army on the

Rio Grande that, under orders, had provoked the attack by Mexican troops in 1846, thus becoming responsible for the shedding of "American blood on the American soil," in President Polk's words.

In subsequent weeks and months Taylor defeated the Mexicans at Palo Alto, at Resaca de la Palma (both on soil claimed by Texas), and at Matamoras. In September 1846 he captured the important city of Monterrey in northern Mexico, and in February 1847, though overextended, defeated Santa Anna at the critical battle of Buena Vista. Taylor's troops were outnumbered about four to one, and "Old Zack" narrowly repelled the persistent attacks by a Mexican army that was near exhaustion from forced marches.

News of the victory at Buena Vista electrified the American people, and one ecstatic citizen was heard to claim that Taylor, a Whig, would be chosen President in the next election by "spontaneous combustion." Slogans that helped his political fortunes were two sayings that he allegedly immortalized during the Battle of Buena Vista, "A little more grape (shot), Captain Bragg" (an artillerist), and "General Taylor never surrenders."

President Polk, a dedicated Democrat, was distressed by the rising acclaim for his two most conspicuous generals, both Whigs. They were "Old Rough and Ready" Taylor, an unconventional dresser, and "Old Fuss and Feathers" Scott, who wore resplendent uniforms. Polk certainly did not go overboard to promote the prospects of these two leading military men as presidential timber for the Whig presidential nomination in 1848. In fact, he detached a large body of troops from Taylor in northern Mexico to support Scott's seemingly suicidal invasion of Mexico City by way of Vera Cruz.

As many pundits expected, and as Polk feared, "Old Zack" Taylor was nominated in 1848 by the Whigs in Philadelphia on the fourth ballot, nosing out the glamorous but perennial Henry Clay and the rival General Scott. Strangely enough, the Whigs had increasingly opposed the Mexican War but chose as their standard bearer the number one hero of that war, at the expense of their long-time professional loser, Henry Clay. For them, it was better to win with a military hero, as they had done with General Harrison, than to lose with a gifted, experienced, and attractive statesman. As events turned out, General Taylor defeated his Democratic opponent, Lewis Cass, by a comfortable margin, with 56 percent of the popular vote. But ex-President

Martin Van Buren, candidate of the antislavery Free Soil party, drained away crucial strength from the Democratic candidate. These votes were probably enough to throw the election to General Taylor.

What manner of man was Taylor, and what qualifications did he have as a politician and a political leader? At the time of his inauguration he was sixty-four years of age, which is old as Presidents go. Five feet, eight inches tall and weighing about 170 pounds, he had a large head, a Roman nose, iron gray hair, hazel eyes, deeply lined cheeks, and a stocky frame set on unusually long legs. Born in Virginia, "The Mother of Presidents," he had never attended college but had received a slender education from a private tutor, who spoke well of him as a student.

General Taylor was well liked by his men, for he was not a strict disciplinarian, like General Scott. Taylor's sloppy attire (sometimes with an old straw hat), his tobacco chewing, and his colorful cursing brought to "Old Rough and Ready" a degree of affection not always found among hard-bitten soldiers. Born in slaveholding Virginia to a family of some prominence, he finally acquired a large plantation in Louisiana, where he owned scores of slaves. Not surprisingly, he believed that slavery should continue where established, but surprisingly he favored its exclusion from the territory recently wrested from Mexico.

Totally inexperienced in political life, Taylor lacked any real claim to being presidential timber. While in the army he evidently had not remained in one place long enough to qualify as a voter and did not cast his first vote until he was sixty-two years of age. When his name was initially mentioned as a candidate, he said, "The idea that I should become President seems to me too visionary to require a serious answer. It has never entered my head, nor is it likely to enter the head of any sane person." Doubt as to what party he would choose was finally resolved when he declared, "I am a Whig, but not an ultra Whig." Actually, he had favored the Whig party since the days of the Democrat Andrew Jackson, whom he did not admire.

A question arose at the outset as to the militancy that would be exhibited by this life-long military man. In his inaugural address he evidently went out of his way to quiet fears on this score. True, he declared that the problem of maintaining the army and navy in "the highest condition of efficiency" would "receive the special attention of the Executive," with of course the "liberality of Congress." But this was really no more than some of his

Democratic campaign cartoon of 1848, charging that Taylor's reputation rested on Mexican skulls. Courtesy of New York Historical Society, New York City.

predecessors had said at one time or another in their communications to Congress.

President Taylor then went on to declare in this inaugural address that the nation would heed the voice of George Washington "to abstain from entangling alliances with foreign nations." Taylor's policy would be to cultivate "peaceful and friendly relations with all powers." He hoped that any possible international dispute could be settled "by wise negotiation." Every nation holding to just principles should "exhaust every resort of honorable diplomacy before appealing to arms."

Designs on Cuba and Hungary

The Ever Faithful Island of Cuba was a problem left to President Taylor by Polk, who bunglingly had tried to buy the outpost from an outraged Spain. In 1849 a Venezuela-born Cuban revolutionist, Narciso López, was organizing a filibustering expedition near New Orleans to free Cuba and presumably annex it to the United States as a slave state. President Taylor was not a greedy expansionist like Polk, and he was fully aware of the dangers of adding more slave territory, especially Cuba, to the United States. The explosive problem of slavery or nonslavery in the territories recently wrested from Mexico, including California, was already vexatious enough.

Whatever his motivations, Taylor issued a ringing proclamation regarding Cuba on August 11, 1849. He declared that it was the "duty of this Government to observe the faith of treaties and to prevent any aggression by our citizens upon the territories of friendly nations." He therefore undertook to warn all American citizens who connected themselves with such an unlawful enterprise that they would "subject themselves to heavy penalties" and "forfeit their claim to the protection of their country." The proposed incursion into Cuba, contrary to the neutrality law of April 20, 1818, was in "the highest degree criminal" and would "endanger the peace and compromise the honor of the nation." Taylor therefore called upon "all good citizens" to do what they lawfully could to halt this enterprise and thus "uphold our sacred obligation to friendly powers."

As befitted a military man, this ringing proclamation was stern and blunt. Although circumstances were different, the episode reminds one of President Andrew Jackson's scorching proclamation against the nullifiers of South Carolina in 1832. But we should note that the severity thus revealed in both cases were directed primarily against fellow Americans in the hope of inducing them to abide by the laws of Congress, in Jackson's case the tariff law, in Taylor's case the neutrality legislation. The first Cuban expedition, like nullification, was nipped in the bud, but in neither case permanently.

The second filibustering expedition of López managed to elude President Taylor's watchdogs at New Orleans, and on May 19, 1848, landed in Cuba, about three weeks before Taylor's death. The oppressed inhabitants failed to rise and embrace their deliverer, so López fled to Florida, one jump ahead of the pursuing Spanish authorities. He obviously had violated the neutrality laws, but sympathetic American juries failed to find him guilty of any crime.

The years 1848 and 1849 experienced an epidemic of revolutions in Europe against monarchial tyranny. Americans applauded these outbursts as flattering imitations of their own War of Independence, won with French help. Of special appeal to the

United States was the gallant struggle of the Hungarians, led by Louis Kossuth. His forces were not crushed by Austria until Russian troops were sent in by the despotic Czar of Russia in August 1849.

In June 1849, before the massive Russian intervention and while hope for success in Hungary still flickered, President Taylor acted. He issued special instructions to A. Dudley Mann, an American diplomat then in Europe negotiating with the German states. Mann was authorized to go to Hungary and, if the liberation of the Hungarians seemed sufficiently assured, was to hold out to the revolutionary new government assurances of formal recognition, as the United States was wont to do.

Mann never reached Hungary, but the Austrian government lodged a strong protest in Washington against this objectionable interference in the internal affairs of a friendly nation. President Taylor resolutely defended his course in a special message to the Senate, March 28, 1850, shortly before his death. He asserted that no diplomatic agent had ever been accredited to the Washington government by the Hungarian rebels. Moreover, no official communication was ever received from the revolutionary government of Hungary. Taylor concluded by declaring that his intention had been to recognize the government of Hungary if it had succeeded in establishing itself on a *de facto* basis, recognizable as such by "the usages and settled principles of this government."

Taylor ended this message to the Senate with a note of defiance, as befitted the no-surrender victor of Buena Vista. Although Hungary "is now fallen and many of her gallant patriots are in exile or in chains, I am free still to declare that had she been successful in the maintenance of such a government as we could have recognized we should have been the first to welcome her into the family of nations."

Isthmian Rivalries and Texan Sensibilities

President Taylor, the man of war, deserves credit as a man of peace in arranging for the negotiation and ratification of the air-clearing Clayton–Bulwer Treaty of 1850. It lasted more than a half-century and may well have averted an armed clash between Great Britain and the United States.

From the days of Balboa onward explorers and other adventurers had dreamed of cutting the earthy cord between North America and South America by means of an isthmian water route. Even while the Mexican War was being fought in 1846, the United States concluded a treaty with New Granada (Colombia) for the transit rights at Panama but failed to secure similar concessions across Mexico's narrowest expanse, the Isthmus of Tehuantepec.

Great Britain, the premier mercantile nation of the world, was acutely sensitive to the problem of an isthmian waterway. In unfriendly Yankee hands, it could be used to cripple British commerce; if in Britain's own hands, a canal could be manipulated to her own advantage. After the early Yankee victories in the Mexican War had advertised American rapacity, the British resorted to aggressive countermeasures.

Already firmly established in British Honduras, Great Britain claimed a protectorate over the Mosquito Indians, who lived near Greytown (San Juan), at the eastern terminus of the proposed Nicaraguan waterway. In 1848 the British intruders seized Greytown, ostensibly to protect their dusky wards against the Nicaraguans.

On the Pacific side of Nicaragua, a British naval officer in 1849 seized Tigre Island, near what was thought to be the most feasible entrance to an isthmian canal. His hasty action was promptly disavowed by the London authorities, but American public opinion was not completely placated. Secretary of State Clayton wrote privately that "a collision will become inevitable if great prudence is not exercised on both sides."

To the credit of Taylor, the man of arms, his communications to Congress on this delicate subject were conciliatory yet firm. The upshot was the Clayton-Bulwer Treaty of 1850, which, though abounding in ambiguities, kept the lid on this explosive problem for a half-century. It was not superseded until 1901, when the second Hay-Pauncefote Treaty gave the United States a free hand to build the Panama Canal.

The controversial but long-lived Clayton-Bulwer Treaty in effect pledged both Britain and America not to obtain exclusive control over any future isthmian canal. They were to keep it open on equal terms to British and Americans alike. The pact also seemed to bar the British from occupying or annexing "any part of Central America," and if this article could be made to stick it would be a signal victory for the recently revived Monroe

Doctrine. All in all, General Taylor's Secretary of State Clayton won a victory in diplomatic generalship for peace, and the President is entitled to share some of the acclaim. He could easily have kicked over the diplomatic applecart.

Yet regarding other diplomatic problems of smaller consequence, Taylor took an aggressive stance. His arbitrary stand in a minor squabble with the French Minister, W. T. Poussin, might well have led to a clash with France, if negotiations had not taken a favorable turn. Moreover, Taylor's adamant position on claims against tiny Portugal has been judged unnecessary, unfair, and unwarranted.

Surprisingly, President Taylor's most dangerous exhibition of bellicosity was directed at fellow Southerners, in this case Texans, rather than at foreign nations. On the issue of slavery, Taylor, though a slaveholder, was of a divided mind. As we have seen, he favored leaving slavery alone where it existed (the slave-cursed South applauded), but barring the spread of black bondage into the newly acquired territories (the antislavery North applauded).

Spurred on by his convictions, Taylor urged the Californians to organize a state government and seek admission to the Union as a free state. As for New Mexico, also acquired by the federal government as free territory, an explosive dispute arose over a claim by Texas to a large part of what is now the state of New Mexico. The Texans were publicly proclaiming their intention of seizing this disputed area with their own state troops; privately Taylor was expressing his determination to fight them, as Andrew Jackson had done with regard to defiant South Carolina in 1832–1833.

Taylor, if anything, was a dyed-in-the-wool military man. He doubtless recoiled from turning the disputed part of free-soil New Mexico over to slaveholders, but he was also Commander-in-Chief of the army. As a general who had never encouraged back talk from the rear ranks, he doubtless resented the defiance of Texas, plus other Southerners, as a challenge to his authority. Like Andrew Jackson, he assumed an inflexible stance, and seemed determined, if need be, to take the field himself and in person crush all "traitors," Texans or not.

When President Jackson had belligerently talked of invading South Carolina in 1832, he was evidently prepared to risk a civil war. But the South Carolinians quickly realized that they would be fighting alone, or nearly alone, because the South had not yet crystalized to a dangerous degree on the issue of the tariff. But in 1850, as in 1860, the Deep South was united in its zeal for slavery expansion, and strong-arm measures against the rebellious Texans could easily have started the Civil War a decade before it blazed forth.

In any event, Taylor's unexpected death in July 1850 almost certainly preserved the peace and made possible ultimate passage of the batch of offsetting measures by Congress known as the Compromise of 1850. In this crunch, as in Jackson's South Carolina crisis, Henry Clay, "The Great Compromiser," played a stellar role. The sticking point of the Texas boundary claim was neatly removed when Congress authorized the federal government to pay Texas $10 million. The area in question was thus saved from slavery, and to this extent Taylor triumphed from the grave without resorting to arms.

CHAPTER 13

MILLARD FILLMORE: THE LAST OF THE WHIGS

We should act toward other nations as we wish them to act toward us, and justice and conscience should form the rule of conduct between governments, instead of mere power, self-interest, or the desire of aggrandizement.

President Millard Fillmore,
First Annual Message to
Congress, December 2, 1850

The Fulfillment of Fillmore

Millard Fillmore's name does not come resounding down through the corridors of time, primarily because he suffered from several serious handicaps. First of all, he was an accidental, act-of-God President, chosen as a vice-presidential afterthought to "balance" the ticket for the presidential nominee, war hero Zachary

Taylor. "Old Zack" was a famous general, from the South, and a slaveowning plantation owner. Fillmore had never served in the U.S. army, hailed from the North, and was willing to compromise on the issue of slavery in the territories recently wrested from Mexico. The irony is that Taylor proved to be a Southern man with Northern principles on slavery extension, and Fillmore proved to be a Northern man with some sympathy for Southern principles regarding slavery. In Fillmore's short term the guns did not boom, and this lack of fireworks is one reason why he is usually written off as colorless and ineffective.

Millard Fillmore was born in upstate New York in 1800, the year of Jefferson's election—the first President born in the nineteenth century. He worked on his father's farm as a youth, while picking up some scanty schooling, which in turn enabled him to teach school for a brief time. As ex-President of the United States in 1855 he declined to accept a D.C.L. degree from Oxford University on the valid grounds that he could present no literary or scientific achievements to warrant such an honor. At one brief stage of his youth he was apprenticed to a wool carder and cloth dresser—hence "His Accidency," "The Wool Carder President." Ultimately finding himself, he read law and became a prosperous practitioner in Buffalo. His sole contact with the military establishment came during the Mexican War, when he commanded a corps of the Home Guard.

Fillmore's experience in politics was marred by considerable frustration and rejection, but he did serve for two years in the New York State Assembly and four terms in Congress. During this time he became chairman of the important House Committee on Ways and Means, where he had a large hand in framing the protective tariff of 1842.

Searching for a Northern Whig nominee to balance Zachary Taylor's Southern Whiggism, the Whigs in Philadelphia turned to Millard Fillmore for their vice-presidential candidate. As ex-officio presiding officer of the Senate, Fillmore presided over the heated debates involving the multipronged Compromise of 1850, always with firmness, fairness, and good humor. President Taylor probably would have wrecked this controversial solution if he had not providentially died, for he was determined to beat the balky Texans into line. He flatly opposed the extension of slavery into the territories, whereas Fillmore, a compromiser in the Henry Clay tradition, was prepared to make significant concessions to the South. Somehow or other, Fillmore has not received the credit he deserves for helping to engineer the compromise legislation of 1850. He signed all of the five component bills, including the ostensibly fair but infuriating fugitive slave law. It was welcomed in the South but condemned in the free-soil North.

The adjective commonly applied to President Fillmore is "colorless," which is another name for what later generations would call "lack of charisma." Yet contemporaries noted that he radiated a dignified and impressive presence, set off by his five feet, nine inches, his well-developed chest, his deep voice, his kindly blue eyes, and his finely chiseled features. Clearly he was one of the most handsome and gracious of all the Presidents.

The five basic bills constituting the Compromise of 1850 were still log-jammed in Congress when Fillmore became President. In a special message to Congress (August 10, 1850), he declared that the deadlock called for "amicable adjustment" by the payment to Texas of "an indemnity for the surrender of that claim." Less than a month later Congress passed the Texas and New Mexico Act, which offered $10 million to the Texans. They accepted, and the Compromise of 1850 emerged triumphant.

Hungary and Cuba Again

The aftershocks of the ill-starred revolt of Hungary against the rule of Austria continued to be felt under President Fillmore. In 1850 Daniel Webster, hero of the Webster–Ashburton negotiations of 1842, had succeeded Secretary Clayton as Secretary of State. The Austrian government had bitterly resented the dispatching of A. Dudley Mann by the United States to grant recognition to the Hungarian rebels whenever the time seemed opportune. After the rebellion was crushed, the Vienna government instructed its representative in Washington to lodge a strong protest against this officious meddling in the affairs of a friendly nation.

Secretary Webster, fearing that the growing controversy over slavery was weakening America in the eyes of foreigners, decided to let fly a patriotic blast. His response (December 4, 1850) was arrogant rather than pugnacious. The tone of his note is best revealed by this high-flown passage: "The power of this republic at the present moment is spread over a region one of the richest and most fertile on the globe, and of an extent in comparison with which the possessions of the House of Hapsburg [Austria] are but a patch on the earth's surface." Webster's stump-speech response evoked an instant and favorable reaction at home from the ranks of both parties, Whigs and Democrats alike. The Austrian government was not pleased, but there was nothing much they could do about the bumptious Yankee.

Louis Kossuth, the exiled leader of the crushed Hungarians, toured the United States late in 1851 to plead for his lost cause. From the diplomatic standpoint, a high point came at a Kossuth banquet, at which Secretary Webster spoke. Possibly overstimulated by champagne, the "Godlike Daniel" would "rejoice to see our American model upon the lower Danube and on the mountains of Hungary." But for the moment he would limit his aspirations to "Hungarian independence, Hungarian self-government, Hungarian control of Hungarian destinies."

American critics interpreted Webster's defiant outburst as a bid for the presidential nomination, to the embarrassment of President Fillmore. For its part, the Austrian government was so deeply offended by this indiscretion that it instructed its representative in Washington to have no further dealings with Webster. Relations continued strained until the eloquent Secretary of State died in the harness in October 1852.

Frustrated filibustering expeditions into Cuba from American ports continued to plague the government in Washington. Having failed twice, Narciso López was scheming to try again. President Fillmore, reluctant to inflame the slavery issue further, issued a ringing proclamation on April 25, 1851. In particular, he did not wish to see his fellow Americans seduced into such forays against a "friendly power" by promises of monetary gain from "plunder and robbery." He sternly warned that under the neutrality statutes of the United States "every person so offending shall be deemed guilty of a high misdemeanor and shall be fined not exceeding $3,000 and imprisoned not more than three years." Fillmore further cautioned that such offenders should "forfeit their claim to the protection of this government," no matter what mistreatment their conduct invited.

Nothing daunted, the Venezuelan-Cuban López completed preparations for his third and last descent upon Cuba from New Orleans. In August 1851 he set sail with about five hundred men, most of them Americans. López landed in Cuba with relative ease, but his tiny force was quickly defeated and dispersed by Spanish soldiers. The intrepid leader and fifty of his followers were put to death, and more than one hundred sixty were sent to Spain for imprisonment.

A number of the "murdered" victims had come from the "best families" of the slavery South, and when the shocking news reached New Orleans patriotic American citizens vented their passions. A local Spanish newspaper was so ill-advised as to gloat over the debacle, whereupon an outraged mob sacked the Spanish consulate, tore up the Spanish flag, and otherwise dishonored Spain.

In Madrid, a mob came near wrecking the United States legation by way of retaliation, and Spanish militants raised angry and bellicose voices. Fortunately for peace, the expansionist and proslavery Democrats were not in power. The Whig President Fillmore, who had warned the filibusterers against expecting American help, was fair-minded enough to remember his proclamation against another Cuban foray. Nor did he forget his threat of no protection if the adventurers ran into trouble.

The Spanish Minister in Washington lodged an angry protest, demanding redress and reparation for damage to property. Secretary Webster, fortunately for peace, did not mount the high horse he had ridden in support of Kossuth. He fully acknowledged the wrong that had been done Spain and promised the necessary amends. The Spaniards, for their part, were thrown off balance by the unexpectedly conciliatory response from Webster. In 1852 the Spanish Queen, by way of reciprocation, pardoned the American survivors of this latest foray. Congress, not to be outdone, appropriately voted $25,000 as recompense for the damage wreaked on Spanish property by the unrestrained mob in New Orleans.

The Caribbean and Japan

Cuba concerned President Fillmore diplomatically in yet another way. Great Britain and France both possessed valuable sugar colonies in the Caribbean, and they both felt increasing concern over what clearly were American designs on Cuba, "The Ever Faithful Isle." The recent filibusterism prompted these two European powers, at the instigation of Spain, to propose a tripartite convention involving the United States. Under it the Spaniards would be guaranteed their possession of Cuba, and the slavery-expansionist United States would never be able to seize this tempting insular prize, so near and yet so far.

Secretary of State Webster, a son of antislavery New England, was rather favorably disposed to such a guarantee regarding Cuba. But he died late in 1852, and the electorate voted for the expansionist candidate, Franklin Pierce, in the fall election. Webster's successor, Secretary Edward Everett, declined to tie America's hands by the self-denying pact into which England and France were trying to lure the United States. Among other reasons for his refusal, Everett invoked the traditional American policy of nonentanglement. He wrote that no Washington government "could stand a day" if it pledged itself never to acquire Cuba.

Fillmore obviously had been at or near Secretary Everett's elbow when this note was written. In his third annual message to Congress, December 6, 1852, the President referred to the Anglo-French scheme to save Cuba and noted that a list of reasons for shunning this entrapment measure would "occupy too much space." But he concluded that "the proposed measure would be of doubtful constitutionality, impolitic, and unavailing." What the Supreme Court would have said on this issue, if anything, was anybody's guess. But for America to team up with hated Britain and suspect France was certainly impolitic, as far as expansionist Americans were concerned. And Fillmore well knew that if enough Americans wanted Cuba urgently enough, they would surely get it, sooner or later.

Yet Fillmore added in this, his last annual message to Congress, the following words of comfort. He had directed the "ministers of France and England to be assured that the United States entertain no designs against Cuba, but that on the contrary, I should regard its incorporation into the Union at the present time as fraught with serious peril." Here spoke no bellicose expansionist, nor even an aggressive Manifest Destinarian.

Fillmore, falsely accused of being proslavery, has received little credit from historians for his key role in engineering the Great Compromise of 1850. He has also garnered scant praise for sending the fleet of four steam warships to Japan, commanded by Commodore Matthew C. Perry, who finally opened the tightly guarded portals of the Mikado's empire to outside influence. This red-letter date in world history dawned in the administration of the forgotten Fillmore's successor, President Pierce, who has received an undue share of the credit.

Yet dispatching the four warships was not evidence of a desire or design on the part of Fillmore to start a shooting war. He evidently intended these vessels to symobolize the Big Stick that later was imperishably identified with the administration of Theodore Roosevelt. The American squadron was under strict orders not to resort to force, except in a situation that required self-defense or resentment of an insult. Fillmore had more pacific objectives in mind.

Ever since 1620 the Japanese, after some unpleasant experiences with foreigners, had banged shut their gates to the outside world. Only the Chinese and the Dutch were allowed to do business through a tiny crack in the gate at Nagasaki, which was atomic-bombed in 1945 by the Americans. Fillmore had cogent reasons for wanting to persuade Japan to consent to reasonably open contacts with the Western world, and he laid them bare in his last annual message to Congress, December 6, 1852.

By 1852 greater commercial contact, as Fillmore pointed out, had been developed by the United States with East Asia, especially since the United States had secured a Pacific frontage, notably at San Francisco Bay. Also, the application of steam to sailing ships accentuated the need for essential coaling stations and supply centers in Asiatic waters. American sailors shipwrecked in or near Japanese waters had been barbarously treated, by allegedly being exhibited as prisoners in cramped cages.

Fillmore concluded in this last annual message that both Japan and the United States would profit from "mutually beneficial intercourse," all the more so since America's "constitutional system excludes every idea of distant colonial dependencies." He had therefore ordered an "appropriate naval force to Japan, under the command of a discreet and intelligent officer of the highest rank known in our service." Perry had been instructed to secure a relaxation of the self-exclusion of Japan and "to remonstrate in the strongest language against the cruel treatment" accorded shipwrecked sailors. Yet Fillmore made clear that the expedition was "friendly and peaceful." Twelve days earlier Perry had already sailed from Norfolk, Virginia, armed with his pacific instructions. What he specifically accomplished belongs under the next administration, that of President Franklin Pierce.

Showing the Flag Abroad

Paralleling the expedition to Japan were additional naval operations in faraway places during the stewardship of President Fillmore. In 1851, after massacres of foreigners (including Americans) at Jaffa in Turkey, the United States Mediterranean Squadron was ordered to the Turkish coast. Apparently no shots were fired. That same year operations were undertaken at Johanna Island, east of Africa, to exact redress for the unlawful imprisonment of the captain of an American whaling ship. In 1852–1853, at different times, U.S. Marines were landed and maintained in Buenos Aires to protect American interests during a revolutionary disturbance. Thus was American naval power brought to bear in remote areas of the globe.

Fillmore, in the light of his record, deserved well of his party at the Whig nominating convention that met in Baltimore in June 1852. Although he led on the first ballot, he could not muster a majority, so the delegates turned on the fifty-third ballot to the remaining great war hero, "Old Fuss and Feathers" Winfield Scott. After all, they had won only with war heroes, Generals Harrison and Taylor. Yet the Whigs took a licking in November of 1852 at the hands of the Democratic nominee, the expansionist Franklin Pierce. The election of 1852 was the last one in which the Whigs ran a candidate, thus leaving Fillmore with an imperishable designation, "The Last of the Whigs."

In 1856 the forgotten Fillmore consented to run for the presidency as the candidate of the Know-Nothing Party. This new grouping, both anti-Catholic and antiforeign, held promise of uniting the country on issues not connected with the burning question of slavery. Fillmore, his luck forsaking him, lost by a wide margin. Ever a compromiser who favored concessions to the South, he opposed Lincoln's prewar and war policies and in 1864, during the Civil War, supported the Democratic candidate, General McClellan, against Lincoln. During Reconstruction Fillmore's sympathies were with President Johnson and the defeated South. If conciliation, moderation, and compromise are the essence of statesmanship, Fillmore has valid claims to being a nonbelligerent statesman. On a pugnacity scale he would receive a low rating, largely because he favored conciliation above coercion.

CHAPTER 14

FRANKLIN PIERCE: THE FORGOTTEN PRESIDENT

Our present attitude and past course give assurances ... that our purposes are not aggressive or threatening to the safety or welfare of other nations.

President Franklin Pierce,
Annual message to Congress,
December 4, 1854

The Accession of Pierce

With wavy black hair and a fine physique, "Handsome Frank" Pierce was of about average height—five feet, ten inches—but his erect military bearing caused him to seem taller. Personally magnetic, genial, and congenial, he was regarded as a hale fellow well met and a fancy dresser to boot. On occasion he would become convivial, sometimes too much so, for he had both an overfondness for alcohol and an allergy to it.

As a youth born in New Hampshire, Pierce was privileged to attend the best preparatory schools. Unlike some of his predecessors, he was a college graduate, in this case of Bowdoin College in Maine, where he rose to high rank in his class. There he made friends with two fellow students who later attained great literary fame, Henry W. Longfellow and especially Nathaniel Hawthorne. After graduation, Pierce turned to the study of law and became a successful practitioner. In 1846 he declined an invitation from President Polk to serve as United States Attorney General; instead he preferred to seek action in the war with Mexico.

Though one of the "forgotten Presidents" of the 1850s, Pierce could claim several distinctions. At age forty-eight, he was the youngest man up to that point to reach the White House. He was the first and only President born in the "Granite State" of New Hampshire, and he came honestly by the sloganized designation, "Young Hickory of the Granite Hills." As a Democratic admirer and follower of "Old Hickory" Jackson, he turned out to be an even darker presidential horse than James K. Polk. Pierce did not receive even a single vote until the thirty-fifth ballot in the Democratic convention at Baltimore, where he finally wound up with 283 votes and the nomination. Democratic Senator Stephen A. Douglas, who had competing presidential ambitions, grimly quipped, "Henceforth no private citizen is safe."

In the ensuing election, Pierce defeated by a considerable margin his former gifted commander in Mexico, "Old Fuss and Feathers" Winfield Scott, the Whig nominee. Yet Pierce had only two short months in which to savor his triumph. Shortly before inauguration in March 1853, the President-elect and his wife suffered the horrifying experience of witnessing the death of their third and only surviving child. Eleven-year-old Benjamin was mangled and killed in a train wreck before their very eyes. Mrs. Pierce, already a fanatic on the twin subjects of alcohol and politics, regarded this tragedy as divine retribution for her husband's acceptance of the presidency. She refused to attend public functions and spent much time writing letters to her dead child. Pierce was distracted by grief, self-reproach, and domestic disharmony at the very time when he desperately needed to concentrate on averting the sectional divorce and conflict between North and South. This divisive issue had already begun to tear the nation apart.

Pierce, though a dark horse, was no tyro in politics. He had served for four years in the New Hampshire House of Representatives, where he was speaker for one year. From 1833 to 1837 he represented his Granite State in the national House of Representatives, and he served in the United States Senate from 1837 to 1842. He resigned out of deference to his wife, who hated both the Washington scene and alcohol, which flowed freely in the capital and further enslaved her husband.

But Pierce was no stranger to military affairs, and his first-hand experience with wholesale bloodshed may have made him a less bellicose President than could have been anticipated. After the Mexican War broke out, he enlisted as a private in the volunteers, rose to the rank of colonel and then brigadier general. He courageously led a detachment of 2,500 men from the fever-cursed Mexican coast for a distance of 150 miles through enemy country to meet General Scott at Pueblo. After this feat he fought in several of the most important battles. At Contreras he suffered an agonizing groin injury while on horseback, after which he fainted, fell, and twisted a leg. Whig foes in 1852 jeered at the "Fainting General," who was the hero of "many a well-fought bottle." Actually, he insisted on participating in the succeeding battles, though decidedly unwell, but was unable to cover himself with maximum glory. Yet his superior officers commended him, and the legislature of New Hampshire presented him with a sword.

Pierce's inaugural address, confidently delivered on March 4, 1853, in a chilling snowstorm, was unique in at least one respect. All of the more than three thousand words were uttered without notes or manuscript, entirely from memory. As leader of the expansive Democratic party of Polk and others, he declared flatly that "the policy of my Administration will not be controlled by any timid forebodings of evil from expansion." Indeed, the situation of the United States rendered "the acquisition of certain possessions not within our jurisdiction [Cuba] eminently important for our protection, if not in the future essential for the preservation of the rights of commerce and the peace of the world." Yet any such acquisitions would be secured, not in a "grasping spirit," but with justice and honor that would "leave no blot upon our fair record."

Pierce went on to say that his goals would best be attained by "peace" and by "kindly and fraternal relations" with neighboring nations. Yet America's rights as a nation "must be sacredly maintained," whether on land or sea. Reaffirming the basic principles of the Monroe Doctrine, without mentioning it by name, he declared as "utterly inadmissible" any "interference or colonization on this side of the ocean by any foreign power."

Pierce probably was thinking of British activities in Central America near a proposed transisthmian route.

Opening Japan and Resisting Austria

The red-letter opening of isolated Japan by Commodore Perry took place in 1853–1854, during the administration of Franklin Pierce, a Democrat. Actually, the fleet had been dispatched from the United States in the previous administration of Millard Fillmore, a Whig. This may be the basic reason why Pierce made only a two-sentence reference to it in his lengthy annual message to Congress of December 4, 1854. He did not even mention Perry by name for his brilliant achievement; perhaps he believed that there was no political profit to be gained by commenting favorably on a project initiated by a rival party.

The drama of opening Japan and then signing the treaty of 1854 is a twice-told tale. But what is seldom stressed, as it must be in the present context, was that force, or the threat of force, went hand in hand with Perry's masterful diplomacy.

When Perry was selected to head this important mission, he wrote to the Secretary of the Navy that he was prepared to assume the leadership, provided that the East India Squadron was greatly strengthened. His suggestion met with favor, and the Fillmore administration decided to dispatch a formidable fleet, hoping that a flexing of naval muscles would facilitate discussions. But Perry was cautioned to use verbal persuasion first, and if this failed he was to change his tone and resort to heavy-handed methods. Yet he was always to keep in mind that his mission was a peaceful one and that the President of the United States had no constitutional power to declare war (although he may start one).

Perry at length reached the beautiful Bay of Yedo (now Tokyo) with four formidable warships on July 8, 1853. Never before had the self-isolated Japanese seen steamers of this type. As Perry's flagship, the *Susquehanna*, and three other warships, belching black smoke, moved steadily up the bay in the teeth of a strong headwind, the onlookers were struck with consternation. The decks of the American fleet were cleared for action, the guns were loaded, and the crews had been called to quarters.

The distrustful Japanese had no way of knowing that Perry carried strict orders never to resort to force except in self-defense or to repay an insult. When Perry was told to repair to ill-starred Nagasaki, one of two ports open to foreigners, he declined to do so. He declared that if rebuffed he would regard such treatment as an insult to his country and "would not hold himself accountable for the consequences"—a delicate reference to force. The Japanese then consented to receive his documents, including a letter from President Fillmore.

At the end of ten days of palaver, Perry sailed away, for he realized that the exposure of Japan to the outside world posed serious problems that required mature deliberation. Before departing, he let fall the veiled threat that he would return in the spring with a much more powerful squadron. True to his word, he then had seven black ships, not just four. He found the Japanese prepared to negotiate, partly for internal reasons, and on March 31, 1854, he signed an epochal treaty of peace, amity, and commerce. As a promising beginning two Japanese ports were to be officially opened to American trade. Such were the immediate fruits of the Perry mission.

Likewise, in the affair of Martin Koszta, a Hungarian by birth, President Pierce inherited a problem that did more than demonstrate the aggressiveness of his administration. It showed that the United States, though not then regarded in Europe as a world power, could and would work its will by force or show of force in a far corner of the globe against a leading European nation.

Martin Koszta, a Hungarian revolutionist, had fled to the United States in 1850, when he formally declared his intention of becoming an American citizen. He later visited Turkey on business. While in the ancient city of Smyrna, he was kidnapped (June 1853) and taken on board an Austrian warship then in the harbor. His captors clapped him into irons with the intention of taking him to Austria, there to face criminal charges growing out of the recent Hungarian revolution. The United States consul in Smyrna, together with the American legation in Turkey's capital, Constantinople, pleaded for Koszta's release, but in vain.

In the nick of time an American warship arrived at Smyrna, and Commander Ingraham, after making the necessary inquiries, concluded that Koszta was entitled to the protection of the United States. As President Pierce reported to Congress, the American commander "took energetic and prompt measures" for Koszta's release. As a matter of fact, Ingraham cleared for action and at eight in the morning demanded the prisoner's release before four in the afternoon. The Austrian commander backed down, although his fire power was evidently somewhat superior to that of the Americans. A compromise was agreed to, under which Koszta was transferred to the custody of the French consul-general in Smyrna, pending agreement between the Austrian and American consuls general as to his disposition. At the time that Pierce reported to Congress, on December 5, 1853, Koszta was in the United States.

Pierce further informed Congress that the Emperor of Austria had responded with a "grave complaint." His Royal Highness claimed that Koszta was still his subject and that Austria was entitled to seize him within the Turkish Empire. Austria therefore demanded the surrender of the fugitive, a disavowal of the action of the Americans involved, and "satisfaction for the alleged outrage." Pierce reported to Congress that the action of the United States had been entirely legal and proper, and consequently "compliance with the several demands of the Emperor of Austria has been declined."

The position of Pierce in this instance was apparently a reaction in part to the pre-1812 days of British impressment of naturalized or partly naturalized American citizens. The Yankees had been compelled to submit to this outrageous treatment because they were almost invariably confronted with greatly superior force. In the Koszta case, the commander of the American warship in the harbor of Smyrna, Duncan Ingraham, seems to have had the armament odds against him. But he presumably was counting on superior American courage and skill. In any event, Ingraham's daring and successful protection of a part-American citizen evoked an enthusiastic response in the United States and in much of Europe. Upon returning to America, Commander Ingraham was greeted by mass meetings in New York and other cities, and Congress awarded him a gold medal. A Vienna newspaper said of the Koszta affair, "We must get out of the way of the Yankee, who is half a buccaneer, and half a backwoodsman, and no gentleman at all."

The Gadsden Purchase and Filibustering Forays

We recall that Pierce had proclaimed in his inaugural address that he would have no "timid forebodings of evil" in connection with extending the territorial domain of the United States. He probably was thinking primarily of Cuba, which the Southern slaveholders coveted but which the United States never acquired. But Pierce did engineer the Gadsden Purchase from Mexico, totaling about 30,000 square miles of land, much of it semidesert or desert.

The story briefly is this. The Mexican War had netted the United States a magnificent Pacific frontage in California. The most feasible southern railway route from the east lay through territory still retained by Mexico under the 1848 Treaty of Guadalupe Hidalgo. President Pierce informed Congress that this area properly belonged to the Mexican Cession because one of the surveyors had incorrectly located the initial base point on the Rio Grande.

With a peaceful purchase in mind, the expansionist Pierce sent to Mexico as Minister a prominent railroad man from the South, James Gadsden. Fortunately for the United States, the slippery Santa Anna was again in power, and as usual in a financial bind. After prolonged negotiations, Gadsden signed a treaty in December 1853. As modified and narrowly approved by the Senate, the pact awarded the Gadsden Purchase territory to the United States for $10 million. Thus, to the extent that the American claim to the area was valid under the Treaty of Guadalupe Hidalgo, the United States bought this barren land twice. The new expanse, which comprises the southern parts of present Arizona and New Mexico, finally gained for the South the coveted railroad route to the Pacific Coast. Best of all, it was secured without bloodshed.

President Pierce informed Congress in December 1853, when negotiations were nearing a favorable conclusion, that he was impressed with "the importance of maintaining amicable relations" with Mexico and "of yielding with liberality to all her just claims." He also expected "a lasting friendship" between the two nations to be "confirmed and perpetuated." This avowal was much too optimistic, but there has been no declared warfare between the two nations since 1848, the date of the Treaty of Guadalupe Hidalgo.

President Pierce soon had an opportunity to back up his declaration of amity regarding Mexico, for this was the decade when filibustering was in flower. Filibustering was a kind of private warfare conducted against weak and disorganized states by bands of armed men assembled by leaders seeking adventure, power, or exploitation. We have already noted that Narciso López attempted three separate and unsuccessful forays against vulnerable Cuba, presumably with the objective of ultimate annexation to the United States. Southerners were generally friendly to filibustering expeditions that held promise of more slave territory for the South.

William Walker, a wispy Tennessean (about 100 pounds), was the most conspicuous, successful, and troublesome filibusterer of the 1850s. As an editor and lawyer in California, this "gray-eyed Man of Destiny" assembled a force of forty-five men, sailed from San Francisco, and landed in Lower California, November 4, 1853. After shooting a half-dozen or so Mexicans, he proclaimed this area an independent Republic and named himself "President." He next "annexed" the neighboring Mexican state of Sonora, but interference by the United States government with his supplies and recruits caused the incursion to collapse. But he would be heard from several years later as a spectacular filibusterer in Nicaragua.

Probably Walker's failure in Mexico was in part the result of President Pierce's stern proclamation against this particular foray on January 18, 1854. Pierce warned American citizens, under penalty of the law, against giving aid and comfort to those who were involved in such "criminal enterprises" as invading a friendly nation. He further called upon the federal authorities, civil and military, to do all within their power "to arrest for trial and punishment every such offender."

On his return to San Francisco, Walker was brought to trial before a sympathetic judge and jury, which promptly acquitted him. Two of Walker's associates were assessed a fine that they never paid. Pierce has been severely blamed for failing to enforce the neutrality laws, but where public opinion is overwhelmingly on the side of the defendants, enforcement breaks down. From the days of the Stamp Act of 1765 through the Embargo of 1807 and prohibition of alcohol in the 1920s, federal laws have been openly nullified.

Nothing daunted, in 1855 Walker accepted an invitation from one of the revolutionary factions in Nicaragua to enter that troubled country with an armed force. He arrived on June 13, 1855, and was made a colonel in the Nicaraguan army; in October he took the key city of Granada in a surprise attack and made himself master of that country. Late in that same year, on

December 8, 1855, President Pierce issued a ringing proclamation warning that American citizens who participated in this revolutionary upheaval would forfeit the protection of their own government. Such interference, he avowed, was "contrary to their duty as good citizens and to the laws of their country and threatening to the peace of the United States."

In May 1856, about six months later, the Washington government judged the new regime to be of sufficient stability to warrant formal recognition, and this was granted. Pierce was condemned by the antislaveryites for seeking to add more slave territory to the Union, but Walker repeatedly disavowed any attention of annexation to the United States. He was enough of an egomaniac to give credibility to his status as a lone wolf.

Reaching for Cuba

President Pierce, though reasonably restrained in other areas, had no "timid forebodings of evil" in connection with the possible acquisition of Cuba. One of his earliest mistakes in this context was to appoint as Minister to Spain one Pierre Soulé, a hotheaded Louisianian of French birth who had been expelled from his native France as a revolutionary. Becoming a naturalized American citizen and a United States Senator, Soulé had caught the eye of the Pierce administration by his overwhelming enthusiasm for annexing Cuba, by fair means or foul. For this reason alone his appointment was an insult to the Madrid government.

The three López expeditions (1848–1851), all aimed at freeing Cuba, had caused the Spaniards there to develop extreme bitterness against the Yankees. A long series of vexations incidents culminated in the seizure in Cuban waters (February 1854) of the *Black Warrior*, an American steamer that had been allowed to ignore the technicalities involved during the thirty or so times that it had previously touched at Havana. A hotheaded reaction in the United States, even in the antislavery North, caused President Pierce to respond with vigor. In a special message to the House of Representatives he assured the country that reparation in proportion to the seriousness of the offense would be demanded. He added that if "an amicable adjustment" with Spain should "unfortunately fail," he would "not hesitate to use the authority and means which Congress may grant to insure the observance of our just rights, to obtain redress for injuries received and to vindicate the honor of our flag." In short, war, if Congress was willing.

Secretary of State William L. Marcy instructed Minister Soulé to ask for an indemnity of $300,000 and to secure "as early a reply as possible." The impetuous Soulé exceeded his instructions when he demanded a reply within forty-eight hours, plus a dismissal of all persons responsible for the seizure of the *Black Warrior*. The Spanish Foreign Minister, sensing that Soulé had grossly exceeded instructions, arranged for a temporary settlement of the incident through direct dealings with the owners, who returned to their regular business. They received an indemnity of $53,000 in August 1855.

Twelve days after Soulé's unauthorized ultimatum, the Crimean War broke out, involving Russia on one side and Britain, France, Turkey, and Sardinia on the other. The British and the French had already made clear their distaste for a Yankee seizure of Cuba, and now was the time for the expansionist Pierce administration to acquire that lush island without fear of European interference.

Taking full advantage of Europe's internal distresses, Secretary of State Marcy instructed Minister Soulé (April 3, 1854) to offer as much as $130 million for Cuba and, if refused, to seek to "detach" the island from Spanish dominion. What Marcy clearly had in mind was to help Cuba to become free so that she could throw herself into the welcoming arms of the United States.

Secretary Marcy sent off supplementary instructions to Soulé on August 16, 1854. Apparently Marcy was motivated by the ever present nightmare in the South that the blacks of Cuba might rise and massacre the whites (as they had earlier done in Haiti). He probably was also willing to take advantage of the preoccupation of the European powers with the Crimean War. In any event Marcy suggested that Soulé arrange a conference with the United States Ministers to France and Britain, exchange opinions, and then report the conclusions in an official dispatch to Washington.

The three Ministers first met for three days in Ostend, Belgium, in October 1854, as the European press buzzed with rumors. Then, evidently seeking greater privacy, the trio adjourned to Aix-la-Chapelle, in Rhenish Prussia, where they concluded discussions nine days later. Their confidential dispatch to Secretary Marcy *recommended* that an immediate effort be made to buy Cuba for a figure not to exceed $120 million (Marcy had mentioned a maximum of $130 million). If Spain refused to sell, and if her continued possession of Cuba seemed dangerous to the United States, then, the dispatch concluded, "we shall be justified in wresting it from Spain."

This was the so-called Ostend Manifesto, a grossly misleading term. It was not drafted at Ostend but at Aix-la-Chapelle. It was not a manifesto, which is a public pronouncement, but only a confidential dispatch drawn up in secrecy and sent by a special messenger to the State Department, where it could be used, if acceptable, to shape policy toward Spain regarding Cuba.

The contents of the Ostend Manifesto leaked out in garbled form even before the official dispatch reached the United States. Pierce was already involved in protecting what he regarded as the rights of the proslavery South in Kansas and Nebraska. The resulting uproar from the abolitionists and free-soilers over the prospective seizure of slave-burdened Cuba was devastating. President Pierce promptly backed away from this diplomatic powder keg and made no mention at all of the Ostend Manifesto in his messages to Congress.

The egregious Aix-la-Chapelle dispatch was never Pierce's settled policy and can hardly be used as proof that he was a militant expansionist as regards Cuba. Actually, on August 1, 1854, some two weeks before Secretary Marcy dispatched instructions for the conference at Ostend, Pierce sent a special message to the Senate deploring filibustering descents on Cuba. He said, "No provocation whatever [e.g., the *Black Warrior*] can justify private expeditions of hostility against a country at peace with the United States."

Fish, Filibusters, and Fire Power

Disputes over American rights to fish in Canadian Atlantic waters continued to bob up repeatedly during the nineteenth century. To the credit of Pierce's pacific disposition, the reciprocity treaty of 1854 with Great Britain (relating to Canada) laid to rest for some time the most serious issues in dispute. In his annual message to Congress of 1853 Pierce reported: "To protect our fishermen in the enjoyment of their rights and prevent collision between then and British fishermen, I deemed it expedient to station a naval force in that quarter during the fishing season."

As a means of preserving order while showing the flag, this precaution served a dual function that reflected favorably on the President.

The Crimean War (1853–1856) had resulted in a heavy drain on British manpower, notably when the Light Brigade charged into a withering fire at Russia's Balaclava. The British Minister in Washington, John Crampton, was authorized to recruit volunteers discreetly in the United States and then send them clandestinely to Halifax, Nova Scotia. This practice proved highly offensive to many anti-British Americans, notably the Irish, and Secretary of State Marcy, evidently with some political motivation, remonstrated strongly. After Crampton had refused to back down, and after London had stubbornly declined to recall him, Marcy abruptly dismissed the Minister, together with three British consuls who were implicated.

London was outraged, and there was some loose talk of war. But this minor affair was too inconsequential to warrant fighting. President Pierce, in his annual message to Congress of December 1855, declared that the United States, having preserved "impartial neutrality" in the Crimea, fully intended to enjoy "its benefits." He concluded with this passage: "And these undeniable rights of neutrality, individual and national, the United States will under no circumstances surrender." This response was firmness rather than pugnacity, and it brought peaceful results.

From 1850, the signing of the Clayton–Bulwer Isthmian Treaty, to 1861, when the American Civil War erupted, the world witnessed a decade of bickering and bitterness in and over Central America. Great Britain and the United States suspected each other of scheming to secure a stranglehold on the key transit routes or potential transit routes. The British were especially sensitive to the activities of the American filibusterer in Nicaragua, William Walker. They suspected or feared, as did the Yankee abolitionists, that he was in the process of adding new slave territory to the rapidly expanding domain of the United States.

Alert Americans, for their part, suspected the British of not only violating the Clayton–Bulwer treaty but also flouting the Monroe Doctrine in their efforts to secure a stranglehold on the Nicaraguan transit route. Most disturbing was the British "protectorate" over the Mosquito Indians of Nicaragua, who occupied tiny Greytown, a place near the mouth of the San Juan River. Its population numbered about three hundred, mostly natives, and the feeble government of Nicaragua had clearly lost control over these lawless elements.

A crisis developed at Greytown in July 1854. Mob outbursts by the Mosquito Indians and their associates included an attack upon the United States diplomatic representative, whose face was bloodied by a broken bottle. A U.S. naval officer, Captain George N. Hollins, commanding the warship *Cyane*, demanded $24,000 as reparation for damage to American property, an apology for the indignity to the injured American diplomat, and assurances of future good behavior. When concessions were not forthcoming, Hollins gave ample warning before turning his guns on Greytown and then putting the torch to the remnant. He thus temporarily blasted and burned the unruly little town off the map. He took no lives but destroyed the property of a number of foreigners, including Britons and Frenchmen. And Captain Hollins got neither reparations nor an apology.

In his annual message to Congress of December 1854, President Pierce went to great lengths to justify this extreme act of retribution. His main point was that because the lawful government of Nicaragua was admittedly powerless to control the outlaws in Greytown, then the United States had an obligation to do so itself. (For a precedent, he might have referred to Jackson's foray into Spain's Florida in 1818.) The Mosquito outlaws were also a standing menace to the lawful transit of all commerce, American or foreign, across the isthmus of Nicaragua. Captain Hollins had acted properly, Pierce indicated, and had resorted to strong measures, without loss of life, when all reasonable requests for satisfaction had encountered silence. Pierce assumed that the Mosquito Indians of Britain's protectorate felt that they could engage in unlawful acts because of a desire to please "a formidable foreign power, which they presumed to think looked with complacency upon their aggressive and insulting deportment toward the United States."

Pierce further stated in this resolute message that the *Cyane* had been ordered to Greytown in the hope that no violence would be needed. But if Captain Hollins, after issuing his demands, had been forced to leave fruitlessly, then he would have encouraged the inhabitants of Greytown to increase their misbehavior. They probably would have been "emboldened" to "grasp at the treasures and valuable merchandise" of all nations attempting to use Nicaragua's transisthmian land-and-water route. As for foreign protests, Pierce noted that in the past other powers under less provocation had laid waste large cities with heavy loss of life.

Secretary of State Marcy spurned claims for damages growing out of the Greytown bombardment. When the lawful government of Nicaragua asked for reparations, Marcy's reply was that if the United States paid Nicaragua damages, then he in turn would have to ask for damages growing out of the inability of the legal regime to preserve order at Greytown. The French claimed damages, which were denied. But the London government, after some irresponsible war talk, took a conciliatory position: Britons living in foreign lands should present their claims to the local government that permitted disorders to occur.

Clearly Captain Hollins had acted within the broad range of his orders, but President Pierce was evidently telling the truth when he reported that he had hoped for less drastic measures. The bombardment was an early but spectacular instance of United States intervention in a disordered Caribbean nation to protect American lives, property, and honor. A handy precedent was thus established for later but less energetic interventions in Latin America and elsewhere in the world.

Elsewhere, between 1855 and 1856, United States forces intervened on three separate occasions to protect American interests in China or to avenge unprovoked assaults. There were also operations, with some landing of U.S. Marines, for similar purposes in the Fiji islands, Uruguay, and the Isthmus of Panama. The last-named intervention came under the preservation-of-order treaty of 1846 with New Granada (Colombia).

Pierce was essentially a man of peace, and the only war he really waged was the minor civil conflict in Kansas that began about 1855 and flared anew in the epochal Civil War of 1861-1865. To a degree Pierce was responsible for the smaller clash because he had backed the Kansas-Nebraska Act of 1854, which brought on localized armed conflict. But evidently he was persuaded that by giving Kansas to the South and Nebraska to the North he would be serving as an even-handed arbiter.

As events turned out, the antislavery North did not want Kansas to become slave soil, so the burning and shooting began. Pierce was forced to send troops into Kansas, not because he was unduly combative but because he wanted to maintain law and order in an area where the local authorities were unable to preserve peace. Some of his predecessors and successors had taken or were to take comparable action.

President Pierce, during an era of turbulence, did not turn out to be a conspicuously bellicose Chief Executive. In foreign affairs, he backed off from more potential conflicts than he embraced. Although pro-Southern, he tried to be fair and compromise between North and South on the issue of slavery but, like many another umpire, endured brickbats from both sides. Retiring to New Hampshire, he criticized the Lincoln administration for provoking the Civil War and attacked Lincoln for overriding the Constitution in prosecuting it. He was antiwar to the end.

CHAPTER 15

JAMES BUCHANAN: THE DOUGHFACE PRESIDENT

We ought to cultivate peace, commerce, and friendship with all nations, and this not merely as the best means of promoting our own material interests, but in a spirit of Christian benevolence toward our fellow men....

President Buchanan,
Inaugural Address,
March 4, 1857

Buchanan's Beginnings

James Buchanan, a lifelong Pennsylvanian, was unique in several respects. After General Harrison, "Old Buck" Buchanan at sixty-six was the second-oldest President thus far elevated to the White House. As the "Bachelor President," he was the first and only lifelong bachelor to become President. The fiancé of his youth had committed suicide after a trivial lovers' quarrel, and he had shunned matrimony thereafter.

As President, "Old Fogey" Buchanan presented an imposing, statesmanlike appearance. Heavy set, he stood an even six feet. Because of defective vision, he carried his head at a tilt, cocked down and to one side. A professional diplomat during much of his career, he got along well with people and impressed many listeners with his gifts as a raconteur.

Buchanan graduated from Dickinson College in Pennsylvania, in the year 1809. After studying law, he was admitted to the bar in 1812 and rose rapidly in his chosen profession. He gained considerable fame as an orator, not only from what he said but also from the impressive way he said it.

As a rock-ribbed Federalist, Buchanan had opposed the declaration of war against Britain in 1812 but patriotically heeded the call to fight for his country. He was among the first to enlist as a volunteer in a company of dragoons for the defense of Baltimore. This episode was his only firsthand experience with waging war, and it no doubt conditioned his thinking regarding it when he became ex-officio Commander-in-Chief of the Army and Navy.

After the War of 1812, Buchanan served briefly in the Pennsylvania House of Representatives and then in the United States House of Representatives for a total of ten years. In 1829 he became chairman of the House Judiciary Committee, which no doubt sharpened his interest and expertise in constitutional law. In 1832–1833 he served capably as United States Minister to Russia. One should note in passing that as President he naturally revealed in his annual messages to Congress unusual concern for foreign affairs.

From 1834 to 1845 Buchanan served as United States Senator from Pennsylvania, and from 1845 to 1849 as Secretary of State under Polk, a post that involved him even more deeply in foreign affairs. We should also observe that he did not share his chief's bellicosity. He opposed going to the brink of war with Britain over Oregon, and he was one of the two members of the Cabinet who objected to sending a war message to Congress before Mexico had spilled "American blood on American soil" in April 1846.

From 1853 to 1856 Buchanan deepened his interest in foreign affairs by serving effectively as United States Minister to Great Britain. As one of the three American diplomats ordered to Ostend in 1854, he was chosen to draft the so-called Ostend Manifesto. Its phrasing was undeniably bellicose, but Buchanan had toned it down considerably from the draft that the impetuous Minister Soulé wanted.

As a result of his numerous positions of responsibility, Buchanan came to be known as "Old Public Functionary," actually his own phrase. After having aspired unsuccessfully to a presidential nomination in 1844, 1848, and 1852, the ever available Buchanan was finally chosen by the Democratic party for the presidency in 1856. A major reason for his success was that he was "Kansasless"—that is, he had been out of the country as Minister to Great Britain when the issue of slavery in territories came to a boil. His Republican opponent was the dashing explorer and free-soiler, John C. Frémont. Many Southern owners of slaves had threatened to secede from the Union if Frémont triumphed, and these scare tactics no doubt helped boost Buchanan into the White House. His victory may have postponed the secession of the South by four years.

Like Presidents Fillmore and Pierce before him, Buchanan was a "Doughface" President—a Northern man with Southern learnings. He believed in standing staunchly by the great Compromise of 1850. The most satisfying advantage that the South had got out of it, after conceding possible gains to the free-soilers in California and the remainder of the Mexican Cession, was the new and iron-toothed Fugitive Slave Act. Yet some of the free-soil Northerners proceeded to break faith with the South by openly and illegally interfering with attempts of Southerners to recover their footloose blacks. Technically, the South was legally right in trying to collect its part of the bargain, but the free-soil North felt that there was a higher moral law than the Fugitive Slave Act passed by Congress. Buchanan, a distinguished legalist, naturally gave the highest priority to the laws and Constitution of the United States. In his presidency, federal enforcement of the Fugitive Slave Act was prosecuted in the teeth of riotous opposition and other forms of illegality.

Cuba and Caribbean Confrontations

In his inaugural address, March 4, 1857, President Buchanan was less blunt than his predecessor, who had disclaimed any "timid forebodings" about expanding the United States. Buchanan, the veteran diplomat, declared flatly, "Our diplomacy should be direct and frank, neither seeking to obtain more nor accepting less than is our due." The nation, he said, "ought to cherish a sacred regard for the independence of all nations" and should "never attempt to interfere in the domestic concerns of any unless this shall be imperatively required by the great law of self-preservation."

Buchanan would also "avoid entangling alliances," in accord with the sage advice of the Founding Fathers. "In short, we ought to do justice in a kindly spirit to all nations and require justice from them in return." The United States, to be sure, had wrested vast areas from Mexico but had honorably paid for them with "a sum which was considered at the time [by Americans] a fair equivalent." "Our past history," concluded Buchanan, "forbids that we shall in the future acquire territory unless this be sanctioned by the laws of justice and honor." Hence no nation could complain if "we shall further extend our possessions."

While standing on the inauguration platform, Buchanan almost certainly had Cuba in mind. Although having softened the Ostend Manifesto of 1854, he had drafted it and no doubt was aware that his active participation had appealed to many Southern voters in his recent run for the presidency.

In three of his four annual messages to Congress, Buchanan urged upon that body the desirability of taking steps to purchase Cuba, including the voting of money. In December 1858 he alluded to the temporary seizure in 1854 of the American ship *Black Warrior*, and then showed unaccustomed bellicosity when he referred to this incident as "an outrage of such a character as would have justified an immediate declaration of war." On this occasion he made an obvious attempt to appease the Northern antislaveryites by pointing out that Cuba was the only place in the world where the African slave trade was legally continuing. To shut it off by securing Cuba would also shut it off at the African source, and thus save the United States and Great Britain the heavy cost of maintaining their ineffective patrols against the merciless slavers. But Buchanan's repeated appeals to acquire Cuba honorably failed to elicit a supportive response from Congress.

In his last annual message, that of December 1860, Buchanan reiterated his pro-Southern plea for the acquisition of Cuba by "fair purchase." He believed that such a transfer would redound to the advantage of both America and Spain, whose "national honor" would not be tarnished by the transaction. Besides, such a purchase would "prove the certain means" of promptly ending "the African slave trade throughout the world." But by 1860 the Cuban issue had been swallowed up by the preliminaries of the Civil War.

In 1858 an explosive development occurred in Anglo-American relations, specifically in the Caribbean area. Early in this year certain overzealous British officers, eager to capture slave ships, began a systematic search of American merchant vessels suspected of engaging in this lawless and loathsome traffic. Her Majesty's searchers even went so far as to fire upon several vessels that refused to display their colors. Actually, a cleverly disguised slaver could not be easily identified unless first boarded for inspection.

But the hoary British practice of visiting and searching American merchant ships brought back ugly memories of the events that had caused patriotic citizens to fight Great Britain in the War of 1812. As indignation mounted, United States warships were rushed to the Gulf of Mexico under orders from Washington to resist with force such objectionable practices. A clash was narrowly averted. When Secretary of State Cass lodged a stern protest in April 1858, the British Foreign Secretary graciously disclaimed any pretense to the right of visit and search in time of peace, African slave trade or no.

President Buchanan, reporting on the crisis in his second annual message to Congress in December 1858, expressed his gratification over the amicable adjustment of the "long-pending controversy" involving "the question of visitation and search." He pointed out that this practice in time of peace had already been overruled by the "most eminent jurists" in Great Britain. What the British had been doing, he declared, was all the more vexatious because it menaced the vital coastwise commerce between the Atlantic and the Gulf states. He had dispatched the emergency naval force to Cuban waters with directions "to protect all vessels of the United States on the high seas from search or detention by the vessels of war of any other nation." These measures had received the "unqualified and even enthusiastic approbation of the American people." Such a reaction was especially noteworthy in the slave-ridden South, for which Buchanan had unconcealed sympathy.

President Buchanan evidently had something of a soft spot in his heart for the British, particularly after his pleasant nineteen months as United States Minister in London. Yet so deep was his Americanism that a strain of pugnacity revealed itself over visit and search. Some kind of shoot-out with the British might well have occurred, with horrendous consequences, but where American lawful rights and honor were concerned Buchanan was prepared to go to the brink. When the North-South secession crisis loomed in 1860-1861, he did not act so resolutely because the Consititution that he had solemnly sworn to uphold, as he read it, did not grant him that authority. So the glorious Union drifted apart—ingloriously.

From Nicaragua to San Juan Island

In connection with filibustering forays into the Nicaraguan transit area, site of the proposed isthmian canal, Buchanan adopted a stern stance against American-launched expeditions. In so doing, he weakened somewhat the accusation that he was a thick-and-thin supporter of the South.

After initial success as dictator of Nicaragua, "General" William Walker was forced to flee and again found himself in the United States. In November 1857 he eluded the federal authorities and sailed from Mobile, Alabama, with a new expedition to battered Greytown. Commodore Hiram Paulding, who was then patrolling these waters for the United States, landed a force of sailors and Marines, captured General Walker, and then sent him back to the United States. There the prisoner was released on the grounds that Commodore Paulding had exceeded his instructions. Evidently this naval officer would have been legally in the clear if he intercepted Walker *before* the filibusterer had reached Nicaraguan soil. But Paulding had no authority—Buchanan so declared in a message to the Senate—to land troops on the soil of any nation, especially one with which the United States was at nominal peace, for the purpose of conducting military operations.

The magnitude of Commodore Paulding's intervention is not generally known. Walker had landed with about 150 filibusterers in defiance of the U.S. armed sloop *Saratoga*. Paulding then threw a force of 350 men ashore, compelled the surrender of Walker without bloodshed, and sent him and his followers home. Such bold action was greeted with warm approval in the antislavery North, but the Buchanan administration freed

Walker and soon relieved Paulding of his command. The grateful government of Nicaragua presented Paulding with a jeweled sword.

Buchanan stated flatly in reporting to the Senate (January 7, 1858) that if Commodore Paulding had captured Walker and his followers *before* they reached the Nicaraguan port, then the American officer could have been commended for a "praiseworthy act." Filibustering, said Buchanan, violated "the principles of Christianity, morality, and humanity." He believed that such adventurism was especially to be deplored in an area where vital transit routes across the isthmus were endangered. The United States could not conduct a successful foreign policy in Central America "or anywhere else" if it had to deal with "lawless military expeditions," such as Walker's, launched repeatedly from American shores. Buchanan followed this pronouncement with a ringing proclamation (October 30, 1858). It denounced a third Walker expedition against Nicaragua that was "being set on foot" on the soil of the United States. Not until August 1860 did Walker land in Honduras, after eluding British and American naval forces. The Honduran authorities tried him by court martial and then stood him before a firing squad, where he died ingloriously.

The dangerous and disruptive misunderstanding between Britain and the United States over the Clayton–Bulwer treaty and its relation to disorders on the isthmus happily came to an end when London made separate treaties with the concerned republics of Central America. The British pact with Honduras in 1859 recognized that the controversial Bay Islands belonged to that small nation. By the treaty of 1860 with Nicaragua, Great Britain also relinquished its claims to the territory of the Mosquito Indians. Reporting to the Congress in his last annual message, that of December 1860, Buchanan could happily state that these two treaties had resulted "in an final settlement entirely satisfactory to this Government."

In another distant area of friction with Britain, President Buchanan managed to keep the peace, albeit with difficulty. The scene was San Juan Island, fourteen miles long and a mile and a half wide, situated among smaller island dots between Vancouver Island and the present state of Washington. The Oregon treaty with Great Britain in 1846, negotiated by Secretary of State Buchanan, had left in dispute the ownership of this small but strategic outpost. Bad feeling between British subjects and American citizens came to a boil in 1859, and about seven hundred United States troops were sent into San Juan Island by the commanding officer for this area. The British, for their part, maintained a powerful naval force in these troubled waters.

With little effort, Buchanan could have started an Anglo-American war over this minor bit of real estate but, as a man of peace, he took the conciliatory path. He dispatched to the disputed area a gifted pacificator, General Winfield Scott, who had helped to calm the Canadian frontier following the insurrections beginning in 1837. Scott managed to work out temporary joint occupation of San Juan Island pending discussions of a permanent settlement at the highest levels in London and Washington. President Buchanan, in his third annual message (December 1859), was glad to report that "there is no longer any good reason to apprehend a collision between the forces of the two countries during the pendency of the existing negotiations." Buchanan had entertained no doubt as to "the validity of our title," and his judgment was confirmed by the arbitral award of 1872.

From Paraguay to Panama to Mexico

In addition to Central America and the Nicaragua transit route, the Buchanan administration became involved in diplomatic problems of a military nature with several countries of Hispanic America. In January 1858 forces from two United States warships landed on the soil of Uruguay to protect American property during a revolution in Montevideo. In September and October 1860 troops went ashore at Colombia's Bay of Panama to protect American interests, including the transisthmian railroad completed by Americans in 1855. But such interventions, which occurred repeatedly to keep the Panama route open, were sanctioned by the treaty of 1846 with Colombia (New Granada).

Paraguay witnessed the most formidable display of Uncle Sam's bulging muscles. In 1853 the United States steamer *Water Witch* was sent to this area to determine the fitness of the La Plata River and its tributaries for navigation by steam. In 1855 the American vessel was fired upon by a Paraguayan fort as it was attempting to make its way up the Parana River. The reason given was that the Paraguayan government had forbidden foreign warships to navigate its streams.

As Buchanan told Congress in his first annual message, such an attack was "unjustifiable" and called for "satisfaction from the Paraguayan government. He argued that the *Water Witch* was a commercial vessel "engaged in a scientific enterprise intended for the advantage of commercial states generally." Besides, one bank of the river belonged to Argentina, and this circumstance, he believed, invalidated Paraguay's claim to sole jurisdiction.

Buchanan went on to say that American citizens in Paraguay had been deprived of their property and had been treated "by the authorities in an insulting and arbitrary manner, which requires redress." Demands would be made "in a firm and conciliatory spirit." But there would be less likelihood of a refusal if Congress clothed him with authority, which he then requested, to "use other means."

We should note that Buchanan, with his reverence for the Constitution, formally asked Congress for permission to use the armed forces in a manner that many of his predecessors and successors did not hesitate to employ scores of times without requesting authority. On June 2, 1858, Congress formally authorized the President to "adopt such measures and use such force as in his judgment may be necessary and advisable" in the circumstances.

The resulting armed expedition was so overwhelmingly powerful as to stifle any impulses to resistance on the part of the Paraguayans. The force consisted of nineteen armed vessels of various sizes, carrying two hundred guns and 2,500 men. Buchanan could therefore inform Congress in 1859 that the difficulties with Paraguay had been "satisfactorily adjusted." The expeditious deployment of so large and well-behaved a force had produced "a happy effect in favor of our country throughout all that remote portion of the world."

Thus ended the bellicose brandishing of what Theodore Roosevelt was to call the Big Stick. But Buchanan did not employ such a weapon against the seceding Southerners, partly because it was nowhere near big enough to achieve the desired results.

During Buchanan's stormy administration, neighboring Mexico again writhed in the throes of civil war, with recurring outrages against American citizens residing there. Buchanan paid particular attention to this troublesome neighbor and in his annual messages to Congress not only used undiplomatic language but also urged that body to clothe him with power to engage in warlike acts. His experience as Secretary of State under Polk evidently had not hardened him sufficiently to the atrocities flowing from disorders in Mexico.

Monetary claims against Mexico had piled up since the Mexican War of 1846–1848 and were continuing to do so. In December 1858 Buchanan told Congress in his second annual message that it was useless to demand payments that then amounted to more than $10 million, because Mexico was "destitute of all pecuniary means to satisfy these demands." He also relayed a message on this occasion from the United States Minister in Mexico City that "severe chastisement is the only earthly remedy for our grievances." "Abundant cause now undoubtedly exists," Buchanan concluded, "for a resort to hostilities against the Government [of Mexico] still holding possession of the capital [Mexico City]."

The only remedy that Buchanan could propose was "for the Government of the United States to assume a temporary protectorate over the northern portions of [neighboring] Chihuahua and Sonora and to establish military posts within the same; and this I earnestly recommend to Congress." He prefaced his remarks by saying, "In such case this remedy of reprisals is recognized by the law of nations, not only as just in itself, but as a means of preventing actual war." In short, make a small war on Mexico to prevent a big war with Mexico.

A year later, in his annual message of December 1859, Buchanan referred again to the recurring outrages against American citizens, including the execution of three physicians. They had been attending to the needs of the sick and dying of the contending factions when hurried away to speedy execution without trial. The President urged Congress to pass a law that would enable him "to employ a sufficient military force to enter Mexico for the purpose of obtaining indemnity for the past and security for the future." He here repeated the recommendation, made in his message of the previous year, that he be clothed with authority to establish "temporary military posts across the Mexican line in Sonora and Chihuahua" to protect the lives of American and Mexican citizens against recurrent lawlessness. Congress refused to respond to these pleas; it was preoccupied with the coming Civil War in the United States.

An observer is impressed with Buchanan's continued reluctance to take any military action against Mexico on his own initiative without receiving clear-cut authorization from Congress. Here was a constitutional lawyer displaying great reverence for the paper shackles created, in his legalistic judgment, by the Constitution. He showed the same reverence for that hallowed document when, in succeeding months, the Union began to dissolve.

On the whole, Buchanan was more bellicose in public than he was in private, and probably for good reason. Behind the scenes he was pushing diplomatic negotiations with Mexico City for valuable transit privileges across the Isthmus of Tehuantepec. He was also actively backing proposals for purchasing Lower California and other valuable territory in northern Mexico for millions of dollars. All these initiatives came to nothing, although a treaty was signed in Mexico City, in December 1859, relating to transit rights across Mexico and other concessions. Sent to the Senate in due course, it was never approved.

In retrospect, Buchanan's aggressive attitude toward Mexico may have been deliberately designed to bully the Mexicans into parting with additional hunks of their neighboring territory. Some of this soil presumably could have been transferred in lieu of payment for mounting claims. Buchanan's stern language in his messages to Congress may also have been designed to deter foreign nations from intervening in defiance of the Monroe Doctrine, as the French ultimately did behind the smoke screen of the American Civil War.

Involvements Far and Near

America's commercial contacts with the enigma called China had begun in 1784 with the voyage from New York of the merchant ship *Empress of China*, five years before President George Washington took the inaugural oath. Trade between the United States and the Middle Kingdom had been put on a formal basis with the negotiation of the famous Cushing Treaty of Wanghia in 1844. But this pact had expired in 1856, the year of Buchanan's elevation to the White House.

Negotiations for a renewal of the epochal treaty had already been launched but had been suspended because of hostilities on the Canton River between Great Britain and the Chinese Empire. President Buchanan either did not know or chose not to mention to Congress that late in 1856 American water-borne forces had joined in the hostilities to protect American interests at Canton and to avenge an assault upon an unarmed boat displaying the American flag.

In his first annual message, Buchanan announced that he had dispatched to China on an American war steamer a special envoy who would seek to effect changes in the old treaty "favorable to American commerce." This diplomat was instructed to "occupy a neutral position" in the current hostilities but to work in harmony with the British and French Ministers to secure the desired commercial concessions.

In his next annual message, that of December 1858, Buchanan informed Congress that he had instructed the new American envoy to cooperate with the British and French envoys "in all peaceful measures." "It was impossible for me," declared the President, "to proceed further than this on my own authority without usurping the war-making power, which under the Constitution belongs to Congress." We should note again Buchanan's proneness to lean over backward in his reverence for what he regarded as a literal interpretation of the Constitution.

The President further stated on this occasion that the nature of American grievances did not warrant a declaration of war by Congress. He was led to this view by "the severe chastisement which had . . . recently been inflicted upon the Chinese by our squadron in the capture and destruction of the Barrier forts to avenge an alleged insult to our flag."

Having opted for peaceful methods, Buchanan reaped what he called peaceful results "of a highly satisfactory character." A few days before the British and French envoys had secured favorable peace treaties as the fruits of their fighting, the American Minister also signed at Tientsin, June 18, 1858, an epochal trade treaty with China. It gave to the United States, free of cost, essentially all the advantages that Britain and France had wrested from the Chinese after costly and bloody naval operations.

In this same annual message to Congress of December 1858 Buchanan could report another victory for peace and commerce. He was "happy to announce that through the energetic yet conciliatory efforts of our consul-general in Japan [Townsend Harris] a new treaty [July 29, 1858] has been concluded with that Empire." The pact could be expected, the President declared, "materially to augment our trade and intercourse in that quarter." At the same time the treaty would free Americans from "the disabilities which have heretofore been imposed upon the exercise of their religion." Townsend Harris thus opened wide the door that Commodore Perry had left ajar and further highlighted the emergence of the United States as a power of consequence in East Asia.

An aggressive Buchanan unquestionably more than measured up to his responsibilities as a constitutional president in his handling of the controversy with the Mormons, the main body of whom had been driven from Missouri and Illinois to Utah. The clash had all the earmarks of a war, except that while American soldiers did not die on the battlefields, a considerable number perished from cold, starvation, malnutrition, and disease.

Buchanan outlined the problem as he saw it from the White House in a resounding proclamation dated April 6, 1858. He declared that the Territory of Utah was an integral part of the United States but that the migrated Mormons, with their unique religious and social structure, were defying the federal laws and intimidating the officers of the Washington government. Buchanan was not begging Congress for authority to act decisively, for his oath of office obligated him to see that the laws of the United States were "faithfully executed." To this end he had ordered troops to march into Utah, although the Mormons had raised and organized an army that was "far from contemptible in point of numbers."

Yet Buchanan's proclamation went on to say that the Mormons had no real grievance against the Washington government. The President was offering "a free and full pardon to all who will submit themselves to the just authority of the Federal Government. If you refuse to accept it, let the consequences fall upon your own heads. But I conjure you to pause deliberately and reflect well before you reject this tender of peace and good will."

A United States Army of 1,500 officers and men set out for Utah from Fort Leavenworth. The Mormons impeded their progress with guerrilla tactics that involved burning or otherwise destroying forts, supply depots, and supplies. The invaders, forced to live in tents rather than barracks, suffered severely from the wintry weather and hunger. Help was summoned with great difficulty from a fort in New Mexico, and 1,500 more soldiers joined the foray. Brigham Young and his polygamous followers were forced to submit, and the federal troops marched into Salt Lake City without bloodshed on June 26, 1858.

A Bungling Buchanan?

Buchanan has gone down in history—way down—as a timorous and vacillating President who permitted the South to secede and who consequently was a spineless, do-nothing incompetent. We have already seen repeatedly that he was a strict constitutionalist who moved only when he felt confident that he had the authority and the means to act effectively. He declared flatly that the slave states had no right to secede, although seven of them did so between the election of Lincoln in November 1860 and the exit of Buchanan in March 1861.

This lame-duck President also stated bluntly that he had no constitutional authority to invade the soil of the wayward Southern sisters and bring them back forcibly. More than that, he did not have a sufficiently large army to do the job. Until the guns of April began to boom in 1861, there was still some faint hope that the seceded states might be coaxed back into the Union. And how does a President prevent a civil war by sending troops into the South and thus starting one?

Much of the downgrading of Buchanan has come from Northern historians, many of whom shared the concern of their section for human rights in the South. In his fourth and last annual message to Congress, nearly three weeks before ringleader South Carolina seceded, Buchanan stated a blunt but disagreeable truth: "The long-continued and intemperate interference of the Northern people with the question of slavery in the Southern States has at length produced its natural effects." All the slave states ever asked for was "to be let alone," and here Buchanan anticipated the very words of President Jefferson Davis of the forthcoming Confederacy. Buchanan added that unless the Northern states repealed their "unconstitutional and obnoxious" laws to thwart the Fugitive Slave Act, "it is impossible for any human power to save the Union."

Buchanan believed that the states had no legal right to secede, but they did have the moral right, as Lincoln later conceded, to resort to "revolutionary resistance." Secession, Buchanan concluded, was "neither more nor less than revolution." "The Union," he added, "rests upon public opinion, and can never be cemented by the blood of its citizens shed in civil war." Accordingly, he recommended the passage of a new amendment to the Constitution guaranteeing to the slave owner the rights to his property at home, in the territories, or in flight. A proposed slave-protection amendment passed Congress in March 1861 but was never acted on by the requisite number of states, because the next month the Civil War erupted with full force. Ironically, the Thirteenth Amendment to *protect* slavery became the Thirteenth Amendment (1865) to *abolish* slavery.

During the secession crisis Buchanan labored earnestly for a peaceful compromise, as did President-elect Lincoln. In fact, their policies were essentially the same. Buchanan in one instance was even more aggressive than Lincoln, because he sent the *Star of the West* to Fort Sumter with reinforcements consisting of some two hundred troops. This vessel, fired on by Confederate batteries, was forced to return. This incident could well have been regarded as triggering the first shots of the Civil War. Yet President Lincoln did not go as far as Buchanan when he ventured to send vessels merely to *provision*, not reinforce, Fort Sumter. The Confederates opened fire—and the four-year bloodbath began.

On the whole, Buchanan was one of the more aggressive, even militant of the Presidents, that is, when he could move within the framework of the Constitution and with fair prospects

Buchanan hard pressed between Southern threats and Northern exhortations to uphold the Constitution. Harper's Weekly, *1861.*

of success. As Chief Executive, Lincoln finally rejected the compromise route with the South and overrode the Constitution. Historians hail him as a great President, although his policies led to the explosion of the Civil War. Buchanan favored concession, compromise, and the Constitution, and managed to keep eight of the fifteen slave states in the Union. Yet historians write him off as a fumbling, bumbling failure.

CHAPTER 16

ABRAHAM LINCOLN: THE GREAT EMANCIPATOR

In stating a single condition of peace I mean simply to say that the war will cease on the part of the Government whenever it shall have ceased on the part of those who began it.

Abraham Lincoln,
December 6, 1864

The Emergence of Lincoln

"Old Abe" Lincoln, the man of many sorrows, was also a man of many contradictions. All told, he attended a grade school for about one year, yet he became a master of English prose. He gained fame as a teller of droll stories, yet he plunged into repeated and bottomless spells of melancholy. He condemned Polk's provocation of the war with Mexico, yet he took steps that the South Carolinians used as an excuse for firing on Fort Sumter and thus bringing on a shooting war. He was known as a man of tender heart and deep compassion, yet he kept the Civil War grinding on for four long years when he had the power in his hands to order the troops home at any time, and thus bring the frightful conflict to an abrupt end.

The major part of the Civil War lasted from April 15, 1861 (after the firing on Fort Sumter) to April 9, 1865 (Lee's surrender), for a total of four years, minus six days. All but forty-eight of Lincoln's days as President were blighted by bloodshed—a conflict that proved to be the costliest in which the United States, as far as its own losses in manpower were concerned, has ever been involved. If nothing else, Lincoln was a war President, and to that extent he was bellicose, whether he wanted to be or not.

Yet there is a gulf between aggressive pugnacity and defensive bellicosity. Whether Lincoln planned it that way or not, he was wise enough to see that if shooting had to come the cause of Northern unity would be served best by having the South fire first. The South Carolinians fell into this trap, if indeed it was a trap, and bombarded Fort Sumter into submission without loss of life on either side.

Lincoln did not have to ask Congress for a declaration of war. To have done so would have been an admission on his part that the Confederacy was a separate nation and not a loose collection of eleven states temporarily in revolt. All that Lincoln did was to declare that an "insurrection" existed and to call for seventy-five thousand volunteers for three month's service to bring the uprising to an end. As has often been true of great wars, this one lasted much longer than the most optimistic "experts" predicted.

Lincoln hated slavery deeply but hated disunion more. He would not have fought solely to free the slaves, but, when attacked, he felt bound to honor his presidential oath and fight to preserve the Union. The fine fabric of the Founding Fathers must be kept intact under the Constitution if a united United States was not to degenerate into a Balkanized cockpit of squabbling and clashing political entities. If the nation should suffer such a fate, it could no longer be the torchbearer of liberty (for whites) and democracy. In this sense, Lincoln's bellicosity was defensively aggressive.

Abraham Lincoln was born in a log cabin on the Kentucky frontier in 1809. Eight years later his family moved to Indiana, and subsequently to Illinois. His schooling was of the scantiest, and his education was primarily self-acquired. As a young man he split rails for fences ("The Railsplitter") and, among other occupations, twice piloted a flatboat downriver to New Orleans. In his prime, the black-haired Illinoisan towered six feet four inches, thereby being the tallest, if not the greatest, of all the Presidents.

Renowned locally as an exceptionally powerful wrestler, Lincoln enlisted in the local Illinois militia to fight the Indians in the Black Hawk War of 1832. Elected captain of his company—to him a most satisfying honor—he was mustered out in July 1832, after eighty days of service, including two reenlistments. He participated in no heavy fighting and later commented jokingly on his "bloody encounters" with the mosquitoes. But he did help bury five men who had been killed and scalped by the Indians. At all events, he got a real taste of the discipline and other problems of military life, and this experience doubtless served him in good stead when he later became Commander-in-Chief of the armed forces of the United States. As President, he studied up on military strategy and became, in the judgment of one eminent scholar, a better general than any of his generals. But he often had bad luck in picking military leaders until he found General U. S. Grant.

In earlier sequence had come "Honest Abe's" candidacy (unsuccessful) for the Illinois House of Representatives, a postmastership at New Salem, service in the Illinois General Assembly, and a move to Springfield, where he was admitted to the bar. The climax of this phase of Lincoln's career came in 1847–1849, when he served as a Whig in the national House of Representatives. Correctly suspecting Polk, a Democrat, of having provoked the border clash with Mexico, Lincoln criticized the way in which the war had begun. He made something of a nuisance of himself in Congress be demanding to know the exact "spot" "on American soil" where American blood had been shed. Little did he realize that in 1861–1865 he would have to reckon with the noisy opponents of his own Civil War.

Until 1854, when Lincoln was forty-five years of age, he had done nothing to attract much national attention. In 1855 he was an unsuccessful candidate for a seat as Senator from Illinois, but the battle over the extension of slavery into Kansas seems to have lighted new fires in him. In 1856, when the newly formed Republican party met in Philadelphia, Lincoln was prominent enough to receive 110 votes for Vice-President. At the Republican state convention in Illinois (June 16, 1858) he startled his audience (and later the nation) by his famous "house divided speech." He declared, "A house divided against itself cannot stand," quoting the book of Mark in the New Testament. He added: "I believe this government cannot endure permanently half slave and half free. . . . It will become all one thing or the other." The antislavery people cheered; the slaveholders jeered.

Growing in confidence, the lanky Lincoln challenged the "Little Giant," Senator Stephen A. Douglas (five feet, two inches), to a series of debates preparatory to the voting in the state legislature for a United States Senator. Lincoln deplored the extension of slavery into the territories; Douglas favored leaving that decision up to the actual settlers. Lincoln made it clear that while he opposed slavery he did not favor "perfect equality" between the two races. "Old Abe" lost the race for the Senate seat, thanks in part to some inequitable apportionment, but he gained a nationwide audience as a result of the seven debates. His debate platforms were among the most important preliminary battlefields of the Civil War.

The Path to the White House

By the mid-1850s the old Whig party was in its death throes, and its place was being taken by the Republican party, which in 1856 selected as its standard bearer John C. Frémont, the dashing Western explorer. But this colorful leader was an antislaveryite, and the Southern hotheads loudly threatened to secede if he should be elected. Frémont ran a spirited free-soil campaign but suffered defeat, partly because many voters took seriously the Southern cries of secession.

By 1860, if not before, Lincoln was an ambitious professional politican, eager to grasp the presidential prize at the end of the Washington rainbow. He received the nomination at Chicago on the third ballot, after his managers had purchased the support of rivals with promises of Cabinet posts. As in 1856, the proslaveryites served notice that the South would secede if the "baboon" abolitionist "railsplitter" should triumph. Lincoln won, the South seceded, and the Civil War erupted. If Lincoln could have foreseen the heap of 600,000 corpses, North and South, that would accumulate as a result of his victory, he might have been willing to bow out of the race. But "Old Abe" evidently believed that the South was bluffing, and that a civil war, if it should come, would be something like the Mexican War, with some 1,700 American battle deaths.

At all events, Lincoln did little to reassure the South during the campaign, and especially during the anxious weeks after his election, when South Carolina and six of her sister states in the Lower South seceded. His attitude was that he had already made clear his reasonable position on slavery, and that issuing further statements would only cause the Southerners to misinterpret him, as they already had done. Because his election led directly to the Civil War, we can conclude, with the perception of hindsight, that he could not have lost much of anything by restating his reasonably tolerant position. He did this in his inaugural address, some four months after his election, a period during which the wholesale secession of seven states had occurred.

Various attempts were made to appease the South by compromise during the tense period before the election in November 1860 and Lincoln's inauguration in March 1861. The most promising of these schemes was the so-called Crittenden compromise being hammered out in the Senate. It contained a proposal by which the old Missouri compromise line of 36° 30′ would be extended westward to the border of free-state California. North of that line, including the Kansas and Utah territories, slavery would be prohibited, thus virtually ensuring that states ultimately admitted from this area would be free soil. South of that line slavery would be protected during territorial status. The hope was thus inspired in the South that the settlers under "popular sovereignty" would make these territories into slave states, even though much of the arid terrain was such as to be inhospitable to crops that could profitably exploit labor under the lash.

The risk that the proposed Crittenden compromise might lead to more slave soil troubled Lincoln deeply. He had run on a platform that rejected the extension of slavery, yet the revived compromise line might open the door to more slave territory. Indeed, at some time in the future the South might manage to acquire all or parts of Mexico and Cuba. So on December 11, 1860, Lincoln wrote to a key member of Congress regarding the proposed Crittenden compromise, "Entertain no proposition for a compromise in regard to the extension of slavery." Thanks in large part to Lincoln's opposition, all attempts at reconciliation failed before the new President was formally inaugurated.

Yet there is scant reason to believe that an affirmative nod from Lincoln would have brought the seven seceding states hurrying back into the Union. As he wrote on December 17, 1860, "The tug has to come, and better now than later." He could have been right, but he evidently overlooked Edmund Burke's dictum that "all government" was "founded on compromise and barter." Compromise had made possible the drafting of the Constitution in 1787 and then had secured its ratification; compromise had held the contentious states together in 1820 and 1850. When it broke down, the Union broke up.

The Road to Fort Sumter

Despite his negative views on compromise with slavery, the new President was notably conciliatory, though firm, in his memorable inaugural address, March 4, 1861. He attempted to reassure the South by saying flatly, "I have no purpose, directly or indirectly, to interfere with the institution of slavery in the states where it exists. I believe I have no lawful right to do so, and I have no inclination to do so." As for returning fugitive slaves to their rightful owners, the Constitution stipulated that this should be done, and Congress was free to devise laws to implement this provision.

Lincoln went on to argue at length that the Union was indissoluble and that individual states had no right to secede. He would therefore abide by his inaugural oath to support the Constitution and to ensure that "the laws of the Union be faithfully executed in all the states." He continued: "I trust this will not be regarded as a menace, but only as the declared purpose of the Union that it *will* constitutionally defend and maintain itself." There did not have to be "bloodshed or violence, and there shall be none unless it be forced upon the national authority."

Sounding much like the outgoing President Buchanan, Lincoln further stated that the country "belongs to the people" and that they "can exercise their *constitutional* right of amending it [the government] or their revolutionary right to dismember or overthrow it." At this point he put himself squarely on record as favoring the proposed Thirteenth Amendment, which bound the Washington government never to "interfere with the domestic institutions of the States," including "persons held to service [slaves]." Because such a proviso was already written into the Constitution, he had no objection to its being made "express and irrevocable."

In concluding his inaugural address, Lincoln counseled against "precipitate action." "In *your* hands, my dissatisfied fellow-countrymen, and not in *mine*, is the momentous issue of civil war. The Government will not assail *you*. You can have no conflict without being yourselves the aggressors. *You* have no oath registered in heaven to destroy the Government, while *I* shall have the most solemn one to 'preserve, protect, and defend it.'"

By this time the fire-eating Southerners were so passionately aroused that they neither heard nor heeded Lincoln's soothing phrases. The seven states that had seceded were seizing federal arsenals, forts, and other government property, thereby literally making war on the Washington government—a fact seldom stressed in connection with Lincoln's so-called aggression. Of the remaining federal forts, the most conspicuous was Fort Sumter, which commanded Charleston, the most important Atlantic seaport of the South. President Buchanan had already undertaken to reinforce this imperiled outpost with two hundred troops, but the transporting *Star of the West* had been driven off with cannon fire. In this instance each side could reasonably charge the other with being the aggressor, although the federal government could claim the legal right to provision its own fort.

Major Robert Anderson, commanding the Union garrison at Fort Sumter, was about to be starved out in April 1861. Lincoln then decided upon a mild act of counter-aggression. He served notice that he was sending a ship containing provisions, but not reinforcements, to the endangered fort. He announced in advance that this was what he proposed to do so that the Confederates would know that he contemplated no aggressive act of war. But before the relief ship arrived, the Confederates opened fire on Fort Sumter and after a prolonged bombardment, which surprisingly took no lives, forced the dazed, hungry, and exhausted Yankee garrison to surrender. From various vantage points the Charlestonians of both sexes turned out to watch the spectacle and cheer on the heroic Southern cannoneers. There were undoubtedly some Carolinians present who had feared that the "cowardly Yankees" would never fight, no matter what the provocation, and that the South would be robbed of its glorious war for independence. Little could they foresee the bloodstained future. Little did they believe that one of their own sons, born in slave state Kentucky, would be so faithful to his inaugural oath as to fight this conflict through to the bitterness of Lee's surrender at Appomattox, four years later.

Lincoln responded promptly to the Confederate bombardment by officially proclaiming that an "insurrection" existed and by calling for seventy-five thousand troops for three months' service to put it down. Hence this bloody conflict was an undeclared war never officially recognized by a resolution of Congress. To the end Lincoln maintained that he was only suppressing an internal insurrection, not fighting a war with a bona fide foreign nation.

Brother Battles Brother

In trying to determine whether Lincoln or the Confederacy was the aggressor at the time of the bombardment of Fort Sumter, historians often ignore or understress several important points. The South looked upon the election of Lincoln, by a minority popular vote of a little less than 40 percent, as an act of aggression by the North against the South. Ironically, a vote for Lincoln could not be legally cast for the Union-splitting "Railsplitter" in the Lower South. His name was not even allowed on the ballot.

Seven Southern states speedily reacted to Lincoln's victory by seceding. In all or almost all of them, state troops had already made bloodless war on the United States government by seizing federal forts, barracks, and arsenals stocked with usable weapons. Louisiana appropriated the arsenal and barracks at Baton Rouge, as well as the United States mint and customs house at New Orleans. In all cases the federal custodians had surrendered without putting up a hopeless fight in the teeth of overpowering force. The revolutionaries ("rebels" in the North) were determined to preserve their way of life, meaning slavery, free from abolitionist nagging, condemnation, and illegal involvement in the freeing of runaway slaves.

Early in the present century economic determinists advanced the thesis that slavery was not the "cause" of the Civil War at all. The real root, they argued, was economic enslavement of the agrarian South by the tariffs and other monopolistic practices of Northern capitalism.

This thesis had delusive appeal to neo-Marxists, but it overlooked several crucial facts. The "servitude" of the South to the North was actually providing prosperity to the producers of Southern raw materials (especially cotton) and to the manufacturers of the Northeast. The states of the Northwest "suffered" gladly under the same kind of profitable "oppression" by the East but did not seriously raise the issue of secession before the Civil War began.

At this point, one should ask a simple but crucial question: Would Civil War have come in 1861 if there had been no institution of slavery? The answer has to be an emphatic no. Lincoln agonized for years over this problem, and as President he must be recognized as something of an authority on it. In 1862 he declared, "I admit that slavery is at the root of the rebellion" and in 1865 he said, "All know that slavery was somehow the cause of the war." In his second annual message to Congress, December 1862, he was more emphatic: "Without slavery the rebellion could never have existed; without slavery it could not continue."

The primary focus of this commentary is on the bellicosity of the President in dealing with foreign nations, not with internal or domestic disturbances. Lincoln was involved in a bloody war, not with a foreign nation but with wayward insurrectionists. To the bitter end he insisted that the Southerners were a large collection of rebels temporarily in insurrection, and that they were to be subdued and brought back into the fold they had never technically left. This harsh aspect of Lincoln's policy was pursued after the war in the reconstruction of the South.

As events turned out, the Confederacy established what most disinterested observers would describe as an independent nation and government. They had a Constitution, a Congress, a President, a Cabinet, a capital city, powerful armies, a small navy, paper money, and other attributes of sovereignty. But the United States government—that is, Lincoln—never recognized the Confederacy as an independent entity, nor did any foreign nation. But Great Britain, France, and other countries did recognize the belligerent status of the Confederacy, partly because they wanted to alert their nationals to the existence of a formal but leaky blockade of Southern ports by the hastily improvised Union navy.

Various deterrents prompted caution in European capitals. If the British, whose thundering navy was most to be feared, should stick their noses too far into a domestic American quarrel, the Yankees would doubtless retaliate. They could unleash privateers against lush British shipping, while seizing Canada as recompense for the loss of the South. In the general uproar, the Confederacy might well have achieved an independence that would gladly be recognized by Great Britain. So the policy of Lincoln's administration was one of restraint, not bumptiousness or belligerence, in dealing with the powerful European nations. One conflict at a time is usually sound policy.

Lincoln prosecuted the war against the South with unrelenting severity, despite the effusion of blood, the lost battles, and the initially inept generals. The "Great Emancipator's" Emancipation Proclamation of January 1, 1863, "freed" only the untouchable slaves in the unconquered South. This decree was designed primarily to weaken Southern resistance, quiet the abolitionists at home, and build up sympathy and hence support for nonintervention among the European powers abroad. Emancipation was initially a policy of both expediency and humanity.

Highlighting Lincoln's policy of one foe at a time was an early encounter with his Secretary of State, William H. Seward, formerly his chief rival for the presidential nomination at Chicago. At the outset, Seward had a low opinion of Lincoln's leadership; he felt that he alone must seize the helm before the ship of state drifted even more dangerously toward the reefs of disaster. In common with many otherwise sensible Americans, the pugnacious Secretary believed that a rousing war against some foreign nation, say Britain, would bring the Southern states flocking back into the Union to fight the ancient foe once more under the glorious Stars and Stripes. He evidently did not reckon with the more probable prospect that the men of Dixie would let the "damn Yankees" stew in their own juice.

Under date of April 1, 1861 (appropriately All Fools Day), Secretary Seward presented to Lincoln an incredible memorandum entitled "Some Thoughts for the President's Consideration." Seward would "seek explanations from Great Britain and Russia" and would "demand explanations from Spain and France, categorically, at once." (Spain had been invited back into Santo Domingo, and France and Britain were reported to be preparing to collect debts from perpetually bankrupt Mexico.) Then, wrote the arrogant Secretary, "if satisfactory explanations are not received from Spain and France, would convene Congress and declare war against them." Seward concluded by writing that he was quite willing to take over these awesome responsibilities himself. Lincoln, who must have been astounded by such impudent irrationality, tactfully refused to adopt Seward's harebrained suggestions and magnanimously forgave him for this lapse from sanity. Taught a lesson, the chastened Secretary settled down and on the whole discharged his duties as Secretary of State with exceptional skill and success.

Britain at the Brink

The long scroll of human folly known as history shows that many, if not most, successful rebellions have been those that have attracted substantial outside aid, as the thirteen seceding colonies succeeded in doing when they allied themselves with France in 1778. The unwritten epitaph on the tombstone of the defunct Confederacy is that the Southerners desperately sought foreign intervention, failed to get it, and lost.

Great Britain was the last best hope of the Confederacy, for the textile mills of England were dangerously dependent for their fiber on the whitened cotton fields of the South. When Southerners flaunted the slogan, "Cotton is King," they believed that in the event of a North-South war the powerful British navy would simply have to break the Yankee blockade to get out the bales of fiber. Southern independence would surely be snatched from the fiery furnace of the ensuing fratricidal conflict.

If the objective of the Southerners was to involve Great Britain in the Civil War, the policy of the Lincoln administration was to handle the ancient foe with kid gloves rather than with the mailed fist. Pugnacity could produce sheer disaster, so negotiations with the British were generally conducted with delicacy and generally with success—that is, keeping Britain out of the war. Diplomacy was mostly handled by Secretary of State Seward in Washington and by Minister Charles Francis Adams in London. In this area President Lincoln had little desire or reason to exhibit bellicosity; he had his hands more than full with trying to whip the wayward states back into line.

In November 1861, about seven months after the bombardment of Fort Sumter, the *Trent* affair brought the United States and Britain to the brink of war. This British merchant ship was carrying to neutral England from neutral Cuba two of the South's best-known statesmen, who were instructed to enlist the support of the leading European powers. In waters near Cuba the *Trent* encountered a Yankee warship commanded by Captain Charles Wilkes. Though unauthorized to do so, he fired two shots across the bow of the merchantman, forcibly removed the two Confederate agents, and permitted the British vessel to continue on to England.

Captain Wilkes, though a headstrong officer, was immediately hailed as a conquering hero in the North. It was great fun to give the haughty British a dose of their pre-1812 medicine and drag men off the decks of their ships for a change. But the British were outraged. Eleven thousand crack troops embarked for Canada, pointedly to the tune of a volunteer band playing, "I Wish I Was in Dixie." If Lincoln's all-consuming purpose was to preserve the Union, he should have reacted instantly against the unauthorized seizure by Captain Wilkes. As it was, he supposed that the two prisoners might yet "prove to be white elephants." A prolonged debate took place in the Cabinet, with the President present and reluctantly going along with the majority. The end result was a painful decision, bound to be politically and patriotically unpopular, to release the two unhappy prisoners.

The case would have been different if the *Trent* had been carrying contraband of war, such as gunpowder, through the Yankee blockade *to* the belligerent Confederacy. Then Captain Wilkes would have been justified, under international law, in bringing the vessel to a United States prize court for adjudication of her status. But the *Trent* appears not to have been carrying contraband, certainly not to the Confederacy, although the two commissioners were alleged to be "personal contraband." In any event, Secretary of State Seward, in a cleverly worded diplomatic note, partially placated Northern opinion by commending the British in effect for finally having got around to recognizing principles for which America had fought Great Britain fruitlessly in the War of 1812.

The *Trent* affair triggered the most serious crisis with Great Britain, primarily because the United States was the offending party, and the Lincoln government appeared to be excessively militant. By contrast, other serious difficulties with Britain cast the British in the role of aggressors, thus leaving the heated remonstrances primarily to Secretary Seward and Minister Adams.

In July 1862 the most famous of the Confederate commerce destroyers built in Great Britain, the *Alabama*, put to sea in the teeth of Yankee protests. British law forbade warships to be built in Great Britain for belligerent nations, but the loophole was to construct the vessel without cannon. In this case the *Alabama* sailed unarmed to the Portuguese Azores, where she received her armament and crew from two other vessels that arrived separately from England. Vigorous and persistent American protests against such bare-faced deception finally led to the payment by Britain of a heavy indemnity to the United States in the Geneva arbitral award of 1872—ten years after the "pirate" *Alabama* had escaped British jurisdiction.

Although the *Alabama* and her sister "pirates" riddled Yankee merchant shipping, the two British-built Laird Rams, ironclads with powerful wrought-iron rams or "piercers," were a greater menace. They threatened to destroy the entire wooden-ship Yankee blockade of Southern ports, and thus incite the North to invade Canada in retaliation. These formidable rams were being constructed in British yards, and in the teeth of the strongest protests from Minister Adams. To this degree he was expressing the defensive pugnacity of the Lincoln government. As a matter of expediency rather than legality, the London government finally detained the Laird Rams and then purchased them for Her Majesty's navy at a figure in excess of the contract price. All parties concerned were happier, except the Confederates.

British Canada also aroused the wrath of the Lincoln administration during the Civil War, even though some forty thousand Canadians, for one reason or another, enlisted in Northern armies. The main bone of contention was the presence in Canada of Confederate secret agents, who were doing all they could to undercut the North and promote the interests of the Confederacy. The Canadian officials did what they could to thwart these plots, but oviously they could not be completely successful. (A reverse parallel presents itself in American unneutral help on the northern border to the Canadian insurrectionists of 1837–1838.)

The most sensational incident was the raid on St. Albans, Vermont, some fifteen miles south of the Canadian border, in October 1864. A party of about twenty-five Southern soldiers, armed but not in uniform, were led by a lieutenant in the Confederate army. They wounded two citizens, set fire to part of the town, scooped up all the money in the local banks ($200,000), and then fled to their secret base in Canada.

No proof ever turned up that the Canadian authorities had guilty foreknowledge of this raid. They jailed the raiders, recov-

"Abe Lincoln's Last Card: or, Rouge-et-Noir." The black ace of spades is the Emancipation Proclamation. London Punch, *1862.*

ered much of the loot, and adopted various precautions to prevent another such hit-and-run raid. But Americans in the North were already alarmed and angry, partly because Confederate agents were known to be busy plotting to burn Yankee cities and wreck railroad trains. Secretary Seward, still relatively pugnacious, gave London the stipulated six months' notice of the termination of the Rush-Bagot agreement of 1819 for naval limitation on the Canadian-American border lakes. Fortunately for the cause of peace, tempers cooled and this notification was withdrawn in March 1865, the month before the Civil War ended.

The abortive abrogation of the Rush-Bagot agreement, at least from Lincoln's point of view, was not prompted solely by spite. Confederate agents had made an attempt to capture the *Michigan*, the only armed American ship on the Great Lakes, but were able to seize only two small boats, later lost. In reporting to Congress in his fourth annual message (December 6, 1864), Lincoln was at pains to say that he did not regard the Canadian "colonial authorities" as being "unjust or unfriendly toward the United States." He had every reason to expect that they would take the necessary precautions, as they did to the satisfaction of the President.

Curiously, American naval power, in concert with that of Britain, was also involved in faraway Japan in 1863–1864, during some of the heaviest fighting of the American Civil War. Japan was suffering civil disturbances of her own, with the ruling Shogun meeting strong opposition from the feudal lords who opposed the westernization of the Island Empire. During these disorders the American legation in Yedo was burned, and American ships were fired upon by the dissidents.

Especially obnoxious was the feudal lord at the strategic Straits of Shimonoseki, where he began to fire upon "barbarian" (foreign) ships. Because the ruling Shogun was not powerful enough to dislodge him, the interested powers (Britain, France, Holland) organized a fleet of sixteen warships to administer a punitive bombardment. American naval power was not then readily available so far from home, so Secretary Seward chartered a small armed ship to show the flag. The obstreperous feudal lord was severely handled, and the Japanese government agreed to pay the Western nations an indemnity of $3 million. This episode marks another step in America's emergence as a Far Eastern power. Charitably, the Washington government later returned its share of the indemnity.

Rather surprisingly, President Lincoln was fully aware of the difficulties that Americans were having with Japan. He referred to these troubles in his annual message to Congress (December 1863), and in 1864 he issued orders that two warships being built in American yards for the Japanese government be held up pending more favorable developments.

The Road to Appomattox

In the closing months of the Civil War, with the corpses and amputated limbs still mounting like cordwood, there was much talk of working out a negotiated peace with the South. In the North, Copperheads and Peace Democrats generally favored negotiation, and this was a burning issue in the election of 1864, when Lincoln defeated the Democratic presidential candidate, General George B. McClellan, who polled 44.8 percent of the popular vote to Lincoln's 55.1 percent. The President actually met with three Confederate Commissioners at Hampton Roads, Virginia, early in February 1865, but he believed that nothing would come of the conference—and nothing did.

The crux of the problem was this: Lincoln was fighting to preserve the Union; the South was fighting to establish its own nationhood. If Lincoln had recognized the Confederate States of America, he would have lost the war, and the enormous effusion of blood would have been all in vain. If the conflict had been a draw, and both sides had stopped fighting, the South would have won. If there had been an armistice of several months, the North might not have had the desire to start up the meat grinder again, and the South would have triumphed. So Lincoln could not and would not accept anything short of "unconditional surrender," a phrase that General Grant had made famous at Fort Donelson in 1862.

If the Confederates wanted peace so much, Lincoln had a surefire formula for lots of it. As he declared in his fourth annual message in December 1864, "They [the Confederates] can at any moment have peace simply by laying down their arms and submitting to the national authority under the Constitution." This is what finally happened at Appomattox. As Lincoln noted in his second inaugural address in March 1865: "Both parties deprecated war, but one of them would make war rather than let the nation survive, and the other would accept war rather than let it perish, and the war came."

There probably would have been no fighting at all if either side could have seen how prolonged and horrible it would be, and how long the vanquished would have to live in the ashes of defeat. By the irony of fate, the kindly Lincoln, though not personally a pugnacious human being, felt obligated by his constitutional oath to fight this war, as he said in his second inaugural address, "until every drop of blood drawn with the lash shall be paid by another drawn with the sword."

This may have been the most brutal statement that soft-hearted "Father Abraham" ever made. He followed it immediately with perhaps his most sublime utterance, "With malice toward none, with charity for all, with firmness in the right as God gives us to see the right, let us strive on to finish the work we are in." Verily, there were at least two Lincolns: the official "Lincoln the Fiend," as he was branded in the South, and the unofficial old "Uncle Abe," as he was affectionately called among pro-Unionists in the North.

Often overlooked is the fact that gentle "Father Abraham" waged two civil wars: one in the South against the secessionists and one in the North against secessionist sympathizers. In order to prosecute the war against the South, he temporarily overrode parts of the Constitution that he was sworn to uphold. Congress was not in session when the shooting started, so Lincoln arbitrarily increased the size of the army, handed out money without Congressional authorization, and suspended the precious privilege of the writ of *habeas corpus*. Federal officials suspended certain pro-Southern newspapers and arrested their editors for obstructing the war. Other dissenters were arrested, jailed, or otherwise harassed. In truth, the tender-hearted Lincoln became one of the most warlike of presidents.

CHAPTER 17

ANDREW JOHNSON: THE TENNESSEE TAILOR

For myself, it has been and will be my constant aim to promote peace and amity with all foreign nations and powers....

President Andrew Johnson,
First Annual Message,
December 4, 1865

The Battler from Tennessee

Andrew Johnson was certainly one of the most contentious men ever to occupy the presidential chair. His entire life was a battle against somebody or something, whether ignorance, poverty, the rich Southern planters, the secessionists, political rivals, Congress, or those who did not interpret his beloved Constitution as he saw it. At his request, he was buried with a copy of that hallowed document as a pillow.

No President, not even Lincoln, ever rose from more inauspicious beginnings. Born to a poor family in North Carolina, he was orphaned at an early age. Thus handicapped, young Andrew appears never to have attended school for as much as one day. Bound as a youthful apprentice to a tailor, at one time he was advertised for as a runaway. He eventually taught himself to read, set up his own tailor shop, and was taught by his wife to write and spell. In short, Johnson was a self-made man and, like many of his kind, inclined to be inordinately proud of his maker.

Endowed with a strong voice and the gift of gab, Johnson early entered the political arena and delighted in battling from the stump—sometimes literally a tree stump, around which hecklers could gather and bait "Old Andy." The aroused speaker would fire back with blasts fully as strong as those he received. He was a fighter to the very end.

Climbing up the political ladder from alderman to mayor, then to Tennessee legislator, Johnson served in the United States House of Representatives from 1843 to 1853. From 1853 to 1855 he held office as Governor of Tennessee and from 1857 to 1862 sat in the United States Senate. A stubborn man to the end, he was the only Senator from the seceded South who refused to go along with his state. His revered Constitution did not sanction secession, and besides "Old Andy," as a once-poor white, hated the wealthy slaveholders, although having little feeling for their slaves. For such devotion to the Union, Johnson was named military governor of reconquered Tennessee with the rank of brigadier general of the volunteers. In this difficult capacity he acquitted himself creditably.

President Lincoln's prospects of reelection were not roseate in 1864, so the Republican managers devised two strategic maneuvers. They relabeled themselves the Union Party or the Union-Republican party, and they chose Johnson as their vice-presidential candidate to "balance the ticket." As a Democrat and a Southerner, presumably he would have some appeal to these antagonistic elements, both in the North and in the South, and thus pull "Old Abe" through to victory. No one could foresee that Lincoln would be shot only forty-two days after his second inauguration, thus leaving almost four full years to Johnson, the forgotten afterthought on the ticket.

As President, Andrew Johnson looked like the fighter he was. Stocky of build, five feet, ten inches tall, with unruly hair, heavy brows, and a grim mouth, he was afflicted with a violent temper. Still a Southerner at heart and also an ardent Unionist, he was prepared to deal leniently with the ex-rebels and readmit the "wayward sisters" to the Union as soon as feasible. At the same time, he was in no particular hurry to confer on the ex-slaves the same civil rights, including the right to vote, that the whites had formerly enjoyed.

The strong Republican majority in Congress, viewing the problem from a Northern exposure, was in no mood to return the seceded Democrats to their prewar voting power. For motives that were both political and humanitarian, the Republicans, especially the Radicals, favored conferring the vote and other civil rights on the ex-slaves. Time and again Republican-sponsored legislation was passed routinely over Johnson's futile veto.

Johnson argued that he was only upholding the Constitution that he revered, but the Republican Congress became weary of his obstruction. They decided to throw him overboard by the impeachment process. The House of Representatives voted to impeach Johnson by a wide margin, and the Senate formally tried him "for high crimes and misdemeanors." He was clearly guilty of intemperate speeches, ill temper, and bad judgment, but the official charges were transparently flimsy. Even so, he escaped removal by the narrow margin of one vote in the Senate.

Andrew Johnson as a parrot. Harper's Weekly.

Johnson's troubles would have been worse if he had not enjoyed the support of Lincoln's Secretary of State, William H. Seward. The long-suffering Secretary had calmed down after his reckless "Thoughts" for President Lincoln's consideration, and he had daringly skated over the thin ice of British-American relations, among others, with commendable skill. Seward stood loyally by Johnson during the latter's nearly four troubled years, during which he helped to write some veto messages and probably some annual messages as well.

It appears that the harassed Johnson gave his experienced Secretary of State a relatively free rein in dealing with the problems in foreign affairs that slopped over from the Civil War or that popped up in unexpected places. But whoever deserves the credit or discredit for what was done or not done, the ultimate responsibility was Johnson's and must be chalked up to his credit or discredit.

Maximilian in Mexico

Behind the billowing smoke screen of the Civil War, two European powers undertook, with complete lack of success, to challenge the Monroe Doctrine. The first of these was Spain, which had been expelled from revolution-ridden Santo Domingo but which, oddly enough, was now invited back by the new regime. In May 1861, the month after Fort Sumter's bombardment, the wayward colony was reincorporated into the Spanish Empire.

Secretary Seward did his duty when he dispatched a note of protest to the Spanish Minister in Washington challenging Spain's right to embrace anew this former outpost. The Spanish Foreign Office did not bother to reply. The United States Minister in Madrid next remonstrated by stating that the Monroe Doctrine was being violated, even though Monroe had said nothing about disillusioned colonials coming back voluntarily into the fold. Seward finally ceased these verbal blasts, no doubt realizing anew that mere words from a nation convulsed by civil war were not going to scare anybody unduly.

The disillusioned Dominicans speedily learned that tyrannical Spain was still oppressive, and they rose again in revolt. Desperate resistance, combined with yellow fever and other diseases, triumphed where Seward's paper protests and the dead hand of

President Monroe had proved impotent. On May 1, 1865, twenty-one days after Lee's surrender, the Spanish Cortes renounced all claim to Santo Domingo, and the Johnson administration was no longer obligated to uphold the Monroe Doctrine in this quarter.

Far more formidable was the challenge to the Monroe Doctrine by Napoleon III of France. This imperial schemer had in mind taking advantage of the internal upheaval in the United States to prop up on the imperial throne of Mexico his Austrian puppet, the Emperor Maximilian. Napoleon III would pull the strings and thus gain glory by resurrecting the colonial empire in America that Napoleon I had so ingloriously tossed away in the Louisiana Purchase. There were actually occasions when Napoleon III would have been willing to intervene in the American Civil War but was held back by a reluctant Britain. Finally, Napoleon decided to go it alone in Mexico.

Supported by the French troops of Napoleon III, the reactionary regime of Maximilian was imposed on the Mexican people, as aroused patriots stepped up their guerrilla warfare. This imposition of monarchy was the most flagrant violation of the Monroe Doctrine thus far in American experience. Yet Secretary Seward was keenly aware that his hands were tied by the all-consuming Civil War. He also realized that if he pushed France too hard he might end by forcing her into the arms of the Confederates. Hence he could do little more than reassert the nation's traditional antipathy to foreign encroachments on the Americas, reserve for the future the right to act, and thus prevent the Monroe Doctrine from expiring by default.

A headstrong Congress got somewhat out of hand when, in April 1864, the House of Representatives passed a resolution expressing displeasure over the erection of a new monarchical government in Mexico on the ruins of a republican government under the auspices of an intervening foreign power. The American Minister in Paris smoothed ruffled French feathers by saying that one legislative branch could not and did not speak for the administration.

As the Civil War thundered to a climactic close, Napoleon III could perceive that he definitely had bet on the wrong horse in backing Maximilian. The triumphant North had 900,000 men under arms, some not far from the Texas border and many of them eager to join with Confederate veterans in running the fancy French "frogs" out of Mexico. But Seward realized that the

French were a proud people, and his policy was to push Napoleon gently with one hand while courteously showing him the door with the other.

Seward next began to turn on the heat by degrees. Not until well into 1865 did he permit anything approaching a threat to creep into his communications with Paris. In September 1865 he injected a definite note of veiled hostility. On February 12, 1866, he declared with diplomatic firmness that the United States would be "gratified" to receive "definitive information" as to the time when French military activity would "cease in Mexico." On April 5, 1866, the Paris government published its decision to pull out French troops over a period of nineteen months.

A new complication arose when word reached America that four thousand Austrian volunteers might sail for Mexico to bolster Maximilian, a fellow Austrian. Not surprisingly, Seward reacted much more vigorously against weak Austria than against strong France. He instructed the American Minister in Vienna to lodge a protest and then demand his passports if the Austrian government did not give satisfactory assurances. Faced with such pressures, Austria knuckled under and Maximilian was left in the lurch. In Mexico, the tragic finale came in June 1867, when the synthetic new Emperor fell before a Mexican firing squad.

So it was that Seward, speaking for President Johnson, pumped new life into the Monroe Doctrine. Napoleon III had taken French leave of his puppet for various reasons, including the uncertain situation at home and in Europe. But the existence of America's big stick behind the door obviously entered into his calculations.

British-Canadian Controversies

Relations between the United States and Canada were seriously strained during and after the Civil War. We have already noted the raid in 1864 of Confederate soldiers into St. Albans, Vermont, from a secret base on Canadian soil. More dangerous than this hit-and-run foray was the open sympathy of Britain for the Confederate cause, notably in permitting the construction in British shipyards of predatory commerce destroyers, particularly the *Alabama*. If Britain and America should go to war over this explosive issue the ancient Yankee cry "On to Canada" would surely be raised anew.

When the Civil War ended, many Union veterans, especially Irishmen, felt the urge to point their bayonets northward toward Canada and there seek revenge, redress, and perhaps annexation. Most conspicuous was the Irish Fenian organization, dedicated to the freeing of Ireland by way of Canada. The most noteworthy of the several northward thrusts by these Irishmen came in the spring of 1866. About a thousand Fenians crossed the Niagara River and then engaged in the somewhat farcical "Battle of Limestone Ridge." There were slight losses on both sides as the Fenians recrossed the river to American soil, leaving behind a few prisoners in Canadian clutches. Some of the returnees and others were arrested by the federal authorities for violating the neutrality laws of the United States.

President Johnson and Secretary Seward had every reason to sympathize privately with the Irish Fenians. Great Britain had not been unduly friendly during the American Civil War, and the large Irish-American vote was both courted and feared by aspiring politicians. But Johnson and Seward realized that if the United States expected Great Britain to make amends for having behaved unneutrally in the recent war, the Washington government would have to honor its own neutrality laws in dealing with Canada. On June 6, 1866, Johnson issued a plain-speaking proclamation, calling upon all federal officials to maintain the "public peace" and uphold the "national honor" in conformity with their "lawful authority." Many of them did so despite widespread sympathy for the Irish Fenians.

In his annual message of December 1866, Johnson referred to his proclamation and his subsequent attempts to cool down the Fenians. He noted that some of the alleged invaders had been brought to trial in Canada "as for a capital offense" and that the Washington government had employed counsel to defend the prisoners. Johnson had also discontinued all prosecutions directed against the defeated invaders. He hoped that the Canadian authorities would regard the recent abortive invasions as of a political nature, for he believed that "severity of civil punishment for misguided persons who have engaged in revolutionary attempts which have disastrously failed is unsound and unwise." President Johnson may not have been thinking primarily of the Irish vote, for he was then dealing with the Southern secessionists with much more clemency than is usual at the end of a bitter civil conflict that has failed. At all events, the Canadians captured some eighty Fenians, a number of whom were condemned to death, only to have their sentences commuted in the face of Yankee protests.

Oddly enough, a unified Canada was in large part the by-product of Yankee greed and Irish intrusion. The sheer necessity of unifying the Canadians against a powerful and vengeful neighbor had much to do with creating a legislative rampart for the protection of Canada. The British Parliament in London was prodded into passing the British North America Act, effective July 1, 1867, under which the Dominion of Canada was born.

But the unification of Canada was not what the Yankees desired, for disunity was the mother of annexation. In Washington an aroused House of Representatives had vented its displeasure by passing a resolution on March 27, 1867, deploring the establishment of the Dominion of Canada as a step toward monarchy and a violation of American principles. This, of course, clearly meant the Monroe Doctrine. The truth is that the British Parliament purposely used the word "Dominion" instead of "Kingdom" lest they wave a red flag in the face of the Yankee bull.

Closely associated with the Fenian incursions, and to some extent prompting them, was the rankling memory of the British role in building the Confederate commerce destroyers. This vexatious issue was to continue to be a running sore until well into the next administration. In his annual message of December 1867 President Johnson alluded to it with considerable tact. He reported that he had felt it to be his duty "to decline the proposition of arbitration made by Her Majesty's Government, because it has hitherto been accompanied by reservations and limitations incompatible with the rights, interest, and honor of our country." But he did not believe "that Great Britain will persist in her refusal to satisfy these just and reasonable claims, which involve the sacred principle of nonintervention—a principle henceforth not more important to the United States than to all other commercial nations."

Despite this setback for arbitration, negotiations were continued in London under Reverdy Johnson, an inept, loquacious, and convivial Marylander. To Americans, he went too far when he courteously shook the hand of John Laird, the Scottish-born and unrepentant builder of the Confederate "pirate" *Alabama*. The ensuing negotiations resulted in the Johnson-Clarendon Convention, signed in January 1869, which provided for arbitration of claims on both sides on a basis of equality. The British expressed no regret and made no reference to "indirect damages" caused to Yankee commerce by the British-built destroyers. For its part, the United States Senate did not appreciate the hasty efforts of the unpopular Johnson administration to patch up the controversy without more regard for American interests, and it delayed action until General Grant became Chief Executive. But at least President Johnson had shown a conciliatory spirit toward Britain, and this he had not done in dealing with those Senators who had sought to reconstruct the ex-Confederate states with iron-toothed measures.

The Seward–Johnson Outward Thrusts

Secretary Seward's purchase of Alaska from Russia in 1867 for the bargain price of $7.2 million still looms as the largest, coldest, and most enduring achievement of the troubled Johnson administration. Actually, Seward deserves the lion's share of the credit, for he was an expansionist of hemispheric voracity.

The truth is that Russia, so it seems, unloaded an immense frozen asset on the gullible Yankees. The huge area had become a liability, for it cost more money to administer and defend than was returned by this "furred-out" domain. The Russians also realized that they were overextended territorially and that in a probable future war with Britain they would lose Alaska promptly to the overpowering naval force of their archenemy. Why not dump this icebound land on the stupid Yankees, who would then protect Alaska against British greed?

Few Americans knew anything about Alaska or felt any need for it, but in the end Seward was able to persuade the Senate that the annexation treaty was worth a gamble and that someday it would pay off, as it has done magnificently. Additionally, President Johnson later informed Congress (December 3, 1867) that the Civil War had demonstrated a need for a naval base in the North Pacific and that Alaska seemed to be the answer.

Yankee naval operations in the recent war against blockade runners and Confederate commerce destroyers had also revealed the need for island naval bases in the Caribbean. The only expansionist scheme of Seward's in this area worthy of mention was the treaty that he negotiated in October 1867 for two of the Danish West Indies (Virgin Islands) for $7.5 million. Hardly was the ink dry when the prospective purchase was ravaged by an earthquake, a hurricane, and a tidal wave. Thus battered, the pact died quietly in the United States Senate, but a half-century later the United States, rightly fearing a submarine war with Germany, paid $25 million for these outposts.

The imperial arm of the United States was also extended to the tiny and uninhabited Midway Islands in 1867, when an American naval officer occupied them. But completely frustrated were Seward's acquisitive designs on Hawaii, Cuba, Puerto Rico, St. Bartholomew's Island (West Indies), Canada, Greenland, Iceland, and, if we may believe his enemies, a part of China. To his credit, Seward did negotiate in Washington the epochal Burlingame treaty of 1867, which expanded trade relations with China. Incidentally, in the summer of 1867, American naval forces had inflicted punishment on a Chinese coastal city for an assault on an American consul.

Turning from continental East Asia, the United States caused its protective arm to be felt in Japan, where grave disorders were occurring during the internal war over the abolition of the Shogunate and the restoration of the Mikado. Chiefly in the spring of 1868, U.S. naval forces intervened to protect American interests in about a half-dozen Japanese localities. President Johnson reported to Congress in his fourth annual message (December 1868) that the United States had "maintained strict neutrality among the belligerents" and had enjoyed the full cooperation of the five other treaty powers, including Britain and France. The long protective arm of the United States was thus felt anew in distant places.

Far to the south the Johnson administration found itself using naval power to uphold American interests and rights. In April 1868 United States forces were deployed once more on the Isthmus of Panama to protect treasure in transit during disturbances attendant upon the death of the president of Colombia. Yet this intervention was in conformity with the neutralization treaty of 1846 with Colombia (New Granada), and it was only one of seven such landings of troops prior to the Yankee-assisted Panama revolution of 1903.

In February 1868 American naval forces were utilized at Montevideo, the capital of Uruguay, to protect foreign residents and the custom house during a local insurrection. This was but one of a number of interventions in the Latin American republics during the nineteenth century, and a foretaste of the wholesale takeovers in the Caribbean that peaked in the Big Stick days of President "Teddy" Roosevelt.

In his annual message of December 1868 President Johnson referred at some length to an altercation that had arisen with Paraguay over the granting of political asylum. The American Minister there had reported that two United States citizens attached to his legation had been seized at his side, jailed, and then subjected to torture to extort confessions of wrongdoing. President Johnson further reported that a new Minister was being sent and that the commanding American admiral in this theater had been directed "to attend the new minister with a proper naval force and to sustain such just demands as the occasion may require, and to vindicate the rights of the United States citizens referred to and of any others who may be exposed to danger in the theater of war."

From 1865 to 1870 Paraguay was engaged in a desperate war with Argentina, Brazil, and Uruguay, during the course of which the luckless Paraguayans, incredible though it may seem, lost about half of their population. In this difficult situation President Johnson was unable to secure satisfaction from the Paraguayan dictator, but none can say that this tempestuous Tennessean was not willing to defend the rights of American citizens abroad to the extent that such protection was possible.

Although a pugnacious man in politics—certainly one of the most pugnacious—Johnson was generally cautious and conciliatory in dealing with foreign nations. With Seward at his side, the Tennessee tailor stayed out of all foreign wars, eased the French out of Mexico, strove to maintain American neutrality during the Fenian invasions of Canada, kept alive United States claims against Britain growing out of the Civil War, acquired gigantic Alaska by peaceful means, and deployed United States naval forces in East Asia and Latin America to protect American citizens during domestic turmoil.

CHAPTER 18

ULYSSES S. GRANT: THE HERO OF APPOMATTOX

In regard to foreign policy, I would deal with nations as equitable law requires individuals to deal with each other, and I would protect the law-abiding citizen . . . wherever his rights are jeopardized or the flag of our country floats.

President U. S. Grant,
Inaugural Address,
March 4, 1869

A Soldier as Commander-in-Chief

General Grant was the first of two West Pointers, Eisenhower being the other, to reach the White House. He was also one of the few professional military men ever to occupy the presidential chair. A number of his predecessors and successors were generals or lesser officers who had entered the service as volunteers, especially during the Civil War, and had risen to high though less exalted rank. One problem is to determine whether or not the reputed fighting instincts of the professional, at least in Grant's case, manifested themselves unduly in the conduct of diplomacy and other civilian affairs.

Grant was the offspring of a farming family in Ohio (the first President born in that state), and was brought up doing heavy farm work. It may even have stunted his growth. Slightly stooped and only five feet, eight inches tall, he did not present a distinguished soldiery bearing. He loved animals, especially horses, and he abhorred hunting and the taking of animal life, especially in bullfighting. He developed a strong distaste for rare beefsteak; it may have reminded him of the gory battles in which "Grant the Butcher" doggedly fought through to ultimate victory over General Lee.

Grant entered West Point in 1839 and four years later graduated with a standing somewhere near the middle of his class. He ranked above average in mathematics, and as a horseman he had no peer. In 1845 he found himself with General Taylor's army in Texas and the next year was near the Rio Grande when the Mexican forces opened hostilities. Never in sympathy with American provocations, he later wrote of the war "as one of the most unjust ever waged by a stronger against a weaker nation." But he served under General Taylor and later General Scott in Mexico with conspicuous valor.

Despite such spirited action, Grant still disliked life in the army, and his fortunes reached a low point when he was stationed at gloomy Humboldt Bay in northern California. Deprived of the company of wife and family, lonely, bored, and underpaid, he began to drink so heavily that he was forced to resign from the army.

After failing to prosper at farming, as a real estate agent, and in other enterprises, Grant was given a job as clerk in his father's leather store in Galena, Illinois, at $50 a month—hardly an American success story—hence the later nicknames "Galena Tanner" and the "Tanner President." When the Civil War erupted in 1861, he offered his services as a volunteer officer, received a commission, and finally emerged from obscurity as the most successful Northern general of the conflict. In July 1866 he was commissioned General of the Army by Congress,

After all the bickering between Congress and President Johnson, the country by 1868 was in a receptive mood for a war-hero president, and the Republicans in Chicago nominated the number one victor, hailed as "The Hero of Appomattox" and "Unconditional Surrender" Grant. He was elected in 1868 and again in 1872 by comfortable margins. Grant's previous experience with civilian political life had been scanty indeed, except for a troubled five-month period as Johnson's ad interim Secretary of War. For various reasons he had voted only once before for president.

While Chief Executive, Grant was repeatedly duped by speculators, peculators, assorted crooks, and other self-servers. The marvel is not that corruption flourished like crab grass during his "eight long years of scandal" but that he acquitted himself as well as he did. "Let us have peace," he declared simply in his letter of 1868 accepting the presidential nomination. Here he struck a responsive chord with a public that was tired of the horrors of fighting the Civil War and the agony of reconstructing the South.

"All Smoke." Cartoonist Nast dismisses Grant scandals. Harper's Weekly, *1872.*

As for foreign relations and foreign wars, Grant had by happy accident selected a high-quality Secretary of State, Hamilton Fish. The harassed Secretary tried repeatedly to resign. But he gave Grant sage advice and deserves much of the credit for the substantial moves toward peace that considerably offset the stench of scandal in Washington.

We recall that an abortive attempt had been made late in the Johnson administration to patch up the grievances against England stemming from the wholesale destruction of American commerce by British-built Confederate warships. These "pirate" craft for the most part had been constructed in British yards, by British workmen, often manned (though not officered) by British subjects, and succored in British ports. While British competitors rejoiced at the losses of their Yankee rivals, Americans spoke bitterly of revenge and reparation. For their part the British had substantial commercial claims growing out of assorted grievances, including the illegal seizures of some of their ships in connection with the Yankee blockade.

The promising Johnson–Clarendon Convention had been signed in London on January 14, 1869, nearly two months before President Andrew Johnson bowed out. Yet it was much too impenitent for Yankee tastes; it provided for the arbitration of claims on each side since 1853, "both batches on an equality." Completely absent was any word of regret about the *Alabama* and her destructive sisters or about "indirect damages" to American commerce inflicted by such predators. With the victorious North in a mood that was anti-British and anti-Johnson, the Senate snowed under the premature pact with Britain by a surprisingly lopsided vote of 54 to 1, on April 13, 1869.

In his first annual message (December 1869), President Grant later praised this rejection by the Senate as "wisely taken in the interest of peace and as a necessary step in the direction of a perfect and cordial friendship between the two countries." He went on to say, "A sensitive people, conscious of their power, are more at ease under a great wrong wholly unatoned than under the restraint of a settlement which satisfies neither their ideas of justice nor their grave sense of the grievance they have sustained."

President Grant concluded this portion of his message (possibly ghost-written by Secretary Fish) by hoping that ultimately a settlement could be reached "with an appreciation of what is due to the rights, dignity, and honor of each" and with a determination "to lay the foundation of a broad principle of public law which will prevent future differences and tend to firm and continued peace and friendship." Luckily for Grant, as we shall presently note, this goal was achieved in the Geneva arbitration of 1872.

An overwhelming burial of the Johnson–Clarendon Convention was such a foregone conclusion that there was no need for oratorical flowers. But the egotistical and combative Senator Charles Sumner of Massachusetts was not content to let the pact die in peace. Resorting to extravagant speech, he delivered a smashing indictment of Britain on April 13, 1869. He charged that the British owed the United States not only for shipping losses but for having prolonged the war by two years, for a total of more than $2 billion. Sumner was supposed to be hinting that because Britain would not or could not pay this preposterous sum, the United States would accept all of Canada in lieu of money.

Red-blooded Americans cheered Sumner's inflammatory oratory; he seemed to be proposing a heavy war indemnity without a war, much less a victory. The British, who believed that they had already made fair concessions in the Senate-spurned treaty, made clear that they would fight before accepting such demeaning terms. Many months would have to pass before the London Foreign Office would again seriously negotiate with Washington on the subject of Yankee demands.

Bickerings with Britain

The prospect of a mutually satisfactory adjustment of the so-called *Alabama* claims was clouded by a renewed quarrel over the perennial question of Yankee fishing rights in Canadian waters. Also involved was the ownership of the tiny San Juan Island, southeast of Vancouver Island. A "Pig War" had started there when an American settler shot a trespassing porker owned by a British subject.

Britain's growing willingness to arbitrate differences with the Yankees was partly related to the explosive situation in Europe. The Franco-Prussian war had been fought in 1870–1871, and the attitude of Russia gravely concerned the British Foreign Office. In the event of Russo-British hostilities, what was to prevent the Russians from building dozens of *Alabamas* in welcoming Yankee ports?

The next logical step was the epochal Treaty of Washington, concluded on May 8, 1871, by commissioners representing America, Great Britain, and Canada. The rather minor San Juan Island dispute was referred to the German Emperor as arbitrator, and he rendered a judgment favorable to the Americans. The fisheries dispute was solved in part by conceding the reciprocal right of Canadian fisherman to operate in American waters as far south as Delaware Bay, where the fish were not comparably plentiful. This tradeoff was so lopsided that the Canadians demanded payment of damages.

More noteworthy in the Treaty of Washington were the arrangements for settling the *Alabama* claims by an arbitral commission meeting in Geneva, Switzerland. The five members were to be named respectively by the rulers of Great Britain, the United States, Italy, the Swiss Confederation, and Brazil. In the recent Treaty of Washington the British had not only inserted an apology for the escape of the *Alabama* but had agreed to a set of rules for neutral conduct. These went beyond generally accepted international law and thus resulted in a virtual surrender of the British case. The arbitral tribunal was reduced to essentially a fact-finding body concerned primarily with awarding dollars and pounds sterling.

After considerable controversy, the Geneva Tribunal granted the United States $15.5 million for direct damages inflicted by the *Alabama* and her sister commerce destroyers. The British were not overjoyed, but they were relieved to get this backfiring precedent out of the way. They subsequently hung the cancelled draft for this penitential payment on a wall of their Foreign Office as a warning to later occupants.

Yet all was not clear gain for the United States. One of the other commissions established by the Treaty of Washington voted compensation to Britain for damages to her shipping growing out of illegal Union blockade practices—a total of about $2 million. Another commission awarded compensation to the Canadian fishermen to the tune of $5.5 million. The United States, under the terms of the Treaty of Washington, netted only about $8 million, or about half of the Geneva award of $15.5 million.

Yet several settlements stand out as landmarks in the long and troubled history of arbitration—and peace. The happy result was primarily the handiwork of Secretary Fish, although Grant received much of the credit. This protracted negotiation looms as an oasis of achievement in a desert of domestic scandal. In his annual message of 1872, Grant rejoiced that the instrumentality of international arbitration had left Britain and the United States "without a shadow upon the friendly relations which it is my sincere hope may forever remain equally unclouded."

Crisis over Cuba

Shortly before General Grant was inaugurated, restive Cuba burst into flames in what came to be labeled the Ten Years' War (1868–1878). American sympathies were deeply involved, as they normally have been toward other nearby peoples struggling to be free. More than that, American lives and property were jeopardized or destroyed in Cuba, and various filibustering expeditions attempted to bring assistance from the shores of the United States.

Pressures finally reached Grant for official intervention in this nearby insurrection, or at least for a recognition of the belligerency of the so-called Cuban government. But such encouragement to rebels would be highly offensive to Spain, just as British recognition of Confederate belligerency had been to the United States. Such dangerous intervention, though only political, might mean war with the Spaniards at a time when the costly wounds of the American Civil War were far from healed.

The fugitive rebel government in Cuba evidently consisted of a few footloose leaders under some palm trees. Yet President Grant yielded to the public clamor by sending a letter to Secretary of State Fish instructing him to issue a proclamation (already signed) recognizing Cuban belligerency. The cautious Fish averted a crisis with Spain by quietly pigeon-holing the explosive orders, while Grant, preoccupied with domestic problems, evidently forgot about his blunder.

Yet the Cuban insurrection continued to grind on, and Secretary Fish, with threats of resignation, finally induced a reluctant Grant to submit to Congress, on June 13, 1870, a special appeal urging strict nonintervention. Alluding to the efforts of Cuban filibusterers and other seeking to entangle the United States, the President stated flatly that he was "unable to see in the present condition of the contest in Cuba those elements which are requisite to constitute war in the sense of international law." In short, Grant concluded, a formal recognition of belligerency might involve the United States in serious difficulties.

The President's special message may have helped his cause, because a resolution recognizing Cuban belligerency was voted down by the House of Representatives on June 16, 1870, by the not too comfortable margin of 101 to 88. Grant's timely but somewhat reluctant move toward nonintervention and peace may have postponed the American war with Spain over Cuba for twenty-eight years.

The most explosive ship in Spanish-American relations, until the *Maine* blew up in Havana harbor in 1898, was the *Virginius*, captured on the high seas by the Spanish gunboat *Tornado* late in October 1873. This vessel had left New York harbor, formally registered as an American merchant ship and flying the Stars and Stripes when captured. The passengers and crew were brought to Santiago, Cuba, where fifty-three of them, including Americans and Englishmen, were shot as pirates after hasty courts martial.

This was a grave affront to the honor of the United States and its flag. In the 1850s the Stars and Stripes had protected slavers, often illegally, and the United States had sternly upheld the principle, as President Grant solemnly informed Congress, that "American vessels on the high seas in time of peace, bearing the American flag," were immune from "any visitation, molestation or detention of such vessel by force" at the hands of a "foreign power." Such action would be "in derogation of the sovereignty of the United States."

The United States rocked with war talk, as well as with war preparations, which President Grant fully supported. The *Virginius* had been involved in carrying arms and men to the Cuban insurgents, and Spain, for her part, was aroused against the Yankees. Secretary Fish dispatched an ultimatum to Madrid demanding an apology and redress within twelve days.

But the United States government soon learned that it was not coming into court with completely clean hands. The *Virginius*, though nominally of legal United States registry and hence entitled to fly the American flag, carried papers fraudulently obtained by the Cuban insurgents. The ship was also transporting arms and a party of revolutionists to Cuba. When Secretary Fish learned of these irregularities, he wisely moderated his demands, and Spain eventually responded with the payment of $80,000 to the families of the Americans who had been so hastily executed. Thus the nonbelligerent course of Fish and Grant surmounted this crisis and postponed the Spanish-American War for about a quarter of a century.

Hidden away in a special message to Congress (January 5, 1874) is further evidence of Grant's moderation in the *Virginius* affair. He declared that if the papers of the ship "were irregular or fraudulent, the offense was one against the laws of the United States" (not international law) and hence "justiciable" only in American tribunals. Accordingly, Grant further announced that "proceedings should be instituted in our courts for the punishment of the offense committed against the United States." For her part Spain was undertaking "to proceed against those [Spaniards] who had offended the sovereignty of the United States, or who had violated their treaty rights."

Among other concessions, Grant stated in this same message, the United States had demanded a "salute to the flag." For her part, Spain had asked to be exempt from this condition, in view of the fraud involved. "I therefore assented," reported Grant, "on the assurance that Spain would then declare that no insult to the flag of the United States had been intended."

Dominion over Santo Domingo

In doggedly fighting for the annexation of Santo Domingo, Grant further proved that he was politically naive and financially inept. This episode also showed that Grant the pugnacious could keep battling long after his cause was lost and retreat was inevitable.

We recall that an independent Santo Domingo had been reoccupied by Spain in 1861 by invitation of the shaky local regime. But the Spaniards, bedeviled by recurrent revolts and yellow fever, had withdrawn in 1865, leaving Buenaventura Báez to seize the presidency for the fourth, but not last, time. Pinched by financial difficulties, he hit upon the scheme of turning over his insecure republic to the United States in return for an assumption of its public debt, with his own private interests protected. Unfortunately for Grant, the whole proposed deal reeked of both peculation and speculation, with the insiders scrambling to feather their own nests.

Yet the proposed annexation of Santo Domingo found favor with American navy men. They were keenly aware that the United States then had no naval base at all in the islands of the Caribbean, and this lack had been a severe handicap in intercepting the swift ships that had run the blockade of the Confederacy. Especially desirable was the splendid bay of Samaná in Santo Domingo, the military value of which Grant, the Civil War warrior, fully appreciated. The whole affair became an obsession with him.

But annexing Santo Domingo was an idea whose time had not come. The preoccupied American people, slowly recovering from the wounds of the Civil War and busy conquering the Great West with settlers and railroads, were not in a mood for overseas expansion. Many citizens felt that the United States had enough Negroes without Santo Domingo, which already supported a large black population.

Grant persisted in pushing this pet project, even after the Dominican treaty had been soundly rejected by the Senate. His chief foe was Senator Sumner of Massachusetts, who assailed the perils of annexation in the most extravagant terms. An angered Grant would shake his fist as he passed the Senator's house, and on one occasion the general hinted darkly that if he were not President there would be a challenge to a duel. Grant lost the treaty, but Sumner lost his proud position as Chairman of the Senate Foreign Relations Committee; the President had vindictively arranged to have the rug pulled out from under him.

Grant had been a real estate man for a brief period in the 1850s, and not a successful one. Yet he had learned enough to perceive the wisdom of playing up all the virtues and advantages of a property being offered for sale. Santo Domingo, as he pointed out repetitiously in successive messages to Congress, came almost as a gift; its soil was about the richest in the world; it could support a population of 10,000,000 people in luxury (not its current 120,000); it grew tropical products that otherwise would have to be purchased from Cuba or some other foreign land; it would enhance American business and water-borne commerce; it would help extirpate slavery in nearby Cuba and Puerto Rico; it would forestall occupation by some greedy European power; and it would strengthen the Monroe Doctrine.

It is fashionable to portray Grant as a clodhopper from Illinois who was taken in by some city slickers with glib talk of enriching the nation. But it is entirely possible, in fact probable, that Grant was thinking primarily of the future defense of the United States, just as Jefferson had been looking ahead in the purchase of Louisiana. The talented Virginian had wanted only an outlet at the mouth of the Mississippi, and to get it he had to take all of the Louisiana territory. Grant wanted the Bay of Samaná, and he had to take the whole island to get it. To justify doing so he felt called upon to list, evidently in an exaggerated fashion, all of the presumed advantages.

Grant even dragged in "Monroe's Doctrine." His argument was that an unnamed foreign power stoody ready "to offer $2 million for the possession of Samana Bay alone." In this event the strategic island would be a pistol pointed at the United States. Monroe had warned the European powers not to secure any more new colonies in the Americas; he had not said (although that was implicit) that one colonial nation could not transfer its territory to another European nation. In connection with Santo Domingo, President Grant was at pains to make this point explicit.

In his message to Congress of May 31, 1870, President Grant included an important milestone in the evolution of the Monroe Doctrine. He said categorically that the exclusionary annexation of Santo Domingo by the United States would be an "adherence to the Monroe Doctrine." Referring to the earlier acceptance of the revered Doctrine by the American people, Grant now deemed it proper "to assert the equally important principle that hereafter no territory on this continent shall be regarded as subject to transfer to a European power." In short, Germany and other European powers were warned to keep their noses out and their hands off.

From Mexico to Korea

During the eight Grant years, from 1869 to 1877, friction along the Mexican border, as before, was endemic. Deeply involved was the sovereign right of Mexico to keep American intruders out of her territory. In 1873 United States troops, under orders, crossed the Mexican border repeatedly in pursuit of murderous cattle thieves and other lawless elements. Obviously these encroachments were technical invasions, or counter-invasions, of Mexican sovereignty, and the authorities in Mexico City protested repeatedly. Agreements between Mexico and the United States, the first of them in 1882, finally legitimized such raids. They continued well into the next century, notably in the Pershing punitive expedition of 1916.

The incursions into and out of Mexico in the nineteenth century often involved uncontrollable bands of Indians, who routinely fled back across the border in attempts to avoid punishment. During the Grant years the United States was having trouble fencing in its own Indians on reservations, and in 1876 Custer's detachment was wiped out to a man at the Little Big Horn. These local wars, being internal, are not of primary concern in the present investigation, but they did elicit from Grant some remarkably humane observations. In his third annual message (1871) he recommended "liberal appropriations to carry out the Indian peace policy, not only because it is humane, Christianlike, and economical, but because it is right."

In his second inaugural address Grant further declared that "wars of extermination," involving a people like that of the United States, "are demoralizing and wicked." He went on to say that America's "superiority of strength and advantages of civilization should make us lenient toward the Indian. The wrong inflicted upon him should be taken into account and the balance placed to his credit." As for trying to civilize the Indians, "If the effort is made in good faith, we will stand better before the civilized nations of the earth and in our own consciences for having made it."

In distant places, American military muscle continued to be exhibited. In February 1874 American forces were landed in the kingdom of Hawaii to preserve order and protect American lives and interests during the coronation of a new king. This was only one of a number of manifestations of United States interest during the nineteenth century in this idyllic outpost.

In the days of President Grant, specifically 1871, the first Korean War occurred. It has been so little recognized by American historians that it is not generally known by that name, if mentioned at all. Like the war of the United Nations against North Korea, beginning in 1950, it was not formally declared by Congress.

In 1871 informal hostilities with Korea, the Hermit Kingdom, followed the killing of Americans who had illegally entered closed ports. An armed American schooner, dispatched to these waters, had suffered the misfortune of running aground on a sandbar. Responding to a royal command, the Koreans burned the ship and murdered its crew.

An American punitive expedition of five or six vessels was dispatched to secure satisfaction. When no response was forthcoming, the warships started to move upriver but were fired upon by masked Korean batteries. The Americans reacted by sending a second expedition to reduce the enemy forts; about five of these bastions were taken and destroyed by landing parties. The Koreans left about 250 dead on the field; the Americans lost only three killed and nine or ten wounded. The Korean king still refused to communicate with foreigners, and consequently this attempt to blow Korea open failed. Eleven years later, in 1882, Commodore Shufeldt, U.S.N., succeeded in negotiating a commercial treaty with the Koreans, the first with any Western power. This achievement bears comparison with Perry's opening of Japan in 1853–1854.

In his third annual message to Congress (1871), President Grant made clear that, provoked by "the barbarous treatment of our shipwrecked sailors on the Korean coast, I instructed our minister at Peking to endeavor to conclude a convention with Korea for securing the safety and humane treatment of such mariners." Admiral John Rodgers was instructed to accompany him, in Grant's words, "with sufficient force to protect him in case of need." The Americans, Grant concluded, had been unable to secure the desired convention, but they had "punished the criminals" and "vindicated the honor of the flag."

We may safely conclude that Grant, although a professional military man, was no more militant than many of his predecessors or successors, and that his administration scored some noteworthy victories for arbitration and peace. His administration of scandal-ridden internal affairs was less commendable.

CHAPTER 19

RUTHERFORD BIRCHARD HAYES: THE MAN OF INTEGRITY

The policy inaugurated by my honored predecessor, President Grant, of submitting to arbitration grave questions in dispute between ourselves and foreign powers points to a new, and incomparably the best, instrumentality for the preservation of peace.

President Hayes,
Inaugural Address,
March 5, 1877

His Honesty: Rutherford B. Hayes

With the exit of General Grant, the country was to have a series of Presidents who, like Grant, had served the nation as officers in the armed services. The list includes Hayes, Garfield, Arthur (but not Cleveland), Harrison, McKinley, and Theodore Roosevelt. Obviously, these new Commanders-in-Chief had previously done some actual commanding and had some firsthand knowledge of warfare.

Until near the end of the century, when an aroused public opinion forced war on Spain in 1898, the United States was overwhelmingly concerned with domestic problems. There was no widespread conflict convulsing Europe, and public attention was generally not focused on friction with foreign nations that might lead to armed combat. As a result, we can pass over this generation of White House warriors much more lightly than we could some of their predecessors.

President Hayes was a prominent Ohioan, five feet, eight inches tall, with sandy red hair and a bushy beard. Unlike some of his predecessors, he had absorbed an excellent education before becoming a lawyer. An honors graduate of Kenyon College in Ohio, he completed a course of lectures on law at Harvard and then established a successful legal practice in Cincinnati. When the Civil War broke out he enlisted, preferring the possibility of dying in battle for the Union rather than living with the shame of not having served.

Young Hayes rose rapidly from the rank of captain of the Ohio volunteers and emerged as a breveted major general "for gallant and distinguished services." He fought in a half-dozen or so of the major campaigns or battles of the Civil War, during which he was wounded in an arm and stunned when his horse was killed. In the second battle of Winchester (Virginia), he was leading an assault on a battery on a hill protected by a morass. His horse became mired down, but Hayes floundered out of the mud, ignored the flying bullets, waved on his following troops, and captured the position in hand-to-hand fighting. Men have received the Congressional Medal of Honor for less spectacular efforts.

Entering politics after the Civil War as a Republican, Hayes was elected to the national House of Representatives and then to the governorship of Ohio, in which capacities he established himself as a man of sterling honesty. In 1876 he ran for the presidency against the Democratic candidate, Samuel J. Tilden. The result was a disputed election, marred by unseemly fraud and violence on both sides, but a special Electoral Commission awarded the prize to Hayes. Thereafter disappointed Democrats called the President "His Fraudulency," "Rutherfraud B. Hayes," and other unkind names, which cut to the quick a man of his integrity.

As a part of the bargain by which the Democrats allowed Hayes to take his controversial seat, the incoming President was committed to withdrawing federal troops from those state governments in the South where Yankee bayonets were still propping up Republican carpetbag governments. Although bitterly criticized by partisan Republicans for doing so, the new President honored this commitment, and the South rapidly solidified as a Democratic stronghold.

Hayes enjoyed a relatively quiet administration as far as hostilities or near-hostilities with foreign nations were concerned. As luck would have it, the most serious outbursts occurred within the domain of the United States. In July 1877 rioting during widespread railroad strikes got out of hand in West Virginia, Maryland, Pennsylvania, and Illinois. The local and state authorities were unable to cope with these disorders, and virtual civil war broke out. The President was called upon, in accordance with constitutional procedures, to send in federal troops. Hayes responded and was happy to report later to Congress that the presence of the federal might was sufficient "to preserve the peace and restore order without the use of force."

Periodic disorders along the border with Mexico, involving raiding Indians and plundering whites, continued to present perennial problems during the 1870s. The Secretary of War issued an order in June 1877 authorizing United States troops to pursue intruders beyond the border with Mexico. The press of Mexico clamored for war, while foes of President Hayes in the United States assailed the administration for having reacted with undue vigor. But such criticism was voiced by relatively few organs of public opinion, and the crisis passed.

A new Mexican dictator finally restored some stability, and, with cooperation on both sides of the Rio Grande, Washington could withdraw the offensive order for invasion. This was done in February 1880. All told, during the decade from 1875 to 1885, troops of the United States pushed into Mexican territory in pursuit of maurauders more than twenty times. And more encroachments were to come.

A potential crisis with Great Britain developed in January 1878 at Fortune Bay, Newfoundland. A local law banned industrial fishing on the Sabbath day, but when the fish were running this restriction made no sense to visiting Yankee fishermen. When they continued to scoop up the catches, as they were entitled to do under the Treaty of Washington (1871), the angered Newfoundlanders drove off the intruders and destroyed much of their gear.

Instead of beating the tom-toms of war, President Hayes calmly had a bill presented to the London government for damages in the amount of $105,305.02. He was able to report in his fourth annual message (1880) that Great Britain had recognized "our right to an indemnity" and had agreed that the conflicting interests of the fishermen on both sides should be peacefully adjusted by "concurrent arrangements between the two Governments." Early in 1871 London paid a scaled-down $75,000.

Chinese Coolies and Samoan Natives

During the 1870s the problem of Chinese immigrants on the Pacific Coast, particularly California, came to a boil. Thousands of laborers had been imported to build the railroads and engage in other low-paid manual labor; by 1880 the Chinese numbered 75,000 in California, or almost 10 percent of the total population.

Thrifty, industrious, and efficient, these Oriental workers were able to subsist on low wages and the "smell of a greasy rag." In the cheap labor market the beef-eater had no chance against the rice-eater, and there was the rub. White laborers, objecting to the "filthy" habits of the Chinese, set upon them and abused them horribly. In 1872 some fifteen "Chinamen" were lynched by an angry mob in Los Angeles. More prolonged was violent anti-Chinese agitation in San Francisco, where in the courts the victim did not have "a Chinaman's chance." He usually came out on the short end, sometimes on the rope's end.

In decades past American citizens and other "foreign devils" had been subjected to corresponding abuse in China. On various occasions, as we have already noted, American naval forces in Chinese waters were used to protect American lives and property. But one should note that during the murdering and lynching of Chinese, especially in California, no Chinese fleet of junks ever showed up to provide protection and inflict reprisals. This fact alone should indicate which of the two nations at that time was a world power and which one was not.

Pressure mounted from the Pacific Coast for Congressional legislation that would bar the Chinese, but such efforts ran into the roadblock of the Burlingame treaty of 1868. This epochal pact had formally granted to Chinese immigrants the unrestricted right of entry. Nothing daunted, Congress passed a bill in 1879 that forbade any immigrant ship to import more than fifteen Chinese laborers on any one trip. The transportation of contract laborers on this small scale was unprofitable; hence the proposed law amounted to virtual exclusion.

President Hayes sympathized with the problem of the white Californians, but he also recognized that the Congress had no constitutional right to modify a treaty by the legislative process. He also perceived that such an exclusionary law probably would anger the Chinese, possibly to the point of inflicting bodily harm on missionaries, merchants, and other Americans residing in China. In a noteworthy veto of the proposed law, Hayes expressed his determination to "maintain the public duty and the public honor." In doing so he may have averted warlike reprisals.

In the states of the American West, the President was widely condemned and even burned in effigy. But his veto and the nation's honor were both sustained. The only honorable way to secure a peaceful exclusion of the Chinese was to revise the Burlingame Treaty of 1868. In 1880 a special commission journeyed to Peking and negotiated the immigration treaty of that year. By its terms the United States could "regulate, limit or suspend" but not "absolutely prohibit" the entrance of Chinese laborers. The Peking government thus saved some face.

During the Hayes years the United States also took gingerly but substantial steps into the deep waters of the Samoan archipelago. Hayes himself could not peer far into the future, but during the subsequent rivalry over these islands the warships of the United States and Germany came dangerously close to opening fire on each other in 1889.

American interest in Samoa, an archipelago of some fourteen idyllic islands in the South Pacific, can be traced as far back as the famous exploring expedition of the American Commodore Wilkes in 1839. With the remarkable expansion of trans-Pacific commerce, and with the growing need for coaling stations to support steam navigation, Uncle Sam began to prick up his ears. The evident covetousness of the latecoming colonial powers, especially Germany, did much to whet the appetite of the government in Washington.

In his first annual message, that of December 1877, President Hayes reported that the government of the Samoans had sent an envoy to the United States to invite the American government "to recognize and protect their independence, to establish commercial relations with their people, and to assist them in their steps toward regulated and responsible government." President Hayes went on to say that the Samoans, having made "progress in Christian civilization" and in trade, "are doubtful of their ability to maintain peace and independence without the aid of some stronger power." In response to this clear invitation to enter the colonial scramble, Hayes declared that the "subject is deemed worthy of respectful attention, and the claims upon our assistance by this distant community will be carefully considered."

A treaty of commerce, signed by the Samoan envoy in Washington and the American Secretary of State early in 1878, was quickly ratified. Among other concessions, it granted to the United States the privilege of using the port of Pago Pago (fully acquired in 1900) as a station for coaling and naval supplies. There were suggestions of a mild entanglement with other powers in Article V, which authorized the United States to "employ its good offices" in any differences that should arise between Samoa and "any other government in amity with the United States."

In his last annual message to Congress, in December 1880, Hayes reported that the government of the king of Samoa, with the support of consuls from the United States, Great Britain, and Germany, had seemingly "given peace and tranquillity to the islands." Hayes went on to say, as was all too true, that "the common interests of the *three great treaty powers* require harmony in their relations to the native frame of government." The four words italicized above are striking evidence that in 1880 the President of the United States not only regarded his nation as a world power but also placed it on an equal footing with Great Britain and Germany. Actually, by 1879, the "harmony" among these three great powers had sunk into acute, swords-drawn disharmony.

Canal Consciousness

Nearer home a more immediate problem confronted the Hayes administration in 1879 with the alarming prospect of a foreign-owned and foreign-dominated interoceanic canal at the narrow isthmus connecting North and South America. An ambitious French company, headed by the elderly but still dynamic Ferdinand de Lesseps, builder of the Suez Canal, was promoting plans for severing the two continents at Panama.

The American people, some of whom had for decades dreamed of achieving this goal themselves, were aroused by the prospect of French control and domination over this strategic American waterway. To be sure, de Lesseps' company was only a private concern, but the government in Paris might one day be forced to intervene for the protection of so costly and valuable an investment. Still fresh in mind was the financial coup by which the British government had won control of the vital Suez Canal in 1875.

Disturbed by these prospects and responding to public agitation, President Hayes sent a special message to both the Senate and the House on March 8, 1880. It breathed a militancy and a sense of urgency that reminded observers of the Monroe Doctrine, to which Hayes on this occasion added another significant corollary.

As the President stated bluntly near the outset, "The policy of this country is a canal under American control. The United States cannot consent to the surrender of this control to any European power or to any combination of European powers. If existing treaties between the United States and other nations or if the rights of sovereignty or property of other nations stand in the way of this policy . . . suitable steps should be taken by just and liberal negotiations to promote and establish the American policy on the subject consistently with the rights of the nations to be affected by it."

Hayes went on to say that the capital invested by other countries "in such an enterprise must in a great degree look for protection to one or more of the great powers of the world. No European power can intervene for such protection without adopting measures on this continent which the United States would deem wholly inadmissible. If the protection of the United States is relied upon, the United States must exercise such control as will enable this country to protect its national interests and maintain the rights of those whose private capital is embarked in the work."

Hayes next declared the proposed canal would "essentially change the geographic relations between the Atlantic and Pacific coasts of the United States and between the United States and the rest of the world. It would be the great ocean thoroughfare between our Atlantic and our Pacific shores, and *virtually a part of the coast line of the United States*." (Italics added.)

Hayes further observed, "Our merely commercial interest in it [the canal] is greater than that of all other countries, while its relations to our power and prosperity as a nation, to our means of defense, our unity, peace, and safety, are matters of paramount concern to the people of the United States. No *other* great power [Hayes here regarded the United States as one] would under similar circumstances fail to assert a rightful control over a work so closely and vitally affecting its interest and welfare."

Determined to drive home his point, the President repeated himself in somewhat different words when he said, "it is the right and duty of the United States to assert and maintain such supervision and authority over any interoceanic canal across the isthmus that connects North and South America as will protect our national interests. This, I am quite sure, will be found not only compatible with but promotive of the widest and most permanent advantage to commerce and civilization."

Although he did not know it, Haye's pointed warning was quite unnecessary. De Lesseps went ahead with his ill-starred project, but after the excavation was about two-fifths completed the whole enterprise collapsed—the victim of ignorance, incompetence, extravagance, corruption, disease, heat, and creeping jungles. But at least Hayes had posted notice in a statement that came about as close to being bellicose as any that he issued during his four years in the White House. Though a Civil War warrior, he was not one of the more warlike Presidents.

CHAPTER 20

JAMES A. GARFIELD: THE MARTYRED PRESIDENT

For mere vengeance [against the South] I would do nothing. This nation is too great to look for mere revenge. But for the security of the future I would do everything.

James A. Garfield, speech in New York on the assassination of Lincoln, April 15, 1865

The Canal Boy President

President James A. Garfield of Ohio was the embodiment of the American success story. The last of the Presidents to be born in a log cabin, he was left fatherless at age two, when his widowed mother was left to bring up her family in grinding poverty. Young Garfield was forced to labor at odd jobs, including work as a canal boy, while scraping together a basic education. He then worked his way through Williams College, from which he graduated with the highest honors. As a teacher of Latin and

Greek, among a half-dozen or so other subjects, he became president of what was later known as Hiram College in Ohio. As a lay preacher for the Disciples of Christ, and widely recognized as an eloquent orator, he was elected in 1859 to the Ohio State Senate.

When the Civil War flared forth, Garfield became a citizen-soldier. He helped to assemble a regiment of Ohio volunteers, of which he was commissioned lieutenant colonel and then colonel. Although much of his knowledge of soldiering was derived from books, he successfully commanded a brigade in a Kentucky battle at Middle Creek, after which he was promoted to the rank of brigadier general by President Lincoln. Garfield served capably at the bloody battle of Shiloh in 1862, and the next year distinguished himself at Chickamauga as Chief of Staff under General Rosecrans, for which service he was named major general of the volunteers. He next went on to make a name for himself in the national House of Representatives, to which he was elected nine consecutive times. Six feet tall, broad-shouldered, heavily bearded, strong-voiced, and well informed, he cut an impressive figure in debate.

These details help make the point that Garfield was a warrior with unquestioned credentials. Elected to succeed Hayes in the presidency, he served only 199 days in that high office, 79 of them while slowly dying in great pain from an assassin's bullet. Whether he would have shown any militancy in foreign affairs if he had not been shot is a matter of conjecture. Despite being a devout Christian he seems to have been willing, if the cause was right, to brush aside the "Thou shalt not kill" injunction of the Ten Commandments.

A few clues to Garfield's future behavior, for example, appear in the presidential documents. In his inaugural address, as he stated with evident approbation, "We ourselves are witnesses that the Union emerged from the blood and fire of that conflict purified and made stronger for all the beneficient purposes of good government." Garfield also noted with approval that the sanguinary quarrel over states' rights was "closed at last in the high court of war."

Later on in this lengthy inaugural address, Garfield alluded to the prospective isthmian canal at Panama—his sole reference to a foreign problem in his published public papers. He avowed that the United States "will urge no narrow policy nor seek peculiar and exclusive privileges." He went on to repeat the words of

President Hayes that it was "the right and duty of the United States to assert and maintain such supervision and authority over any interoceanic canal across the isthmus that connects North and South America as will protect our national interest."

So spoke this servant of the Lord—and mankind.

CHAPTER 21

CHESTER ALAN ARTHUR: THE DUDE PRESIDENT

But if we heed the teachings of history we shall not forget that in the life of every nation emergencies may arise when a resort to arms can alone save it from dishonor.

President Arthur, annual
message to Congress,
December 6, 1881

Arthurian Beginnings

Chester Alan Arthur, the fourth "accidental President" of the United States, could boast of no log-cabin-to-White-House background. He was the son of a Baptist preacher in Vermont and an honors graduate of Union College in Schenectady, New York. At the time of his elevation to the White House he had gained recognition as a wealthy New York lawyer-politician, living in the lap of luxury. He dined well and dressed well. Six feet, two inches tall and well proportioned, he sported elegant sideburns and a drooping mustache. Reputed to have eighty pairs of trousers in his wardrobe, he came honestly by such nicknames as "The Dude President," "Elegant Arthur," and "Prince Arthur."

Shortly before the coming of the Civil War, Arthur joined the staff of the New York Governor as engineer-in-chief, with the rank of brigadier general. After the shooting started at Fort Sumter, he became acting quartermaster general, and bestirred himself with preparing and forwarding the state's quota of troops. In 1862 he was appointed inspector general, with the rank of brigadier general, and then examined the New York troops serving with the Army of the Potomac. General Arthur was never a combat officer, but he rendered valuable services to his state, which provided the largest number of troops to the Union cause.

"Elegant Arthur" inherited from the murdered Garfield an aggressive and glamorous Secretary of State, James G. ("Jingo Jim") Blaine. The Secretary had an enthusiastic following, but he never was able to attain the presidency, largely because of widespread doubts about his honesty in public life. As a close friend of Garfield, Blaine did not hit it off well with the accidental President and left the State Department in December 1881, after only nine and a half months of service.

Yet during his brief tenure Secretary Blaine managed to stir up hornets' nests, despite some good intentions. He undertook, without much success, to mediate disputes between Mexico and Guatemala, Colombia and Costa Rica, and Chile and Peru. The upshot was that he angered some of these smaller countries, for they resented officious interference by Big Brother.

We have already noted that both Presidents Hayes and Garfield regarded the future Panama Canal as a part of the "coastline" of the United States. Blaine reacted similarly when rumors began to circulate that the great powers of Europe were planning to conclude a joint agreement guaranteeing to France the prospective Panama Canal. Secretary Blaine dispatched an identical instruction to the United States Ministers in the European capitals; it served notice that any such joint agreement would be regarded by the United States as an unfriendly act. This was about as far as a diplomat dared go without using the short and ugly word, "war."

Some four months later "Jingo Jim" Blaine responded to mounting public pressure when he entered upon an aggressive but futile diplomatic interchange with the London Foreign Office. He argued that the bothersome Clayton–Bulwer Treaty of 1850, in which both Britain and America had renounced exclusive ownership of any future canal, was outmoded. The pact offended, Blaine claimed, "our rightful and long-established claim to priority on the American continent." The British Foreign Office, skillfully parrying Blaine's futile thrusts, stood squarely on the mutually hand-tying bargain of 1850.

Yet during these Arthurian years relations with Britain, on the whole, continued to be unusually amicable. As "Prince Arthur" reported in his first annual message (December 1881), "The feeling of good will between our own Government and that of Great Britain was never more marked than at present." In recognition of the new era of good feelings, Arthur further stated that he had directed "that a salute be given to the British flag" on the occasion of the celebration at Yorktown of the last great defeat of the British forces in the Revolutionary War. In more concrete terms, the President also reported that the London government had paid in full the sum of £15,000 as compensation for the injuries inflicted on American fishermen in the Fortune Bay incident in Newfoundland in 1878.

In his second annual message (December 1882), Arthur referred delicately to the "slight differences" with Britain that had recently arisen and that were "likely to reach an early adjustment." He then referred to American citizens of Irish ancestry who, under their cloak of United States citizenship, had returned to Ireland to engage in anti-British revolutionary activities. Some had been jailed for their pains, with a consequent "extended correspondence." This problem recurred throughout succeeding administrations, which were always sensitive to the presence of the Irish vote in the great cities of the Eastern Seaboard. Happily for peace, the activities of these transplanted American-born Irishmen never precipitated a major crisis.

Of a different magnitude was the problem of the Panama Canal, which, Arthur informed Congress in 1881, had assumed "grave national importance." He reaffirmed the reaction of his "lamented predecessor" in informing the "European powers" that the injection by them of a joint guarantee of the neutrality of Colombia (and the canal) "might be regarded as a superfluous and unfriendly act." We recall that Colombia had already invited such a joint guarantee of the neutrality of the projected

Panama Canal. In any event, the multipower joint guarantee never jelled.

Mexico, Chile, Egypt, and China

In dealings with Spain and Mexico, President Arthur could sound a familiar refrain. Revolutionists in Cuba were continuing their agitation, and some of them, as he said, were "abusing the sacred rights of hospitality which our territory affords" by using American territory as a staging base for operations. Arthur had ordered the proper officials to "prevent infractions of our neutrality laws at Key West and other points near the Cuban coast." Such precautionary measures, he declared, had been blessed with success.

During these yeasty years both Mexico and the United States continued to be harassed by the forays of reservation Indians breaking loose from either side of the Rio Grande. In his second annual message (December 1882) Arthur could report, "A recent agreement with Mexico provides for the crossing of the frontier by the armed forces of either country in pursuit of hostile Indians." In his message of December 1883 the President related, "A raid from Mexico into Arizona was made in March last by a small party of Indians, which was pursued by General Crook into the mountain regions from which it had come." This was only one of the many precursors of General Pershing's punitive expedition of 1916.

The major armed conflict in South America between Chile on one side and Peru and Bolivia on the other finally resulted in a crushing victory for the elongated republic in 1884, with Bolivia losing her entire seacoast. The United States had interceded to the extent of sending a special mission to the belligerent parties. It urged, without success, that victorious Chile accept a monetary indemnity in lieu of seizing so much enemy territory.

President Arthur had earlier reported to Congress, in December 1882, that the United States was unwilling to impose its will on Chile "without resort to measures which would be in keeping neither with the temper of our people nor with the spirit of our institutions." To interfere in Peru to "dictate peace" would "almost inevitably lead to the establishment of a protectorate—a result utterly at odds with our past policy, injurious to our present interests, and full of embarrassments for the future." Thus spoke a noninterventionist and anti-imperialist, whose advice could well have been heeded by President William McKinley, the reluctant imperialist at the end of the century.

In the relatively peaceful days of President Arthur, American naval power, in conformity with established policy since the days of Jefferson and the Barbary pirates, was used primarily to protect American lives and property. In 1882 American Mediterranean interests were involved during the large-scale warfare between the British and the Egyptians. The city of Alexandria was looted and burned by starving Arabs. In his annual message of that year, Arthur reported that "the timely presence of American vessels served as a protection to the persons and property of many of our own citizens and of citizens of other countries, whose governments have expressed their thanks for this assistance."

The treaty of 1880 with China, we recall, gave the United States the right to "regulate, limit or suspend" but not absolutely prohibit the immigration of Chinese laborers. Congress in 1882 passed a bill suspending such immigration for twenty years. To President Arthur, as to the Chinese, this restriction seemed like an absolute prohibition, and hence a breach of the treaty. He vetoed the bill but suggested that a less harsh suspension might be acceptable to all parties concerned. Congress obliged with a substitute that suspended the entry of skilled and unskilled Chinese laborers for a period of ten years, and this compromise was properly signed.

Arthur was obviously concerned about the national honor in his efforts to deal fairly with China. As he said in his veto message, "A nation is justified in repudiating its treaty obligations only when they are in conflict with great paramount interests. Even then all possible reasonable means for modifying or changing those obligations by mutual agreement should be exhausted before resorting to the supreme right of refusal to comply with them."

Arthur and the New Navy

President Arthur is sometimes labeled the "father" of the modern American steel navy or what came to be called the New

Navy. Such a martial designation carries with it the implication that he was something of a saber-rattler and a big-stick flourisher. Nothing could be further from the truth. As a matter of sober fact, the old Civil War navy, including its wooden ships and outmoded ironclads, was a national disgrace. Its worm-eaten state reflected an almost incredible indifference to the outside world and to possible attacks upon the nation's valuable but vulnerable coastal cities and shipping. The whole rotting and rusting collection of "floating washtubs" reminded one outspoken American admiral of the dragons that the Chinese painted on their forts to frighten away the enemy.

An initial step toward the construction of the New Navy came when President Arthur, in his first annual message (December 1881), directed attention to the recent report of a naval Advisory Board. This body had been instructed, as Arthur stated, "to report as to the character and number of vessels necessary to place" the Navy "upon a footing commensurate with the necessities of the Government."

Arthur went on to say, "I cannot too strongly urge upon you my conviction that every consideration of national safety, economy, and honor imperatively demands a thorough rehabilitation of our Navy." He was well aware that such a building program would involve "a large expenditure of the public moneys," yet, he added, "Nothing can be more inconsistent with true public economy than withholding the means necessary to accomplish the objects intrusted by the Constitution to the National Legislature," including "common defense." Obviously nothing was "more essential to the defense of the United States and of all our people than the efficiency of our Navy."

Arthur followed with a classic statement regarding the wisdom of naval preparedness: "We have for many years maintained with foreign governments the relations of honorable peace, and that such relations may be permanent is desired by every patriotic citizen of the Republic." But, as he said, past experience had demonstrated that emergencies could develop that would require an armed response to uphold the national honor.

Arthur then assured the Congress that "No danger from abroad now threatens this people, nor have we any cause to distrust the friendly professions of other governments. But for avoiding as well as repelling dangers that may threaten us in the future we must be prepared to enforce any policy which we think wise to adopt."

More specifically, Arthur declared, "We must be ready to defend our harbors against aggression; to protect by the distribution of our ships of war over the highways of commerce, the varied interests of our foreign trade and the persons and property of our citizens abroad; to maintain everywhere the honor of our flag and the distinguished position which we rightfully claim [as a world power] among the nations of the world."

By Act of August 5, 1882, Congress authorized the construction of two steam cruising vessels of war, to be made of steel and of domestic manufacture. With this rather feeble catch-up beginning, the new steel navy expanded until by 1898, the year of the Spanish-American War, it ranked about fifth among the navies of the world.

Chester A. Arthur is not commonly ranked as one of the better Presidents. The only office he had ever held before coming to the White House, aside from important military posts, was Collector of the Port of New York, and from this lucrative post he was removed by President Hayes for overzealous political activity. He was subsequently put on the ticket with President Garfield in a vain attempt to appease a disgruntled faction of the Republican party. When the bullet that killed the President elevated Arthur to the White House, people exclaimed. "My God! 'Chet' Arthur President of the United States!"

But the office dignified the man, and Arthur gave his countrymen a far abler administration than they deserved for having elected him to the Vice-Presidency in the first place. If one good term deserves another, he richly merited being elected President in his own right, but the politicians shoved him aside. Yet he had achieved a commendable balance between preparedness on the one hand, and on the other a willingness to fight for American security, rights, and the honor of the flag.

CHAPTER 22

GROVER CLEVELAND: THE VETO PRESIDENT

There are no questions of difficulty pending with any foreign government.

President Cleveland, First
Annual Message to Congress,
December 8, 1885

"Old Grover's" Beginnings

As a personality, the short-tempered and stubborn Grover Cleveland was one of the most militant presidents, especially in fighting for what he conceived to be the right. Fortunately for international peace, most of his pugnacity was directed at domestic corruption and other wrongdoing in public life, not at the misbehavior of foreigners. On coming to Washington, he possessed little knowledge of foreign affairs and manifested small concern for them. At the same time, he was evidently more interested in property rights than in human rights.

Grover Cleveland, the son of a Presbyterian clergyman, was born in New Jersey and reared in New York State. He received an ordinary common school education but did not attend college. After reading law for a period, he was admitted to the bar and established a successful practice in Buffalo, New York.

Although young and able-bodied, Cleveland never served in the Civil War and evidently had no compelling urge to do so. To his lasting political disadvantage, he proved to be the only President from Buchanan in 1857 to Taft in 1909 who had never been at least a temporary part of the military establishment. Obligated to support his widowed mother and two sisters while his two brothers were away fighting for the Union, he borrowed $150 to induce an illiterate Pole to serve as a substitute in his place, an acceptable legal practice then to avoid the draft. Later accused by Civil War veterans of having been a slacker, he conspicuously incurred their wrath when as President he vetoed scores of questionable or fraudulent private pension bills. He also came under especially heavy verbal fire from the Union veterans of the G.A.R. (Grand Army of the Republic) when in 1887 he ordered a return of captured Confederate battle flags. He had hoped to close the "bloody chasm" between North and South, but the resulting uproar forced him to revoke this sportsmanlike order. (The banners were finally returned in 1905, when passions had cooled and Colonel Roosevelt was president.)

Cleveland, ever a slave of conscience, was the kind of man who saw his duty—and overdid it. As sheriff of Erie County in New York, he hanged two murderers with his own hands, although "The Hangman of Buffalo" could have delegated this unpleasant chore to subordinates. In his meteoric rise as "reform mayor" of Buffalo and the "unowned" Governor of New York, he came honestly by the nicknames "Veto Mayor," "Veto Governor," and later "Veto President." When he was nominated for the presidency at Chicago in 1884, the orator who placed his name before the convention proclaimed that the young men of the Democratic party loved Cleveland especially "for the enemies he has made," including crooks, nest-feathering politicians, and other unworthy citizens.

Strong men make strong enemies, and Cleveland, "the unowned candidate," made many enemies of the right kind. Hot-tempered, he would profanely put his foot down instead of sliding it down, and this tactlessness was much resented. Moreover, Cleveland was the first Democratic president since the Civil War and thus indelibly tainted with the party of the rebellion.

Such was the background of walrus-mustached "Grover the Good" as he took the inaugural oath on March 4, 1885. There he stood, a bull-necked and portly bachelor (married the next year), five feet, eleven inches in height, and about 250 or 260 pounds in weight. Undoubtedly an independent and unowned man of principle, he had so much backbone, remarked one crit-

Cleveland files rough edges from tariff. Harper's Weekly, *1888.*

ic, that it made him "stick out in front." Tactless as a mirror and direct as a steamroller, he remained outspoken, unbending, and self-righteous to the end. In keeping with his innate pugnacity, Cleveland directed most of his fire at domestic political foes during his first term, and much of it at Great Britain during his discontinuous second term, notably during the dangerous blowup over the Venezuela boundary.

In his inaugural address of 1885 Cleveland sounded like the dove of peace. He declared that the "genius of our institutions" and the "needs of our people in their home life" dictated "the scrupulous avoidance of any departure from the foreign policy commended by the history, the traditions, and the prosperity of our Republic." America's historic course had been a "policy of independence, favored by our position and defended by our known love of justice and by our power. It is the policy of peace suitable to our interests." In brief, the republic would pursue a "policy of neutrality, rejecting any share in foreign broils and ambitions upon other continents and repelling their intrusion here."

In his first annual message to Congress—one of the longest on record—Cleveland still preached peace: "It is gratifying to announce that the relations of the United States with all foreign powers continue to be friendly." Historically, America's position furnished "proof of a political disposition which renders professions of good will unnecessary."

Cleveland probably meant that there were no difficulties liable to produce war, because there were then minor problems being settled or in the process of settlement with a number of foreign nations, great and small. When all else failed, the United States could usually count on some recurrent squabble with Canada, probably the age-old dispute over joint custody of the fish.

President Cleveland revealed anew his aversion to unnecessary foreign complications in his first annual message, when he referred to a treaty that President Arthur had submitted to the Senate. It had provided for the construction of a canal "by and at the sole cost of the United States" through the territory of Nicaragua. Cleveland observed that "the tenets of a line of precedents from Washington's day" flatly forbade "entangling alliances with foreign states," and consequently he had withheld the proposed pact "from resubmission to the Senate."

Another minor problem, and one that caused an international scandal, involved Cleveland's appointment of Anthony M. Keiley, a prominent Democratic politician, as Minister to Austria. He was first named Minister to Italy, which refused to receive him because he had publicly criticized Italy's usurping of the Pope's authority. Clumsily, Cleveland then appointed Keiley to the legation in Vienna, but the government of Austria-Hungary also found him unacceptable. The Vienna regime judged him *persona non grata* because his wife was a Jew and hence subject to rebuffs in diplomatic circles.

Short-tempered Cleveland was not pleased. As he asserted in his annual message to Congress, he could not acquiesce in a species of discrimination that would violate his "oath of office" and the "precepts of the Constitution." That sacred charter rejected "a religious test" as a qualification for holding office. To demonstrate his displeasure, Cleveland announced that the Vienna legation would be left without a Minister, and that any necessary business would be conducted by a "chargé d'affaires ad interim."

Chinese Coolies and Native Americans

In the days of Hayes in the 1870's, we recall, brutal treatment of Chinese laborers in California had escalated, and the Burlingame treaty of 1868 was modified in 1880 so as to regulate the Oriental influx. In his inaugural address in 1885 Cleveland showed little sympathy for the Chinese newcomers. "The laws," he said, "should be rigidly enforced which prohibit the immigration of a servile class to compete with American labor, with no intention of acquiring citizenship, and bringing with them and retaining habits and customs repugnant to our civilization."

Cleveland gradually developed more sympathy for Chinese workers in America. The most outrageous incident of all occurred in Rock Springs, Wyoming, in September 1885, when white coal miners, many of alien birth, armed themselves and attacked some five hundred docile Chinese miners, killing twenty-eight of them in cold blood and wounding some fifteen others. In November 1885 Cleveland ordered the federal authorities to disperse white rioters in the Territory of Washington. In February 1886 anti-Chinese riots in Seattle, Washington, drove some four hundred of the Orientals from their homes, some as far as San Francisco, with the result that federal troops were summoned by presidential direction to restore order.

In his annual message of December 1885, Cleveland avowed, "All the power of this government should be exerted to maintain the amplest good faith toward China in the treatment of these [Chinese] men, and the inflexible sternness of the law in bringing the wrongdoers to justice should be insisted upon." In February 1887 Congress voted the sum of $147,748 as an indemnity to the Chinese for the Rock Springs massacre of 1885.

The next year the long naval arm of the United States was felt in East Asia. In June 1888 American armed forces were employed to protect American residents in Seoul, Korea, during unsettled political conditions. In November 1888 American naval strength in Samoan waters was used to safeguard American citizens and the American consulate during a native civil war.

There were also troubles in the Caribbean. Pursuant to the treaty of 1846 with Colombia, in January of 1885 some five hundred U. S. Marines were landed in Panama to protect the transit of American property during revolutionary activity. In December 1888 the navy was also involved in persuading the government of Haiti to release an American steamer. It had been seized on the charge of having breached a blockade.

In January 1889 Cleveland sent a special message to Congress in which he reported that during the recent disturbances in Samoa "one or more vessels of war have been kept in Samoan waters to protect American citizens and property." Repeatedly, in communicating with Congress, the President deplored the decrepit condition of the post-Civil War navy and urged faster progress in building, from feeble beginnings, the new steel fleet. Cleveland was not an apostle of the big stick, but he recognized the drawbacks of not having one. As he proclaimed in his first annual message in 1885, "The nation that cannot resist aggression is constantly exposed to it. Its foreign policy is of necessity weak and its negotiations are conducted with disadvantage because it is not in a condition to enforce the terms dictated by its sense of right and justice."

In Cleveland's first administration the last major Indian war in the Southwest ended. In May 1885, after earlier destructive forays, the Apache Chief Geronimo embarked with a considerable following on the last, bloodiest, and most spectacular campaign of his career. Pursued doggedly by United States troops into Mexico, he and his band were finally forced to give up the struggle in 1886, many months later. Geronimo and his followers were shipped off to Florida and were never allowed to flee back to their native haunts.

Cleveland had no sympathy at all for the sentimentalists who favored returning the Apaches once more to their reservation in Arizona. He stated in his fourth annual message in 1888, "Experience has proved that they are dangerous and cannot be trusted. This is true not only of those who on the warpath have heretofore actually been guilty of atrocious murder, but of their kindred and friends, who, while they remained on their reservation, furnished aid and comfort to those absent with bloody intent."

The Sackville-West Blunder

During the first Cleveland administration, to no one's surprise, the perennial fishing squabble with the Canadians bobbed up again. The problem of sealing by British subjects on or near America's Alaskan (Pribilof) islands also was developing more urgency, particularly when, on four occasions in April 1887, sealing ships flying the British flag were seized by American patrols.

The fishery provisions of the Treaty of Washington in 1871 had proved unsatisfactory, and the United States gave official notice of their termination, effective July 1, 1885, in accordance with a joint resolution of Congress in 1883. In retaliation, the Canadians began to seize American fishing schooners for alleged violations of previous regulations. Congress passed a bill early in 1887 that authorized reprisals, but Cleveland, though signing it, regarded it as only a padded club with which to extort concessions. The upshot was the negotiation with the British in 1888 of the Bayard-Chamberlain treaty, which yielded substantial advantages to each party.

Blatant election politics now intruded. Cleveland, a Democrat, was the logical candidate to succeed himself in the election of 1888, and the Republican Senate could not allow him to get credit for negotiating the Bayard-Chamberlain treaty. This forward-looking pact was fatally undercut by politics, although an existing working arrangement with the Canadians was continued.

Cleveland responded cleverly with some counter-politics of his own. He sent a stern message to Congress on August 23, 1888, recommending that this body clothe him with the authority to suspend the transportation of all bonded goods across the Canadian border. He had no intention of using such drastic retaliation; but he was courting the anti-British and anti-Canadian vote, which was heavily represented by Irish-Americans. In the end Cleveland's ploy worked beautifully. The Republicans in Congress would not give Cleveland the retaliatory bludgeon that he recommended, and thus caused themselves to appear to be pro-British.

Cleveland's pro-Irish strategy was largely canceled out in 1888 by an indiscreet private letter penned by the British Minister in Washington, Sir Lionel Sackville-West, in 1888. A California resident wrote him asking how a former British subject should vote in the forthcoming presidential election—for the Republican Harrison or the Democratic Cleveland. The indiscreet diplomat unwisely replied in effect that a vote for Cleveland was a vote for Great Britain and her interests.

This explosive letter, though carefully labeled private, was gleefully emblazoned in Republican headlines. A shocked British Foreign Office did not want to recall this blundering envoy until after a deliberate official investigation. But the election was only a few days off, and the Irish vote was fast slipping away from the Democrats. Cleveland then made one of the few weak moves in his political career: He bundled the "damned Englishman" off home. Cleveland narrowly lost reelection in 1888, but whether or not his defeat was a result of this unfortunate letter we shall never know for certain. But we do know that the loser was angered by this ugly turn of events. The British, in turn, showed their displeasure by not sending a new Minister until Cleveland had left office several months later.

Nearly a month after his defeat for reelection in 1888, Cleveland reported to Congress in his fourth annual message on the "unpardonable conduct" of Sackville-West. The British Minister had interfered "by advice and counsel with the suffrages of American citizens" and also by his "subsequent public declarations" inpugning the President and the Senate "in connection with important questions" still under discussion between the two nations. Cleveland concluded: "The offense thus committed was most grave, involving disastrous possibilities to the good relations of the United States and Great Britain, constituting a gross breach of diplomatic privilege and an invasion of the purely domestic affairs and essential sovereignty of the Government to which the envoy was accredited."

Cleveland's unhappiness over having lost the election by a narrow margin was so great that his agitation is understandable. Sackville-West's initial indiscretion was committed in a purely private letter, designed to be helpful to an unknown inquirer. His real sin was in blundering into a Republican entrapment.

During his rather uneventful first term, Cleveland's chief battles developed with Republican politicians. He revealed no serious willingness to engage in armed combat with foreign nations. But after the four-year Harrison interlude, his ire was so aroused that he skirted close to the abyss of war with Great Britain, not over American rights or honor, but over what he conceived to be the rights of weak Venezuela (see Chapter 24). He may have been swayed in part by having lost reelection as a result of the shortsighted interference of the British Minister in Washington.

CHAPTER 23

BENJAMIN HARRISON: THE CENTENNIAL PRESIDENT

The dealings of this Government with other states have been and should always be marked by frankness and sincerity, our purposes avowed, and our methods free from intrigue.

President Benjamin Harrison,
Message to Congress,
December 3, 1889

Young Tippecanoe

Benjamin Harrison, born in Ohio in 1833, was a grandson of William Henry Harrison, the one-month President known as "Old Tippecanoe" or "The Hero of Tippecanoe." The younger Harrison, five feet, six inches in height and heavily bearded, did not present the imposing military presence of his distinguished grandfather. Yet when running for the presidency "Little Ben" was hailed by Republican followers as "Young Tippecanoe," "Young Tip," and "Our Tippecanoe."

The son of a Congressman, young Harrison graduated from Miami University (Ohio) in 1852. Admitted to the bar the next year, he rapidly rose to a position of prominence in the law and ultimately became a member of the United States Senate.

When booming cannon heralded the fall of Fort Sumter in 1861, Harrison responded to the call of duty. He assisted in raising an Indiana regiment of volunteers and was commissioned its colonel. His command saw action in Kentucky and subsequently in Georgia, where Harrison was directly involved in some of the heaviest fighting of the war. When mustered out in 1865, he had received a commission as brevet brigadier general.

Harrison's field experience in fighting with his troops may have had some relation to his inherent pugnacity, notably in the near-war with Chile. This background also explains his more than ordinary concern in various messages to Congress with the slow building of the new steel navy, as well as with the decrepit coastal defenses.

Much of the militancy exhibited by the Harrison administration was the work of Secretary Blaine, though the ultimate responsibility was the President's. "Jingo Jim" Blaine had a tendency to "take the hated foreigner by the beard," and with his background as a newspaperman rather than a diplomat, he was prone to tackle diplomatic problems, especially with the British, with a startling lack of tact. Yet he made some promising strides toward peace, particularly in promoting Pan-Americanism and also reciprocity in trade with the nations of Latin America.

In his inaugural address, Harrison devoted an unusual amount of attention to foreign affairs. He observed that the United States had traditionally pursued a policy "of avoiding all interference with European affairs." He felt that the nation had a right to expect reciprocal treatment, and he anticipated that no European power would attempt to dominate the proposed isthmian canal—the "shorter waterway" between the two Americas. As Monroe had proclaimed in effect, there were to be no more "colonial dependencies upon the territory of these independent American states." On the other hand, Americans involved in trade abroad "will have our adequate care in their personal and commercial rights." Once the United States had "fairly obtained" coaling stations and similar privileges (in Samoa or Hawaii), "our consent will be necessary to any modification or impairment of the concession."

Harrison further served notice that "we shall neither fail to respect the flag of any friendly nation or the just rights of its citizens, nor to exact the like treatment for our own. Calmness, justice, and consideration should characterize our diplomacy."

To this end "friendly arbitration" would make "our contribution to the world's peace."

Seals and Samoa

Friction with British Canada over the Newfoundland fisheries, as we have seen, had continued intermittently ever since the United States formally won its independence in 1783. A new dimension was added to the problem with the slaughter of American fur seals in the North Pacific in the 1880s.

With the purchase of Alaska the United States had acquired complete jurisdiction over the immense fur seal herds on the Pribilof Islands within the three-mile territorial waters. But increasingly the furry creatures that ventured out beyond such limits were being harpooned by men from sealing ships, most of them British-owned. At the rate the slaughter was continuing, the vast seal herd faced extermination.

In March 1889 Congress, responding in part to the persistent seal lobby, formally authorized President Harrison to seize sealing vessels encroaching on American rights in the Bering Sea. Two of these ships were captured that same month on the high seas. Ironically, for once the Americans, not the British, were flouting freedom of the seas.

As Secretary of State and protector-in-chief of the seals, Secretary Blaine went to the mat for alleged American rights over these sleek mammals on the high seas. In his lengthy diplomatic duel with the London Foreign Office, Blaine resorted to bellicose language when he wrote, "The law of the sea is not lawlessness." He also declared, "One step beyond that which Her Majesty's Government has taken in this controversy and piracy finds its justification." In response, the British government took its stand on the unassailable ground that, except for piracy or under mutual agreement, no nation in peacetime could legally seize the ships of another on the high seas.

Ugly talk of war burst forth in the United States. But Blaine, who had done his best as the attorney for a bad case, finally arranged for arbitration. A mixed tribunal met in Paris in 1893, but the United States lost on every one of the five major counts. The end result was a loss for the seals and American pride, but a gain for the principle of arbitration, which Harrison had warmly favored in his inaugural address. To its chagrin, the

United States was required to pay $473,151 for the losses involved in the seizure of Canadian sealing schooners. Not until 1911 was the seal herd finally saved by international agreement.

In the faraway South Pacific the Samoan archipelago had meanwhile for many years been a magnet to American whaling and shipping interests. After the Civil War, the United States went so far as to negotiate a significant treaty in Washington (1878) with the "tattooed prince" of the islands. It specified that in return for rights to a coaling station at the spacious harbor of Pago Pago, the United States would use its good offices to smooth out any differences that should arise between Samoa and a foreign power. At the outset this pact did not seem like a "foreign entanglement," but in truth it was the genesis of an alarming one.

The next year, 1879, both Great Britain and Germany also received treaty rights in Samoa, and the elbowing for advantage spread. Each of the three powers was deeply suspicious of the designs of the others on these lush islands, which soon became a cauldron of intrigue, as Samoan brother killed brother and as the various consuls hoisted the flags of their respective countries.

On March 14, 1889, ten days after his inaugural oath, President Harrison took a significant step toward peace when he appointed three delegates to attend a conference in Berlin on the explosive Samoan question. Two days later a tropical hurricane intervened. Tensions were approaching the breaking point in the harbor of Apia, where lay a fleet of ships representing Germany, the United States, and Great Britain, all with guns presumably loaded for action. At this critical juncture the winds descended with tremendous force. All three American warships, plus three German warships, were wrecked, sunk, or driven upon the beach. The one British warship, with boilers straining, headed out to sea into the teeth of the storm and ultimate safety.

The next month, April 1889, the scheduled three-power conference met in Berlin, with the atmosphere definitely improved by the cataclysmic fury of nature. Secretary Blaine was expected to take a bellicose stand, but he proved to be surprisingly reasonable. The upshot was a three-power protectorate—definitely an entanglement—while the native dynasty nominally ruled from the royal hut. This clumsy arrangement inevitably spelled trouble, but the Harrison administration must be credited with having opted for what it thought would be a peaceful course.

In his first annual message to Congress, December 1889, President Harrison referred to the completed Samoan treaty, which would be submitted to the Senate. He hoped that "the efforts which have been made to effect an adjustment of this question will be productive of the permanent establishment of the rights and interests of the natives as well as of the treaty powers." We are struck with Harrison's pacific stance, quite in contrast, as we shall note, with his pugnacious approach to the crisis with Chile in 1891-1892 over the *Baltimore* affair. Possibly he was remembering well that the new navy was still in the building process, that three precious warships had been lost in the hurricane, that Germany was a first-rate military and naval power, and that Great Britain was Mistress of the Seas.

Lynching Italians

In 1891, two years after Harrison took office, the United States became embroiled in its first major diplomatic crisis with Italy. A mob in New Orleans lynched eleven cowering Italians who were then being jailed for allegedly having plotted the recent Black Hand murder of the local chief of police.

The outraged government in Rome demanded punishment of the lynchers and indemnity for the heirs of the victims. The Italian masses responded with heated meetings and indignities to Americans. Under heavy fire, the shaky Rome ministry withdrew its ambassador in Washington, and the United States retaliated by bringing home its Minister on a leave of absence. But diplomatic relations were not completely severed because each legation was left in the hands of a chargé d'affaires.

President Harrison and Secretary Blaine found themselves impaled on the horns of a legal embarrassment. In matters of municipal policing, the local and state authorities had complete jurisdiction, and the federal government was powerless to interfere or act. This gap in federalism, which could spark a war that all the other states would have to fight, was to continue to vex the Washington government for many years to come.

The Rome government could not understand why a great sovereign nation was powerless to intervene in the police affairs of municipalities. In response to the criticisms of the Italian Minister in Washington, Secretary Blaine responded with some belligerent and undiplomatic journalese: "I do not recognize the right of any government to tell the United States what it should do. We have never received orders from any foreign power and we will not begin now. . . . It is a matter of total indifference to me what persons in Italy may think of our institutions. I cannot change them, still less violate them."

In Italy there was much talk of fighting the United States. As for armored ships, the Italian navy outnumbered the embryonic American fleet nineteen to one, and in theory it could have gutted America's coastal cities. Even so, war with an aroused American giant was not to be undertaken lightly, especially since Italy had no refueling or naval bases in the Americas.

With the passage of time, tempers on both sides of the Atlantic Ocean cooled. The Italian government felt less unhappy when it discovered that only three of the eleven victims were unnaturalized Italian subjects. International law conferred no right on a mother country to intervene in the killing of naturalized Americans. The storm blew over when the United States, as a friendly act, paid an indemnity of $25,000 or more than $2,000 a head.

If President Harrison had matched the bellicosity of the Italian government, war might have resulted. In his third annual message (December 1891), he referred to the New Orleans lynchings as "a most deplorable and discreditable incident." But, he added, the affair did not "have its origin in any general animosity to the Italian people, nor in any disrespect to the Government of Italy, with which our relations were of the most friendly character." Actually, "the fury of the mob was directed against . . . the supposed participants or accessories in the murder of a city officer." Harrison "regretted that the manner in which these claims were presented was not such as to promote a calm discussion of the questions involved." Then, speaking as a lawyer, he hoped that Congress would make such offenses against resident foreigners "cognizable in federal courts."

The Chilean Crisis

Elongated Chile did not applaud the return of James G. Blaine to Washington for a second stint as Secretary of State in 1889. The Chileans could not forget that in 1881 Blaine had interceded in the war between Chile, on the one hand, and Peru and

Bolivia, on the other. Even so, he had failed in his attempt to rob Chile of the complete fruits of victory.

Disorders again broke out in Chile in 1891, when the Congressionalists revolted against the president, who was accused of trying to seize dictatorial power. The rebels triumphed, but they could not forget that the United States had interfered with the sailing of one of their ships that was supplying arms. Nor could they overlook the role of the United States Minister in Chile, Patrick Egan, who had granted political asylum to a number of prominent Chileans fleeing the vengeance of the victors.

With feeling against the Yankees still running high, the captain of the U.S.S. *Baltimore* unwisely gave shore leave to about 120 unarmed but uniformed men at Valparaiso. In the afternoon of October 16, 1891, a riot broke out in the True Blue saloon after a Chilean had allegedly spat in the face of an American sailor. In the resulting brawl two uniformed American seamen were killed, one reportedly receiving eighteen bayonet and knife wounds. Seventeen were injured, while some of the rest were beaten up and imprisoned. Shockingly, the local police allegedly helped the Chilean rioters assault the Yankees.

At home, the American public reacted angrily and bitterly. To red-blooded citizens this was no mere lynching, American style, of Italians or Chinese laborers. It was an insult to the uniform and flag of the United States, as well as a stain on the national honor. Days dragged by without an apology from Chile, or even an expression of regret. The Acting Secretary of State (Blaine was then ill) dispatched a sharp note complaining that Chile was remiss in not acknowledging responsibility. The Chilean Foreign Minister delayed, failed to present an acceptable apology, and vaguely declared that justice would be done.

President Harrison, after his experience in the Civil War commanding men who had worn the American uniform worthily, could not laugh off this outrageous insult to the uniform and the flag. In a special message to Congress (January 25, 1892), he avowed, "If the dignity as well as the prestige and influence of the United States are not to be wholly sacrificed, we must protect those who in foreign ports display the flag or wear the colors of this Government against insult, brutality, and death inflicted in resentment of the acts of their Government and not for any fault of their own."

One gathers from Harrison's public utterances, which could well have been less harsh than those in private, that he was much more deeply aroused than the "spirited" Blaine, who had never worn the uniform at all. ("Invincible in peace, invisible in war," Blaine's enemies jeered.)

In his annual message to Congress of December 1891, Harrison hoped that the investigation of the *Baltimore* incident then under way would bring full satisfaction. But he ended his discussion of the affair on this ominously belligerent note: "If these just expectations should be disappointed or further needless delay intervene, I will by a special message bring this matter again to the attention of Congress for such action as may be necessary." This is about as close as a Chief Executive could come to hinting at a recommendation to declare war. Angered by Harrison's unsubtle threat, the Foreign Minister of Chile poured further fuel on the flames by spreading broadcast a note of rebuttal in which he assailed Harrison's good faith and truthfulness.

War fever now rose dangerously high in both Chile and the United States. The American people had experienced no such excitement since the *Virginius* affair with Spain in 1873. One Kentucky Congressman boasted that a million men would respond to a call to arms, thus further reuniting the North and South. The naval yards in both countries became ominously active.

The warlike Chileans, intoxicated by relatively easy victories over their weaker neighbors, boasted loudly of what their navy would do. It was in fact decidedly superior to that of the United States in torpedo boats in the Pacific Ocean, and for a time panic struck the undefended California coast. But the United States had a population of sixty-three million to three million for Chile, and ultimate victory for Yankee arms was a foregone conclusion. War probably would have been suicidal for Chile, and not altogether honorable for the overpowering Colossus of the North.

Meanwhile the Department of State had been active. On January 21, 1892, Blaine sent an ultimatum to Chile that had been drafted by President Harrison: "I am now . . . directed by the President to say that if the offensive parts of the [Chilean] dispatch of the 11th of December are not at once withdrawn, and a suitable apology offered, with the same publicity that was given to the offensive expressions, he will have no other course open to him except to terminate diplomatic relations with the Government of Chile." This, of course, was the usual prelude to war during the nineteenth century.

The new Foreign Minister of Chile bowed to the inevitable when he knuckled under with an apology that was evidently wholehearted. But while this pacific response was being decoded, Harrison sent a bellicose special message to Congress (January 25, 1892), in which he outlined the *Baltimore* episode at length and submitted the relevant papers for the "grave and patriotic consideration" of Congress and "for such action as may be deemed appropriate." This virtual invitation to vote a declaration of war, at a time when the Chilean capitulation was momentarily expected, caused Democratic partisans to bring down a storm of criticism on Harrison, the Republican candidate for reelection. They claimed that he was hoping to provoke a war so that he could sweep to victory with the hoary slogan, "Don't swap horses in the middle of the stream." Whatever Harrison's objectives, the Chilean apology ended the crisis, and the government of Santiago finally paid $75,000 to the injured men and to the families of those killed.

Secretary Blaine has been accused of excessive harshness in his demands during the Chilean crisis and of having used a sledge hammer to crush a butterfly. To his credit, scholars have discovered that the fiery Secretary actually restrained the President's determination to preserve unsullied the honor of the old uniform. Yet the Chileans could not forgive the Yankees, then or later, for having forced them to knuckle under.

Revolution in Hawaii

In dealing with the problem of Hawaii, President Harrison unwittingly became one of the impulses behind the imperialistic tidal wave that welled up in the United States in the 1890s. He apparently did not authorize some of the irregular steps that were taken toward the annexation of this island paradise, but he seemed quite willing to garner the fruits of those indiscretions.

America's acquisitive interest in Hawaii had developed initially with an almost glacial slowness. Beginning in the 1820s came the New England missionaries, who were eclipsed in numbers by the visiting seamen from the numerous American whalers, who there found relaxation of various kinds from their arduous duties. In 1842 the Washington government declared that although the United States had no intention of annexing these islands, it would not stand idly by if some European power, particularly Britain, should attempt to acquire them. This warning was a virtual extension of the Monroe Doctrine and was reaffirmed in this sense by succeeding secretaries of state.

Ties between the tiny Kingdom of Hawaii and the United States grew closer in 1875, when a commercial reciprocity treaty was concluded between the two mismatched nations. By its provisions Hawaiian sugar and other products were to come in free of tariffs, to the distaste of competing American producers. This reciprocity treaty was renewed in 1884 and formally approved in 1887, when the Senate attached an amendment securing exclusive rights to the priceless Pearl River Harbor as a naval station. We should note that in his annual message of December 1891 President Harrison strongly recommended that "provision be made for improving the harbor of Pearl River and equipping it as a naval station."

For a few years the sugar interests in Hawaii prospered, especially those owned and operated by Americans. But in 1890 Congress passed a tariff act that put sugar on the free list, while providing a bounty of two cents a pound for American planters. The Hawaiian sugar producers quickly perceived that the only way to get around this discriminatory legislation was to annex their lush islands to the United States.

The worries of the American colony in Hawaii deepened when a new potentate, Queen Liliuokalani, ascended the rickety Hawaiian throne in 1891. Resenting the growing influence of the while elite, she attempted to establish by royal edict a new and autocratic constitution.

Thoroughly alarmed, the white leaders organized a revolution, working hand in glove with the United States Minister in Honolulu, John L. Stevens, a notorious annexationist. The coup occurred on January 17, 1893. Responding to the cry of the white revolutionists for help, Stevens arranged for the landing of more than 150 Marines from the U.S.S. *Boston*, then in Honolulu harbor. Ostensibly he was protecting American life and property; actually he was supporting the revolutionists. The troops in question were not stationed near American property at all but near the royal palace, where their artillery could help overawe the Queen and her supporters.

Minister Stevens, although without authorization, speedily accorded formal recognition to the shaky revolutionist regime. Queen Liliuokalani, with both the United States and the small group of revolutionists arrayed against her, yielded her scepter under protest and surrendered to the United States. Two weeks later, the energetic Stevens declared Hawaii an American protectorate, hoisted the Stars and Stripes over the government building in Honolulu, advised the State Department that the Hawaiian pear was "fully ripe," and expressed the fear that if the United States did not pluck it, the British might be forced to do so.

Events now moved rapidly in this rush-order annexation. Three days after the one-day revolution, a five-man Hawaiian commission was hurrying to Washington to lay these priceless islands on the doorstep of the United States. The five "Hawaiians" consisted of four Americans and one Englishman, while the large body of natives was unrepresented.

The Harrison administration was not caught completely off guard by these curious developments. Secretary of State Foster, probably with the President's knowledge, had permitted Minister Stevens' ardor for annexation to go unchecked. In fact Foster had been preparing American public opinion quietly for a takeover of the islands. In this favorable atmosphere, negotiations for a treaty of annexation proceeded rapidly, and President Harrison submitted the signed pact to the Senate for its approval in a special message, February 15, 1893, less than one month after Queen Liliuokalani's downfall and about two weeks before the end of his own term.

Near the beginning of his brief message to the Senate (about seven hundred words), Harrison explained that it had been "the policy of the Administration not only to respect but to encourage the continuance of an independent government in the Hawaiian Islands so long as it afforded suitable guaranties for the protection of life and property and maintained a stability and strength that gave adequate security against the domination of any other power."

Harrison went on to gloss over the unauthorized doings of Minister Stevens by saying the "overthrow of the monarchy was *not in any way promoted by this Government* [italics added], but had its origin in what seems to have been a reactionary and revolutionary policy on the part of Queen Liliuokalani." She had "put in serious peril not only the large and preponderating interests of the United States in the islands, but all foreign interests, and, indeed, the decent administration of civil affairs and the peace of the islands." Her restoration was "undesirable, if not impossible."

Harrison further argued that only two courses were "now open." One was "the establishment of a protectorate by the United States, and the other annexation full and complete." The treaty being submitted to the Senate would be in "the best interests of the Hawaiian people, and is the only one that will adequately secure the interests of the United States." It was "essential that none of the *other great powers*" should secure these islands.* Such a possession would not consist with our safety and with the peace of the world."

"Prompt action upon this treaty," concluded Harrison, "is very desirable." But he had not answered certain questions about the irregularities of Minister Stevens, and the pact was still before the Senate when President Cleveland was sworn in for a second term. As we shall see in the next chapter, Cleveland strongly suspected that the Harrison administration, including the enthusiastic Minister Stevens, had not done right by Queen Liliuokalani.

Everything considered, General Benjamin Harrison was one of the more bellicose Presidents, possibly in part because of his previous martial experience. Some of the military tone was promoted by Secretary Blaine, but one finds it difficult to believe that the President was left completely in the dark in regard to foreign affairs. Especially in dealing with Chile in the *Baltimore* affair, Harrison displayed the clenched mailed fist. He was also supporting the relatively small white revolutionist minority in Hawaii, even though he may not have directly authorized the intervention of American forces. Harrison thus caused the United States to look embarrassingly like just another imperialistic land-grabber. At least his successor, President Grover Cleveland, thought so.

*Harrison, like a number of his predecessors, regarded the United States as a "great power."

CHAPTER 24

GROVER CLEVELAND: DEFENDER OF THE UNDERDOG

Further, though the United States is not a nation to which peace is a necessity, it is in truth the most pacific of powers and desires nothing so much as to live in amity with all the world.

Grover Cleveland,
Fourth Annual Message,
December 7, 1896

"Old Grover" Spurns Hawaii

In 1892 Grover Cleveland became the first and only President to be reelected to his high office after having been turned out of the White House four years earlier by a defeat in the anachronistic Electoral College. Actually, he polled some 100,000 more popular votes than Harrison in 1888 and in this sense was elected for three consecutive terms instead of two discontinuous ones.

Between his two nonconsecutive terms, Cleveland retired to practice law in New York City, where many of his clients were wealthy citizens. With the passing years he grew more conservative but no less combative. In his first term he had waged lengthy battles on the domestic front with unworthy pension claimants and with the advocates of high tariffs; in his second term he fought against the free-silver inflationists and for sound money, all the while battling the miseries of the Panic of 1893.

In the first annual message of his second term (December 1893), Cleveland gave a prominent place to the recent irregularities in Honolulu. He reported correctly that they had caused the government under his predecessor "serious embarrassment." Accordingly, he had withdrawn the rush-order treaty of annexation from the Senate and had sent to Hawaii a special investigator in the person of a former Confederate colonel and a long-time Congressman from Georgia, the Honorable James H. Blount.

After an "exhaustive examination," Cleveland now announced, Blount had submitted a report "showing beyond all question that the constitutional Government of Hawaii had been subverted with the active aid of our representative to that government [Stevens] and through the intimidation caused by the presence of an armed naval force of the United States, which was landed for that purpose at the instance of our minister." Cleveland thereupon concluded that "the only honorable course for our government" was to undo this grave wrong and "to restore as far as practicable the status existing at the time of our forcible intervention." To remedy this "unjustifiable interference," the new Minister in Honolulu had "received appropriate instructions to that end."

Two weeks later, on December 18, 1893, the President reviewed the Hawaii affair at great length in a special message to Congress, evidently relying heavily on the report of Commissioner Blount. The ardent annexationists insisted that this agent was biased unduly against the white revolutionists, and in truth he apparently had not interviewed as many of their leaders as he might have done. In any event Cleveland seems to have drawn most of his facts or alleged facts from Blount's report.

Near the outset of his message Cleveland declared that the new white regime was the result of neither "popular revolution nor suffrage." He stressed the "extraordinary haste" with which the new revolutionary government had moved toward getting a treaty of annexation before the Senate—thirty-two days since the uprising in Honolulu, fifteen of them consumed by the commissioners in transit to Washington. In an unusual jab at a predecessor, Cleveland insisted that Harrison had been "misled" when he declared that "the overthrow of the monarchy was not in any way promoted by this Government." Cleveland regarded the whole episode as one involving "the subversion" of the existing constitutional government of Hawaii and the installation of a provisional government.

President Cleveland was further disturbed by the obvious fact that a dusky native regime had been overthrown by a white Committee of Safety consisting of thirteen "Hawaiians," seven of them foreigners: five Americans, one Englishman, and one German. The landing of more than 150 Marines with two pieces of artillery had been "an act of war," because the reigning royal regime had not asked for such protection. If the troops had been deployed for the safeguarding of American life and property, they should have been stationed in another part of the city, near American residences and official buildings, rather than near the Queen's headquarters, where they could best subserve the interests of the tiny group of insurrectionists.

Cleveland interpreted the strange doings in Honolulu as an indelible stain on the nation's honor. On the face of it, an imperialistic United States had openly conspired with the tiny revolutionist minority to achieve the annexation of the Island Kingdom. The Queen's government had not been overthrown by a popular uprising; in fact, no one was claiming that if the legitimacy of the government had been submitted to a vote of the entire population, including the native Hawaiians, it would have achieved the necessary support. The brutal truth was "that the Provisional Government owes its existence to an armed invasion by the United States." In these circumstances, "the United States cannot fail to vindicate its honor and its sense of justice by an earnest effort to make all possible reparation."

Cleveland finally informed Congress that he had advised the deposed Queen of his willingness to restore her status as it had existed before "the lawless landing" of the United States forces in Honolulu. But he expected "clemency as well as justice to all parties concerned." Yet these conditions had not "proved acceptable to the Queen," who evidently was determined to see rebel heads roll. Cleveland had clearly run into a stone wall, but he was willing to cooperate with Congress in "any legislative plan which may be devised for the solution of the problem before us which is consistent with American honor, integrity, and morality."

But Cleveland simply could not stick the fallen fruit back on the tree. The only possible way by which he could restore the Queen's rule was by armed intervention. A color-conscious America would not stand for killing white men, especially white Americans, to set a Polynesian potentate back on her throne. After impassioned debate in Congress, during which Harrisonian Republicans verbally battled the anti-annexationist Cleveland Democrats, two resolutions of noninterference were passed. The annexation of Hawaii would have to wait until 1898, when the partially Americanized republic of Hawaii threw itself into the arms ofthe United States during the Spanish-American War.

Cleveland's motives, in a day of frantic land-grabbing by the other powers, were honorable to himself and his country. It is true that he displayed pugnacity against the Harrisonian Republicans, the white oligarchy in Honolulu, the scheming sugar barons of Hawaii, and others who would feather their own nests. But at the same time he brandished the sword of righteousness on behalf of justice for the weak rather than selfishness for the strong.

Bickerings with Britain

Cleveland could hardly be expected to avow much love for Great Britain, since a large part of his Democratic constituency consisted of Irish-Americans. Also, as we have seen, it was the blundering British Minister in Washington, Sackville-West, who had written the indiscreet letter that had helped cost Cleveland reelection in 1888. Yet initially the President showed remarkable patience and reasonableness in dealing with the London Foreign Office.

We recall that the forays of British-Canadian sealers in open waters outside the three-mile limit of America's Alaskan islands had led to the seizure of the offending vessels, followed by some heated diplomatic interchanges. The dispute had been settled temporarily through mutual consent, by means of the Paris Tribunal of Arbitration (1893). This agency placed certain illusory restrictions on sealing in the open seas, and in addition assessed damages against the United States in excess of $425,000. Cleveland revealed a growing interest in arbitration when he recommended in his second annual message (1894) that this sum be promptly paid. He was convinced that the settlement was "equitable and advantageous."

In his third annual message (1895), Cleveland brought up the subject of seals again. The slaughter was continuing, he noted, either because the new regulations were inadequate or because they were not being strictly enforced. Even so, he was still of the opinion that the arbitral settlement was "a judicious and advantageous one" for the United States. He regretted that Congress had not honored his recommendation and voted the $425,000 awarded Great Britain, and strongly urged that it be favorably reconsidered. If Congress was still of a contrary mind, the federal government was "bound by every consideration of honor and good faith to provide for the speedy adjustment of these claims by arbitration as the only other alternative." A draft treaty of arbitration had been agreed upon, Cleveland added, and would "immediately" be laid before the Senate. As we shall presently note, a general treaty of arbitration, submitted by Cleveland on January 11, 1897, was defeated by the Senate several months after his term had expired.

When all Spanish America had belonged to Spain, precise boundary lines were of little significance. But with independence came many disputes, including the one between Venezuela and British Guiana. In 1840 Britain had authorized a careful survey of this line by Sir Robert Schomburgk, but the Venezuelans, expecting much more, rejected all such approaches.

The dispute remained in complete deadlock after the British had repeatedly spurned arbitration. The Venezuelan claim was extravagant, and London knew that arbitrators have a tendency to split the difference. Venezuelan propagandists were busy in Washington, and Cleveland was easily persuaded that the voracious British lion was up to no good in South America. The President's problem as an arbiter was complicated by Venezuela's having rashly broken off diplomatic relations with Great Britain.

In his second annual message (December 1894), Cleveland reported that he would renew the efforts of the Washington government to settle the Venezuelan boundary dispute. He believed that "its early settlement on some just basis alike honorable to both parties" was "in the line of our established policy to remove from this hemisphere all causes of difference with powers beyond the sea." He would try "to induce a reference to arbitration," a device that Britain "so conspicuously favors in principle and respects in practice and which is earnestly sought by her weaker adversary."

The British refused to be alarmed by these gentle nudgings. They did nothing, even after a resolution favoring arbitration was adopted early in 1895 by both houses of Congress. A disturbing new provocation took place in April 1895, when the British occupied the port of Corinto in Nicaragua in an effort to secure reparations for recent disorders. Upon receiving satisfaction, the intruders quickly withdrew. But this incursion was too close to the proposed Nicaraguan canal for comfort. The American press gave vent to a loud outcry, and some editors dubbed the Monroe Doctrine an impotent "scarecrow." Such charges, coming on top of Cleveland's having hauled down "Old Glory" in Hawaii, may have helped to prod the President into intemperate action.

Barging into a Boundary Dispute

Cleveland's bellicose interference in the ancient boundary dispute between Venezuela and British Guiana came about as close to a war with Great Britain as was possible without actual shooting. "Old Grover" was lucky to get out of this quarrel without a bloody nose. But pugnacious though he proved to be, his Venezuela intervention was really none of his business and was evidently undertaken largely because of his concern for an underdog that was being bullied, he thought, by the British bulldog.

We remember that Cleveland's support for Queen Liliuokalani and his subsequent battle with the annexationists and others were largely motivated by his solicitude for the injured party. In Hawaii or Venezuela he was not seeking the aggrandizement of the United States, only what he conceived to be plain justice. In the case of Hawaii he was endeavoring to redress a wrong perpetrated by the United States; in the case of Venezuela he appeared to be a busybody concerned with what he regarded as a wrong perpetrated by land-hogging Britain.

Cleveland's Secretary of State was a combative railroad attorney, Richard Olney, who had few obvious qualifications for delicate diplomatic negotiations. It was he who had persuaded the conservative President Cleveland to send in federal troops to break the Pullman railway strike in Chicago in 1894—another prime example of the President's pugnacity on the domestic front. As for Venezuelan arbitration, Olney drafted a defiant note to the British Foreign Office that generally made a favorable impression on Cleveland, who undertook to soften the wording here and there. This was the bombshell note of July 20, 1895, some ten thousand words in length.

Olney's main thrust was that the British were violating the Monroe Doctrine by bulging the boundary of British Guiana deep into Venezuelan territory and then declining to submit the dispute to arbitration. Olney declared that the doctrine meant that any European (British) interference among the nations of the New World would be regarded by the United States as an unfriendly act. When we recall that the Monroe Doctrine was aimed primarily at preventing the powers of the Holy Alliance from imposing their monarchial systems on the ruins of the recently independent nations of Latin America, we must conclude that the application of this dictum to the boundary line of a long established colony in South America was indeed far-fetched.

Olney concluded his long-winded note with a startling burst of bombast: "Today the United States is practically sovereign on this continent, and its fiat is law upon the subjects to which it confines its interposition." The giant republic ruled the roost because "in addition to all other grounds, its infinite resources combined with its isolated position render it master of the situation and practically invulnerable as against any or all other powers." Olney was indeed shaving rather close to the teeth of the British lion.

Cleveland and Olney fully expected the British to sit up and take notice, or at least keep the negotiations moving. But the Foreign Office waited a maddening four months before responding to Olney's ten-thousand-word note, which Cleveland later dubbed a "twenty-inch gun" effort. The Foreign Secretary declared that the hoary Monroe Doctrine was seventy-two years old and not applicable to modern conditions; that the Venezuela dispute had no real relevance to an area which Britain had held as a united colony since 1831; that the boundary controversy had no connection with colonizing in the Americas; and that the affair had no relation to transplanting a European form of government and imposing it in South America. The dispute simply involved "the determination of the frontier of a British possession which belonged to the Throne of England long before the Republic of Venezuela came into existence."

If Olney and Cleveland erred in being too bumptious and bellicose, Lord Salisbury erred in not parrying their thrusts more urbanely, and above all by not keeping the ball in play with some kind of counterproposal. Olney had asked the British if they would arbitrate, and the answer was a flat "No."

Brinkmanship with Britain

When Cleveland read the condescending dispatch of Lord Salisbury, he felt, as he stated privately, "mad clear through." He sat up most of the night drafting a special message to Congress, and on December 17, 1895, he submitted this smashing pronouncement. Near the outset, Cleveland deplored the rebuff of his friendly attempt to end the dispute, partly because this ancient boundary controversy might result in war between Britain and Venezuela and threaten the peace of the American people. Up to this point he had not undertaken to determine who was right in the dispute, but the time had come to judge where the boundary line should be drawn. Accordingly, he urged Congress to pass an appropriation to finance an investigative commission.

Cleveland went on to serve notice: "When such report is made and accepted it will, in my opinion, be the duty of the United States to resist by every means in its power, as a willful aggression upon its rights and interests, the appropriation by Great Britain of any lands or the exercise of governmental jurisdiction over any territory which after investigation we have determined of right belongs to Venezuela." Then Cleveland added, "In making these recommendations I am fully alive to the responsibility incurred and keenly realize all the consequences that may follow." In other words, the United States would arrange to have the correct boundary line determined and then fight Britain, if necessary, to maintain it.

Cleveland concluded this amazing message with some lofty thoughts. He deemed it "a grievous thing" to regard the two great English-speaking nations as other than "friendly competitors in the onward march of civilization." Still "there is no calamity which a great nation can invite which equals that which follows a supine submission to wrong and injustice and the consequent loss of national self-respect and honor, beneath which are shielded and defended a people's safety and greatness."

Congress and country were immediately swept off their feet by Cleveland's two-fisted, tail-twisting, star-spangled message. The fighting President was the hero of the hour; he would show the toplofty British a thing or two. Congress promptly, uproariously, and unanimously approved appropriation of $100,000 for the expenses of the boundary commission. War seemed possible, even probable, and to many sterling patriots desirable. A tidal wave of jingoism swept the country. Few citizens knew or seemed to care that the British had thirty-two warships of the big battleship class to five for the United States, and that America's rich coastal cities were all vulnerable to destructive bombardment by warships based at Halifax.

Happily, most Americans gradually regained their senses. The "Rule Britannia" class in England, at first bent on flogging the upstart Yankees, began to sober down. Canada was vulnerable to Yankee invasion, and British shipping would be exposed to Yankee predators. Britain had no allies and few real friends in Europe, and the erratic German Kaiser bared his teeth menacingly when, at a critical moment, he dispatched a telegram to the Dutch-descended Boers in South Africa congratulating them on having repelled a recent English raid.

The upshot was that the British came down off their high horse and cooperated admirably in providing the American boundary commission with data. The result was a treaty signed by both Venezuela and Britain in 1897. The new pact made provision for the settlement of the boundary dispute by an arbitral board but exempted from its purview those areas that had been held by either party for fifty or more years. Here the British won an important point, because from the outset they had refused to expose to arbitration their subjects living in the area east of the Schomburgk line. Even in what seemed defeat Britain succeeded in winning her main point of contention.

Two and one-half years later, in October 1899, the arbiters handed down their decision. Ironically, it was not much out of kilter with what the British had on several occasions offered the Venezuelans. So it was that a battling Cleveland won for the Venezuelans this somewhat hollow victory after skating dangerously near the brink of war.

The proverb tells us that there never is a great calamity without some small good for somebody. It is true that following Cleveland's exhibition of pugnacity a new spirit of jingoism welled up in America, foreshadowing the imperialistic debauch at the end of the century. The United States, having forced the proud British to knuckle under, obviously gained greater stature as a world power, and Cleveland may be regarded as one of the unwitting fathers of the new imperialism at century's end.

We should also note that much of Latin America (except disappointed Venezuela) was pleased with the protective bombast of Uncle Sam. Anglophobia suffered a setback, as an epochal new cordiality developed between a shaken Britain and an ebullient America near the turn of the century. An era of America's "twisting the British lion's tail" was succeeded by one of Britain's "patting the eagle's head." Now dedicated to the principle of arbitration, the Cleveland administration negotiated a general arbitration treaty with Britain in January 1897, some two months before "Old Grover" left office. But early in the days of McKinley, as we shall note, this promising pact was disemboweled by amendments and then rejected by the Senate.

Cuba Again in Convulsion

In February 1895 the island of Cuba again erupted in revolt. President Cleveland was thus presented with the agonizing problem of whether to support the ruling Spanish regime or the insurgents, who were striving desperately to throw off the oppressor's yoke. The internal uprising continued until 1898, when the United States won the war to free Cuba. Cleveland, despite his demonstrable pugnacity, clung to his hands-off principles and passed the problem of possible intervention on to his more pliant successor, President McKinley.

The population of Cuba then numbered about 1,500,000, of whom about two-thirds were whites; the remaining one-third were black, mulatto, or Indian. The directing Cuban junta, operating openly in New York, raised funds and arms. The United States was the chief base of supplies. Indeed, some forty filibustering expeditions left American shores in two years, and about fifteen of them reached Cuba after eluding Spanish patrols and those of the United States.

Guerrilla warfare in Cuba was both brutal and bloody. Thousands of well-armed and disciplined Spanish troops occupied the cities and more thickly settled areas, while the insurgents roamed the countryside in pursuit of their scorched-earth policies. They adopted the practice of burning the buildings and sugar cane fields in the hope of rendering the island so worthless that the Spaniards would withdraw in defeat. Many Yankee holdings were thus destroyed. Harsh measures of retaliation by Spain also affected adversely the property of American investors, who in 1895 were involved to the extent of about $50 million.

The United States had been torn by rebellion during the Civil War, and President Cleveland in 1895 was aware of the nation's obligation to observe and preserve a state of neutrality. To this end he issued the standard proclamation warning American citizens to observe "the obligations of the United States toward a friendly power" and to observe faithfully the neutrality laws, especially as they forbade "setting on foot" various "military enterprises." In short, Cleveland conceded the existence of a state of rebellion rather than formally recognizing the belligerency of the Cuban rebels, with inevitable entanglements.

Despite Cleveland's stubborn efforts to be fair to Spain, agitation for intervention gained great momentum in the United States. In April 1896 Congress passed a concurrent resolution that went so far as to recognize Cuban belligerency, but this measure did not require Cleveland's signature and consequently did not bind him. The President was demonstrably a bullheaded man, and when there was talk in Congress of declaring war over his head, he was reported to have said that as Commander-in-Chief he would refuse to order the armed forces into action.

In his third annual message (December 1895), Cleveland discoursed at some length on the painful problem of Cuba. He referred to his efforts to prevent American territory "from being abused" as a base for insurgent activity. He believed that despite the hereditary sympathy of the people of the United States for neighbors struggling to be free, his "plain duty" required him "to observe in good faith the recognized obligations of international relationship."

In December 1896, in his last annual message, Cleveland referred at even greater length to the current Cuban uprising. The insurgents, he believed, were roaming "at will over at least two-thirds of the inland country." He dismissed the proposal that the United States buy the now devastated island from Spain; he also rejected the more extreme alternative of going to war with Spain to end the strife. The United States, he said, had "a character to maintain as a nation, which plainly dictates that right and not might should be the rule of its conduct." Peace to the Americans was not a "necessity," yet the nation desired nothing "so much as to live in amity with all the world." As for Cuba, "genuine autonomy" for the Cubans would seem to be a reasonable alternative. Indeed, the United States had already intimated to Spain that the Washington government would help in supporting "such guaranty" with its "friendly offices."

Finally, Cleveland more than hinted that conditions in Cuba might degenerate intolerably. Despite "the international duty we owe to Spain," the United States might be constrained by "considerations of humanity" to take steps that would enable "Cuba and its inhabitants . . . to enjoy the blessings of peace." This sounded like armed intervention, which indeed came two years later under Cleveland's successor, President McKinley.

Whether in dealing with the Hawaiian revolutionists, the Venezuelan boundary, or the Cuban insurrection, Cleveland exhibited his stubborn combativeness. But it was pugnacity for peace and nonintervention, and in support of what he regarded as the policy that best comported with the nation's honor. Except for the dispute with Britain over Venezuela, he set his jaw like flint against the clamor of the crowd.

Latin America, East Asia, Armenia, and Samoa

Cleveland's concern with points south was by no means limited to Venezuela and Cuba. In 1894 Brazil was caught in the grip of a civil war, and the United States strengthened its naval force in the harbor of Rio de Janeiro in a successful attempt to afford protection to American commerce. No landing was attempted. In his second annual message (1894), Cleveland reported that the United States forces had maintained a "firm attitude of neutrality" to the end. Such opposition as the insurgents "encountered was for the protection of our commerce and was clearly justified by public law."

In this same message Cleveland devoted a long paragraph to recent revolutionary disorders in Nicaragua in the summer of 1894. The ruling regime had expelled a dozen or so foreigners, including two Americans, for alleged complicity with the rebels. One or two American warships had been stationed in nearby waters, and their "constant exhibition of firmness and good judgment contributed largely to the prevention of more serious consequences and to the restoration of quiet and order." The two ejected Americans had been permitted to return to their peaceful business. As a follow-up, in May 1896 American naval forces made their presence known as Corinto, Nicaragua, during political unrest.

Likewise, turbulent East Asia found itself in more than normal ferment during Cleveland's second four years. From 1894 to 1896, during and following the Sino-Japanese War, U.S. Marines were present at or near Seoul, Korea, and a guard of Marines was kept at the American legation most of the time.

In his second annual message (1894), Cleveland deplored the war between China and Japan, with Korea caught in the middle. Referring to American commercial interests in East Asia and the safety of American citizens there, he made clear that his good offices were available at any time to bring to an "honorable termination" the lamentable hostilities between Japan and China. Later in the same message he noted that the "war now in progress between China and Japan has rendered it necessary or expedient to dispatch eight war vessels to those waters." And this was four years before the United States became a world power—at least, according to popular legend.

In 1894–1895 Marines were stationed at Tientsin, China, and they came relatively near Peking for the purpose of protecting American missionaries and others during the Sino-Japanese War. In his third annual message (1895) Cleveland deplored the antiforeign outbursts that had occurred against missionaries and others during the Sino-Japanese War, although only "one American citizen was reported to have been actually wounded." The demands of the United States and other powers for the punishment of provincial officials involved in fomenting these disorders had resulted in the imposition of the death penalty on a number of those adjudged guilty.

In a distantly related area, Cleveland concerned himself with the frightful massacres of Christians in Armenia at the hands of the Turks. No Americans had been reported killed, he announced in his third annual message (1895), but damage to the property of American missionaries had undoubtedly occurred. He had ordered American warships to these waters, as close as it was "possible for them to go, where they offer refuge to those obliged to flee." Several of the great powers of Europe had the treaty right to intervene on behalf of all foreign nationals, and Cleveland hoped that these guardians would move energetically.

Troubled Samoa provided Cleveland with yet another opportunity to reveal his ingrained distaste for imperialism, as he had also done in Hawaii. We recall that the Treaty of Berlin in 1889 had provided for a three-power protectorate by Germany, Britain, and the United States. Too many cooks spoil the broth, we are told, and in this case the cooks were not only numerous but also working at cross purposes in pursuit of their own interests. Local insurrections among the natives continued, with all three powers employing naval forces and backing their favorites.

Cleveland alluded to the nonentanglement precepts of the Founding Fathers, as he had done several times previously, when he declared in his third annual message (1895) "that our situation in this [Samoan] matter was inconsistent with the mission and traditions of our Government, in violation of the principles we profess, and in all its phases mischievous and vexatious."

On March 4, 1897, Cleveland turned over the presidency to the incoming William McKinley. As a private citizen, "Old Grover" was doubtless relieved when in 1899 the Samoan islands were divided outright and amicably. The United States made off with several highly desirable outposts, including Tutuila, with its valuable harbor of Pago Pago, in which American seamen and merchants had shown an active interest for about half a century.

Rugged "Old Grover" Cleveland must take high rank as one of the most combative of the Presidents. But his adversaries were mostly domestic antagonists, including the land-grabbing apostles of American imperialism. Cleveland became involved in no foreign war, though he went to the brink with Britain over the Venezuela squabble. To the end he was a friend of the underdog and a foe of the nest-featherer. His deathbed words were, "I have tried so hard to do right."

CHAPTER 25

WILLIAM McKINLEY: THE RELUCTANT IMPERIALIST

Gentlemen, let us ever remember that our interest is concord, not conflict, and that our real eminence rests in the victories of peace, not those of war.

President McKinley's last public statement before assassination, Buffalo, New York, September 5, 1901

A Napoleon for Peace

William McKinley, the twenty-fifth President, was born in Ohio in 1843. His father and one grandfather were iron manufacturers who probably helped to spark the grandson's passionate advocacy of the protective tariff. His elementary education was absorbed at the public schools, and his more advanced instruction at Allegheny College in Pennsylvania. Like his father he became and remained a devout Methodist, as attested by repeated references in his public addresses to the workings of Divine Providence.

McKinley's war record was impressive. In 1861, when only eighteen years of age, he enlisted as a private in an Ohio volunteer regiment to fight in the Civil War. He found himself in the thick of the shooting in West Virginia, Maryland (Antietam), and Virginia, where he had a horse shot from under him. In recognition of his services, involving exceptional gallantry, he rose from the rank of private, to sergeant, to second lieutenant, to first lieutenant, to captain, and then to brevet major of volunteers. He had served successively on the staffs of General Rutherford B. Hayes (the future President), General George Crook, and General W. S. Hancock, a future Democratic presidential candidate.

Although urged to remain in the army, McKinley returned to civilian life, began the study of law, and ultimately established a remunerative practice in his native Ohio. After successfully engaging in local politics, he served for fourteen years in the House of Representatives. Then, after a defeat for reelection, he held office as Governor of Ohio for four years. In the frenzied free-silver campaign of 1896, "Gold Bug" McKinley handily defeated William J. Bryan for the presidency in a memorable battle for the gold standard.

In mature life Major McKinley bore a striking resemblance to Napoleon Bonaparte and was frequently cartooned as such. One of his commonest nicknames was "Napoleon of Protection"—that is, a high protective tariff, which he resolutely supported. Like Napoleon, he was short (five feet, six inches), stout, and dignified in bearing. He was notably calm in temper and was famous for his spotless white vests, which he changed several times a day, especially in the Washington heat before the advent of air conditioning some four decades later. He had a gift for saying "no" in such a gracious manner that aspiring politicians would go away from the White House glowing over the red carnations that McKinley had placed in their buttonholes. Some of them seemed to be happier than they would have been if they had received a coveted office. McKinley was no brusque, impatient Grover Cleveland.

For thirty years McKinley was married to Ida Saxton. After four years of matrimony, she suffered a breakdown following the death of two infant daughters. She ultimately became a tormented epileptic, who, contemporaries thought, was bordering on insanity. On state occasions President McKinley overrode protocol and seated her by his side so that he could cover her face with his handkerchief if she should suffer an epileptic seizure. When the President was shot in 1901, he gasped, "My wife, be careful how you tell her—oh, be careful."

Major McKinley was perhaps the most gentle, kindly, compassionate, and peace-loving man ever to take up residence in the White House. Yet he relentlessly prosecuted a war against Spain and an even bloodier war against the Filipinos, who wanted nothing but the independence they had long been fighting for in vain.

In his inaugural address, March 4, 1897, President McKinley noted that American policy "since the foundation of the Government" had been "to cultivate relations of peace and amity with all the nations of the world, and this accords with my conception of our duty now." In the past the United States had cherished a "policy of noninterference with the affairs of foreign governments," a policy introduced by President Washington. The republic had thus kept itself "free from entanglement, either as allies or foes," and willing to leave undisturbed to foreign nations "the settlement of their own domestic concerns."

McKinley further declared that his aim would be "to pursue a firm and dignified foreign policy." It "shall be just, impartial, ever watchful of our national honor, and always insisting upon the enforcement of the lawful rights of American citizens everywhere. Our diplomacy should seek nothing more and accept nothing less than is due us. We want no wars of conquest; we must avoid the temptation of territorial aggression [in Cuba?]. War should never be entered upon until every agency of peace has failed; peace is preferable to war in almost every contingency."

The President then went on to say, "Arbitration is the true method of settlement of international as well as local or individual differences." He recalled that recently, on the initiative of the United States, a general treaty of arbitration with Britain had been signed in Washington in January 1897, and then sent by Cleveland to the Senate for approval. Favorable action was urgent, McKinley felt, because the United States had taken the lead; because arbitration long had been "the leading feature of our foreign policy"; because arbitration presented "to the world the glorious example of reason and peace, not passion and war, controlling the relations between two of the greatest nations in the world"; and because this splendid example was "certain to be followed" by other nations. McKinley then "respectfully" urged the Senate to move expeditiously on the pending arbitration treaty, "not merely as a matter of policy, but as a duty to mankind."

Indeed, concluded McKinley, the "importance and moral influence of the ratification of such a treaty can hardly be overestimated in the cause of advancing civilization." The pact could "well engage the best thought of the statesmen and people of every country, and I cannot but consider it fortunate that it was reserved to the United States to have the leadership of so grand a work."

Despite the high-flown endorsement by President McKinley, the general arbitration treaty with Britain did not fare well under senatorial hatchets. The "best people" of the country, urging a favorable vote, deluged the Senate with petitions, letters, and telegrams. But the Irish-Americans did not want peace with Britain; nor did other hereditary Britain-haters and Britain-baiters. England was also dedicated to upholding the gold standard at a time when fanatical America silverites were numerous and vocal. Finally, the Senators were jealous of their own prerogatives, which they did not want to hand over on a platter to foreign arbiters.

Methodically, the Senate proceeded with its job of butchering. First, it eviscerated the treaty by tacking on amendments which would exempt altogether certain crucial questions from arbitration. As for the remaining controversies, a two-thirds vote of the Senate would be required before submitting them to an arbitral board. Having chopped off or immobilized the main limbs of the treaty, the Senate showed its mettle by rejecting the miserable remnant on May 5, 1897, two months after McKinley's earnest appeal. A change of three votes would have ensured the necessary two-thirds.

Explosive Cuba

Tradition has it that on inauguration day, March 4, 1897, the departing President Cleveland remarked to the incoming President-elect McKinley, "I am deeply sorry Mr. President to have to pass on to you a war with Spain." Whether these words were uttered or not, the conflict did erupt some thirteen months later.

In 1896 the Spanish government had sent over General Weyler to crush the rebellious Cubans. He reasoned that the best way to combat the shadowy enemy was to imprison the civilians in barbed wire enclosures, where they could not supply the rebels with food and other necessities. Lacking sanitary arrangements, men, women, and children died like flies in "Butcher" Weyler's reconcentration camps.

Mounting atrocities in Cuba were meat for America's emerging yellow press, which featured the frenzied competition for circulation between William R. Hearst and Joseph Pulitzer. Conditions in the island were admittedly horrible, but the "Czars of sensation," unrestrained by formalized ethics, either exaggerated or fabricated many of their most lurid tales. But a turn for the better came late in 1897, when a liberal Spanish regime rose to power. It was prepared to offer the Cubans a species of autonomy, which was so objectionable to Spanish loyalists in Cuba that riots broke out in Havana. Such disturbances pointed to the desirability of sending a United States warship to the scene, where it could provide some protection to American lives and property, as well as remind the Spaniards that there were more battleships back in the United States.

On January 25, 1898 the battleship *Maine* arrived in Havana harbor for a "friendly visit." Three weeks later the vessel mysteriously blew up with a loss of more than 250 officers and men. Many Americans jumped to the conclusion that the Spaniards had treacherously destroyed the visiting ship, but many other citizens were willing to wait for the outcome of the official investigation. Theories regarding the explosion ranged from spontaneous combustion of the coal bunkers near the powder magazine to a mine deliberately set by the Spanish officials. Two inquiries were launched. One was undertaken by the Spanish officials in Havana, and although the Americans would not permit them to examine the wreck, the Spaniards blamed the disaster on an internal accidental explosion. The American investigators, numbering four naval officers, pointed to a supposed submarine mine planted by persons unknown, a category that could have included Cuban insurgents or Spanish officials. Of all possible theories, the one implicating the Spanish authorities was inherently the least plausible; these officers did not want war with the United States. As the saying went, "Spain was 3,000 miles away, America was 90 miles distant, and God was high in the heavens."

War with Spain over the intolerable conditions in Cuba probably would have come anyhow, so inflexible was Madrid. But the explosion on the *Maine* so greatly influenced the American people (and the yellow press) against Spain that the dogs of war were almost bound to be loosed. Yet the irony is that the Spaniards were right; they had nothing whatever to do with blowing up the *Maine*.

Seventy-eight years later, in 1976, Admiral Hyman G. Rickover, under the auspices of the United States Navy, published an exhaustive book, with diagrams, on how the *Maine* was destroyed. His convincing conclusion was that spontaneous combustion in one of the coal bunkers (not uncommon in those days) had spread to an adjacent powder magazine, thus touching off the explosion. This was essentially the finding of the excluded Spanish investigators. In 1898 the Madrid government proposed submitting the issue to arbitration, but President McKinley, who had warmly praised arbitral methods in his inaugural address, would have nothing to do with this kind of foreign intervention.

On March 21, 1898 the American naval court of inquiry sent its report on the *Maine*, unfavorable to Spain, on to the White House. Twenty-two days later the President presented his message to Congress asking for authority to make war on Spain in Cuba. During this period much had happened on the diplomatic front, as well as in McKinley's mind.

Despite the clamor of the yellow press and the American masses for war, the influential business community was inclined to hold back. American capitalists had sunk about $50 million into the island, and their highly vulnerable trade with Cuba amounted to about $100 million annually. Businessmen like Mark Hanna, McKinley's backer, had reason to fear that a war with Spain would retard returning prosperity, weaken the economic structure, generate inflation, and expose American shipping to Spanish warships.

Knowing war at first hand and hating it, McKinley ventured as far as he dared into the jungle of diplomacy. He managed to induce the Spanish government to revoke the herding of civilians in the disease-ridden camps. A few days later, on April 9, 1898, the Madrid regime agreed to grant an armistice to the Cuban insurgents. Yet there was a catch. One nation can order a cease-fire by its own forces, but it takes two to make an armistice, which requires an agreement between or among the contending powers. The Cubans, with American intercession imminent and victory presumably around the corner, were in no mood to consent to an armistice. So the gory struggle would have to grind on—a consideration that figured largely in McKinley's thinking.

With prospects of a peaceful solution in Cuba slowly fading, the responsibility for doing something or nothing rested squarely on McKinley's shoulders. A kindly man, he recoiled from the prospect of war with Spain. On the other hand, the longer the United States kept hands off, the longer the inhumanity in Cuba would persist. Not until after McKinley's death did the public learn that he had anonymously donated $5,000 to the sufferers. His leadership of his own party was threatened, notably by young jingoes, conspicuous among whom was a future Chief Executive, the fiery Theodore Roosevelt, who exploded privately, "The President has no more backbone than a chocolate eclair." The truth is that more backbone was required to resist warlike pressures than to get into the war itself.

McKinley Opts for War

Prolonged nonintervention in Cuba was also playing into the hands of the Democrats. A President can do the maximum good, or what he conceives to be good, only if he is continued in office. McKinley, a staunch Republican and gold-standard man, shrank from the prospect of having the Democrats sweep him out of power in 1900 with "Free Cuba" and "Free Silver" emblazoned on their banners. In the mid-term elections of November 1898 the war hysteria might sweep into Congress a majority of war hawks, who in turn might pass a humiliating resolution for intervention over McKinley's head. The masses seemed desperately determined to have war anyhow, so why not cooperate with the inevitable rather than resist it? War would be inhumane, as all wars are, but armed intervention would put an end to the prolonged inhumanity in Cuba, as in fact it did. Further futile negotiations with Spain would merely prolong the agony.

McKinley was a servant of the people, rather than their dictatorial master, and as a champion of democracy he believed in giving the people what they wanted. His penchant for ear-to-the-ground politics has caused him to be labeled a spineless President, which he was not. Almost certainly more people would have died in Cuba, including Cubans and Americans, if the United States had not intervened.

On April 11, 1898, only two days after Spain had made her partial and illusory capitulation regarding an armistice for the Cuban insurgents, McKinley sent his incendiary war message to Congress. He referred to "the grave crisis" that had developed between Spain and the United States as a result of the warfare that had been raging "for more than three years" in "the neighboring island of Cuba." After describing at considerable length the destruction, terror, and inhumanity in Cuba, all of which had affected Americans and their interests adversely, McKinley summarized in four categories the grounds that he felt would justify intervention by the United States.

First, "the cause of humanity" required "an end to the barbarities, bloodshed, starvation, and horrible miseries now existing there, and which the parties to the conflict are either unable or unwilling to stop or mitigate. It is no answer to say this is all in another country, belonging to another nation, and is therefore none of our business. It is specially our duty, for it is right at our door.

"Another Old Woman Tries to Sweep Back the Sea." Public opinion in favor of war overwhelms McKinley. New York Journal, *1898.*

"Second: We owe it to our citizens in Cuba to afford them that protection and indemnity for life and property which no government there can or will afford, and to that end to terminate conditions that deprive them of legal protection.

"Third: The right to intervene may be justified by the very serious injury to the commerce, trade, and business of our people and by the wanton destruction of property and devastation of the island.

"Fourth, and which is of the utmost importance: The present condition of affairs in Cuba is a constant menace to our peace and entails upon this Government an enormous expense." Here McKinley referred to injuries to the persons and property of American citizens in Cuba; the seizing of American ships by Spain; and the suppression of filibustering expeditions. The result was "strained relations" and "a constant menace to our peace," which compelled the United States "to keep on a semi-war footing with a nation with which we are at peace."

McKinley next referred to the "inexpressible horror" of the destruction of that "noble vessel," the *Maine*. The unanimous report of the American naval court of inquiry commanded "the unqualified confidence of the Government." The investigators had found the lethal explosive to be "a submarine mine," but the responsibility "remains to be fixed."

Whether the Spaniards or others had planted and detonated the mine, McKinley further stated, the disaster "is a patent and impressive proof of a state of things in Cuba that is intolerable. That condition is thus shown to be such that the Spanish Government can not assure safety and security to a vessel of the American Navy in the harbor of Havana on a mission of peace, and rightfully there." (This verdict indeed sounds strange in view of the later finding by Admiral Rickover of an internal accidental explosion.) McKinley concluded his mention of the *Maine* by saying that he had "made no reply" to the Spanish offer "to submit to arbitration all the differences" arising from the loss of the *Maine*.

Near the close of his momentous message McKinley declared that the sole "hope of relief and repose from a condition which can no longer be endured is the enforced pacification of Cuba. In the name of humanity, in the name of civilization, in behalf of endangered American interests which give us the right and the duty to speak and to act, the war in Cuba must stop."

The President then asked for authority from Congress to employ the army and navy to bring an end to existing hostilities and to establish a stable government, though not specifically an independent one. In short, a war to end the three-year war.

At the very end of this message urging armed intervention, McKinley referred to the arrival the day before of telegraphic word from Madrid that the Spanish Queen had directed General Blanco in Cuba to "proclaim a suspension of hostilities, the duration and details of which have not yet been communicated to me." McKinley assumed that this message, plus other evidence, would be carefully considered by the (war-mad) Congress as it debated its future course. If peace should result, "then our aspirations as a Christian, peace-loving people will be realized. If it fails, it will be only another justification for our contemplated action."

This belated reference to the concession from Madrid is a noteworthy example of what President Harry S Truman later called "passing the buck." Critics of McKinley have pointed out that with the stakes so high he should have waited a few days to study with great care the latest proposal for a cease-fire, while simultaneously communicating by cable with the United States Minister in Madrid. But the President had already drafted his war message; Spain had repeatedly held out false hopes; a unilateral cease-fire was not a true armistice; and the chances were good that the war would grind wearily along, with one more disappointment to lament. So McKinley dumped the burning issue into the lap of a war hawk Congress, all the while reasonably certain about the result. In short, he had made up his mind that the United States would have to fight to abate a nuisance.

McKinley's prognosis about the futility of a cease-fire proved to be correct. Eight days later, on April 19, 1898, General Calixto Garcia, still the rebel commander in eastern Cuba, sent a circular to the commanders of the three rebel armies. He ordered them to keep on "shooting up pueblos" and "causing as much damage as possible" until Spain was willing to grant "absolute independence."

On April 19, 1898, eight days after McKinley's war message, Congress passed a fateful joint resolution that was equivalent to a declaration of war. It declared Cuba free; demanded that Spain withdraw; authorized the President to use the army and navy to achieve these objectives; and disclaimed any purpose of annexing Cuba. Two days later Congress formally declared war on Spain, with an overwhelming 310 to 6 vote in the House and a closer 42 to 35 vote in the Senate.

Blundering into Empire

The primary concern of this study is with presidential pugnacity as it relates to the coming or provocation of wars and near-wars. Once the shooting has started, the only way out is forward, at least if the honor of the country is a major consideration.

Secretary of War Russell Alger was an obvious incompetent, so war veteran McKinley to a degree was his own chief of staff. The American navy, with a combination of aggressiveness and good luck, covered itself with glory when Commodore George Dewey destroyed the overmatched Spanish fleet in Manila Bay, and when the American commanders completely wiped out the escaping Spanish fleet near Santiago, Cuba. United States troops, featuring Colonel Theodore Roosevelt's heroics, ultimately captured the city of Santiago. By this time the Spaniards had shed enough blood to satisfy their honor, and they arranged for a protocol through the French Ambassador in Washington (August 12, 1898). This preliminary pact terminated hostilities and roughly outlined the future terms of peace.

A peace commission representing the United States and Spain assembled in Paris in October 1898, and as a result the Spaniards surrendered all title to Cuba. Together with many other American citizens, McKinley believed that the only sure way to prevent recurrent rebellions against Spanish misrule in the Americas was to deprive the Spaniards of the last two major remnants of their once magnificent colonial empire in the Americas, Cuba and Puerto Rico. This solution was in complete accord with McKinley's message to Congress—that is, make war to ensure peace.

The United States also acquired from Spain the South Pacific island of Guam, which was of minor significance, and the Philippine islands, which were of enormous significance. Because their acquisition led to a bloody, protracted, and dishonorable war with the Filipinos, this clash must be regarded as a responsibility of McKinley. Ironically, one of his most compelling motives for taking on the islands was to head off a war among the colony-conscious great powers, as had almost flared forth in Samoa in 1889.

At this time in 1898, McKinley was presented with various alternatives—all bad. He could have kept only the main island, Luzon, but the remaining islands would probably be scooped up by competing colonial powers, including Germany, thus outflanking the American position. Or the American forces in the Philippines could just sail away and leave the powers to scramble for the spoils, like apes for nuts, while possibly triggering a world war into which the United States might be sucked.

The most honorable alternative of all would be to turn the Philippine islands over to the natives, many of whom, like the Cubans, had been fighting the Spaniards for many years. Their leader, Emilio Aguinaldo, had been brought back from exile in Asia by Admiral Dewey, and he and his insurgent forces had cooperated helpfully with the Americans in the capture of Manila. They had evidently been assured, or had convinced themselves, that in return for their help they would receive complete freedom. In his annual message to Congress of December 1899, McKinley "categorically denied" that such assurances had been given by anyone in authority.

McKinley evidently came to believe, or so claimed, that it would be dishonorable to give the Filipinos their complete freedom without significant restraints. They did not appear to be ready for self-government. As a consequence, factions would start fighting among themselves, and bloodshed would go on interminably, as in Cuba. The Americans, having wiped out the rule of Spain, allegedly had a moral responsibility to remain in the islands until order could be guaranteed.

This was an era of worldwide imperialism, and the United States was feeling the oats of its exalted status. Nations that were great powers seemingly had to have imperial headaches. But British poet Kipling was trumpeting the virtues of taking on "the white man's burden" of clothing, feeding, educating, governing, and Christianizing colored peoples—those "lesser breeds without the law." In the case of the Philippines, there were also rich natural resources to be tapped, and McKinley was not deaf to the preachments of Mark Hanna and other apostles of big business. As one historian has slyly paraphrased McKinley, "God directs us, perhaps it will pay." Ironically, the richer the natural resources of the Philippines appeared to be, the less capable the

Filipinos seemed to be of exercising independence, at least in the eyes of American exploiters.

So it was that McKinley cabled the peace commissioners in Paris their final instructions, which were to take all the Philippines. The Senate narrowly approved the treaty in due season, but Congress, as we see it now, made one costly oversight. It failed to pass at the same time a resolution declaring, as it had done in the case of Cuba, that as soon as order was restored in the Philippines, the islands would be turned over to their inhabitants. The natives feared that they had merely changed Spanish misrule for American tyranny, and on February 4, 1899, they rose in revolt against the occupying United States troops. In annexing an empire, McKinley had annexed a war.

The Philippine Liability

Like Abraham Lincoln, also a compassionate man, McKinley prosecuted with vigor the war launched by the rebels against the mighty United States. He believed that he had at heart the best interests of the Filipino people in his determination to civilize, educate, and otherwise uplift them. He would bring "peace and tranquility" under a "beneficent government," as he declared in his third annual message (December 1899). The few ambitious insurgents, he believed, did not represent "the wishes and aspirations of the great mass of the Filipino people."

The inglorious Philippine insurrection dragged on from 1899 to 1902, lasting longer than the "glorious" war with Spain and involving, all told, some 120,000 American soldiers. The insurgents, defeated in open warfare, resorted to guerrilla tactics and barbarities. As often happens when civilized people fight primitive tribes, counter-atrocities occurred, with the Americans viciously holding up their end. The United States, having professedly taken on the Philippines so as to benefit the Filipinos, created an international scandal by torturing and murdering some of them, as happened later in Vietnam.

Yet McKinley told Congress that the rebellion must be "unflinchingly crushed." Many *insurrectos* would have to be shot so that the United States could do the remaining masses good; they would have to be destroyed, as later in Vietnam, in order to be saved. In his annual message of December 1900 McKinley, without mentioning the atrocity scandals besmirching American honor, referred to having secured control of "the greater part of the islands." He would confer on the masses "fuller measures of local self-government, of education, and of industrial and agricultural development." In short, these Filipinos were "the wards of the nation."

In his second inaugural address (March 1901) McKinley praised his nation for having taken the uplifting imperialistic path. The war with Spain had become "inevitable," though he had done "all that in honor could be done to avert it, but without avail." The conflict had "imposed upon us obligations from which we cannot escape and from which it would be dishonorable to seek escape. We are now at peace with the world, and it is my fervent prayer that if differences arise between us and other powers they may be settled by peaceful arbitration and that hereafter we may be spared the horrors of war." Ironically, he had not responded at all to Spain's offer to arbitrate the *Maine* mystery in 1898.

McKinley went on in this second inaugural address to deny that "we lose our own liberties by securing the enduring foundations of liberty to others." And were "not those we serve [Filipinos?] lifted up and blessed?" The conflict in the Philippines, he added, was in its last phases. "Our countrymen should not be deceived. We are not waging war against the inhabitants of the Philippines Islands. A portion of them are making war against the United States." The American nation "will not leave the destiny of the loyal millions in the islands to the disloyal thousands who are in rebellion against the United States." Nor was this all. "Order under civil institutions will come as soon as those who now break the peace shall keep it."

The Filipino insurrection supposedly came to an end in 1902, the year after McKinley's assassination. But sporadic fighting in the jungles dragged on for several more years, and the United States did not rid itself formally of these enormously expensive islands until the Fourth of July, 1946, when the Philippines became a completely independent nation, at least officially. A controversial defensive obligation remained for many years thereafter.

By happy contrast, Commodore Dewey's bothersome victory at Manila sped a joint resolution for the annexation of the Hawaiian Islands through Congress. McKinley signed it on May 4, 1898. We recall that President Cleveland had withdrawn the hurry-up Hawaiian treaty of 1893 from the Senate. Another treaty was negotiated in June 1897 by the incoming McKinley administration, but the Senate rejected it, unwilling to take Hawaii even as a sugar-coated gift.

Dewey's smashing victory at Manila Bay changed everything. Hawaii was evidently needed as a way station for sending troops and supplies to Dewey across the broad Pacific. So why not accept the islands, exclude other rival powers, extend the defensive coastline of the United States some 2,000 miles out, and fulfill America's manifest destiny? The joint resolution of annexation passed both houses of Congress overwhelmingly, 209 to 91 in the House and 42 to 21 in the Senate. President McKinley, who signed the next day, remarked perceptively, "Annexation is not change; it is consummation."

Involvement in China

For a half-century or so the United States had been deploying warships in Chinese waters and landing Marines on China's shores. This problem gained greater prominence later in the nineteenth century, after the Sino-Japanese war of 1894–1895 had revealed the vulnerability of the sprawling Chinese empire. Predatory imperialistic powers, notably Russia and Germany, moved in and, much like vultures tearing blubber from a stranded whale, wrested from the Chinese government valuable leaseholds and economic spheres of influence.

The multipower scramble in China provided not only the combustibles of war but the disagreeable prospect of excluding American commerce from some of the richest Chinese areas. In the summer of 1899, McKinley's Secretary of State, John Hay, leaped into the breach with his Open Door notes, addressed to all of the major powers. He called upon them to proclaim that within their acknowledged leaseholds and spheres of influence they would respect certain Chinese rights and permit fair competition. In short, a fair field and no favors.

The great powers, thus smoked out, paid lip service to the ideal of an Open Door, except for Russia, which in effect declined. Yet Hay, like a clever salesman, accepted the Russian refusal as an acceptance. The next year, in July 1900, he unilaterally attempted to widen the Open Door principle to preserve additionally China's "territorial and administrative integrity."

But the concept of the Open Door, never well hinged, was engulfed by the outbreak of the Boxer rebellion in 1900.

Open Door or no, nationalistic Chinese did not care to be used as the door mat. A super-patriotic group known as the "Boxers" rose up and gave vent to the frenzied cry, "Kill Foreign Devils." More than two hundred missionaries and other stranded whites, including the German Ambassador, were brutally murdered. A considerable number of foreign diplomats, all entitled to immunity under international law, were beseiged behind improvised barricades in Peking. Their stubborn resistance stands out as an epic of heroism.

An international rescue force of some eighteen thousand men, hastily assembled, fought its way to Peking and arrived just in time to rescue the beseiged foreigners. This multi-uniformed army consisted of troops from Japan, Russia, Britain, France, Germany, and the United States. The American warriors were dispatched from the Philippines, to which they had come to fight the Filipinos, and all told they numbered about 2,500. Here we witness contradictory foreign policies at work. Joint intercession by the Americans, especially in far-off Asia, ran counter to George Washington's fixed policy of nonentanglement and noninvolvement. On the other hand, the Adams-Jefferson concern for protecting American lives and property took priority during an urgent crisis. As a matter of fact, in 1898- 1899, well prior to the Boxer intervention, the United States provided a guard for the American legation at Peking and the consulate at Tientsin during a contest between the Dowager Empress and her son.

Angry and vindictive, the victorious invading powers in 1901 saddled the beaten Chinese with an excessive indemnity of $333 million, of which some $25 million was apportioned to the United States. When the McKinley government discovered that this sum was more than adequate for losses incurred, it remitted about $18 million. A grateful Chinese government, as a prolonged gesture of reciprocal good will, used the refund to educate a selected group of Chinese students in the United States, thus contributing to the partial westernization of China.

To the end McKinley insisted that he bore no malice toward the Chinese people as such. "Our declared aims," he told Congress in his fourth (and last) annual message, December 1900, "involved no war against the Chinese nation. We adhered to the legitimate office of rescuing the imperiled legation, obtaining redress for the wrongs already suffered, securing wherever possible the safety of American life and property in China, and preventing a spread of the disorders or their recurrence." To the very end, McKinley would wage war in China only to do the natives good, as in Cuba and the Philippines.

In the area of relatively minor disturbances during McKinley's administration, the documents show that in 1898 and again in 1899 American armed forces were employed in Nicaragua to protect American lives and property in this sensitive area tentatively earmarked for an isthmian canal. And in 1899 the Germans, British, and Americans in Samoa ceased their feuding long enough to divide the spoils amicably, with the United States obtaining outright the long-coveted naval base at the harbor of Pago Pago. The far-flung American empire was expanding, in this instance by peaceful means.

President McKinley presents a perplexing paradox. A benign man who had seen enough of war, he reluctantly led his nation into a conflict with both Spain and the Filipinos. Had wiser policies prevailed, both of these ugly episodes might have been avoided.

CHAPTER 26

THEODORE ROOSEVELT: BRANDISHER OF THE BIG STICK

Generally peace tells for righteousness; but if there is conflict between the two, then our fealty is due first to the cause of righteousness. Unrighteous wars are common, and unrighteous peace is rare; but both should be shunned.

President Roosevelt,
Annual Message,
Dec. 6, 1904

A Cowboy President

"Teddy" Roosevelt, elevated to the White House by an assassin's bullet, was clearly one of the most pugnacious men ever to appear in American public life. In hotness of temper and bellicosity, Andrew Jackson may have exceeded him, but not by a wide margin. Before becoming President, Roosevelt fought with fists and words; Jackson fought most conspicuously with knife and dueling pistol. Still, responsibility sobered both leaders, for the record reveals that neither of these two Presidents either started a major war or got into one.

Theodore (Teddy) Roosevelt, the fifth cousin of the future President Franklin Delano Roosevelt, was born to a Dutch-descended patrician family in New York City. His early education came largely from tutors and travel abroad, including Germany and Egypt. As a spindly youth, young Teddy was severely handicapped by asthma and an extreme case of shortsightedness. His vision was finally corrected by thick-lensed, pinch-on spectacles, and his body was strengthened by a self-imposed regimen of exercise, which he maintained in the White House and even later. In his prime he was a stocky and muscular five feet, ten inches, with a heavy brown mustache that only partially concealed strong white teeth.

At Harvard young Roosevelt graduated in 1880 with Phi Beta Kappa honors and also competed on the Harvard boxing team, surprisingly as a lightweight. By his own admission he did only moderately well in this sport, but he did develop an enduring love for "the manly art of self-defense." In later life he made the acquaintance of a number of leading professional pugilists, and repeatedly put on the gloves with friendly opponents at the White House. In one of these impromptu bouts, Roosevelt received a punch in his left eye that resulted in partial blindness in it for the rest of his life. Yet he rejoiced that his right eye was spared for marksmanship, and he repeatedly urged boxing as a recreational sport for the armed services. In his view this masculine but brutal exercise helped to keep alive the virile juices and virtues.

Leaving Harvard in 1880, young Roosevelt had a brief bout with the study of law, which he found too slow and stuffy. He then turned to politics for three years, during which he served in the New York State Assembly. Before doing so, he exhibited his interest in fighting men by publishing a highly creditable book on *The Naval War of 1812* (1882), the first of about twenty of his literary contributions.

Then came two years as a cattle rancher in the Badlands of the Dakotas, into which he sank $50,000 of his patrimony. He lost most of his money but gained a muscular physique that later served him in good stead. At first the rough and tough cowboys did not know what to make of this bespectacled tenderfoot, but "Four Eyes" gained much respect when he knocked out a bully with his bare fists. One of his favorite sayings became, "Never hit if it is honorably possible to avoid a fight, but never hit soft." At the time of another dispute in the Dakotas, there was some talk of a challenge to a duel. Roosevelt reportedly remarked that he would name rifles at twelve paces, whereupon the subject was dropped.

The dream of assembling a volunteer regiment of Rough Riders came to Roosevelt at an early date. During recurrent disturbances near the Mexican border, and particularly during the crisis with Chile in 1891, he toyed with the concept of getting into action at the head of tough fighting men. When the Venezuela boundary dispute ballooned into a crisis with Great Britain in 1895, he ardently hoped for war, since he felt the country had gone soft and needed a rousing foreign blood-letting to stiffen its backbone. He realized that the British navy would probably bombard and lay waste the coastal cities, but the Middle West would still be there. Patriotic Americans in the interior would spring to arms and settle matters victoriously at gunpoint in Ottawa, Montreal, and Quebec.

As a reward for political campaigning, President McKinley appointed Roosevelt Assistant Secretary of the Navy in 1897, a position in which the ebullient Teddy displayed an excess of zeal that greatly embarrassed his immediate superior. But the young upstart did manage to get George Dewey chosen as commander of the Asiatic fleet. During these months T.R. was on fire to plunge into war with Spain to free Cuba despite the cautious McKinley, who, Roosevelt indicated privately, did not have the backbone of a jellyfish.

When war finally came, the impatient cowboy, a man of action, resigned his naval post and organized a volunteer regiment of "Rough Riders," consisting of cowboys, ex-college boys, expolo players, ex-convicts, and other rugged characters. Roosevelt was made a lieutenant colonel under Colonel Leonard Wood, although totally without military experience and dangerously near-sighted (he brought along a dozen spare pairs of spectacles cached on his person or nearby).

Roosevelt's Rough Riders got to Cuba all right, but in the confusion they left most of their horses behind. Their glory-hungry leader outflanked rival regiments to get into action, shot a Spaniard with his revolver, exposed himself and his men recklessly, and later boasted that his command suffered heavier casualties than any other American regiment. After a brisk engagement at Kettle Hill, he was made a full colonel but thought he deserved the Congressional Medal of Honor as well. He published a book the next year about his exploits entitled *The Rough Riders* (1899), which a leading contemporary humorist thought should have been entitled "Alone in Cubia [sic]."

The colorful, controversial, and combative Rough Rider emerged as the one enduring hero of the Spanish-American War. A master of keeping himself in the limelight, at a wedding he eclipsed the bride, at a funeral the corpse. Capitalizing on his martial fame and elected Governor of New York, he was uproariously nominated for the vice-presidential slot in 1900 on McKinley's Republican ticket by a vote of 925 to 0. Big business was acutely unhappy with this choice, because it regarded Roosevelt, "that damned cowboy," as a bull-in-the-China-shop radical. "Don't you realize," one industrial giant reportedly shouted, "that there is only one heartbeat between that madman and the presidency of the United States?" The worst fears of Big Business were realized, for President McKinley died from an assassin's bullet in September 1901, and Roosevelt, at age forty-two, became the youngest President up to that point in American history.

In domestic affairs, President Teddy Roosevelt was constantly assailing someone—or so it seemed. His most spectacular efforts came in public speeches, which he delivered with a high, piercing voice, sometimes between clenched teeth. His hands, fists, and arms would flail the air, as though he were a man fighting bees instead of his assorted foes. He had a "bully time" knocking heads together, for apparently this exercise kept his virility alive. On a visit to Rome after leaving the White House he got into what he called an "elegant row" with the Vatican.

Rumor had it that certain metropolitan newspapers set up permanent headlines with the words "Roosevelt Flays," followed by whatever he happened to be flaying on that particular day. His formidable list of foes included Congress, crooked politicians, big business, the trusts, plutocrats ("malefactors of great wealth"), the grabbers of public land, the dogooders ("Muckrakers"), the Democrats, birth control advocates, divorce, patent medicine vendors, impure food, national dishonor, "civilized softness," and doctrinaire pacifists ("flubdubs" and "mollycoddles").

Venezuelan Vexations

If Roosevelt was a two-fisted fighter before coming to the White House, and if he was pugnacious in assailing assorted domestic foes, he managed to keep a fairly level head in his management of foreign affairs. His basic policy , of course, was that of the Big Stick. He enjoyed quoting a proverb: "Speak softly and carry a Big Stick, [and] you will go far." The Navy was his stick behind the door, and no President has ever pushed so hard and so often for more big battleships than the ex-Rough Rider, especially in his annual messages to Congress. When he left the White House in 1909, the United States Navy was about second in the world, clearly ranking far behind that of Great Britain.

The rationale behind the Big Stick was quite simple. If a nation had no effective bludgeon, it could shout and screech, and nothing good would happen. If it had a big stick, it could

Teddy and the big stick against trusts and other foes. New York Globe.

speak softly and work its will without having to resort to force. At times Roosevelt, although he had the Big Stick, would raise his shrill voice, but he did not need to. Despite some obvious bluster, he achieved his major objectives without having to fire a shot. Weaker nations did not enjoy being pushed around, but there was nothing they could do about it except to knuckle under.

Roosevelt's repeated applications of the Big Stick came most spectacularly and permanently in the Caribbean area, just below the soft underbelly of the United States. The first conspicuous trouble spot involved Venezuela, then under the iron heel of an unscrupulous dictator, Cipriano Castro. Recurrent civil war there had been ruinous to the investments of foreigners, notably the British and the Germans, and these two powers were sorely tempted to intervene. Roosevelt himself did not regard the Monroe Doctrine as a deterrent to the collection of valid debts from irresponsible Latin Americans. Time and again the United States itself had intervened all over the world to protect American lives and property. As Roosevelt wrote privately in 1901, "If any South American country misbehaves toward any European country, let the European country spank it." He told Congress in December 1901, "We do not guarantee any state against punishment if it misconducts itself, provided that punishment does not take the form of the acquisition of territory by any non-American power."

Reassured by Roosevelt's tolerant attitude, British and German naval units, later joined by the Italians, mounted a "pacific blockade" of Venezuela in 1902. The Germans sank two gunboats, and the allies captured several more. Thus properly "spanked," dictator Castro cried aloud for the arbitration that he had earlier spurned. The Roosevelt government, ostensibly acting only as a messenger boy, forwarded this proposal to London and Berlin, both of which accepted arbitration in principle. The case was closed after the Hague Court ruled on the Venezuelan claims in 1904.

Thirteen years later, in 1915, the same German Kaiser had brutally invaded "poor little Belgium," and Roosevelt, who had never admired Wilhelm II, felt free to tell the whole story behind the story. He related how in 1902 he had called in the German Ambassador, laid down a stern ultimatum, threatened to send Admiral Dewey to Venezuelan waters with the American fleet, and thus had forced the Kaiser to consent to arbitration.

The weakness of Roosevelt's story is that there is not a shred of evidence in the German archives to support it. Either the incident never happened, or it was never reported by the German embassy in Washington, or the Berlin records were deliberately destroyed. Roosevelt's private presidential letters contain several veiled allusions to the Venezuelan episode, significantly before he left the White House and while the details were presumably fresh in mind. He refers delicately to an untold tale about how he got the Kaiser out of Venezuela (1902–1903), and indicates that someday he would come clean with the full story. In short, if he dreamed up the tale, he evidently did so before he ceased to be President and at a time when he had no special reason to portray the Kaiser in an unfavorable light. It is conceivable that he exerted some behind-the-scenes pressure on the German Emperor, although not in the spectacular fashion that he later described with such evident relish. Actually, Dewey's fleet was in Caribbean waters, and its very presence was a veritable threat.

But the Big Stick was really not needed during the Venezuela episode, and for this reason Roosevelt may not have used it. American public opinion was being aroused against the British and German seizures and sinkings, and that was pressure enough. Although Roosevelt may have thought it proper for foreign nations to do a little "spanking," not all Americans were prepared to interpret the Monroe Doctrine so laxly. What the powers were up to in Venezuela looked more like the iron fist than the velvet glove. To many red-blooded Americans the musty Monroe Doctrine had more relevance than Roosevelt was willing to acknowledge.

The Big Stick in Panama

If doubt lingers as to whether or not Roosevelt clubbed the Kaiser out of Venezuela, none whatever exists as to his having big-sticked Colombia out of Panama. The United States is still doing penance for the impetuosity and bellicosity of the Rough Rider in 1902.

Interest in an artificial waterway at the isthmus rose to new heights in the United States during and after the Spanish-American War. In particular, trade with the nation's new Pacific possessions, notably Hawaii and the Philippines, obviously would be benefited by such an engineering miracle. The victorious war with Spain had dramatically advertised the need for a canal that would permit vessels of the United States Navy to be shuttled from one ocean to the other without having to triple the length of their voyage by steaming all the way around South America.

Initial obstacles to digging the isthmian canal were diplomatic rather than physical. By the yellowing Clayton-Bulwer treaty of 1850 with Great Britain, the United States could not honorably construct the proposed waterway and retain exclusive control over it. After protracted negotiations with London, the Hay-Pauncefote treaty of 1901 was negotiated and ratified. By its specific terms the United States was permitted to construct, control, police, and fortify the proposed isthmian waterway.

The next problem was the precise location. A commission of engineers appointed by President McKinley recommended the Nicaraguan route as against the Panama route. Among other advantages, Nicaragua was many sailing hours nearer the United States. The French-spawned New Panama Canal Company, eager to salvage some $40 million from the United States for its isthmian holdings, then got busy with its persuasive lobbyists in Washington. A bill passed the House of Representatives providing for the Nicaraguan route, but the Senate amended the measure in such a way as to give preference to the Panama route. Yet the needed right of way had to be secured "within a reasonable time and upon reasonable terms." If the President failed to do so, he would have to turn from Panama to Nicaragua.

Using the Nicaragua alternative as a lever, the State Department extorted a treaty from Colombia that was highly advantageous to the United States. Roosevelt was to secure in perpetuity a canal zone for a cash payment of $10 million and an annual payment of $250,000, to start in nine years. The Colombian Senate in Bogotá, obviously wanting more money for this valuable natural asset, voted unanimously (August 12, 1903) to reject the draft treaty, although favoring a renewal of negotiations with Washington.

Seldom a patient man, Roosevelt reacted with fury. The Republican National Convention loomed only some ten months away, and as an accidental President he was desperately eager to win the nomination in his own right. Delay would hurt his chances, but making the dirt fly at Panama would do more than anything else to impress the American people. Eventually, more kinds of dirt flew than he had anticipated.

At various times, mostly in private, Roosevelt bitterly condemned the "corrupt pithecoid community" in Colombia as "inefficient bandits," "foolish and homicidal corruptionists," "contemptible little creatures," "jack rabbits," and "cat rabbits." He insisted that the situation was "exactly as if a road agent had tried to hold up a man," and he declared that the "blackmailers of Bogotá" should not be allowed to bar civilized progress. Roosevelt actually went so far as to prepare a message, which he finally withheld, urging that the canal zone be taken by force of arms. But Secretary of State John Hay did cable a virtual ultimatum that the Colombians bitterly resented.

Roosevelt's fighting instincts, always rather close to the surface, caused him to react unfairly. A sovereign nation, for whatever reasons, will not willingly accept terms that it regards as unsatisfactory. And the United States Senate, like the Senate in Bogotá, has been known to reject treaties.

Like Roosevelt, the Panamanians were greatly distressed by the Colombian rejection, though for different reasons. They had counted on the enriching prosperity that would come with the Panama Canal, and they feared that Roosevelt would honor the law passed by Congress and turn to Nicaragua after this unwelcome roadblock. Panama was ripe for revolt from Colombia; by Roosevelt's count there had been fifty-three uprisings in fifty-seven years, Under the time-honored treaty of 1846 with Colombia, the United States had been granted the right to preserve the neutrality of the isthmus so that commercial traffic could flow back and forth without interruption. On about seven different occasions the United States had landed troops to ensure "free transit," but always with the approval or consent of the Colombian authorities. A reading of the treaty of 1846 makes clear that "free transit" was to be ensured to the advantage of the Colombians. Otherwise, one cannot imagine why they should have accepted such a hand-tying pact.

Not unexpectly, the Panamanians rose in revolt in November 1903, nearly three months after the "blackmailers of Bogota" had killed the treaty. Roosevelt resorted to his trusty Big Stick when he dispatched the warship *Nashville* to Colón, on the Atlantic side, where it prevented the Colombian troops from landing, crossing the isthmus to Panama City on the Pacific side, and thus crushing the uprising. Roosevelt then and later insisted that he had merely honored the treaty of 1846 with Colombia and had kept the transit route open. He did not add that all the previous Yankee interventions under that agreement had been to assist Colombia, not to aid the rebels. On November 6, 1903, after an indecently short wait of only three days, Washington extended *de facto* recognition to puppet Panama.

A scheming Frenchman, Philippe Bunau Varilla, again appeared on the scene as an agent of the newly fledged Panamanian government. More interested in securing the $40 million in salvage for the French canal company, he hastily signed an epochal treaty, although two bona fide Panamanians were on their way to Washington. The new pact, concluded on November 18, 1903, granted to the United States in perpetuity a canal zone ten miles wide instead of six miles, as well as extraordinary sovereign rights. The financial terms were the same as those rejected by "the blackmailers of Bogotá," $10 million at the outset and $250,000 a year.

Critics of Roosevelt's imperialistic intervention in Panama condemned him for having sullied the good name of the United States. Abroad, and especially in Europe, the press jeered that the Americans could no longer adopt a holier-than-thou attitude toward foreign imperialists. Roosevelt was evidently not directly involved in plotting the revolution in Panama, but he certainly had more than a vague idea of what was going on. And he deliberately and knowingly used the Big Stick to achieve success when he issued orders to prevent the Colombian troops from landing and crushing the rebels.

For the rest of his life the Rough Rider defended his conduct in this shabby affair with vehemence, if not discretion. In his next annual message to Congress he avowed that he had acted in response to "a mandate from civilization" to brush aside the highwaymen of Bogotá. But he neglected to say that an act of Congress required him to turn next to Nicaragua, where no revolution was needed, where the local government was eager to have the canal, and where American experts had decided that a waterway could be built that was more advantageous to the United States. But regarding this pro-Nicaragua act of Congress, Roosevelt allegedly shouted in private, "Damn the law. I want the canal built!"

As time wore on and the Panama Canal neared completion, Roosevelt became more defiantly indiscreet. In a famous speech in Berkeley, California (1911), he reportedly boasted, "I took the Canal Zone and let Congress debate; and while the debate goes on the Canal does also." In short, the end justifies the means.

Various attempts in the United States to placate Colombia were aborted or fell short of the mark while the noisy Roosevelt was still alive. There would be no apology or "blackmail" balm, he cried, except over his dead body. He came to believe that Colombia had wronged the United States by not allowing herself to be benefited. By 1921 oil had been discovered in Colombia, and American developers were being given the cold shoulder. The more this oil gushed from Colombian soil, the more tears of remorse gushed from the eyes of certain Yankee promoters. Roosevelt was now dead, and a treaty was finally approved by the Senate in 1921 which granted Colombia some $25 million in conscience money or what some wit has called "canalimony." The irony is that if $15 million had been offered Colombia in 1903, the original treaty probably would have been approved and a vast amount of controversy and bad feeling would have been averted. The Rough Rider had acted more roughly than necessary.

Roosevelt's brandishing of the Big Stick against Colombia in Panama doubtless helped him win the Republican nomination "in his own right" at Chicago, June 23, 1904. He received all 994 votes on the first ballot, a rare achievement, and the nomination was then formally made unanimous. The Panama coup was evidently not needed for this victory at the convention.

Nor was the famous Perdicaris incident. Ion Perdicaris, a Greek subject, who may or may not have been a naturalized citizen at the time, had been seized in Morocco by a brigand named Raisuli. United States warships (the Big Stick) were rushed to Moroccan waters, although these vessels could not have done much fighting in the mountains and desert.

Arrangements were soon made for the release of Perdicaris, but the Chicago nominating convention, so Roosevelt thought, needed to be sparked into life. Ever the showman, he arranged for a cablegram to be dispatched to the American consul general in Morocco: "Perdicaris alive or Raisuli dead." This was red-blooded stuff, and when read to the Republican delegates it excited loud cheers for the two-fisted Roosevelt, who was nominated the next day. But the message was completely unnecessary and hence a cheap effort at rabble-rousing; in fact the unread part of the telegram gave orders not to use force without specific instructions. The State Department later ruled that Perdicaris had been a naturalized citizen all along.

Caribbean Confrontations

In bothersome Cuba, the recently acquired protectorate, Roosevelt also wielded the Big Stick, but reluctantly, temporarily, and with circumspection. He had inherited this headache from McKinley, in whose administration Congress had adopted the Platt Amendment (1901). By its terms the "Queen of the Antilles," as Roosevelt called the lush island, was to discourage any foreign lodgment, avoid excessive indebtedness to foreigners, provide naval and coaling stations for the United States (Guantánamo), and permit American armed intervention to preserve order and maintain Cuban independence.

As the event proved, Roosevelt had no annexationist designs whatever on Cuba. After a semblance of order had been restored in 1902, he withdrew American troops, to the amazement of cynical European imperialists. But in 1906 the insurrectionary habit reasserted itself, and disorders burst forth anew. Roosevelt wrote privately that he was "so angry with that infernal little Cuban republic that I would like to wipe its people off the face of the earth. All that we wanted from them was that they would behave themselves and be prosperous and happy so that we would not have to interfere."

Fearing that foreigners would intervene, Roosevelt sent American troops into Cuba in 1906, all in the interests of peace, law, and order. Luckily, the Yankees were able to restore a semblance of harmony, and in 1909 the United States troops were withdrawn, the month before the Rough Rider left office.

Roosevelt feared that some foreign power, perhaps Germany, would secure a lethal lodgment near the Panama Canal lifeline. One consequence was a deep and prolonged involvement by the United States in Santo Domingo. The government of this "wretched" republic had indulged in the "insurrectionary habit" so long that foreign debt collectors might come and stay. If they remained they would violate the Monroe Doctrine, with the consequent danger of war. Because the United States would not permit European powers to intervene, Roosevelt argued that he had a strong obligation to collect the necessary money himself, remit it to the creditors, and thus keep them safely on the other side of the Atlantic. This policy, popularly known as the

Roosevelt corollary to the Monroe Doctrine, meant in effect that the United States itself would intervene to prevent foreign intervention. The Rough Rider vehemently disclaimed any desire to annex troublesome Santo Domingo, any more than "a gorged boa constrictor" would want "to swallow a porcupine wrong-end-to."

Roosevelt's next move was to secure control of the Dominican customs houses, for they produced the revenue that the grafters found so juicy. After a show of force (the Big Stick), the island regime reluctantly "invited" the Colossus of the North to step in. An agreement was reached under which the Yankees would collect all customs duties, retain 45 percent for running the Dominican government, and allocate 55 percent to pay off outstanding foreign indebtedness. Roosevelt did all this under an executive agreement, to the acute dissatisfaction of his critics, but in 1907 a treaty passed the Senate approving the caretaker scheme.

Financially, the Rooseveltian intervention in the Dominican Republic was a gratifying success—to the Yankees. Customs receipts swelled, debts decreased, and revolutions declined. Most unhappy were the grafting Dominican politicians, who valued sovereignty above solvency, especially where lush pickings were within reach. At the time other Latin Americans did not protest with undue vehemence, but they did in later years when the Roosevelt corollary to the Monroe Doctrine was used to justify elsewhere a lengthening list of Caribbean interventions. Mistakenly, many Latinos cursed the unoffending and long-dead Monroe instead of the highhanded wielder of the Big Stick.

During the rule of Roosevelt, from 1901 to 1909, armed interventions occurred in Columbia (1901, 1902), Honduras (1903), the Dominican Republic (1903), Panama (1903–1914), the Dominican Republic (1904), Korea (1904–1905), Cuba (1906–1909), and Honduras (1907). Obviously, the Big Stick gathered no cobwebs, although most of these interventions were in the interests of peace—that is, to protect American lives and property, to prevent greater disturbances, or to avert foreign intervention.

Japan a World Power

Oddly enough, Theodore Roosevelt, the fight-thirsty warrior of 1898, became the conciliator of 1905 and winner of the Nobel Peace Prize in 1906. How did this near-miracle come about?

Lethal rivalry between Japan and Russia over territory in

East Asia, notably China's Manchuria, led to a sanguinary conflict between these two nations. It began with a devastating sneak attack on Russian naval units in Chinese waters at Port Arthur in February 1904. The small but efficient Japanese soldiers next administered a humiliating series of beatings to the inept Russians, both on land and on sea. But as the strain and drain of war continued, little Japan began to run short of manpower and money—of men and yen. Not wishing to betray such weakness to the enemy, the Japanese secretly approached Roosevelt with the request that he mediate a peace between the two belligerents.

The fighting President was not eager to get involved in this fight, for he was well aware that honest mediators suffer brickbats from both sides. But he also realized that if either Japan or Russia collapsed, the Asiatic balance of power would be upset and the victor would pose a threat to American interests in Eastern Asia, notably the Philippine Islands, not to mention America's commercial and missionary interests elsewhere.

Accordingly, Roosevelt subordinated his personal interests to what he conceived to be the national interest and reluctantly consented to serve. Under his vigorous proddings, the negotiators of Russia and those of Japan met in 1905 near Portsmouth, New Hampshire. The politely bowing Japanese, fully aware of their substantial victories, demanded a huge indemnity to pay for the cost of the war, plus the Russian island of Sakhalin. Roosevelt found both sides stubborn, even though he blustered behind the scenes. He finally induced the Japanese to give way by abandoning their demand for an indemnity and by agreeing to take only half of Sakhalin Island.

Great was the disappointment and bitterness in Japan, where the President's picture was turned to the wall. Nor were the Russians happy; they fatuously believed that with one more campaign they could have beaten their tenacious foe. Russian officials spread the tale that Roosevelt was not of Dutch descent at all but of a Jewish line named "Rosenfelt." The Rough Rider no doubt took pride in the Nobel Peace Price of 1906, which his strenuous efforts as a mediator merited. Probably he would have preferred the Congressional Medal of Honor for his derring-do in Cuba in 1898.

As events turned out, two historic friendships wilted on the wind-swept plains of Manchuria. The relationship between the United States and Russia, already sickly, fell upon more evil days. Relations with Japan underwent a severe strain. During the Russo-Japanese War of 1904–1905 Japan had emerged as a great power, much as the United States was generally thought to have come of age as a result of the war with Spain in 1898. The two nations were now Far Eastern rivals, as feelings of jealousy, suspicion, and fear substantially displaced the formerly happy relationship of teacher and protégé. To many Americans, including Theodore Roosevelt, the Japanese were getting too big for their kimonos.

Following the burdensome Russo-Japanese war, hundreds of Japanese laborers with their families began to leave their tax-burdened rice paddies for the spacious and fertile valleys of California. Old-time residents began to fear this new "yellow peril," which supplanted the earlier one spawned by the Chinese. Following the ruinous earthquake and fire in San Franciso in 1906, the local Board of Education, cramped for space, set aside a segregated school, which all Oriental children of all ages would have to attend, regardless of inconvenience. The reason openly given was to reduce overage crowding in the white schools, but probably important also was a desire to express dissatisfaction with the continuing influx of so much cheap Oriental labor.

In Japan public opinion reacted angrily and dangerously. The victorious Japanese, feeling their muscles after defeating Russia, were quick to resent any suggestion of racial inferiority, especially in relation to children. There was even much irresponsible talk of war in the Japanese press, which did not understand that the powerful Washington government had no control whatever over local school affairs. President Roosevelt was deeply worried, writing his son that the "infernal fools in California" seemed bent in provoking a war that the whole nation might have to fight.

Unable to control the school board, Roosevelt gave full vent to his pugnacity when, in his annual message to Congress (December 1906), he blasted the objectionable school order of the San Franciscans as a "wicked absurdity." He also hinted at strong measures. The Japanese were pleased, but the Californians were sorely displeased, and they reacted bitterly against Roosevelt's bullying with his verbal Big Stick.

Roosevelt soon realized that brandishing his trusty club at the Californians was getting him nowhere. He thereupon invited the eight-man school board of San Franciso to come to Washington at government expense. When these small-time politicians, the head man under indictment for graft, reached the rarefied atmosphere of the White House, they fell under the spell of both the Big Stick and Roosevelt's torrential verbosity. They finally agreed to a compromise by which Japanese children of proper age and preparation would be permitted to enter schools beside Caucasians. In return, Roosevelt agreed to negotiate an executive agreement with Japan by which the Tokyo government itself, without undue loss of face, would deny passports to coolies coming directly to the mainland of the United States. Such an understanding was concluded with Tokyo in 1907–1908, and the storm clouds disappeared.

We should note that in connection with the Japanese schoolboy incident Roosevelt vented his Big Stick pugnacity at the "wicked" Californians, not at the Japanese, whom he rather admired, not least of all for their proven martial prowess. Although he had been thirsting for war with Spain in 1898, he drew back from fighting Japan in 1906. He thought that the Californians were in the wrong, and he knew that the Japanese could easily seize the Philippines—what Roosevelt called America's "heel of Achilles." He was aware that the Russian Baltic fleet had sailed about halfway around the world, only to be utterly destroyed by the Japanese at the straits of Tsushima, near Japan's main islands, in May 1905.

The Great White Fleet

Roosevelt was no coward in a physical sense. This impatient warrior, who had enjoyed a "bully time" charging through the hail of bullets in Cuba, needed no certification of his bravery. But of one stigma he was clearly afraid, and that was the reputation of being afraid. His successful browbeating of the Californians and his concurrent appeasing of Japan sparked rumors that he had acted as he did because he was afraid of Japan's recently demonstrated military and naval strength against Russia.

Partially to spike rumors of cowardice, Roosevelt decided to send the entire battleship fleet around the world—by far his most spectacular flourishing of the Big Stick. There were other motivations as well, including a desire to remind Japan that the United States was then about number two in naval power, behind Britain, while Japan was only number five. But Roosevelt was not at pains to say that if the United States attacked Japan in Japanese waters, the odds would greatly lengthen against the attacker. With his considerable experience with naval affairs, especially as Assistant Secretary of the Navy, he could hardly have avoided such a conclusion.

The spectacular world cruise of the battleship fleet was obviously designed as a warning to Japan, probably more so than as a threat against Japan. Some of the more perceptive Japanese leaders recognized the mailed fist and reacted angrily against it, mostly in private. The cruise was also designed to impress Congress, which Roosevelt was constantly nagging for increased appropriations to build up the navy.

The battleship fleet of sixteen great warships left Virginian waters late in 1907, as its commander said, ready for "a feast, a frolic, or a fight." Conservative Easterners were afraid that the vessels might be lost in the Straits of Magellan or fall victim in some way to Japanese treachery, but Commander-in-Chief Roosevelt blithely ignored such prophets of doom. Initially, he described the operation as a peacetime "practice cruise" designed to transfer the entire fleet from one ocean to the other. Then, and only then, could he make sure that the shift could be made in wartime. But against whom, if not the Japanese?

Once the fleet had reached the peninsula of Lower California in safety, thus proving that the transfer could be made, Roosevelt felt free to announce that the battleships would continue all the way around the world. Invitations were received from Australia and Japan, among others, and in both places the visiting armada received an uproarious reception. In particular, the Japanese masses made clear their eagerness to revive the ancient friendship and avoid war with the United States. The junketing fleet returned by way of Europe and reached home waters in February 1909, just in time to usher out Roosevelt's "bully" seven-year "reign" in a blaze of glory.

Yet Roosevelt's dispatching of the sixteen seaworthy battleships into Japanese waters proved to be an unnecessary, even a desperate, gamble. The Great White Fleet was completely dependent on foreign colliers for coal, and these supply ships, as neutrals, would have had to depart in case war broke out, leaving the obsolescent battleships to certain destruction. The Japanese were by no means overawed, and shortly after the visiting fleet departed they paraded 123 warships of all classes (including torpedo boats) in a line twenty miles long. The visiting Americans had no protective destroyers or other small escorts of any kind.

When Roosevelt was nominated for the vice-presidency in 1900, conservatives had loudly questioned his sanity. The provocative sending of the battleship fleet into Japanese waters was a throw of the dice worthy of a madman: Little was to be gained aside from thus displaying America's muscle. And everything could have been lost.

Of course the Rough Rider had calculated the chances of this demonstration and had concluded that all would go well. But a gun could have discharged by accident, or a ship could have blown up from internal combustion (as the *Maine* had in 1898), with highly unfortunate consequences. The fleet was not supposed to be Roosevelt's plaything: It belonged to the American people, countless numbers of whom in the Eastern states regarded the whole exhibition as crack-brained. Indeed, Roosevelt overlooked a fundamental maxim of diplomacy and warfare: Especially when the stakes are high, never take a leap into the dark unless you have to.

The air-clearing fleet cruise did spark more Congressional interest in the navy, although not as much as Roosevelt had hoped. The demonstration also widened the global focus of the American people; improved to some extent diplomatic relations with Japan; and gave added impetus to the explosive naval race among the great powers. In his memoirs the pugilistic Roosevelt wrote that the world cruise was "the most important service that I rendered to peace." Enamored of grand flourishes, he evidently felt that provoking a possible war with Japan was more worthy of the Nobel Peace Prize than mediating an end to the actual war between Japan and Russia. To a degree, Roosevelt remained a man of Mars to the very end.

From Morocco to Alaska

The overblown Perdicaris incident of 1904 was but a curtain raiser to a really serious involvement by Roosevelt and his Big Stick in Morocco. French imperialists were then seeking political and economic control in this independent nation, which by the treaty of 1880 had granted protective rights to the nationals of thirteen foreign countries, including the United States. The Germans, traditional enemies of the French, resented this attempt by France to slam the open door on the fingers of their merchants. In March 1905 the theatrical German Kaiser journeyed to Morocco, where he delivered a saber-rattling speech. The long-predicted European war seemed at hand, with Germany fighting on one side and France and Britain on the other.

The jackbooted German armies were not yet ready to march, so the Kaiser urged Roosevelt, who did not much like him, to support the call for an international conference. The Rough Rider did not relish getting involved, for America had only a small commercial interest in Morocco. Reluctantly, Roosevelt decided to bring pressure to bear on Britain and France to attend the proposed multipower conference, which met at Algeciras in southern Spain in January 1906. In attendance were delegates from the interested countries, including two from the United States.

At the Algeciras conference Germany had a majority of the votes against her, including a determined Anglo-French bloc. Germany had to yield or fight, and she was not yet ready to fight in 1906. Roosevelt, who was definitely pro-French, exercised a strong influence behind the scenes on the Kaiser and hence on the final settlement. Yet he exaggerated, as he was prone to do, when he wrote privately, "You will notice that while I was most suave and pleasant with the Emperor [Kaiser], yet when it became necessary at the end I stood him on his head with great decision."

The result of the conference was a compromise settlement, signed in 1906, that may well have deferred World War I for eight years. The sovereignty of the native sultan of Morocco was guaranteed by the conferees, as was the Open Door principle for foreign commerce. But Spain and France were left in a privileged position with the native police force, and the French slowly proceeded to take over Morocco.

The Senate of the United States approved the Algeciras convention with some reluctance, and with an added reservation that reasserted the traditional policy of American nonentanglement. To many Americans the pact seemed like a strange departure from George Washington's and Thomas Jefferson's policy of no entangling alliances. Yet Roosevelt assured Congress that the Algeciras convention merely "confers upon us equal commercial rights with all European countries and does not entail a single obligation of any kind upon us." The new treaty, he felt, was merely perpetuating unbroken the protection of American commerce that had continued for about 120 years, beginning with the treaty of peace and friendship with Morocco in 1787.

Few people, if any, ever accused Roosevelt of being an excessively modest man. Proud as he was of his role, he could have made much more than he did of the fact that his intervention did much to head off World War I in 1906. But the Treaty of Portsmouth, signed September 5, 1905, had brought a shower of brickbats on him from the disappointed Japanese and Russians. The Algeciras pact was signed on April 7, 1906, and approved by the Senate on December 12. By this time Roosevelt had learned the wisdom of keeping a low profile in such controversial negotiations. He does not mention the Algeciras Conference in his autobiography, published in 1913.

All his life the fight-loving Roosevelt disliked dreamy-eyed pacifists, and he remained suspicious of arbitration. In 1897, when Assistant Secretary of the Navy, he delivered a speech at the Naval War College in which he conceded that arbitration was all right but "those who wish to see this country at peace with foreign nations will be wise if they place reliance upon a first-class fleet of first-class battleships." In 1911, two years after leaving the White House, he wrote in a magazine, "It would be not merely foolish but wicked for us as a nation to agree to arbitrate any dispute that affects our vital interest or our independence or our honor." Of course, the great flaw in any true arbitration of the national interest was that the United States might lose.

The Alaska boundary dispute best illustrates Roosevelt's impatience with arbitral processes. The panhandle of this vast area is indented by deep inlets, and the Canadians advanced the claim that the Canadian-American boundary should not follow the sinuosities of the coast but should run in a straight line. This redrawing of the demarcation line would leave the Americans with a long string of disconnected headlands, while the Canadians smugly occupied the strategic heads of the inlets. This absurdly awkward arrangement was obviously not what the negotiators of the Anglo-Russian Treaty of 1825 had intended.

Roosevelt wrote privately to Secretary Hay in 1902 that the Canadian contention was "outrageous and indefensible." He moved troops into the disputed area, ostensibly not to browbeat the Canadians and British but to prevent disturbances by the roughneck American miners and others.

Hoping to head off a clash, Secretary Hay negotiated a convention in 1903 with the British. By its terms "six impartial jurists of repute" were to meet in London and by majority vote decide where the boundary should run. The tribunal was to consist of three Americans, two Canadians, and one Englishman. This arrangement, be it noted, did not create a true arbitral body, because the decision was not left in the hands of third parties.

Leaving nothing to chance, Roosevelt handpicked the three Americans in the certain knowledge that they would support his claim. The swing man was the one Englishman, Lord Alverstone. Behind the scenes Roosevelt went into action with his trusty Big Stick. In letters and conversations he announced with great vehemence that if the tribunal did not support the American position, he would pour troops into the disputed area and run the line according to his own lights. Such an arbitrary course was bound to trigger war, and almost certainly Lord Alverstone was made aware of this dire possibility. He ultimately embraced the main American contention, which the tribunal finally supported with a 4-to-2 vote.

We shall probably never know how Lord Alverstone would have voted if Roosevelt had not applied pressure, but the Rough Rider left little to chance. The Canadians, who seemed to be angrier with the English Lord than with Roosevelt, gained some unappreciated consolation when the United States received a somewhat narrower strip of territory than claimed, but the Alaska panhandle remained unbroken.

The President had clearly rigged the game but, to his credit, had managed to end a dispute that might have escalated into war. His Big Stick threats, though perhaps bluffs, were at least sanctified by success. With obvious lack of candor, he told Congress in December 1903 that the outcome of the Alaska settlement "furnished signal proof of the fairness and good will with which two friendly nations" can resolve their differences.

As a fight-lover, Theodore Roosevelt had clearly one of the most pugnacious personalities of all the Presidents. But the responsibilities of office sobered him somewhat, and he not only avoided war but also managed to settle some war-fraught disputes. He even endorsed American participation in the Second Hague Conference of 1907, which failed to adopt an American-proposed World Court. But after Roosevelt left office, his inherent bellicosity reasserted itself. He first hand-picked his successor, William H. Taft, and later engaged in an unseemly name-calling fight with him. The upshot was that the Republican party was split in two, with the further result that the Democratic Party under Woodrow Wilson took over in 1913.

An embittered Roosevelt was savagely critical of President Wilson's efforts to avoid war with Mexico and then with Germany. The frothing Rough Rider was one of the most pugnaciously active figures in the preparedness movement of 1915–1916, which was designed to raise an army to fight Germany. The bitterest disappointment of Roosevelt's life came when Wilson denied the aged and ailing warrior the joy of raising and then leading a latter-day Rough Rider division pell-mell against the Germans through the barbed wire and trenches of France. The former President condemned the armistice with Germany in 1918, for it did not require unconditional surrender, and he died in 1919 bursting with hate for Wilson, who had just arrived in Italy with what Roosevelt regarded as the soft-on-Germany Fourteen Points.

Theodore Roosevelt had entered public life as a fighter, and he still was one as he lay on his deathbed. He believed that it was better to burn out than to rust out, and he burned out at age sixty.

CHAPTER 27

WILLIAM HOWARD TAFT: APOSTLE OF DOLLAR DIPLOMACY

Our international policy is always to promote peace. We shall enter into any war with a full consciousness of the awful consequences that it always entails, whether successful or not, and we, of course, shall make every effort consistent with national honor and the highest national interest to avoid a resort to arms.

President William H. Taft,
Inaugural Address,
March 4, 1909

"Peaceful Bill" Taft

Teddy Roosevelt's Rough-Riding act was a hard one to follow; anyone who came after T. R. was bound to suffer by comparison. That unfortunate successor happened to be good-natured and somewhat lethargic William H. Taft—"Smiling Bill" as he was often called—and the impression left with the voters was that the nation had suffered something of a letdown. The overweight Taft—five feet, eleven inches, and more than 300 pounds—

lacked the aggressiveness and combativeness of his predecessor, and although he was basically a judicial and judicious man, Roosevelt finally goaded him into as bitter a brawl as American political history has to offer. Taft's "milktoast" disposition has been overemphasized.

Taft was born in Ohio to a distinguished family; his father had been in Washington as Attorney General under President Grant in 1876-1877. As a youth he went to Yale University, where he graduated as class orator and number two scholastically in a class of 121. Naturally judicious and judicial in temperament, he attended law school in Cincinnati, practiced law, and later served as a prosecuting attorney, as Solicitor General of the United States, and as a United States Circuit Judge. He loved the law and was thoroughly at home in it; the dearest wish of his life was to rise above the hurly-burly of politics and become a Justice of the Supreme Court—a position that he belatedly attained in 1921 after he had been turned out of the presidency under a cloud of alleged failure. In his private correspondence one finds the revealing complaint, "politics makes me sick."

When it came to war, Taft was no rank greenhorn. In 1900, with savage guerrilla fighting still going on, he had been appointed head of the Philippine Commission and then, from 1901 to 1904, civil governor of the islands. From 1904 to 1908 he had served ably as Secretary of War in Roosevelt's Cabinet. As President, Taft's detailed messages to Congress show a keen appreciation of the necessity of following in Roosevelt's footsteps by keeping the army and navy at a high peak of effectiveness. After all, Roosevelt handpicked Taft as his successor, and he certainly would not have done so if he had suspected that "Peaceful Bill" was "soft" on preparedness.

As a confirmed legalist, Taft did not think it proper to go around the world intimidating nations with the bullying Big Stick. So T. R.'s trusty bludgeon gathered cobwebs, and the public, thus deprived of fireworks, felt let down. Beyond a doubt Taft was more friendly to international arbitration than the Rough Rider, although he did not shrink from warlike action if American honor, security, lives, property, and other vital interests were at stake.

So, as events turned out on inauguration day 1909, the setting sun (Roosevelt) eclipsed the rising sun (Taft). The rotund Ohioan was not an exhibitionist; he could not play to the galleries and stoop to cheap electioneering tricks like "Perdicaris alive or Raisuli dead." But Taft did deal firmly with foreign nations, especially in cases involving American lives and property. His most spectacular exhibition of pugnacity came in 1912, when he was forced to reply in kind to Roosevelt's unfair strictures during the party-splitting Bull Moose campaign of 1912.

Diplomacy of the Dollar

As for Europe, Taft pursued more of a hands-off policy than the two-fisted Roosevelt. In contrast with the Rough Rider's intervention in the Morocco dispute, Taft followed a strictly neutral policy in 1911 during the second Morocco crisis. The Kaiser's government had stirred up this hornets' nest anew by sending a German warship to Agadir to safeguard German interests. Likewise, during the Italo-Turkish war of 1911 and the First Balkan War of 1912, Taft, the peace-lover, favored mediation, not meddling.

Taft's Secretary of State, a domineering corporation lawyer named Philander C. Knox, fully realized that the United States had now attained the rank of a major commercial and financial power, with surpluses of all kinds to export and overflowing capital to invest in foreign climes. Accordingly, Knox enlisted the full cooperation of President Taft in pursuing a spirited commercial foreign policy, known popularly as Dollar Diplomacy. Thus the Big Dollar subtly supplanted the Big Stick.

Taft's aggressive Dollar Diplomacy was double-barreled. First, Washington would use its influence to secure new pastures of profit for the dollars of American industrialists and bankers in foreign lands. The federal government would protect these investments, so far as feasible. It would also encourage American bankers to pump money into areas, such as the approaches to the Panama Canal, that would protect and promote the national interest. In this way the Taft administration would achieve a degree of security that might otherwise have to be established later by using force. As the President told Congress, his policy was one of "substituting dollars for bullets."

Dollar Diplomacy ran a curiously unprofitable course in its attempt to preserve the integrity of China, especially against the intruding Japanese. A consortium of British, French, and German bankers was proposing to build the Hukuang Railway in central and southern China, with a consequent increase of European influence. Apparently unaware that dollar entanglement is one of the most dangerous forms of foreign enmeshment, President Taft used his influence with the Chinese prince regent to have an American banking group admitted to the European consortium in 1911. As a result, the imperialistic powers were embittered, little railroad building was achieved, and anemic China was still left to the mercy of foreign predators.

The Taft-Knox duo blundered even more ineptly in Manchuria, which was an important part of underdeveloped China. There the Russians enjoyed a dominant position with their railroad in North Manchuria, and the Japanese had infiltrated the area with their railroad in South Manchuria. Secretary Knox, with good reason, perceived that the presence of the Russians and Japanese alike boded ill for the integrity of China and for America's Open Door policy. So he came up with a half-baked scheme in 1909 for having American and European banking groups lend the Chinese government the money with which to buy the railroads in question from the Russians and Japanese.

The clumsy Knox-Taft attempt to purchase peace in Manchuria with a deluge of American dollars failed dismally. The Russians and Japanese, recently at each other's throats, were driven into each other's arms. The reluctant dollar was forced to beat an ignominious retreat because Washington had not discreetly sounded out the interested parties in advance. An alarmed Roosevelt wrote privately to Taft scolding him for bluffing and pointing out that the task of defeating the Japanese in Manchuria "would require a fleet as good as that of England, plus an army as good as that of Germany." Pushing war-provoking policies with dollars was not only dangerous but counterproductive.

Disorders triggered in China by the great Kuomintang rebellion in 1912 led to a prolonged series of armed United States landing parties for the protection of American lives and property. Such incursions occurred at various points from 1912 to 1941. The American guard at Peking and along the route to the sea was actually maintained intact until 1941. By 1927 the United States had 5,670 troops ashore in China, plus forty-four naval vessels in Chinese waters. Although this new series of interventions began in 1912, Taft's last year, such operations to protect

American interests in this turbulent Asiatic country were based on treaties dating as far back as 1858.

Latin American Entanglements

Taft's strategy of using the Big Dollar instead of the Big Stick led to a curious experiment with battleship diplomacy in South America. The Washington administration used high-pressure salesmanship on certain Latin American countries to induce them to buy their warships from private American yards. On the one hand, the Yankee shipbuilders would profit and not abandon a critically important business; on the other, the purchasers would help Uncle Sam by adding more and bigger dentures to the Monroe Doctrine. In his second annual message (December 1910), Taft informed Congress that it "gratifies me exceedingly" to report that the Argentine government had placed a contract with American yards for the construction of two battleships.

Business is business, but in this case considerable unpleasantness developed when the Washington officials, seeking to safeguard their naval secrets, applied pressure to prevent a resale of the battleships elsewhere. But the American builders gladly pocketed their profits, the essential armor plate industry in the United States received welcome tonic, and the naval race in South America gathered more steam.

Much more important than "battleship diplomacy" was Taft's aggressive Dollar Diplomacy, primarily in the Caribbean Sea. The prospective completion of the Panama Canal, the veritable jugular vein of Yankee sea power, sharpened the concern of the United States for this area. Chronic disorders in the bankrupt "banana republics" of Central America, formerly regarded as rather minor vexations, could no longer be laughed off. If chaos should lead to foreign intervention near the Panamanian artery, a ruinous war might easily result.

Taft's revised version of Roosevelt's Dollar Diplomacy led to his vigorous efforts to thrust America's financial empire deeper into the Caribbean. In 1909 Washington became deeply concerned over friction that Honduras was generating with British bondholders, and the Taft-Knox regime made a determined effort to interest Wall Street bankers in refinancing the Honduran debt. But the Senate of the United States spurned the treaty designed to achieve this objective. In the end, U.S. Marines went ashore to safeguard American property. And in 1912 American forces landed in Santo Domingo to restore order and protect the custom house, a main source of revenue and a major magnet for local grafters.

Fourteen long years after nominal freedom, nearby Cuba continued to churn up problems. A black insurrection caused the U. S. Marines to land at Guantánamo and also at Daiquiri in 1912. This intervention was all perfectly legal under the Platt Amendment, agreed to by Cuba after the Spanish-American War. Late in 1912 a treaty was concluded with the Cubans under which the United States yielded its reserved rights at Bahia Honda for increased advantages at the naval base of Guantánamo. The Taft administration regarded this move as elemental protection, not dollar imperialism.

Troublesome Nicaragua proved to be the focal point of one thrust by Taft's Dollar Diplomacy into the Caribbean. In this tiny republic the economic stake of American investors was comparatively small, but the strategic stakes for the United States were high. Here lay the alternate canal route, which Taft would not permit to slip into foreign clutches. Yet, as bad luck would have it, Nicaragua had fallen under the iron rule of a notorious troublemaker, one José Zelaya. He reportedly jeered, "I ridicule the United States, laugh at Germany, spit on England."

Not surprisingly, an anti-Zelaya revolution, partly fomented by American firms, erupted in 1909, and Zelaya sought safety in flight. During the fighting that ensued two American citizens, both involved with the insurgents, were promptly executed. Secretary of State Knox summarily dismissed the Nicaraguan chargé in Washington and then refused to recognize the new government until it had borrowed funds from American bankers with which to pay off the debt owed to British investors. Washington also dispatched a warship to Nicaraguan waters to ensure the acquiescence that followed this flexing of Uncle Sam's naval muscles.

Late in 1911 an American citizen, Colonel C. C. Ham, was named collector of the graft-riddled Nicaraguan customs, with the approval of the New York bankers—and the new Nicaraguan government. The next year, 1912, about 2,500 U.S. Marines and bluejackets disembarked to protect American life and property during the widespread disorders. The main body of Yankee troops departed in 1912, but a legation guard lingered for thirteen years, until 1925. Such was the persistence of "dollar imperialism" in Nicaragua.

Taft's concern over these disorders in Central America was largely eclipsed by a revolutionary upheaval in neighboring Mexico. At issue was the dictatorial rule of Porfirio Díaz, whose presidential "Diazpotism" for some thirty years had become unbearable to the masses, even though massive amounts of foreign capital had been attracted. For if Mexico was rich in natural resources, the Mexican masses were desperately poor. Conspicuously opulent were foreign exploiters of oil, minerals, and other sources of great wealth. Prominent among these newcomers were some 40,000 or more American citizens, who by 1913 had invested an estimated $1 billion in this slumbering volcano.

The inevitable revolution erupted in 1910, and the subsequent fighting between Díaz's Federals and the rebels often raged near the Mexico-United States border, with "wild bullets" occasionally striking American citizens. Taft ordered some 20,000 soldiers dispatched to the danger areas, plus standby battleships and cruisers, where they would all be at hand if intervention proved necessary. But the President was at pains to assure Congress that, as a constitutional ruler, he would not invade Mexico unless authorized by that body to do so. He described his policy to Congress (December 1911) as one of "strict impartiality as to all factions in Mexico."

Taft was savagely condemned in much of the American press for not intervening to protect American lives and property. But the mere existence of the Yankee troops appears to have had a sobering effect on the clashing Mexicans. Taft's accusers to the contrary, the President was not a peace-at-any-price man, but he remembered all too keenly the results of guerrilla fighting in the Philippines. In his messages to Congress he made it clear that he was willing to intervene in Mexico if absolutely necessary and if the legislators would grant him the necessary authorization. But he probably was hoping that he could pass on this hot potato in 1913 to President Woodrow Wilson, and this he did, undoubtedly with great relief.

Battling for Peace and Arbitration

The other side of the coin of pugnacity is what one may call pacificity. In 1911 the Taft administration concluded a treaty involving the four powers most interested in America's North Pacific seals—Russia, Japan, Britain, and the United States. The end result was the preservation and rehabilitation of the fast disappearing herd inhabiting Alaska's Pribilof Islands. This decades-old problem was at last settled by banning the killing of seals in open waters, and also by dividing the profits from the regulated land kill of the surplus males among the signatory nations. This was a landmark triumph for environmentalists and for the fur seals.

Paralleling this victory for peace, sanity, and posterity, the Anglo-American Convention of 1912, initiated under the Roosevelt administration, was concluded in the days of President Taft. It brought a peaceful end to the century-old squabble between the North Atlantic fishermen of Canada and the United States. A permanent body of adjudicators was established to settle individual disputes as they arose.

Less happy were Taft's strenuous efforts to effect a reciprocity agreement with Canada. Under it various commodities would be reciprocally admitted to both countries free of duties or with reduced duties. The relevant enabling legislation passed the House of Representatives in 1911, but the Senate, responding to pained American critics, adjourned without taking action. For once the fighting spirit of the easygoing occupant of the White House was aroused, for he had expected more cordial relations with Canada to flow from reciprocity. He summoned Congress into special session in the heat of a torrid Washington summer, and in the end forced reciprocity through that perspiring body. But in his support of this forward-looking measure, he indiscreetly gave the impression, as did many other advocates, that his scheme was a gilded trap that would hasten the annexation of Canada.

As events turned out, the Canadians preferred their connection with the British Empire to absorption by their powerful and aggressive neighbor to the south. In the end they threw reciprocity back into the mustached face of the well-meaning Taft. After fighting so hard for a peaceful relationship, the luckless President had little but bruises to show for his pains.

Not dissimilar to Taft's experience with rejected Canadian reciprocity was his failure to shepherd genuine arbitration treaties safely past the Senatorial gauntlet. Roosevelt's Secretary of State, Elihu Root, had negotiated twenty-five arbitration pacts with various nations. But they turned out to be worthless paper because, among other restrictions, they exempted from arbitration any dispute affecting the "vital interests, the independence, or the honor of the two contracting parties." This was a sure-fire escape hatch for those nations who did not want to be dragged into court.

Taft, the conservative lawyer and judge, favored peace and order, and he was eager to obtain treaties that were more binding than those negotiated under Roosevelt. In 1911 two new pacts, designed as models, were negotiated with Britain and France. They provided for the arbitration of all "justiciable" questions, not even excepting "vital interests" and "national honor." Naturally opposition began to gather steam in the Senate.

Again Taft's fighting spirit was aroused for peace. He went before the country on a vigorous speaking tour, during which he castigated the "emotionalists and neurotics." He was so indiscreet as to declare that the Spanish-American War was an unnecessary conflict—a thrust that brought an anguished outcry from the Rough Rider, whose special war it had been. Roosevelt struck back at the proposed arbitration treaties in a militant magazine article. President Taft was not far from the mark when he declared privately that Roosevelt's dearest wish was to be a Napoleon and die at the head of his regiment.

A stubborn Senate stuck grimly to its task of watering down the treaties by exempting from arbitration just about every question of any importance that an aggrieved nation would want to arbitrate, including Oriental immigration, states' debts, and the Monroe Doctrine. On March 7, 1912, the Senate approved the two pacts, helplessly cluttered though they were with exemptions, by the lopsided vote of 76 to 3.

A crestfallen Taft, having lost the fight with this mockingly affirmative vote, sighed resignedly, "We shall have to begin all over again." As he later remarked, he hoped that "the Senators might change their minds, or that the people might change the Senate; instead of which they changed me."

Battling the Bull Moose

Our primary concern is with presidential pugnacity in relation to foreign nations, not with regard to Congress, political rivals, or other friction points of the domestic scene. An exception must be made in our consideration of both the good-natured Taft and the combative Roosevelt, for they got into an unseemly row with each other that brought out the worst in both of them. More important, they changed the course of history by enabling Woodrow Wilson to win the presidency and hence lead the United States into World War I, which in turn paved the downhill path for Hitler and World War II.

Teddy Roosevelt had engineered the nomination and election of Taft as his successor in 1908 because he had confidence that the amiable Ohioan, an excellent administrator and a reliable "yes man," would carry out "my policies" faithfully. T. R. then left for a long-desired lion hunt in Africa, while wealthy businessmen in their exclusive clubs reportedly drank the toast, "Let every lion do its duty." One problem with Roosevelt was that he had enjoyed a "bully" time occupying the White House pulpit, and he had left the seat of power at the early age of fifty, still bursting with energy. For him, any experience after leaving the White House would have to be anticlimactic.

Taft was supposed to "carry out" Roosevelt's reformist plans and other forward-looking policies, but extreme liberals began to suspect that he was carrying them out to the garbage heap. The country was moving more rapidly to the left than the lethargic Taft, who by comparison seemed to be standing still. Indeed, Progressive insurgents secured enough votes in the House of Representatives in 1910 to shear from Speaker Cannon much of his ruthless power.

Taft's record as a liberal or progressive was not at all bad. He actually had prosecuted and "busted" more trusts than had Roosevelt, the great "Trust Buster," although in fairness one must add that some of these important legal actions had been initiated under Roosevelt. Taft's record in rescuing the public lands from the predatory interests, as Roosevelt had done spectacularly, was remarkable by any standard.

As Roosevelt was returning from Africa by way of Europe, talebearers brought him stories of how the mildly progressive Taft was selling out to the "standpatters" of the Old Guard. Up to this time Roosevelt had honored his promise, impulsively made when overwhelmingly elected in his "own right" in 1904, that he would never be a candidate for a third term. But in February 1912 he announced that his earlier spurning of a third term had applied to three *consecutive elective* terms. And Taft's four years had broken the sequence. Exuberantly T. R. declared, "My hat's in the ring!" and "The fight is on and I am stripped to the buff!" As for his once handpicked rival, he conceded that although Taft meant well, "he means well feebly." The once-placid "Big Bill," now in a fighting mood, retorted publicly that Roosevelt's supporters were "emotionalists and neurotics." He was quoted as saying, "Even a rat in a corner will fight"—thus giving the impression that he would fight like any other rat.

Early in the superheated campaign of 1912 Roosevelt swept most of the primary elections in states that held them, including Taft's home state, Ohio. But "Smiling Bill" Taft and the Republican Old Guard controlled the delegates to the Chicago convention, notably those who hailed from the Solid South, where the Republicans had not won an electoral vote for decades. Ironically, the convention "steamroller," which Roosevelt had used in 1908 to nominate Taft, ran over the Roosevelt delegates, whereupon the corpulent incumbent was renominated. In the end, the Roosevelt adherents, crying "fraud" and "naked theft," refused to vote.

Roosevelt, the avid sportsman, proved to be a poor sport. Virtually frothing at the mouth over this "barefaced fraud," he joined his Progressive following at a new convention, held elsewhere in Chicago, by seceding delegates, who organized the Progressive party. With the enthusiasm of a revival meeting, Roosevelt's following applauded uproariously as their hero cried in a fighting speech, "We stand at Armageddon, and we battle for the Lord!" The theme songs of this starry-eyed convention were "Onward, Christian Soldiers" and "The Battle Hymn of the Republic," Roosevelt's favorite song. Bursting with righteous wrath, T. R. declared that he felt "as strong as a bull moose," and this powerful animal was henceforth identified with Roosevelt's newly born Progressive party in the American political zoo, along with the Republican elephant and the Democratic jackass.

Roosevelt the Indian giver. Knecht in the Evansville (Indiana) Courier.

The Democrats nominated Dr. Woodrow Wilson, but his campaign was largely eclipsed by the unseemly name-calling battle between Roosevelt of the Progressive Party and Taft of the Republican Party. The Rough Rider had earlier exchanged mild pejoratives with Taft, but now the two antagonists tore into each other as only former friends can. "Death alone can take me out now," avowed the once-jovial Taft, as he branded T. R. a "dangerous egotist," a "demagogue," and a "brawler." Roosevelt, fighting mad, called Taft "an apostate," a "weakling," and a "fathead" with the brain of a "guinea pig."

The angry passions of the campaign peaked when Roosevelt, while campaigning in Milwaukee, was shot in the chest by a fanatic. With Bull Moose gameness, he insisted on delivering his scheduled speech with a bloodstained and bullet-holed manuscript in his hands, while his spellbound audience feared that he would collapse and die at any moment.

Any politician with postadolescent acumen could have predicted that Taft and Roosevelt, by splitting the Republican vote, would almost certainly permit Woodrow Wilson, the Democrat, to slip under the wire as a minority winner. This is precisely what happened, for the victorious Wilson won only 41 percent of the popular vote. As one cynic quipped, the only question was which corpse, Taft or T. R., would get the more flowers in the form of ballots. The graveyard winner in this phase of the contest was Roosevelt, 27 percent to 23 percent of the popular vote.

After the Bull Moose convention in Chicago, one prominent newsman wrote, "Roosevelt bit me and I went mad." When the smoke of battle had cleared away, an observer could almost conclude that Roosevelt, the vindictive poor loser, had bitten himself in his anger and pugnacity, and then had gone mad. He ultimately buried the hatchet with Taft, as both bitterly opposed President Wilson. But the patched-up friendship was never the same again.

The Progressives had made such an impressive showing in 1912 on short notice under Roosevelt that they nominated him again in 1916. He declined the nomination and then supported the Republican nominee, Charles E. Hughes. By this time his head had cleared and he could see that as a third-party candidate he would only guarantee the reelection of the "hypocritical" Wilson, who had been "too proud to fight" the Germans and Mexicans, and whose guts Roosevelt hated. T. R.'s final decision was a sound one politically, but the Progressive party perished when their chosen leader left them at the altar. So much for the politics of pugnacity.

Neither Roosevelt nor Taft was a pacifist, or even close to being one. At heart Roosevelt loved the clash of battle, with its bullet-defying bravery, but Taft, the ex-Secretary of War, was not one to beat a quick retreat where the nation's interests and honor were involved. Roosevelt, who did not believe in real arbitration, won the Nobel Peace Prize for his role in mediating the Russo-Japanese War. Taft, who vigorously supported real arbitration, put up a gallant fight for it against the Senate but lost. There were many who thought that he was more deserving of the Nobel Prize than Roosevelt and some other subsequent winners.

CHAPTER 28

WOODROW WILSON: THE IDEALISTIC WARRIOR

There is a price which is too great to pay for peace, and that price can be put in one word. One cannot pay the price of self-respect.

Woodrow Wilson, Speech,
February 1, 1916

The Scholar in Politics

Thomas Woodrow Wilson, a devout Presbyterian and eloquent lay preacher, hated war. Yet he presents the paradox of an idealistic Princeton professor, dedicated to peace, who led the United States into World War I—the greatest foreign war up to that point in its history. He also presided over formidable shooting incursions into European Russia and Russian Siberia, as well as into Mexico and Haiti, to mention only the most conspicuous of some fifteen armed interventions during his occupancy of the White House.

Born in Virginia in 1856, little Tommy Wilson was taken at age two by his parents to Augusta, Georgia, where his father served as a Presbyterian clergyman. As an impressionable youth, the lad was able to see at first hand the devastation that the "damnyankee" invaders had inflicted and the misery they had continued to inflict on the South during the ordeal of Reconstruction. He would have been stupid indeed if he had not learned that war does not pay, especially for losers. The Confederates had fought in vain for self-determination, and President Wilson's later espousal of this concept worldwide may have sprung in part from the scorched soil of the war-ravaged South.

After receiving his A.B. degree from Princeton University in 1879, Wilson attended law school at the University of Virginia. Then came a brief but frustrating bout with the law in Atlanta. He next returned to the academic world, received his Ph.D. from the Johns Hopkins University, published scholarly books, advanced rapidly up the academic ladder, and became President of Princeton University in 1902. There he distinguished himself as a visionary who was an uncompromising fighter for what he regarded as the right. He did manage to reform the curriculum and institute small-group instruction to supplement the usual formal lectures, but he failed in his stubborn attempt to restructure Princeton into residential colleges.

Wilson's biggest battle of all at Princeton resulted in his academic undoing. He insisted that a proposed graduate college be located near the center of the University, where it would elevate the frivolous undergraduates. But Dean Andrew West, long-time head of the Graduate School, feared that the undergraduates would pull the graduates down to their own level. West won this struggle, and thereafter Princeton was not big enough for both scholars. Wilson then accepted the Democratic nomination for the governorship of New Jersey, thus landing squarely on his feet in politics.

Wilson was a square-jawed fighter with high ideals and lofty principles who would break before he would bend, just as he did later in unsuccessfully championing the League of Nations. Dean West could have been right on the issue of the graduate school, but there was no way of peering into the future, and Wilson could have been wrong. In perspective we can speculate that the precise location of the graduate college probably would not have made enough difference to warrant the donnybrook that resulted. Wilson was not only inflexible, but he plainly lied during the academic investigation, especially when he denied having read a report by Dean West whose proof sheets he had personally corrected. We now know that Wilson had suffered the first of a series of minor strokes in 1896 and 1906 and that at times his mind could have gone blank.

By 1910 the nationwide tide of progressivism was setting in, and the Democrats of New Jersey needed a liberal candidate like Wilson for Governor. The controlling bosses of the state were confident that if they elected "the Professor" they could lead him about by his long academic nose. Once nominated, Wilson put on a fighting campaign. "God, look at that man's jaw," one listener was heard to say. Upon being elected, "the scholar in politics" turned against the scheming bosses who had elected him and appealed over their heads to the sovereign voters. He fought so vigorously against special privilege that New Jersey, "The Mother of Trusts," became a model state with its program of political, social, and economic reform. Yet Wilson did not think of himself as a wild-eyed radical but as "a progressive with the brakes on." By this time he had become a national figure, and in 1912 he received the Democratic nomination for the presidency. Thanks to the disastrous split between Taft and Roosevelt, Wilson won the presidential plum. Back in Princeton Dean West is supposed to have groaned, "My God, I've made Wilson President of the United States."

Preliminary Battles

A fighting Wilson, standing a lean five feet, eleven inches, came to the White House in 1913 prepared to lead Congress in a massive assault on "the triple wall of privilege." This bastion embraced the highly protective tariff, the bloated trusts, and the horse-and-buggy system of banking and currency.

Tackling first the tariff early in 1913, Wilson summoned the Democratic Congress into special session and appeared before it to deliver his earnest appeal in person—the first President to do so since John Adams in 1800. But in the Senate he ran head-on into the well-paid lobbyists, those "tools" of the special interests who constituted the unofficial "third house of Congress." Executing an end run around this roadblock, the embattled Wilson, with his appeal habit, issued a dramatic plea to the voters over the heads of the stubborn legislators. This "pitiless publicity" evidently helped to beat the Senate into line, and that windy body passed the controversial legislation late in 1913, after six months of stormy debate. Round one for Wilson.

The President's next major clash with Congress involved the big bankers. Again Wilson appeared in person before Congress to demand overdue reform. But well-financed opposition rapidly developed, and Representative Carter Glass, chief sponsor of the the reformist bill, spoke dejectedly to the President of resigning. "Damn it, don't resign, old fellow," interjected Wilson in a rare outbreak of profanity, "outvote them." The aggressive tactics of the President finally prevailed, and the epochal Federal Reserve Act was signed late in 1913. Round two for Wilson.

Hardly pausing for breath, the pugnacious Princetonian pressed forward to the last towering rampart of the "triple wall of privilege." Again the aggressive "schoolmaster in politics" appeared before Congress to demand legislation that would loosen the iron grip of monopolists and other foes of free enterprise. After nine months of verbal infighting there emerged the epochal Federal Trade Commission of 1914, which substantially curbed or prevented unfair or otherwise harmful practices. Round three for Wilson.

Other laws were passed under Wilson's tireless prodding, including the somewhat illusory Clayton Anti-Trust Act of 1914. But by late 1914 conditions changed when the World War erupted in Europe, and the Democratic majority in the House suffered a sharp reduction in numbers. The glory days of Wilson's whip-and-spur legislation had passed.

Wilson, the hater of war, turned out to be preeminently a war President, but in fairness one must note that in certain areas he also fought hard for peace. Secretary of State Bryan, an avowed pacifist, was permitted to negotiate some thirty conciliation pacts with various nations. This approach was not formal arbitration but involved what were known as "cooling off" treaties. The signatories agreed to submit all insoluble disputes to international commissions and not to resort to war until a recommendation was forthcoming, ordinarily within a year. The disputants could then accept these findings or reject them, as the case might be, but by that time they probably would have cooled off. We shall never know what cooling off these treaties would have achieved, because World War I flared forth in Europe in August 1914.

A sworn foe of monopolies and giant banks, Wilson deplored Taft's Dollar Diplomacy for the benefit of Wall Street investors. Among other objections, defense of the American dollar abroad might result in warlike entanglements. Wilson was not slow in exercising his powers. Speaking abruptly and unceremoniously in the early days of his administration through the newspapers, he openly repudiated his predecessor's policy of pumping dollars into Latin America and Asia. Taft had more or less forced the big bankers into the six-power railroad consortium in China; Wilson forced them to back out. This they did without undue protest.

Self-centered California stirred up a new crisis with Japan in 1913 by barring Japanese from owning land in the Golden State. Powerless to intervene effectively in a local dispute, Wilson dispatched the eloquent Secretary Bryan to California to plead with the state legislature. It finally defied him and passed a new exclusion bill, but the language was so softened as not to mention the word "Japanese." This conciliatory intervention by the Washington government enabled Wilson to surmount the crisis without a resort to shooting.

President Wilson, an admirer of England and things English, also managed with extreme difficulty to patch up a hot dispute with Great Britain regarding the Panama Canal tolls. The British had yielded their right to joint control of a canal, written into the Clayton-Bulwer Treaty of 1850, by substituting the new Hay-Pauncefote Treaty of 1902. The words stated that the canal tolls should be exacted of "all powers observing these rules on terms of entire equality." In the subsequent legislation passed under Taft, the Congress had exempted all American coastwise traffic, notably that sailing from New York to San Francisco, from paying any tolls. The justification was that foreign nations, under existing law, could not engage in this coastwise traffic anyhow. Hence, to American legalists, the phrase "all powers" meant "all other powers" than the United States that used the Panama Canal.

The British, as the leading maritime people, were outraged by this "Yankee dodge" to circumvent the plain English of the pact. They pointed out, as was true, that if American coastwise ships paid nothing at all, then the cost of their transit would have to be added to the tolls of all other users. The American response was that foreign nations were getting a relatively free ride from the enormous amount of money that the United States alone had poured into the canal.

Wilson, the good Christian, found this canal quarrel highly embarrassing, in part because he had been elected on a platform that had favored the exemption of American coastwise traffic from paying tolls. After wrestling with the problem, he decided that the basic issue involved was national honor, and that if reasonable doubts existed they should be resolved in an honorable way. This solution he urged upon Congress, and after a bitter fight the tolls exemption for American coastwise traffic was repealed. By thus fighting for national honor and then winning the battle, Wilson swept away the last major controversy bedeviling Anglo-American relations. Otherwise the United States might not have entered the coming World War I of 1914–1918 on the side of Britain in 1917.

Dollar Diplomacy Reverses Wilson

Wilson deplored Taft's Dollar Diplomacy, but the facts of political life, especially in the Caribbean, forced him to carry the same policy through to a bloody conclusion, especially in the strategic approaches to the Panama Canal. His armed interventions were not only about as numerous as those of Roosevelt and Taft but also far more bloody.

First came Haiti in 1915, where an enraged mob cornered the brutal president-dictator and literally tore him limb from limb. Germany and France had earlier landed troops on a temporary basis, and their obvious interest generated fears in the United States about the Monroe Doctrine and the Panama Canal. Reluctantly, Wilson concluded that he would have to intervene in what he regarded as the national interest.

The U.S. Marines landed on Haitian shores in 1915 and remained for nineteen years, with Washington's fiscal control continuing until 1947. Order was thus restored, but Haitian sovereignty was flouted. The occupying and "pacifying" Marines averaged about two thousand in number, and in the bitter struggle that followed their coming about two thousand black Haitians were killed. Actually, they were fighting for what they conceived to be their liberties, even the liberty to engage in graft and otherwise misgovern themselves. In short, the peace-loving Wilson, in the national interest, involved the United States in a bloody and prolonged war in carrying to the ultimate the protectively interventionist policies of Roosevelt and Taft.

Santo Domingo, like its western neighbor Haiti, continued to be a potential menace to both the Monroe Doctrine and the Panama Canal. In the summer of 1914 the U.S. Navy used gunfire to stop the bombardment of Puerto Plata, and in the spring of 1916 the "leathernecked" Marines landed in force and remained until 1924. A military government was established under the jurisdiction of the Navy Department in Washington.

Some Dominican nonconformists ("bandits") were shot during the pacification, as bayonet-imposed order was restored. But most of the Dominicans, like their Haitian neighbors, preferred their own misrule to orderly rule imposed by foreigners. After 1917 critics of Wilson, especially Theodore Roosevelt, accused the President of arrant hypocrisy in fighting to make the world safe for democracy and self-determination, except notably in Haiti and Santo Domingo. In short, such ideals wither under the white heat of national interest as represented by the Monroe Doctrine and the Panama Canal. On the other hand, Wilson's "missionary diplomacy" was evidently motivated in part by the Christian desire of a do-gooder to lend a helping hand to root out endemic civil war, disease, and starvation.

We recall that in Mexico the three-decade dictatorship of Porfirio Díaz was overthrown in May 1911 by revolutionists under the leadership of a Democratic reformer, Francisco Madero. His liberal regime in turn was overturned in February 1913 by the reactionary General Victoriano Huerta, a full-blooded Indian who evidently arranged for the subsequent murder of Madero.

Wilson resolutely refused to recognize the bloody-handed Huerta, a "desperate brute" who clearly was thwarting the masses of the Mexican people in their desire for an orderly representative government. Up to this time the traditional policy of the United States had been to recognize *de facto* governments firmly established in power, regardless of whether murder, dictatorship, or other irregularity was involved. Wilson's Christian heart bled for the Mexican masses, who had been crushed for so long under the heel of dictatorship. He was determined to oust the "unspeakable Huerta" in favor of the democratic forces by withholding recognition and by permitting democratic foes of the dictator to import arms from the United States. Ex-Professor

Wilson told a visiting Briton, "I am going to teach the South American republics to elect good men."

So the President stood firm, and by not intervening actually intervened. Thus he prolonged the revolutionary disorders. Foreign investors, including many Americans, much preferred the calm of despotism and deplored the continued destruction of multimillion-dollar investments and the taking of scores of lives, including Americans. An angry cry for intervention arose from two-fisted Yankees, including Theodore Roosevelt, who excoriated Wilson for having "kissed the blood-stained hand that slapped his face." The President's policy of "watchful waiting," as he called it, was widely condemned as "deadly drifting," while the stubborn Huerta refused to resign.

An explosion finally occurred at Tampico, a key Mexican port on the Atlantic Ocean, in April 1914. An unarmed party of nine men from the U.S.S. *Dolphin* docked in a whale boat to load supplies, with the Stars and Stripes plainly displayed in bow and stern. By error they had entered a restricted zone, so two American seamen were arrested in their boat by the Mexican authorities and then marched with the others through the streets for having violated martial law. An hour and a half after the arrest they were all released, with verbal expressions of regret from the commanding officer than an uninformed subordinate should have sparked the incident.

But the American Admiral Mayo, clearly a stickler for military protocol, wanted a stiffly formal apology for this affront to the Stars and Stripes. He hastily presented an ultimatum to the commanding general in Tampico, demanding that it be complied with in twenty-four hours. The conditions were that there be a more formal disavowal and apology for the insult, assurances that the Mexican officer responsible would "receive severe punishment," and guarantees that the American flag be publicly hoisted in a prominent position on shore and saluted with twenty-one guns. The salute would then be returned by an American warship.

The commanding Mexican general at Tampico had promptly expressed his regret in writing for the Tampico incident, and the harassed Huerta announced that he deplored the distressing incident. But he flatly refused to salute the American flag unless the United States guaranteed a gun-for-gun response. There was indeed some inconsistency in Admiral Mayo's having demanded a formal salute from a government that Washington would not even recognize. In fact, one reason why Wilson would not sanction a return response was that such action might be construed as meaning formal recognition.

This whole affair is a classic case of a petty incident, for which adequate apology had been made, blown up into a bloody confrontation. Yet once Admiral Mayo's ultimatum was issued, both the pacific Secretary Bryan and President Wilson believed that the dignity and honor of the United States required that the superpatriotic admiral be supported. The visionary Wilson, in particular, seems to have felt that he could use this seemingly trifling affair as a pretext to seize Vera Cruz, cut off customs duties and shipments of arms, and thus put enough pressure on the hated Huerta to force him out of office. Yet one prominent Republican journalist cried out, "What legal or moral right has a President of the United States to say who shall or shall not be president of Mexico?"

Warring on Mexico

A determined Wilson, the good Christian who hated war, stood before Congress on April 20, 1914, and in solemn tones asked for authority to intervene with American armed forces in Mexico. He made it clear that the Tampico affront was only the most recent in a long series of disagreeable incidents and other grievances, many of them aimed at Americans and not at other foreigners. His quarrel, he insisted, was with the despotic Huerta, not with the Mexican people. He denied that the incident was a "trivial one," because the two men in the flag-protected boat were taken from "the territory of the United States"—a statement that was open to challenge. After two days of debate, Congress voted its approval of the proposed intervention.

The shooting showdown came on April 21, 1914, the day after the House of Representatives had voted for armed intervention but the day *before* the Senate gave its approval. A German freighter was fast approaching the Mexican port of Vera Cruz with a huge shipment of arms and ammunition, which Huerta might use effectively against the United States. Wilson was aroused at the White House from a deep sleep shortly after midnight in the morning of April 21 and apprised of the danger. Groggily he telephoned orders to seize the port, as he was entitled to do as the constitutional commander-in-chief of the armed forces. Evidently he expected little or no resistance. Critics then and later have concluded that a President should never have to make so momentous a decision with a brain still fogged by sleep.

American Marines and bluejackets stormed ashore at Vera Cruz and, after heavily bombarding key centers, captured the city. The defending Mexicans, many of them snipers, lost about 126 killed and 195 wounded of all ages and both sexes, while the attacking Americans suffered 19 dead and 71 wounded. This was waging an undeclared war on Mexico, for its own "good," with the primary objective of toppling the Huerta regime that had seemed so offensive to Wilson. Ironically, the German ammunition ship moved down the coast of Mexico and discharged her cargo, too late to be of much use to Huerta.

Wilson's heart was torn by the deaths of the nineteen American servicemen killed at Vera Cruz, and he felt it his duty to travel to New York City and speak at the biers of those who had sacrificed their lives. Touching on the theme that he was only trying to "serve the Mexicans" by liberating them from the grip of a dictator, he solemnly declared, "A war of aggression is not a war in which it is a proud thing to die, but a war of service is a thing in which it is a proud thing to die." Here was the starry-eyed idealist administering patriotic soothing syrup.

Despite this sacrifice of American blood in behalf of Mexican humanity, much of the rest of the world, including especially the Latin Americans, regarded the Yankee incursion as an indefensible assault over what appeared to be a small matter of punctilio. Wilson had definitely worked himself out onto the end of a limb. After so much sacrifice of lives, he could not risk the humiliation that would result from not securing an apology from Huerta. Yet a full-fledged Mexican War, guerrilla or not, would be immensely costly, bloody, and probably frustrating. It would also be in conflict with Wilson's hands-off policy regarding Latin America that he had nobly proclaimed at Mobile, Alabama, in October 1913.

At this critical juncture, like angels from heaven, the ABC powers of South America (Argentina, Brazil, Chile), came forward with an offer of mediation. Wilson gladly and gratefully made use of this escape hatch. The ABC delegates, conferring at the Canadian side of the Niagara falls with representatives of the United States and Mexico, agreed on a plan. But it proved ineffectual because Venustiano Carranza, the chief liberal foe of Huerta, flatly refused to accept it. Yet the Niagara Conference did enable Wilson to avoid war and at the same time partially quiet the fears of the rest of the world regarding Yankee designs on a southern neighbor.

The "unspeakable Huerta" at last crumpled under a combination of difficulties, including Wilson's pressure, and finally fled to Spain in July 1914. He was succeeded by the leading democratic revolutionist, "First Chief" General Carranza. With some misgivings, Wilson formally recognized his regime in October 1915 as the *de facto* government of Mexico.

Once secure in office, Carranza began to show increasing indifference to the reforms that he had earlier championed. A chief lieutenant, Francisco Villa, an illiterate combination of bloodthirsty bandit and open-handed Robin Hood, led a sanguinary revolt. Scheming to embroil Carranza in war with the North American gringos, Villa's horsemen thundered across the border and sacked the town of Columbus, New Mexico (March 9, 1916), killing seventeen Americans and wounding others, and then fleeing deep into the recesses of Mexico.

The Columbus raid presented a clear-cut case of American blood being shed on American soil, clearer in fact than President Polk's border incident in 1846. Several months earlier Villa had shown his contempt for the gringos by killing in cold blood eighteen American mining engineers seized at Santa Ysabel, deep in northern Mexico. Wilson, understandably regarding Villa as a mad-dog outlaw, undertook to end such outrages. He ordered General John J. Pershing, with several thousand men, mostly cavalry, to pursue Villa into Mexico and destroy his bandit following. President Carranza took a distrustful view of this invasion of sovereign Mexican territory, even in hot pursuit of a foe. But he grudgingly and belatedly consented to a face-saving agreement that permitted the reciprocal chastisement of outlaws by either nation in the future, presumably in small force.

The Pershing punitive expedition ("the perishing expedition," it was dubbed), penetrated deep into the vastnesses of Mexico, ultimately with more than eleven thousand men, mostly cavalry. They scattered Villa's following and narrowly missed bagging the bandit leader himself. But the farther Pershing pushed into Mexico (more than 300 miles) the rougher the terrain became, and the more hostile the people seemed. There was mounting friction with the regular Carranzista troops, for Carranza had never agreed to an invasion of this magnitude. At Parral a body of Mexican soldiers opened fire on the Americans as they were leaving town, and in the subsequent shooting forty Mexicans and two Americans died. At Carrizal a clash resulted in the killing of twelve Americans and the capture of twenty-three. The Mexicans lost their commander, plus twenty-nine soldiers, as an all-out confict seemed perilously near. Wilson even prepared a war message that he never delivered.

As the hopelessness of the chase became more apparent, as the hostility of the Mexicans seemed more threatening, and as the current submarine crisis with Germany grew more menacing, Wilson wisely withdrew the last men of the Pershing expedition on February 5, 1917. But he left behind an outraged Carranza, a defiant Villa, long-lived Mexican bitterness, and a revolution that had yet to run its course. The visionary President had waged an undeclared but fruitless war on Mexico, whether he called it that or not. He never did bring peace to this troublesome neighbor, but his great contribution to the Mexican masses, willy-nilly, was to permit them to have their democratic revolution. The high-browed Wilson turned out to be more of a warrior than anyone would have predicted, but he showed great patience most of the time with what he repeatedly called his policy of "watchful waiting." But his attempt to "shoot men into self-government" left hateful memories. One must be wary of do-gooders who are trying to do you good; they may do you in.

The U-Boat Peril

Woodrow Wilson had preached peace and brotherhood for all nations, which included Mexico, Haiti, and Santo Domingo. But he led the American people over the edge into the bloodbath of World War I. Why and how?

As has been true of all of America's major foreign wars, Wilson got involved in this conflict because it already existed. It was there, inflicting serious side blows on the United States, from August of 1914 to April of 1917. The republic, true to form, was finally sucked in.

President Wilson, like his Cabinet and an overwhelming majority of the American people, was pro-Ally, especially pro-British. His mother was English born; he admired British statesmen, political philosophers, and writers; and he was at home with English culture, having visited the British Isles a half-dozen or so times. To him it appeared as though the arrogant German

Kaiser had forced war on the French and British by invading and laying waste "poor little Belgium."

Despite his built-in pro-Ally bias, Wilson at the outset preached strict neutrality. He issued an appeal on August 20, 1914, urging all citizens to be "impartial in thought, as well as in action." But this was the counsel of perfection, for people could refrain from acting but could not refrain from thinking. Critics responded by saying that only "moral eunuchs" or people "mentally unsexed or paralyzed" could follow Wilson's counsel of perfection.

Lurid and even lying propaganda, which stressed German atrocities in Belgium, further turned the American people against the Kaiser, "the Beast of Berlin." The fear pervaded America that when Emperor Wilhelm II had knocked France and England out of the war, he would flout the Monroe Doctrine and invade the United States with millions of helmeted goose-steppers.

With the exception of the pacifist Secretary of State, William J. Bryan, each member of Wilson's Cabinet was pro-Ally. Bryan was in fact so neutral that his colleagues regarded him as pro-German. As the war took its gory toll, Wilson found himself becoming increasingly pro-Ally, despite considerable friction with Britain. On one occasion in private he burst out, "England is fighting our fight!"

The British navy controlled the high seas, thus virtually ending America's commerce with Germany. In its place sprang up enormous exports of munitions and other materials of war to Great Britain and the other Allies. When these beneficiaries ran short of funds, American bankers advanced huge sums of money with which to purchase urgently needed military supplies. To Secretary Bryan the selling of ammunition with which to kill Germans seemed unneutral, especially since the Germans could not import American arms with which to shoot the British and French. America's answer to this criticism was that American manufacturers of munitions ("merchants of death") would be delighted to sell arms to the Germans if only the buyers would come and transport them. America's economic chariot thus became so tightly tied to the bankers and munitioneers that a dreary business recession would probably have set in again if this lucrative trade had been halted. And no sane politician wants a recession when his party is in power.

Shortly after the guns began to boom, the London government established an unorthodox, even illegal, "starvation" blockade of Germany. Previously warships had stood off the coast of an enemy, usually outside the three-mile line, to intercept all objectionable shipping, especially those vessels carrying contraband to the enemy. But because of lurking submarines, the British added a refinement to their blockade. They would stop all merchant shipping on the high seas, and if a vessel appeared to be carrying contraband of war to the enemy, the victim would be shepherded into a British port for a safe and leisurely search. London justified its highhanded tactics by pointing to the "unusual," "peculiar," and "unconventional" nature of the war, especially the new dimension introduced by the German submarine.

What is sauce for the goose is supposed to be sauce for the gander. The Germans naturally felt at liberty to establish a submarine war zone around England, also because of the "unusual," "peculiar," and "unconventional" nature of the war. But the Wilson government, which did not formally protest against the illegal British blockade, protested bitterly against the German submarine blockade. Defenders of the illegal British system argued that it did not take innocent lives, whereas the German U-boat zone resulted in the torpedoing of many innocent ships and a heavy loss of life. Nor did Wilson stress the fact that the British also had planted stationary mines in the open sea, thus creating an announced war area as a major means of supporting their long-range surface blockade. If the United States and other neutrals had tried to bull their way through these lethal minefields without British pilots, heavy loss of life would have resulted.

On February 4, 1915, Berlin announced that Germany would establish a war area around the British Isles and attempt to destroy all enemy ships encountered within that zone. The official declaration noted that Germany had been driven to this expedient as a result of the acquiescence by neutrals in the illegal, long-range blockade by Great Britain. Neutrals were warned to avoid sailing on enemy ships and to keep their vessels out of these waters, lest mistakes be made. In a diplomatic note from the State Department, approved by Wilson, Germany was sternly informed that she would be held to "strict accountability" if American lives or vessels were lost in the newly announced German zone. This phrase was perhaps the most dangerous one used by

Wilson before formal war with Germany, because the time soon came to honor or retreat from his bellicose words.

On May 7, 1915, a German submarine torpedoed and sank a palatial British liner, the *Lusitania*, near the southeast coast of Ireland. A tragic total of 1,198 persons perished, 128 of them Americans and many of them women and babes in arms. The wholesale inhumanity of the incident shook Wilson to his depths. True to his "strict accountability" warning, he upheld the "indisputable" right of American citizens to sail on a British-owned vessel that was a munitions-carrying blockade-runner transporting neutral passengers as a shield. More than that, Wilson demanded a specific disavowal of the act, plus reparations for damages. The Berlin Foreign Office stiffly replied that because of a cargo of munitions (4,200 cases of rifle ammunition) and other circumstances, the *Lusitania* was not just "an unarmed merchant vessel." Moreover, and probably unknown to Wilson, the captain of the *Lusitania* was carrying orders to ram any hostile submarine on sight, and as a result his vessel could be regarded as offensively armed and hence subject to sinking without warning.

Wilson's second note to Germany was so bellicose that Secretary of State Bryan, a dedicated pacifist, resigned from the Cabinet rather than sign it. Not until February 1916, some ten months after the torpedoing, did Germany reluctantly assume liability for the sinking of the *Lusitania* and agree to pay an indemnity, which was collected after the war. Meanwhile the German Ambassador in Washington had given assurances on September 1, 1915, following the *Arabic* incident, involving the sinking of a British vessel with the loss of two American lives. Henceforth passenger ships were not to be sunk without warning and without provision for the safety of noncombatants aboard, "provided that the liners do not try to escape or offer resistance."

Early in 1916 Congress threatened to get out of hand and undercut Wilson's inflexible pro-Ally leadership. Two resolutions were being debated that would require American citizens to be warned against traveling (as protectors) on armed belligerent passenger ships. But a proud Wilson, resenting this challenge to his authority and the nation's honor, sent a strong letter to Congress saying that if this concession were made to Germany, then the "whole fine fabric of international law might crumble under our hands piece by piece."

The two "scuttle resolutions" of Congress were finally sidetracked, and Americans continued to embark on British liners carrying American contraband and under orders to ram submarines on sight. Proving that legislators can indeed learn from history, we should note that in 1935—nineteen years and one world war later—Congress passed a neutrality act authorizing the President to warn American citizens that they could travel on belligerent passenger vessels only at their own risk. In short, what was intolerable to a sensitive Wilson in 1916 became mandatory to a realistic Franklin Roosevelt in 1935.

The *Sussex* Blank Check

An English-owned cross-channel ferry boat, the *Sussex*, burst into the headlines in March 1916 and proved to be, diplomatically, the most important merchant ship of the war. While flying the French flag it was torpedoed by a German submarine, whose commander allegedly mistook her for a warship. Although badly damaged, she limped into port after having suffered some eighty dead or injured, including injuries to several American passengers.

Mistake or not, this torpedoing was a gross violation of the German pledge, following the *Arabic* affair, not to torpedo without warning unresisting and nonescaping passenger ships. Wilson was deeply angered by what he regarded as German duplicity, and he unwisely authorized Secretary Lansing to dispatch a harshly uncompromising note. It served notice that unless Germany immediately abandoned "its present methods of submarine warfare against passenger and freight-carrying vessels," the United States would "have no choice but to sever diplomatic relations." Such a rupture in these circumstances was almost certain to bring on a shooting war.

The German reply promised that no more unresisting merchant ships would be sunk without warning and without the proper humanitarian precautions. But Berlin added one "string," and that was a demand that Washington require the blockading powers to respect "the laws of humanity" and force Britain to relax her "starvation blockade." Wilson accepted the no-torpedoing pledge of Berlin but ignored the "string." Here he revealed a curious contradiction that betrayed all too well his pro-Ally sympathies. He had been inexpressibly shocked by the inhumanity involved in the *Lusitania* disaster. But, oddly enough, he ignored the brutal truth that the five-year Allied "hunger blockade" of Germany, grimly retained for about seven months after the armistice in 1918, was taking or would take a toll of tens of thousands of human lives.

The President's *Sussex* ultimatum, which robbed him of all freedom of maneuver, proved to be a colossal diplomatic blunder—that is, if his primary objective was to keep America out of war. In effect, Wilson handed the Berlin Foreign Office a blank check. When the German warlords filled it out with unrestricted U-boat warfare, he would have no choice, being a man of the highest honor, but to sever diplomatic relations completely—the usual prelude to war.

Some six months later, in November 1916, Wilson was reelected President by a paper-thin margin. The winning slogan, which almost certainly pulled him through, was "He Kept Us Out of War"—that is, war with Germany. But inherent in this potent campaign cry was the implication that Wilson was pledged to continue to keep on keeping out of the world conflict. He disliked the slogan, although he could not publicly repudiate it, because he was well aware that peace lay at the mercy of any trigger-happy U-boat commander.

In December 1916, the month after his reelection, Wilson tried desperately to mediate a peace between Germany and the Allies. But both sides had already sacrificed so much that they had to have some gains to show for their pains. Moreover, the Allies, ignoring this "peace threat," could confidently count on Wilson's not throwing his support to the German side. After much prayerful thought, Wilson delivered a memorable address to the Senate—and the world. He warmly endorsed a league of nations for establishing worldwide accord and declared that only "peace without victory" could endure. Subsequent events proved that a victor's peace had much to do with bringing on World War II.

Berlin responded to Wilson's pacific plea with a verbal kick in the teeth by proclaiming an unrestricted submarine campaign on January 31, 1917. German U-boats would try to sink *all* ships of any nationality or description in the proclaimed submarine war zone around the British Isles. As a special concession to the United States, one well-marked and well-lighted American passenger ship, flying the Stars and Stripes and carrying no contraband, might sail each week "in each direction" to and from Falmouth, England. This arrangement probably would ensure the safe shipment of essential diplomatic dispatches and the transportation of most Americans who urgently needed to travel.

Wilson regarded Berlin's important concession of one well-marked ship a week (actually two ships) as insulting and as a further breakdown of the "whole fine fabric of international law." Ever since 1915 the Germans had proposed arrangements for a special safe conduct for plainly marked and properly lighted American ships, but Wilson would not betray the other neutrals—and humanity—by accepting such a concession. His warped conception of the American tradition of freedom of the seas involved the "right" of Americans to sail with safety as "shields" for British munitions carriers serving as blockade runners through the proclaimed German war zone. His inflexible stand led him directly down the slippery path to the hell pits of Europe.

The German warlords, goaded in part by Wilson's pro-Ally leanings, had taken a carefully calculated risk. The British "starvation blockade," in which Wilson reluctantly acquiesced, would in time drive the Fatherland completely to the wall. The Germans planned on knocking England out of the war in a few months by sinking all essential supply ships. They almost succeeded and would have achieved their objective if the British had not been forced to adopt the lifesaving convoy system.

The German warlords were not greatly worried about America's coming into the war, partly because the President had built up no formidable military deterrent. Not until December 1915—fifteen long months after Europe had exploded—did Wilson belatedly ask Congress to gird the country for defense. As a result, he had no army of any consequence to send to Europe when the challenge came, and he lacked the ships with which to transport the raw troops. Britain would surely be knocked out, the Germans reasoned, before America could pull together her immense latent strength and intervene effectively.

Obligated by the *Sussex* ultimatum, Wilson severed relations with Germany. But he could not make himself believe that the German warlords were going to sink American ships wholesale; he would wait patiently for overt acts, while keeping guard with an ineffective armed neutrality. In mid-March 1917 German U-boats ruthlessly sank four unarmed American merchant ships, and Germany was indubitably making war on the United

States. On April 2, 1917, Wilson went before Congress and in a loftily idealistic message asked that body to accept the status of belligerency that had been "thrust" upon the United States. Congress speedily and overwhelmingly obliged.

It is clear that Germany would not have "thrust" war on the United States if Wilson had been willing to do what Congress was to do some twenty years later: bar American merchant ships from venturing into the war zones. But Wilson was more concerned about American rights and honor, as he conceived of them, than he was about keeping out of the fray. So the war came.

The northern neutrals—Norway, Sweden, Denmark, and Holland—altogether lost hundreds of ships and thousands of lives to German marauders. Their honor was certainly compromised to a high degree. But none of the four declared war on Germany, primarily because they were under the Kaiser's gun and sure to suffer invasion or other savage reprisals. Pocketing their pride and their profits, the northern neutrals carried on. Nations, including the United States, do not ordinarily go to war unless they feel that they have at least a long-shot chance of winning. Then their honor becomes highly sensitive.

A Martyr to Humanity and Idealism

Our primary concern is with presidential pugnacity that led to war or near war. Wilson did not really want to get into the fray, but he insisted on taking steps that led the nation inexorably over the edge. Once in the conflict, the only honorable way out for the nation was forward, and Wilson keyed his people up in a tremendous crusade to make the world safe for democracy and to fight a war to end war. Strong men in America shed tears when the armistice of 1918 was concluded before they could get "over there" and fight in so noble a cause.

Wilson made the costly mistake of overdoing his lofty aims, for the inevitable "slump in idealism" was bound to come when the war ended and Europe's scramble for the spoils began. Ironically, on the home front the President dealt harshly with those who opposed his idealistic war, including the Socialist leader Eugene V. Debs, who was sentenced to ten years' imprisonment in 1918 for a speech assailing the government's prosecution of persons accused of sedition.

Pugnacious in war, once it had come, Wilson was pugnacious for peace once the shooting had ended. He fought stubbornly at Paris for a lasting settlement based on his Fourteen Points, some of them idealistic and including his hope-giving League of Nations to preserve the peace. Forced to compromise at Paris with the European victors, Wilson refused to compromise with the Republican Senate over the imperfect Treaty of Versailles, with the League of Nations firmly welded into it. As was his "appeal habit," and against the advice of physicans, the weary and sickly Wilson undertook a transcontinental speaking tour of the country to fight for the treaty and the League. As events turned out, he would have been better off remaining in Washington and trying to compromise with the Senators whom he was combating.

After an impassioned appeal in Pueblo, Colorado, Wilson was whisked back to Washington, where he suffered a severe stroke. Secluded, out of touch with public opinion, and with a damaged brain, he sent word from the White House to the Democrats in the Senate to vote down the treaty with fourteen Republican reservations attached. The Democrats followed their fighting leader's command, in the vain hope of getting something better, and the last chance for the League of Nations in the United States went down the drain. The broken Wilson had his back up to the end—with tragic results for himself, the nation and, ironically, humanity.

"Going to Talk to the Boss." Wilson appeals to public opinion. Chicago News.

CHAPTER 29

WARREN G. HARDING: THE APOSTLE OF NORMALCY

We want to do our part in making offensive warfare so hateful that Governments and people who resort to it must prove the righteousness of their cause or stand as outlaws before the bar of civilization.

Warren G. Harding,
Inaugural Address,
March 4, 1921

"Wobbly Warren" Harding

Warren G. Harding, the short-term president from 1921 to 1923, when he died in office, was a man of peace. With World War I ended, his problems were those of returning to "normalcy." Not only was he an easygoing, "folksy" person, but the pressures for new armed interventions were virtually nonexistent. Yet he kept the Marines in Haiti and Nicaragua, in line with the established policies of his predecessors. And in September and October 1922 a United States landing force was sent ashore, with the consent of Greek and Turkish authorities, to protect American lives and property when the Turkish Nationalists entered Smyrna.

An Ohio politician, Harding was a well-built six-footer, with whitish hair, blue eyes, and a smooth complexion. His slightly dark coloration provided some basis for the campaign accusation that there was a strain of Negro blood in his family. Whatever the truth, there could be no doubt that he was one of the handsomest men to ever occupy the White House. His good looks may have had something to do with his having been an unfaithful husband before becoming President. One of two major scandals is fully documented with a packet of love letters in his own handwriting.

The pre-presidential career of the amiable, weak-willed Harding may be compressed into a few words. For three years he attended Ohio Central College, an institution of academy grade in Iberia, Ohio, but evidently he earned no degree. Born the year the Civil War ended, and fifty-two years of age when America entered World War I, he understandably had no military record whatever. Affable, glad-handing, and somewhat gullible, his pugnacity pressure was extremely low. He was so humane that he would carefully brush off ants rather than crush them.

After attending college, Harding tried teaching, selling real estate, and then journalism, in which capacity he became editor-owner of the small-town Marion *Star*. After serving in the Ohio State Senate and as Lieutenant Governor, he was elected to the United States Senate in 1914, the year war broke out in Europe. As a Senator who had attracted little notice, he joined many other Republicans in attacking Wilson's "watchful waiting" in Mexico while American lives and property were being lost. He also supported the formal declaration of war against Germany, as did the great majority of his colleagues of both parties. He had early learned that the best way to get along was to go along. As a staunch Republican, he likewise supported the fourteen "strong" Lodge reservations to the Treaty of Versailles, which embodies the League of Nations.

As a Republican party stalwart and a strong-voiced orator of some repute, Harding had been chosen in 1916 to deliver the keynote speech at the National Convention in Chicago. Even then there was some mention of him as a possible dark horse nominee at the next great convocation.

Four years later, in 1920, the Republicans met again in Chicago, and the two leading candidates, General Leonard Wood and Governor Frank Lowden ruined each others' chances by becoming completely deadlocked. After extensive wheeling and dealing in smoke-filled hotel rooms, the Senate oligarchy got behind the supposedly enemyless Harding and helped to engineer his overwhelming nomination by the convention. Harding was not so much a dark horse as a little-known horse, actually a third choice. As one Republican Senator shortsightedly said, the times did not demand "first raters."

The ensuing campaign, pitting Harding against Governor James Cox, also of Ohio, was supposed to be, as the sickly Wilson had unwisely proclaimed, a referendum on the League of Nations. Yet it was not and could not be a referendum on anything. Harding straddled on the League issue, condemning Wilson's creation in harsh terms, while promising to work for "an Association of Nations." In short, a League but not this one. Such a dodge worked beautifully: Anti-League Republicans were satisfied that there could not possibly be a competing Association of Nations; pro-League Republicans were persuaded that there might be one.

Harding's straddling on the League issue probably was not necessary to achieve victory. He won by an awesome landslide, amassing 61 percent of the popular vote, a prodigious plurality of over 7 million ballots. The sovereign voters were tired of idealism and moral overstrain, as well as disillusioned with the land-grabbing Allies. They were weary of Wilson and all his works; "Back to Normalcy" was the winning slogan. To say that Harding killed the League and future peace by befogging the issue with the Association of Nations is to overlook an essential fact. Any other Republican stalwart, including Calvin Coolidge, almost certainly would have won, perhaps by as impressive a margin.

The Disarmament Delusion

One obvious reason why Harding did not get involved in a major war was that much of his truncated administration was deeply involved in patching up a peace following the recent one. The remaining "boys" had to be brought home from Europe. Treaties of peace had to be signed with the defeated enemy powers, now that the Treaty of Versailles (with its engrafted League of Nations) had been voted down by the Senate.

Harding and other critics of the League, chiefly Republicans, argued that far from keeping America out of future conflicts this foreign trap would ensnare the United States in another European war. Awed, even frightened, by the landslide vote of 1920, the new administration would have no official contact with the League of Nations. As a consequence, agents of the mighty United States hung around the outskirts of the League in Geneva, much like detectives shadowing a criminal.

In August 1921, nearly three years after the shooting had ceased, the United States signed separate peace treaties with Germany, Austria, and Hungary. All these late-coming pacts specifically reserved to America such rights and privileges as the victorious Allies had wrested from the defeated enemy. In this way Washington could claim benefits without responsibilities. Wilson's ideals to make the world safe for democracy and end war thus got lost in selfish, lone-wolf deals. In January 1923 the American Army of Occupation on the Rhine was ordered home by Harding, and the Stars and Stripes were hauled down. The next month Harding in a special message urged America's adherence to the World Court, the judicial arm of the League of Nations, but the Senate refused to act affirmatively on this recommendation.

Harding's major push for peace through the so-called Washington Disarmament Conference of 1921–1922 is to his credit, but the praise has been overdone. The truth is that many Republicans suffered from guilty consciences over the defeat of the League of Nations in the United States, and American taxpayers were worried about the senseless naval race that the victorious powers, including America, had kept up after the guns had grown cold in Europe. Japan's building of warships was of grave concern.

Public pressure at home mounted for calling a conference in Washington of nine of the major and minor powers most involved. Harding, with some initial reluctance, finally issued invitations to Great Britain, France, Italy, Japan, Belgium, China, The Netherlands, and Portugal. Outcast Bolshevik Russia and beaten Germany were not invited, and hence not bound by the deliberations.

After much haggling in Washington, a ten-year moratorium on building capital ships was adopted. The United States agreed to scrap enough of its tonnage, already built and being built, to conform with the following scaled-down ratio: United

States (5), Britain (5), Japan (3), France (1:7), and Italy (1:7). This formula applied to equality or inferiority in capital ship tonnage, but the naval race could go merrily on in submarines, destroyers, and cruisers—and this it did. Great Britain and Japan, like the United States, also scrapped aging capital ships.

From this historic Washington Conference emerged not only the Five-Power Naval Treaty but also the Four-Power Pacific Pact, which provided for mutual respect of one another's rights in the Pacific Ocean by Britain, America, Japan, and France. Finally came the Nine-Power Treaty, in which all the attending powers bound themselves to respect the "sovereignty, the independence, and the territorial and administrative integrity of China." The signatories also agreed on paper to uphold "the principles of the Open Door" and to assist China, "the sick man of the Far East," in forming a stable government.

The Washington "peace conference" of 1921–1922 ended with much fanfare and with considerable credit to the pacific proclivities of the Harding administration. Critics complained that "Uncle Sam" had agreed to scrap too many ships, built and building; and comedian Will Rogers was prompted to jeer, "The United States never lost a war or won a conference." He was wrong on both counts, but the Harding administration purchased about ten years of peace, broken conspicuously by Japan's lunge into Manchuria in 1931. Even ten years was no mean achievement when one considers the frustrations and hates generated by World War I. Harding, the nonwarrior, was the beneficiary of a peace of exhaustion.

CHAPTER 30

CALVIN COOLIDGE: THE SPHINX OF THE POTOMAC

The foreign policy of America can be best described by one word—peace.

Calvin Coolidge, Acceptance
Speech, August 14, 1924

A Political Accident

Calvin Coolidge, the dour Vermonter, did not look like a pugnacious President, and was not one. Five feet, ten inches in height, with reddish hair, a pale and freckled complexion, and blue eyes, he presented no heroic figure. He looked, one contemporary sneered, as though he had been "weaned on a pickle." "Silent Cal" indeed had a reputation for pinch-penny frugality and taciturnity, though he could be positively voluble on occasion with his high-pitched nasal twang.

Born on the Fourth of July in tiny Plymouth Notch, Vermont, this penny-pinching Yankee graduated from Amherst College. He established himself as a lawyer in Northhampton, Massachusetts, and rose gradually from mayor of his home city to Governor of his adopted state in eight easy stages. He burst into the limelight during the Boston police strike of 1919, which was accompanied by looting and other violence. He called out the state troops and the police were losing out when labor leader Samuel Gompers fired off a telegram to Governor Coolidge complaining that the strikers were being mistreated. Coolidge, now that it was safe to speak up, responded resoundingly that there was "no right to strike against the public safety by anybody, anywhere, any time." This unnecessary and belated blast by Coolidge made him a national hero overnight, and it accounted for his nomination for the vice-presidency on the same ticket with Harding at Chicago in 1920. "Coolidge luck" continued when Harding died in 1923, and the dour President-by-accident was overwhelmingly elected in his own right in 1924. Winning slogans were "Keep Cool with Coolidge" and "Keep Cool and Keep Coolidge."

As President for nearly six years, Coolidge was not bursting with either energy or pugnacity, like rough-riding Teddy Roosevelt. He took two-hour afternoon siestas and kept a mechanical horse in the White House for exercise. He could have been renominated easily for a second elective term, but announced, "I do not choose to run in 1928"—a typically laconic statement that was interpreted by many Coolidge-watchers as a desire to be drafted. If so, he was disappointed and was lucky to leave the White House a few months before the Great Depression began to overwhelm Herbert Hoover. He died at age sixty in 1933, two months short of the four years for which he almost certainly could have been elected. A worsening heart condition probably contributed to his decision not to run in 1928.

Mexico, Nicaragua, and the World Court

Friction with Mexico, an oft-told tale, again came to a head in the Coolidge years. In 1925 the Mexican president reversed the calming assurances of his predecessor and made retroactive the seizure of subsoil properties under the constitution of 1917. An outraged cry rose from American oil companies and other investors in Mexican land, and once again there was wild talk of invading Mexico.

At this critical point, in September 1927, President Coolidge had the foresight or good luck to appoint his Amherst College classmate, Dwight W. Morrow, as Ambassador to Mexico. A wealthy Wall Street banker, Morrow had none of the stuffiness of the white-spatted professional diplomat. "I know what I can do for the Mexicans," he remarked. "I can like them."

Morrow's friendliness and tact generated popularity with the Mexican masses, and he achieved an epochal breakthrough. Agreements were reached under which the land-seizure program was slowed down, and foreign companies that had actually begun to work their subsoil properties before the constitution of 1917 might retain ownership. The friendlier atmosphere that followed could be regarded as a promising overture to the Good Neighbor Policy formally inaugurated by Coolidge's successor, Herbert Hoover.

Elsewhere in Latin America President Coolidge achieved significant gains for peace and good will. In September 1924 came the final removal of the U.S. Marines and their gear from Santo Domingo, followed by a treaty ending American military government.

In August 1925 the Marines also left Nicaragua, for by then the nervous New York bankers had been paid off. The local Liberals, long out of power, were free to rise in revolt against the Conservatives, so the Marines returned the next year, 1926. Concerned about preserving American property, the United States supported the puppet Conservative regime of Adolfo Díaz. At his request, President Coolidge finally landed several thousand Marines to fight what critics called Coolidge's "private war."

The uproar of protest in the United States, chiefly among opposition Democrats, prompted President Coolidge to dispatch to Nicaragua, as his personal representative, Colonel Henry L. Stimson, the future Secretary of State under Hoover. By persuasive diplomacy he induced most of the factions to give up their rifles and consent to American-supervised elections. Stimson's remarkable success as a negotiator greatly enhanced the reputation of President Coolidge as a waver of the olive branch.

The U.S. Marines lingered in Nicaragua from 1926 to 1933, chiefly because of the prolonged resistance of the elusive "bandit," General Sandino, and his ragtag following. In 1934, after Sandino had finally laid down his arms, he was treacherously shot by officers of the *guardia*. Appropriately enough, those Nicaraguans who revolted against the dictatorial Somoza regime in 1979 were called "Sandinistas."

President Coolidge had shunned the League of Nations as a thing unclean, yet he came out in support of the World Court, the judicial arm of the League, in his first annual message to Congress, December 6, 1923. The next year he repeated his recommendation through the same medium. Finally, in 1926, the United States Senate tentatively approved adherence to the World Court, with five reservations, which were the crippling handiwork of isolationists and other foes of the League.

Representatives of the signatory powers of the League met in Geneva to consider America's qualified acceptance, and they finally agreed to go along with the United States, except for the fifth reservation. It stipulated that the Court should never entertain a request for an advisory opinion in a dispute affecting the United States, unless the Washington government first gave its consent. Further attempts to work out an accommodation failed, and America never did join the World Court, although an American jurist always sat on the tribunal. This failure of the United States was mainly the responsibility of isolationists in the Senate, not of the successive American Presidents, in this case Coolidge.

Outlawing War and Collecting Debts

In the sense that he was President when it all happened, Coolidge deserves what little credit can be squeezed out of the illusory Kellogg–Briand Peace pact.

For some years naive but well-meaning elements in the United States had been urging action to stamp out war by declaring it unlawful. The idea gained considerable starry-eyed momentum, and in April 1927 the French Foreign Minister, Aristide Briand, announced that France was prepared to enter into a pact with the United States for the mutual outlawry of war. Secretary of State Kellogg, not wanting to be sucked into defending France in Europe, reacted coldly. But public opinion in the United States was mightily aroused for peace, and Kellogg finally suggested to Briand that the proposal be enlarged to include all powers. The Frenchman consented with considerable reluctance.

The Kellogg–Briand Pact, also known as The Pact of Paris, was formally signed by fifteen powers on August 27, 1928, and in later months by virtually all other sovereign nations. In its final form it would permit wars of self-defense but would outlaw war as "an instrument of national policy." The relatively few skeptics who raised their voices sneered at this "international kiss," this "letter to Santa Claus," and this "New Year's Resolution." The pact was so nonbinding that the normally suspicious Senate approved it 85 to 1, although attaching an "interpretation" that reserved the right to self-defense, the right to fight for the Monroe Doctrine, and the right not to punish violators.

The skeptics were correct. The Kellogg–Brian Pact did not abolish war, only declarations of war in the upcoming heyday of the dictators of Germany, Italy, and Japan. As for offensive wars, the aggressors could always trump up some claim of self-defense, as Hitler conspicuously did. Yet the Kellogg-Briand pact finally did serve one useful purpose: When the war that it had outlawed was over, it was used to help convict the losers in the memorable war crimes trials in Nuremberg, Germany.

On balance, the Kellogg–Briand pact did little to avert war, in fact may have encouraged it by lulling the peace-hungry nations and encouraging the dictators to push ahead with their schemes. The irony is that the reluctant Secretary Kellogg was pushed into immortality when he won the Nobel Peace Prize in 1929. He was not the last recipient to receive this high honor for not having achieved peace.

Trouble was brewing on yet another front. Its root was America's policy after World War I of cracking the whip to recover some $10 billion in loans to the recent Allies, notably Britain, France, and Italy. As events turned out, this dunning was directly related to the phenomenal rise of Adolf Hitler and his subsequent launching of World War II. Harding and Coolidge were not seers, but in an indirect sense they were both partially to blame for the catastrophe that befell the world. Actually, the United States had advanced little gold, but mostly war supplies on credit. And American "merchants of death" had turned a pretty penny while doing so.

With the wisdom of 20-20 hindsight we can now see that the statesmanlike policy would have been to forgive these European debts incurred in a common cause, especially in view of the subsequent defaults. In 1921 the Allies finally presented Germany with a staggering reparations bill totaling about $32 billion. On paper, this colossal figure could have been reduced to more manageable dimensions if much of it had not been earmarked for the United States in repayment for the wartime loans. The resulting burden on the German economy was one of Hitler's great grievances as he shouted and screamed his way to power.

Washington finally threshed out individual agreements with the debtor nations in the 1920s, with installments to be paid over a period of sixty-two years. Journalist Walter Lippmann pointed out that to Europeans this scheme was like being forced to pay for the damage caused by one's grandfather at a wild party. War-torn Italy and France put up strong resistance but finally were pressured into terms by "Uncle Shylock." In all instances the standard interest of 5 percent on the unpaid balance was reduced to 3.3 percent or below, and in the case of France this concession amounted to a cancellation of about 60.3 percent of the original principal of $3.4 billion.

To a host of Americans the reduction of interest, plus the long term for repayment, seemed eminently fair. President Coolidge, who was no great expert on international finance, certainly thought so. "They hired the money, didn't they?" he is supposed to have twanged. He merely followed the policy established by Harding and warmly endorsed by the American people, who were becoming increasingly disenchanted with the colony-grabbing ex-Allies.

Japanese Exclusion and Disarmament Deadlock

Japan was one ex-Ally not enmeshed in a quarrel over the war debts, but in the days of Coolidge she became involved in a face-losing problem loaded with high explosives. The issue was Oriental immigration, which was pushed to the fore by the flood of destitute refugees pouring in from Europe. The proposed law of 1924, then before Congress, would allow foreign countries to send a number of immigrants each year that would represent 2 percent of those already in the United States in 1890. If the Japanese had been granted this same privilege, they could have sent legally about 250 a year—certainly not a "yellow horde."

As the result of loud outcries and other pressures from the Pacific Coast, especially California, the immigration bill of 1924 was amended in Congress so as to bar completely all Orientals from entering the United States, even students. This restriction would be a rude abrogation of the Gentlemen's Agreement of 1908, which had worked reasonably well, for the Japanese government had itself undertaken to withhold passports from prospective coolie emigrants.

Secretary of State Hughes, greatly alarmed by the proposed abrogation in Congress, urged the Japanese Ambassador in Washington to act. This envoy was advised to prepare an explanation of Japan's position and the desirability of putting the Japanese on the regular quota basis. Ambassador Hanihara obliged, and Hughes regarded the Japanese note as an admirable summation of the Gentlemen's Agreement. Yet in the concluding paragraph the Ambassador unwisely referred to the "grave consequences" that would result if Japan were excluded from her fair quota. Secretary Hughes regarded "grave consequences" as unacceptably provocative, for in the understated language of diplomacy this phrase could mean war. But Congress was on the verge of voting, and there did not seem to be time for a reworking of the note. So Hughes sent it up to Capitol Hill.*

The explosive note had an effect that was the reverse of the one intended. Here Coolidge's brilliant Secretary of State made a serious error of judgment, although the pending legislation probably would have been passed anyhow by a wide margin. An angered Congress, professing to be threatened, vindictively voted for complete Japanese exclusion by overwhelming majorities.

Coolidge signed the resulting Immigration Law of 1924 with great reluctance, primarily because the country needed it to stem the influx pouring in from postwar Europe. If the Japanese exclusion clause had been a separate act, the President almost certainly would have vetoed it. In any event, the Japanese people were gravely offended. Boycotts of American goods were launched; the American flag was publicly desecrated; and one patriot disemboweled himself near the American embassy. A day of national humiliation was proclaimed. The friends of America in Japan were discredited; the war-bent military elements finally forced their way into the saddle and savored the sweet joys of revenge at Pearl Harbor in 1941.

As a man of peace, Calvin Coolidge hoped to win plaudits by convening a new disarmament conference, as President Har-

*The present author first obtained this information in an interview with Mr. Hughes in Washington, D.C., in 1937.

ding had done so spectacularly in 1921–1922. Actually, such a conclave was urgently needed because the race in constructing warships had shifted to cruisers from the capital ships that had been tightly restricted by the Washington Conference. From 1922 to 1930 the number of warships laid down or funded numbered 125 for Japan, 119 for France, 82 for Italy, 74 for Britain, and 11 for the United States. In this race Uncle Sam had been left almost at the starting gate.

Coolidge's intentions regarding disarmament were good, but he dealt himself a losing hand. He hastily issued the call for a parley at Geneva, Switzerland, without proper preparations and without having done all his diplomatic homework. Britain and Japan sent acceptances, but the French and Italian rivals, for various reasons, sent declinations. The Geneva conclave was thus doomed from the start.

The American negotiators at Geneva sought to apply the 5-5-3 formula for capital ships to smaller vessels and also to bring about a reduction in cruiser tonnage. The question of cruiser size quickly produced a deadlock between Britain and the United States. Naval officers from the concerned countries were much in evidence and inclined to view global disarmament through a porthole. They were reluctant to sink either their differences or their ships. To confound the confusion, a clever lobbyist for three American shipbuilding firms operated smoothly behind the scenes to promote discord. After six weeks of futile, fur-flying sessions, the Geneva conference broke up in utter failure. Among the debits were embittered British-American relations, a defeat for the further limitation of armaments, and a disappointment for the complaining American taxpayers. But Coolidge's desire for arms reduction and peace was commendable.

Aside from the landings of the U.S. Marines in Nicaragua, already mentioned, the Coolidge years witnessed a number of armed interventions, more or less routine in nature and designed to promote the long-established American policy of protecting American lives and property abroad, where possible. One episode occurred in Honduras in February, March, and September 1924, primarily on behalf of American lives and interests during the election hostilities. In April of the next year American forces came again to safeguard foreigners during a political upheaval. And in Panama, in October 1925, strikes and rent riots led to the landing of about six hundred American troops to preserve order and to protect American property.

In faraway China there was a surprising amount of intrusive activity by the United States. In September 1924 U.S. Marines were landed in Shanghai to protect Americans and other foreigners during Chinese riots and other disturbances. In 1926 American forces went ashore at Hankow and Kiukiang for protective purposes, and in 1927 American forces also intervened at Shanghai and Nanking, where American and British destroyers used shell fire to protect Americans and other foreigners. Coolidge probably did not know much about any of these interventions, for they were in line with standardized policy of protecting American lives where possible. But they did occur during his administration and are included to fill out the full-length picture of this man of peace.

CHAPTER 31

HERBERT HOOVER: THE GREAT HUMANITARIAN

Surely civilization is old enough, surely mankind is mature enough so that we ought in our own lifetime to find a way to permanent peace. . . .

Herbert Hoover, Acceptance Speech, August 11, 1928

A Political Greenhorn

Herbert Hoover did not look like a bellicose man, and in fact was not one. Five feet, eleven inches tall, with broad shoulders, a round face, ruddy complexion, and straight parted hair, this extraordinary man was coldly reserved in appearance. During his four years, the United States fought no war, invaded no one's territory (for the first time in many decades), and in fact withdrew the Marines from Nicaragua in 1933, after a lingering visit of some twenty-one years.

How can one account for Hoover's pacificity? One explanation is that he was a devout Quaker by upbringing, and this sect militantly eschews the sword. Also, he had lived abroad on five continents as a mining engineer and consultant, during which he had amassed a fortune reputedly amounting to $4 million. He had seen enough of imperialistic foreigners, including the British, to be distrustful of them, although he was dubbed "Sir Herbert Hoover" by his political enemies. And in Europe he had witnessed enough of the horrors of war and war-spawned famine to abhor the clash of arms.

Hoover had been in China at the time of the Boxer outbreak in 1900 and had been involved in the defense of Tientsin. When World War I engulfed much of Europe in 1914, he was made chairman of the American Relief Committee in London, and in this capacity he assisted the homeward passage of a host of stranded American tourists. From 1915 to 1918 he served as Chairman of the Commission for Relief in Belgium, in which capacity he played a stellar role in feeding the starving victims of the ruthless German invasion.

In 1917–1918 Hoover made the headlines as United States Food Administrator, and this superefficient "Knight of the Lean Garbage Can" taught Americans to "Hooverize" so that they could send the maximum quantity of food to Europe. After the war he continued to direct the American Relief Administration, and in this role he saved millions of Russians from starvation during the devastating famine of 1921–1923.

Hoover, the "miracle man," was chosen Secretary of Commerce in the Harding and Coolidge administrations and he succeeded in elevating that office to new heights of importance. So awesome was his reputation as an organizer and achiever that, although a political greenhorn, he was overwhelmingly elected President in 1928 over the Democratic nominee, jaunty, wisecracking Al Smith of New York.

There are at least two tried-and-true ways of involving one's nation in war. The first is to launch an attack, declared or undeclared. The other is to pursue policies that result in a conflict between other nations into which one's own country is drawn, sooner or later. With these two alternatives before us, we can best determine how well Hoover fared.

Good Neighbors to the South

Franklin Roosevelt, who overwhelmed Hoover at the polls in 1932, is hailed as the author of the Good Neighbor Policy, with special reference to improving troubled relations with Latin

America. The truth is that although Roosevelt carried this concept to a new plateau, the path to this friendly policy had already been partially prepared by President Hoover, to go no farther back among Roosevelt's predecessors.

Shortly after Hoover's spectacular success at the polls in November 1928, the President-elect undertook a seven-week goodwill tour that brought him to the shores of more than half of the Latin American republics. Legend to the contrary, his reception was not overwhelmingly enthusiastic. He arrived on a big battleship rather than on a more modest cruiser, thus reminding those he visited of the scores of landings by U.S. Marines. In addition, Hoover had been indirectly tarred by the interventionist policies of Harding and Coolidge, under whom he had helped serve big American bankers abroad while Secretary of Commerce.

Yet on balance Hoover's goodwill tour seems to have promoted a modest amount of amity. The previously snubbed and invaded republics to the south must have been flattered to some extent by this sudden show of interest after so many years of neglect. The warmest receptions appear to have been evoked in Brazil, the biggest nation of them all and the traditional friend and coffee bag of the United States. In addition, the visitor's repetition of the felicitous phrase, "Good Neighbor," gave promise of happier days to come.

After Hoover was officially sworn in as President, he made clear his determination to retreat from Yankee imperialism in Latin America. In his inaugural address he ringingly proclaimed that "we have no desire for territorial expansion, for economic or other domination of other peoples." In his first annual message to Congress (December 1929), he referred to the presence of U. S. Marines in Nicaragua and Haiti, and added pointedly that "we do not wish to be represented abroad in such a manner." True to his word, he withdrew the troops from Nicaragua in January 1933, some two months before leaving office.

Also heartening to Latin Americans, but only mildly so, was the publication in 1930 of the Clark *Memorandum* relating to the Monroe Doctrine. Prepared in 1928 by J. Reuben Clark, Under Secretary of State under President Coolidge, it challenged the interventionist twist given to the Monroe Doctrine under Theodore Roosevelt. The Clark pronouncement did not surrender the right to intervene in all cases, only the alleged right to intervene under the Monroe Doctrine, which the United States had designed in 1823 to keep the European powers away. Colonel

Henry L. Stimson, Hoover's new Secretary of State, approved the Clark *Memorandum*, although it was not published until 1930, the year after the new President took office. Hoover and his subordinate officials in the State Department regarded the document as unofficial and rather unimportant, yet this self-denying pronouncement helped to foster the emerging spirit of Good Neighborism.

The Great Depression severely tested the new policy of nonintervention as set forth in the Clark *Memorandum*. Partly because of contagious economic maladies, a rash of revolutions broke out in Latin America, notably in Mexico and Brazil. But the once-meddling Uncle Sam kept his hands off and refused to use President Wilson's nonrecognition bludgeon, whether the new regime was headed by legitimate rulers or bloody-handed usurpers.

But what Hoover gave with one hand, he unwittingly snatched away with the other. He signed with reluctance, but he did sign, the Hawley-Smoot Tariff of 1930, which boosted to new heights many categories of imports from abroad, including Latin America. Presumably, a veto of this controversial measure, among other drawbacks, would have damaged relations with his own Republican party, dedicated as it was to a high tariff. The Latin Americans reacted bitterly, for they were already sinking deeper into the quicksands of depression and had long resented Yankee barriers erected against their products. Regarding the latest tariff as a blow below the trade belt, they vented their anger accordingly.

"Sweet are the uses of adversity," as Shakespeare noted. Owing to the Great Depression, the American investors had less money to invest in Latin America, and billions of dollars in Yankee funds were lost by default. The Yankee exploiters thus became the exploited. Dispatching more Marines would be pointless, for these fighting men, though formidable, could not pin down the vanishing dollars with bayonets.

Plainly the time had come for troop withdrawals. In 1932, in the trough of the Great Depression, the Hoover administration negotiated a treaty with Haiti that provided for the exit of the last Marines. The legislature of Haiti finally rejected the proposed withdrawal because of a remnant of financial supervision, yet the end of foreign occupation was clearly in sight. The departing Marines folded their tents two years later, under President Franklin Roosevelt. In 1934, also under Roosevelt, the Marine buglers sounded their last shrill notes in Nicaragua, and silence fell after twenty years of occupation. Thus Herbert Hoover, the Engineer in Politics, engineered the emplacement of some of the foundation stones of what would become Roosevelt's Good Neighbor Policy.

Debt Defaults and Japanese Aggressors

In Latin America, as noted, Hoover gave Good Neighborism with one hand but used the other to jerk it away with the Hawley-Smoot tariff. In Europe the concessions made to the European debtors were substantially canceled out by repercussions in Germany against the extraction of reparations.

President Hoover favored the debt settlements with the ex-Allies that had been negotiated by his immediate predecessors, but he narrowly insisted that technically the Allied war debts were not connected with the payment of reparations by Germany. In theory, he had a point; in practice, he was wrong. After World War I ended, American bankers had invested more than $2 billion in the revival of German industry, much of it later used by Hitler's war machine. Much of this money was paid to the ex-Allies in reparations, and in turn these funds substantially found their way back to the United States in the form of payments on the Allied war debts. Gullible old Uncle Sam, in this roundabout way, was transferring money from one pocket to another.

The depression that descended on America with the stock market crash of 1929 gradually spread its economic blight to Europe and the rest of the world. American loans to the Germans dried up, reparations payments from Germany dried up, and payments to the United States on the Allied war debts began to dry up. Accelerating this arid process was the short-sighted Hawley-Smoot tariff, which Hoover signed with considerable reluctance but defended with verbal vigor.

International trade is a two-way street, and if the ex-Allies could not boost their goods into America over the new tariff barrier, they could not repay their obligations as debtors to Uncle Sam. The stock replies from Washington were "try harder" and "pay anyhow." In the end, many foreign nations jacked up their tariff walls in retaliation, and the resulting economic isolation worsened the financial chaos that contributed mightily to the rise of Adolf Hitler.

A millionaire businessman, Hoover was inflexibly opposed to the cancellation of war debts, but he was sharp enough to perceive that the alternatives were now either generous cancellation or just plain default. He compromised when he arranged in 1931 for a one-year moratorium on the payments on war debts owed the United States. Pundits predicted correctly that when the moratorium ended in 1932 the emphasis would be on "more." With the United States still demanding payments on what it regarded as just debts, six of the debtor nations defaulted outright in December 1932. From then on repayment was virtually a dead horse.

If Hoover had been able to foresee the inevitable more clearly, and if he had been willing and able to persuade Congress to cancel or greatly reduce the war debts—big "ifs" indeed—the result could have been happier. The rise of Adolf Hitler to the Chancellorship of Germany in 1933, as well as World War II, might conceivably have been averted.

America's response to Japan's incursion into China's Manchuria and Shanghai, in 1931–1932, also presented President Hoover with a painful dilemma. He could either join with the other powers in forcing Japan to withdraw or he could stay out altogether. Being a Quaker and a pacifist, he did neither but resorted to paper preachments instead.

In 1931 the Japanese warlords lunged into China's Manchuria, took it over, and renamed it Manchukuo. In so doing they defied their commitment to the League of Nations (of which the United States was not a member), to the Nine Power treaty (signed by the United States in 1922), and to the Kellogg–Briand Pact of 1928, engineered and signed by the United States. The Japanese proved abundantly to Mussolini and Hitler that treaties and leagues could be defied with impunity. If the United States had offered to join the other powers in energetic armed action, would Japan have been forced to knuckle under, and would World War II have been averted? We shall never know, and little can be gained by wearisome speculation.

Secretary of State Stimson, something of a "hawk," at the outset rebuffed overtures from the League of Nations, though responding that the United States "probably" would not interfere with an embargo against Japan. Britain and France, both knee deep in the Depression and both fearing for their trade and investments in the Far East, had no stomach for resolute action. Possibly they would have been more willing to act decisively if the United States, the most potent foreign power, had been willing to take the lead. But this again is speculation.

Secretary Stimson, held in leash by the Quaker Hoover, evolved the Hoover–Stimson doctrine, which proved to be worth no more than the paper on which it was written. This pronouncement was aimed directly at Japan's aggressions in China, and in effect stated that the United States would not recognize any changes, territorial or otherwise, effected by force of arms. Sticks and stones may break bones, but paper bullets and moral sanctions can be useless, as indeed they were in this case, except perhaps to salve the national conscience.

Smarting from a Chinese boycott, the Japanese attacked China's Shanghai in January 1932, and largely with aerial bombing killed or wounded thousands of men, women, and children. An outraged American public launched boycotts of Japanese goods and knicknacks in the department stores. Secretary Stimson favored joining hands with the League of Nations in imposing a boycott, but Quaker Hoover turned a deaf ear. To his way of thinking, boycotts spelled bayonets and embargoes spelled bombs. Instead, he would rely on paper pills and moral sanctions, with the result that the other powers found in Washington's aloofness further encouragement for their own timorous course. A five-man commission of the League of Nations, after a lengthy on-the-ground investigation, formally condemned Japan's rampage. But instead of driving the Japanese offenders out of Manchuria, the condemnatory powers merely succeeded in driving Japan out of the League of Nations. In a very real sense, the Open Door was kicked in the panels, the League disintegrated, collective security died, and World War II started in 1931 on the chill plains of Manchuria.

The League of Nations and Disarmament

Japan's thrust into Manchuria highlighted the increasing concern of President Hoover with the League of Nations, which Harding and Coolidge had shunned as one would avoid a leper. Unofficial "observers" from America gradually sat with League committees to discuss important nonpolitical problems in a "consultative" capacity, especially health problems. By 1930, Hoover's second year, the United States had participated in more than forty League conferences, all presumably nonpolitical. By 1931 the once standoffish Americans had five permanent officials stationed at Geneva, all committed to cooperation without political involvement. All told, Hoover and Secretary Stimson together negotiated twenty-five treaties of arbitration and seventeen of conciliation.

A significant break with tradition followed the Manchurian crisis of 1931. In response to an invitation from Geneva, Washington designated a representative to sit in judgment on Japan with the Council of the League of Nations. But he received clear-cut instructions to participate in the discussions only when they related to America's obligations under the Kellogg–Briand Peace Pact of 1928. The offending Japanese, noting America's previous aloofness from the League, naturally resented the presence of the American representative as a deliberately unfriendly act.

A peace-loving Hoover was eager to achieve the success in the arms limitation (not "disarmament") that Coolidge had failed to win at Geneva in 1927. The Washington Conference of 1921–1922 had placed limits only on capital ships, while the mad race still went on with smaller craft, conspicuously destroyers and cruisers. Representatives of the United States, Britain, Japan, France, and Italy met in London early in 1930. After prolonged argument, the argumentative quintet of nations emerged with a "disarmament" treaty of sorts. A shell-shocked France, still obsessed with security, demanded assurances of military support in a crisis. But Hoover, at heart an isolationist, rejected the support that he knew the American public would not approve. The result was that France and Italy subscribed to only unimportant parts of the Treaty of London. Yet for the first time the United States was granted parity with Britain in all classes of ships, while the Japanese improved their ratio somewhat.

American taxpayers were disappointed, for about a billion dollars would be needed for the additonal construction to achieve the parity granted on paper. But Hoover rather deviously argued that the London Conference had saved the United States a billion dollars when compared with what had been discussed at Coolidge's abortive Geneva Conference of 1927. A distrustful Senate finally approved the Five-Power Naval Pact but accompanied its action with a resolution that the United States would not be bound by any secret understandings.

Hoover conspicuously cooperated with the fifty-one nation World Disarmament Conference, which convened at Geneva early in 1932 under the auspices of the League of Nations. The conferees were getting nowhere after five months of argument when Hoover electrified the conclave with a spectacular proposal. He urged the abolition of offensive weapons and the wholesale reduction of existing arms by about one-third. After an initially enthusiastic reception, the Hoover proposals were buried beneath a heap of oratorical flowers.

The good Quaker President was surprisingly naive. Arms are not so much a disease as manifestations of such maladies as insecurity, fear, and predatory ambitions. In certain circumstances arms races can reach the point, as in 1914, when they are a part of the disease itself. As for the distinction between "offensive" and "defensive" arms, to which Hoover adhered, there are few offensive arms that cannot in certan circumstances be used for defensive purposes. A bomber that destroys airplane factories manufacturing offensive aircraft is serving in a defensive capacity. Bayonets that are used in an assault can be used to drive back an invading enemy. And what aggressor nation in history, if it had chosen to, could not have claimed self-defense, however hollowly?

Hoover was unquestionably a man of peace and justifiably honored as "The Great Humanitarian." The irony is that shortly before his administration ended he gave the orders that resulted in the eviction from Washington of thousands of veteran bonus marchers in the inglorious "Battle of Anacostia Flats," July 28, 1932. It is true that their presence was a menace to the public health, that they had been trying to intimidate the Congress into awarding them their bonus prematurely, and that their ranks contained a relatively few Communists and other left-wingers. But all these did not justify brutal treatment.

The eviction of bonus marchers by American troops under General Douglas MacArthur, though undertaken under Hoover's orders, was carried out with far more severity than the President had envisaged. The soldiers used bayonets, torches, and tear gas. Though suffering some slight injuries from flying bricks and other objects, the troops wiped out the whole collection of pathetic shanties. An eleven-month-old "bonus baby" died, allegedly from exposure to gas. In cynical Democratic eyes "The Great Humanitarian" and "Friend of Helpless Children" became "The Hero of Anacostia Flats," and this distressing eviction no doubt contributed to Hoover's overwhelming repudiation at the polls some three months later, in November 1932.

CHAPTER 32

FRANKLIN DELANO ROOSEVELT: THE MAN OF DESTINY

I have said not once but many times that I have seen war and that I hate war. I say that again and again.

Roosevelt's radio address,
September 3, 1939, the day
Britain and France declared
war on Germany

The Squire of Hyde Park

Franklin Roosevelt, unlike his distant cousin, the Rough Riding Theodore Roosevelt, hated war yet managed to involve his nation in the most frightful conflict in history. Along the slippery path to the abyss he pursued a zig-zag course, a part of the time taking significant steps toward peace, some of the time moving toward warlike confrontations, at other times fighting defensively in his efforts to get lend-lease supplies to England and Russia. Wilson had more or less blundered into World War I; Roosevelt got into World War II with his eyes open. He was willing to risk shooting in what he regarded as the interests of the nation and humanity.

Franklin Roosevelt was born in 1882 on the family estate at Hyde Park, New York. The father and mother were wealthy, and the son was pampered. Educated at Groton and Harvard, Roosevelt subsequently studied law at Columbia University. Then, after practicing it with considerable distaste for several years, he tried his hand at politics. He was elected as a Democrat to the New York State Senate for the term from 1911 to 1913. When the Democrats came to power under Woodrow Wilson in 1913, Roosevelt was appointed Assistant Secretary of the Navy. He evidently thought on a grand scale, served usefully, and learned much about naval problems—information that he would later put to good use after Hitler and the British began their death struggle in 1939 for control of the seas.

Young Roosevelt was on fire to get into action when America slithered into the war against Germany in 1917, but he was told by his superiors that he could serve the common cause more usefully by remaining at his desk job. There was no question then about his physical fitness. Handsome as a Greek god and superbly built, Roosevelt stood six feet, two inches. But he did manage to travel across submarine-infested waters to the Western Front in France on an inspection tour in the summer of 1918. He got near enough to the action to see dead men lying in the mud, with many of the survivors bleeding or "coughing out their gassed lungs," as he told a radio audience in 1936 while President. He added that he had seen "children starving," as well as "the agony of mothers and wives. I hate war." One can believe that he did.

Roosevelt was added to the Democratic ticket as the vice-presidential candidate in 1920, and he staged a vigorous but fruitless campaign in behalf of Wilson's peace-oriented League of Nations. But the voters, weary of Wilson and all his works, buried the Cox-Roosevelt ticket in an avalanche of ballots.

Returning to his rather distasteful law practice in 1920, Roosevelt was crippled the next year in both legs by a devastating attack of polio. Thereafter he was largely confined to a wheelchair or locked in steel braces. But nothing had gone wrong with that vibrant golden voice, and he was persuaded to run successfully for the governorship of New York in 1928 after Al Smith had pointed out that being an acrobat was not a necessary qualification for a potential governor of the state.

The worried voters, rendered desperate by the Great Depression, turned overwhelmingly against the harassed Hoover and in favor of Roosevelt in the presidential election of 1932. With jauntily upturned cigarette holder, the smiling New Yorker exuded confidence as bands blared "Happy Days Are Here Again." He would give the people action, he would try new experiments until he found ones that worked, and he would balance Hoover's unbalanced budget. Popular slogans that later made ironical reading were "Throw the Spenders Out" and "Out of the Red with Roosevelt."

Good Neighbors All

One of Franklin Roosevelt's most significant moves for peace was to carry forward to new heights the Good Neighbor policy already pioneered by President Hoover and others. Roosevelt's overwhelming preoccupation was obviously the Great Depression, but toward the end of his inaugural address he incorporated this paragraph: "In the field of world policy I would dedicate this nation to the policy of the good neighbor—the neighbor who resolutely respects himself and, because he does so, respects the rights of others—the neighbor who respects his obligations and respects the sanctity of his agreements in and with a world of neighbors."

Roosevelt was speaking of world neighbors, not just those to the south, with whom he was to achieve his most noteworthy successes. To this end, he worked hand in glove with his patient Secretary of State, Cordell Hull. Finally, the Reciprocal Trade Agreements Act passed Congress in 1934, under which existing tariffs could be mutually reduced by as much as 50 percent. From 1934 to 1945 Washington concluded twenty-seven trade treaties, a large number of them with Latin American countries. These concessions managed to take much of the sting out of the unpopular Hawley-Smoot tariff enacted under president Hoover in 1930.

Late in 1933 Secretary Hull journeyed to Montevideo, Uruguay, where he became something of a hero at the Seventh International Conference of American states. When he arrived he was jolted by placards proclaiming "Down with Hull," but he delighted the delegates by backing a pact which flatly declared, "No state has the right to intervene in the internal or external affairs of another." Improbably, the Senate of the United States subsequently approved the Montevideo treaty without a dissenting vote and with only one minor reservation.

The watershed policy of nonintervention, thus formally adopted, meant that Roosevelt was abandoning, even reversing, the preventive intervention sanctioned by his cousin in the Roosevelt Corollary to the Monroe Doctrine. Late in 1933 an uprising in Cuba against "Butcher" Machado brought Yankee warships to Cuban waters, but no landing of troops. After calm was restored, the United States formally released Cuba from the restrictive hobbles of the Platt Amendment in May 1934. This step was immensely popular in Latin America, and later in the same year Roosevelt ordered the Marines to pack up their gear and depart from Haiti. For the first time since 1915 no United States troops "polluted" the soil of Latin America, as local politicians charged. No further such landings of United States forces occurred until 1965, when President Lyndon Johnson intervened in the Dominican Republic under circumstances to be recounted later.

In 1936, with Hitler and Mussolini darkening the European horizon, Roosevelt proposed a special Inter-American Conference for peace. The suggestion flowered into a special inter-American conclave in Buenos Aires, Argentina, to which the President journeyed by sea as "a traveling salesman for peace." His dramatic proposal to make the Monroe Doctrine multilateral against the European dictators was not then accepted, but he laid the groundwork for the more significant conferences that came later at Panama and Havana. Nonintervention by the United States was reaffirmed at Buenos Aires.

Roosevelt's new hands-off policy received another crucial test in Mexico, which in 1938 expropriated foreign oil properties. American investors, valuing their holdings at some $260 million, clamored for armed intervention. A compromise settlement was finally reached in 1941, with the American capitalists being awarded about one-sixth of what they demanded. But Roosevelt solidified his Good Neighbor Policy by honoring his nonintervention pledge, and the crisis in Mexican-American relations passed into history.

Under Franklin Roosevelt, Good Neighborism was extended, without conspicuous success, to the Soviet Union. Ever since the Bolshevik Revolution of 1917 and the Soviet declaration of ideological warfare on the capitalist world, Washington had declined to recognize the Communist regime in the Kremlin. Among assorted sins, the Soviets had repudiated Tsarist debts to the United States, and they had continued their propaganda in America for Communist world revolution.

By 1933 the picture was changing dramatically. The Great Depression in America had proved devastating, and an enriching trade might conceivably be developed with the Soviet Union. Dictatorial aggressors were on the rise in Germany, Italy, and Japan, and a bolstered Soviet Union might yet serve to restrain them. With such inducements in mind, the liberal Democratic regime of Roosevelt did what his conservative Republican predecessors had refused to do—extended formal recognition to a nation that occupied one-sixth of the earth's surface. Yet the Communist propaganda did not cease, and the hoped-for trade did not develop. In any event, mutual name-calling was now on an official basis.

Roosevelt's Path to Peace

High hopes generated by President Harding's conference in Washington on the limitation of (some) arms had merely resulted in an acceleration of the frantic race to build noncapital ships. Coolidge's abortive Geneva conference in 1927 had only deepened suspicions, and the disputatious London Conference of 1930 in Hoover's day proved to be a delusion. The war-bent Japanese were distressed by being left on the short end of the 5-5-3 ratio, which to one of their spokesmen sounded like "Rolls-Royce—Rolls-Royce—Ford." In December 1934 Tokyo formally served notice that in two years it would terminate its subordinate connection as spelled out in the Washington Naval Treaty of 1922.

The Second London Naval Conference convened late in 1935. The Roosevelt administration, responsible for defending America's two long coastlines and far-flung insular possessions, including the Philippines, was unwilling to concede 5-5-5 parity to the Japanese, who then stalked out of the conference. The resulting pact was virtually toothless, and this meant that by 1938 the naval powers had tossed overboard virtually all the meaningful restrictions on further naval construction.

Roosevelt was an experienced naval man who perceived the need for a two-ocean navy and who recognized the danger of falling perilously behind in a madly rearming world. In January 1938 he asked Congress for a $1 billion naval appropriation. With Hitler, Mussolini. and the Japanese warlords on the march, Congress obliged, but not until May 1938. With dangerous belatedness, the United States finally had both feet in the most costly naval race thus far in history.

Meanwhile, in 1934–1935, a phobia had developed in America against the "merchants of death"—that is, the munitions manufacturers and bankers who allegedly had dragged the United States into World War I in pursuit of their ill-gotten gains. With Mussolini threatening to touch off World War II with his invasion of Ethiopia, Congress hastily passed the Neutrality Act of 1935. In brief, its terms were that whenever the President proclaimed the existence of a war, he was to bar the sale or transportation of munitions to the warring nations. With disaster ships like the *Lusitania* still vividly in mind, the Chief Executive was empowered to warn American citizens not to travel on belligerent passenger ships except at their own risk. The Neutrality Act of 1935 won overwhelming support in Congress, but Roosevelt signed it with reluctance. He had privately concluded that the most practicable approach to peace and neutrality was to deny munitions to the aggressor while supplying them to the victim.

A new Neutrality Act, that of 1937, reaffirmed the nonsale of munitions to belligerents while making travel on belligerent passenger ships completely unlawful. As a concession to American merchants, belligerents might purchase the raw materials of munitions, such as copper and lead. But these buyers would have to pay cash on delivery and take the purchases away in their own ships on a "cash and carry" basis.

Roosevelt did not really believe in storm-cellar neutrality, and he managed to have the existing legislation modified and then virtually repealed in 1939 and 1941. He was thinking primarily of the national interest, the ultimate peace and security of the United States. When Japan wantonly attacked China in 1937–1945, in one of the longest and bloodiest conflicts in history, Roosevelt did not proclaim the existence of a war, as he was technically bound to do. Like most Americans, he favored China against Japan and did not want to cut off the trickle of munitions being sent to the embattled Chinese.

The Japanese assault on China evidently aroused Roosevelt to the necessity of averting a general blowup by the dictators, including Hitler and Mussolini, that would involve a peace-seeking United States. In his sensational "Quarantine Speech" in Chicago, in October 1937, he proposed that "positive endeavors to preserve peace" be made by quarantining the war-bent dictators. But the blacklash from the isolationists in America was so violent that Roosevelt dropped this frontal approach.

Then came the Munich crisis of 1938, fueled by Hitler's fanatical determination to add the Sudetenland, inhabited by Germans, to the German Reich. World War II seemed inevitable. Roosevelt feared that America would be drawn in, and in desperation he cabled two last-minute appeals to Hitler and one to Mussolini. The Italian dictator called Hitler on the telephone, and the Fuehrer reluctantly consented to a conference at Munich. Whether or not Roosevelt's intercession saved the day cannot be determined, but at least he tried.

At Munich both Great Britain and France abandoned Czechoslovakia to Hitler, and the new world war was averted for about one year. This was the classic case of appeasement, or surrender on the installment plan. America rejoiced that shooting had been averted, not realizing that worse was yet to come.

Hopes for peace with Germany were dashed in March 1939, nearly six months after the Munich capitulation, when Hitler's troops took over the rest of Czechoslovakia. The next month Mussolini, Hitler's partner in the Rome–Berlin alliance, overran Albania. Roosevelt, greatly fearing that the fragile peace of Europe would soon be shattered, cabled the two dictators. He rather naively asked for pledges from both that neither would overrun thirty-one specific countries that embraced all of Europe, plus some of the Near East. In the interests of world peace and humanity, Roosevelt requested assurances of nonaggression for at least ten years.

Nothing could better highlight Roosevelt's desperate desire for peace. Hitler responded, not in a direct rebuff to the President, but in a two-hour harangue to his puppet Reichstag. Its members roared with laughter as the Fuehrer read off in mock tones the names of the thirty-one nations, including tiny Luxembourg. After roundly insulting Roosevelt as a loathsome meddler, Hitler declared unrealistically that he would negotiate peace guarantees with the specific thirty-one nations, provided that they took the initiative and settled for absolute reciprocity.

He omitted from the list nearby Poland, which he was planning to invade and in fact did overwhelm some four months later. Roosevelt, the earnest peacemaker, was indignant over this insulting rebuff, but he recognized the futility of trying to reason with an unreasonable dictator obviously hell-bent for war.

Fearful of Hitler, the Soviets under Stalin were negotiating with the British for some kind of defensive alliance. When Great Britain would not offer enough soon enough, the double-dealing Stalin turned the tables and negotiated instead a nonaggression pact with Hitler on August 23, 1939. It gave the Fuehrer a green light to attack Poland and formally launch World War II on September 1, 1939. On September 3 both Britain and France honored their commitments to Poland and declared war on Hitler's Reich.

That night Roosevelt declared in a fireside radio chat from the White House, "I hope the United States will keep out of this war. I believe that it will. And I give you assurances that every effort of your government will be directed toward that end." F.D.R. would have been on safer ground if he had said that he would make every effort to stay out of a declared war or a full-scale war. His efforts actually had been directed to that end. Up to this point his record as a general peacemaker had been praiseworthy; he had gone beyond the call of duty in trying to restrain Hitler, only to be kicked in the teeth.

Unneutral Neutrality

In his fireside chat to the nation on September 3, 1939, Roosevelt not only promised to try to keep out of the war but also promised, "This nation will remain a neutral nation." But he quickly added, with an obvious thrust at Chancellor Hitler, "Even a neutral cannot be asked to close his mind or conscience."

The simple truth is that the people of the United States were never neutral during this war: Overwhelming majorities of them distrusted, hated, or feared the dictators, chiefly Hitler. From the early beginnings of the conflict the Washington government was pro-Ally, and as Hitler swept to successive triumphs, the time-honored concepts of neutrality went out the window. Strict neutrality probably would have resulted in total victory for the aggressors, with all that this tragic result portended for the possible enchainment of the United States. Roosevelt's unneutrality was designed primarily for the security and peace of his own country.

The disagreeable truth is that the dictators openly flouted both international law and their treaty commitments, particularly the Kellogg–Briand peace pact. They had made or were making nonaggression treaties that were callously designed to lull their prospective victims into a false sense of security. Hitler's submarines made a mockery of international law by torpedoing merchant ships without proper regard for the safety of passengers and crew. In a grim game of this kind, if one side is bound by the rules and the aggressor is not, the law-abiding nation is almost certain to lose. From the vantage point of Washington, the only realistic course was to fight the devil with fire. Roosevelt felt that he had to combat such unlawful aggressors by brushing aside the laws of neutrality, especially those that prevented aid from being sent to the victims of aggression. In the end, the war-hating Roosevelt pursued a flagrantly unneutral policy of helping the Allies, not the Axis powers, in what he conceived to be, with good reason, the national interest.

In the early days of the Hitler war, Roosevelt arranged to have U.S. Navy patrols radio the presence of German merchant ships in plain English to nearby British destroyers. To help the democracies resist aggression, he called Congress into special session to revamp the hand-tying neutrality legislation. This step was taken after Poland fell to Hitler's mighty war machine. After prolonged debate the revised neutrality act became law in November 1939. It lifted the former ban on exporting munitions of war, while requiring that such material be purchased on a cash-and-carry basis and then carried away on the purchaser's ships. As a concession to the isolationists, American merchant vessels were forbidden to enter the danger zones proclaimed by the Germans and British. In short, the so-called Neutrality Act of 1939 turned out to be unneutral because it permitted arms to go to the democracies and not to the dictators.

Amid rumors that Mussolini was about to join Hitler in the German attack on France, Roosevelt appealed to Premier Mussolini on April 29, 1940, to exert his influence for peace. The President repeated his plea three times during the following month, but to no avail. Mussolini, jackal-like, attacked France from the rear on June 10, 1940, as Roosevelt reported with evident anger when he spoke at the commencement exercises at the University of Virginia.

Roosevelt's unneutrality (under the now defunct rules) was so blatant that one need not belabor the point. But several of the most famous (or notorious) incidents should be mentioned. In September 1940, as Britain appeared to be in imminent danger of invasion by Hitler's warriors, Roosevelt transferred an unprecedented fifty overage destroyers from the U.S. Navy to that of Great Britain. In return the United States received long-term, rent-free leases for base sites on eight Atlantic locations, mostly insular, ranging from Newfoundland to British Guiana. The Newfoundland and Bermuda leaseholds came as outright gifts. Roosevelt consummated this deal as an executive agreement, without consulting a Congress that would have generated furious opposition to what was essentially an act of war.

In March 1941 Roosevelt signed the epochal (and grossly unneutral) Lend-Lease Act, which he had shepherded through a refractory Congress. To avoid another era of ill feeling over war debts, this bill provided that the United States would lend the materials of war without stint to those governments "whose defense the President deems vital to the defense of the United States." All told, some $50 billion in lend-lease was sent to Hitler's foes, including some $11 billion to the Soviet Union. This open-handed legislation was more than abandonment of neutrality; it was an unofficial declaration of war on the ruthless dictators, or rather a sweeping recognition of the fact that in effect Hitler and Mussolini had already declared war on all democracies, including the United States.

In August 1941 Prime Minister Winston Churchill of Great Britain met informally with President Roosevelt on a splended new British battleship off the coast of Newfoundland. They concerted plans for the ultimate defeat of Hitler and issued a blueprint for the kind of peaceful new world they envisioned, once the dictators were crushed. American isolationists cried out that the President of a neutral United States had no business concocting plans with a leading belligerent. These critics missed the point. The United States was no longer neutral, if she ever had been, and the Atlantic Charter in effect was the fruit of a tacit alliance with Great Britain.

On several occasions during this anxious period of undeclared warfare, German submarines had torpedoed American merchant ships. More alarming were the clashes in the North Atlantic between American destroyers and German submarines.

Some of the earlier shipments of lend-lease material to England had been sunk by German submarines in the North Atlantic. Roosevelt finally concluded that such cargoes should be escorted with the aid of American destroyers, because Congress, in voting for lend-lease, evidently expected the supplies to get to their destination. Acting under the President's orders as Commander-in-Chief, these speedy U.S. warships were not to seek out German submarines in European waters. Rather, they were to fight off U-boats attacking convoys of lend-lease supplies sailing from Canada to England, often by way of Iceland.

In September 1941 the American destroyer *Greer* had a brush with a German submarine but escaped undamaged; in mid-October 1941 the U.S. destroyer *Kearny* was torpedoed and badly damaged, with a loss of eleven lives, but finally made port in Iceland. Late in October the U.S. destroyer *Reuben James*, engaged in convoy duty, was torpedoed and sunk in the North Atlantic, with the loss of more than one hundred officers and men. Indisputably, Roosevelt was fighting German submarines preying on lend-lease cargoes, and the U-boats were fighting back in a vicious undeclared war.

Fighting for Peace

Critics used to argue, and some still do, that Roosevelt was deviously trying desperately to get into the all-out shooting war with Hitler, and that he was deliberately having his destroyers attack the U-boats so that Congress would be stampeded to a declaration of war. An exhaustive examination of all the evidence, both American and German, results in a more favorable conclusion.

By December 1941, at the time of Pearl Harbor, Hitler still did not want war with the United States, largely because his available ground and air forces were tied down by the far-flung invasion of the Soviet Union. When he had the Soviets at his mercy, he could turn his attention to the United States and Roosevelt. Meanwhile the German submarines were under orders not to fight U.S. destroyers except in self-defense.

Roosevelt sensed that he had Hitler over a Bolshevik barrel. All that the President really wanted was to get the lend-lease shipments to Great Britain, from which some of them could go to Soviet Russia. The British and the Russians could thus keep Hitler at bay, and perhaps the war in Soviet Russia would be fought to a stalemate without the necessity of a total American involvement. If Roosevelt had desired to fight more directly with Hitler, he could have used U.S. destroyers to hunt down German submarines in European waters. As it was, these warships tangled with the U-boats only to protect convoys on the North Atlantic run.

Roosevelt's game of only limited shooting was working beautifully in the Atlantic until the Japanese burst out in the Pacific at Pearl Harbor on December 7, 1941. Japan declared war on the United States, as did Hitler and Mussolini, with Congress responding in kind. The evidence is overwhelming that Roosevelt did not "plan it this way." American public opinion, according to the polls, strongly favored lend-lease aid to England, even at the risk of war. Roosevelt invited a limited, undeclared war in the Atlantic but got all-out war in the Pacific as well, largely because of the embargoes he had clamped on war supplies going to Japan. He had acted in this remote theater in the interests of China and America's security in East Asia and the Pacific. He wanted no war in the Pacific area in large part because, as he wrote privately to Secretary Ickes, he did not have "enough navy to go round."

Roosevelt's subsequent leadership in fighting World War II is not evidence of unusual pugnacity. As was true of Lincoln and Wilson of an earlier day, the only way out was forward. Roosevelt worked intimately with Prime Minister Churchill, and finally overbore him in insisting on a cross-channel invasion of Hitler's Fortress Europa. The President took this direct route, not because he was especially pugnacious by temperament, but primarily because he wanted to win the war before Hitler could come up with secret weapons that would make the conflict unwinnable.

German scientists had made disquieting progress toward an atomic bomb by the early stages of the conflict, and the fear prevailed among Jewish refugees in the free world that Hitler might develop this city-busting weapon and enchain at least all of Europe. The letter that the famed Jewish scientist, Albert Einstein, had sent to Roosevelt on this subject in October 1939 evidently had something to do with the President's decision to create the atomic bomb. It was put together with every intention of using it on the Nazi fanatics who had blasted Rotterdam, Coventry, London, and other cities. But Hitler's Germany surrendered before the completion of the bomb, and, ironically, the Japanese were the ones who suffered in this regard for the sins of Hitler.

"The Three Musketeers," F.D.R., Stalin, and Churchill, drawn by Manning in the Phoenix Arizona Republic. *Reprinted by permission of the McNaught Syndicate, Inc.*

To the very end Roosevelt carried forward Wilson's ideal of an international league for peace. Late in the war, and shortly before Germany surrendered in May 1945, he sent out invitations to the fifty nations that were to meet in San Francisco, from April 24 to June 26, to hammer out the charter of the United Nations. Despite many shortcomings, the U.N. lives in New York and has rendered useful service in the preservation of peace.

Roosevelt was both a man of peace and a man of war. The evidence more than suggests he was a happier warrior when he was fighting for peace and his New Deal. Personally pleasant, outgoing, smiling, bantering, he was not basically pugnacious; for the most part he seemed to enjoy political strife rather than armed combat. In peace and war he kept uppermost in mind what he conceived to be the national interest. If he could have had his choice between the clash of ballots and the whine of bullets, we can be reasonably sure that he would have opted for politics and peace.

CHAPTER 33

HARRY S. TRUMAN: THE MAN OF INDEPENDENCE (MISSOURI)

I have always been opposed even to the thought of fighting a "preventive war." There is nothing more foolish than to think that war can be stopped by war. You don't "prevent" anything by war except peace.

Harry S. Truman,
Memoirs, 1952

The "Gutty" Man from Missouri

"Give 'Em Hell Harry" Truman was a born fighter, but not with his fists. Largely because of extreme shortsightedness and thick-lensed spectacles, he was reared as a "mama's boy," and he spent much of his boyhood practicing on the piano or keeping his nose in a book. Even as a mature man, he was referred to by the press as "little," although he was five feet, nine inches in height and weighed 167 pounds. Except where the bullets had whistled in France, he did his fighting with pen and tongue, both of which revealed his penchant for salty language, perhaps picked up from his mule-trader father.

As a fighting President, Truman took on a host of foes, ranging all the way from Republican partisans, to the "do-nothing Congress," to Korean Communists, to "Uncle Joe" Stalin himself. Along the way the peppery Missourian would dash off SOB letters to assorted critics, including one who had criticized the singing ability of his darling daughter. Truman was the only future President since Theodore Roosevelt to have served in the nation's armed forces—and bravely under heavy fire in France at that. He was the only Chief Executive in American history to bring to a victorious conclusion one titanic war, fight another major war (Korea), and then embark for a second time upon reconstruction. Meanwhile he was fighting the Cold War to stem what he and the American people regarded as the expansive aggressions of Soviet Communism.

Truman was common clay—uncommon common clay. Born in Missouri to a farming family, he attended public school in Independence, graduated from the local high school in 1901, and then earned his living by working at various white-collar jobs. He was one of the minority of American Presidents who never attended college, although he did study law on the side from 1923 to 1924 at the Kansas City Law School. As a student he earned good grades and developed a lifelong interest in reading history. He especially admired the pugnacious President Polk, who had provoked the war with Mexico.

From 1906 to 1917, Truman worked as a partner on his father's farm, beginning the year after he joined the National Guard of Missouri as a charter member. In 1917, with the great conflagration raging in Europe, he helped to organize the Second Missouri Field Artillery, and later the 129th Field Artillery, 35th Division. By June 1918 he was in France as the bespectacled captain of Battery D, 129th Field Artillery. He subsequently saw heavy action, especially at St. Mihiel and during the Meuse-Argonne offensive. He was discharged as a major in 1919, having won the lasting esteem of his comrades, many of whom kept in touch with "Captain Harry" in later years.

As a returned veteran, Truman embarked upon the haberdashery business in Kansas City in 1919-1921, but these years embraced the postwar recession, and the enterprise, along with many others, finally failed. This shirt-losing experience evidently had a substantial impact on "Haberdasher Harry." As President he was nattily dressed, and his Jewish partner in the venture, Eddie Jacobson, apparently had a strong influence on President Truman's decision to help create and then hastily recognize the state of Israel in 1948.

After a course of study in the Kansas City Law School, Truman became presiding judge of the county court, Jackson county, Missouri, from 1926 to 1934. He had the support of the unsavory Pendergast political machine, but he seems to have come away from this experience with relatively clean hands. Next elected to the United States Senate from Missouri in 1935, he gained fame as chairman of a special committee to investigate excessive expenditures in the national defense programs. His persistent probing saved the government billions of dollars and gained him headline fame.

When the Democrats met in Chicago in 1944 to nominate Franklin Roosevelt for the fourth time, a strong movement developed to "dump" Henry A. Wallace, the incumbent Vice-President. He had proved to be too much of a starry-eyed liberal for his own good. Roosevelt was willing to substitute the toothy, owlishly bespectacled Harry Truman, and the vice-presidential persimmon went to the Missourian. Little sober thought was being given to the declining state of Roosevelt's health.

As a forgotten Vice-President for nearly three months, Truman was kept largely in the dark regarding Roosevelt's policies and commitments, especially in relation to the Soviet Union. When "The Chief" died unexpectedly in April 1945, the whole responsibility descended on the man from Missouri, as he put it, like a load of hay. But this average man's average man quickly pulled himself together and did what he described as his "damndest." As he put it more graphically, "If you can't stand the heat, get out of the kitchen." The motto on his White House desk was "The Buck Stops Here," meaning that too many decisions had been "bucked" up to the White House, beyond which they could not properly go.

Communism on the March

Truman proved to be an aggressive President, at times a pugnacious one, though he regarded his first major acts of aggression in foreign affairs as defensive ploys to thwart Soviet encroachments. Such also was his goal when in 1950 he initiated American financial and advisory aid to the French colonists in Vietnam, and when he entered the Korean conflict in 1950 (without a formal declaration of war) under mandate of the United Nations. Yet while warring with one hand, with the other he was supporting the United Nations and approving various pacts designed formally to end World War II and avert other conflicts in the future. On balance, he appears to have been somewhat less combative than his popular image represents him to have been. Even so, he was prone to go off half-cocked and "shoot from the lip."

There can be no doubt that Truman supported the decision, also reached by his advisers, to drop an atomic bomb on Hiroshima and then on Nagasaki. The reasons that he gave were that the shock would shorten the war (as it no doubt did) and hence save the lives of thousands of American soldiers earmarked for the invasion of Japan. As Truman declared later, he was not thinking so much of the Japanese civilians as of the American soldiers entombed in the hulk of the battleship *Arizona* at Pearl Harbor—victims of the Japanese "sneak attack."

With all the advantage of hindsight, various scholars and nonscholars have turned out numerous articles and books questioning the wisdom of destroying these two Japanese cities. But Truman was not in possession of all the relevant facts now available to researchers. The decision to use the atomic bomb had to be approved by him ("The Buck Stops Here") in the light of the information that was at hand. As a former soldier, he made up his mind as a military man confronted with a military situation during a frightful war. He then lost little sleep over what he had done. More than that, he defiantly defended his decision as time wore on.

President Roosevelt had bent over backward to conciliate and coexist with "Uncle Joe" Stalin. On one occasion he had allegedly remarked, "I can handle that old buzzard." But Roosevelt's efforts aimed at a united United Nations failed, and a bitter exchange of messages with Stalin marred the last few days of the placatory Presient. When Harry Truman grasped the scepter of power in April 1945, he discovered that the Soviets were infiltrating and trying to communize much of Eastern and Central Europe, contrary to what Washington regarded as binding pledges of restraint given at the Yalta Conference attended by Roosevelt early in 1945.

In March 1947 Greece and Turkey appeared to be in grave danger of being sucked into the Soviet orbit. After conferences with his advisers, Truman went before Congress to enunciate his epochal Truman Doctrine. Asking for an appropriation of $400 million for military and financial aid to Greece and Turkey, he concluded that "it must be the policy of the United States to support free peoples who are resisting attempted subjugation by armed minorities or by outside pressures." One should note that his all-embracing formula was not confined solely to Greece and Turkey, or even Europe, but could be applied to Asia, including Vietnam.

After considerable debate, Congress approved the Truman Doctrine by wide margins when it appropriated the requested $400 million. The new formula completely reversed the nonintervention dictum of the Monroe Doctrine of 1823 but, like the Monroe Doctrine, was aimed at long-range defense. The Truman Doctrine led by direct steps to the immensely more important Marshall Plan of 1948 and the North Atlantic Treaty Organization (NATO) of 1949, both of them major aggressive steps designed to counter what was regarded as Soviet expansionism.

Truman is widely but inaccurately condemned by certain "revisionist" historians for having started the Cold War. Actually, the "cold" or bloodless war between the Soviet Communists and the American capitalists had already begun. In 1917 the Bolsheviks had seized power in Russia and declared open and undying ideological warfare on the "rotten" capitalistic world, including the United States. From 1941 to 1945, after Hitler's devastating invasion and America's involvement as an ally of Stalin, the Soviets put this cold conflict on the back burner. But when the war crashed to a close in 1945, the marriage of convenience melted away. Truman and his advisers recognized this alarming turn in events, and the President struck back bloodlessly with the doctrine that bears his name.

Foreign Entanglements

The epochal Marshall Plan of 1948, designed to rescue much of prostrate Western Europe, was branded by the Kremlin as an aggressive act by President Truman. It was admittedly a major thrust in the Cold War, but it proved to be an aggressive act only in that it was designed primarily to counter the worrisome westward push of Soviet Communism, especially into Germany, France, and Italy. In addition, the United States was deeply concerned about the prospect of another Great Depression, and Washington recognized that a revived Europe would enrich American commerce.

The Marshall Plan, a classic example of humanitarian self-interest, was approved overwhelmingly by Congress. It provided more than $12 billion over a period of about four years to lift the West Europeans off their backs and onto their economic feet. Truman thus won a great victory for humanity in what appeared to be the Communist-provoked Cold War. Communism fattens on misery, and partly for this reason Moscow seems to have spurned an invitation to join in the Marshall Plan.

One frightening response of the Soviets to the Marshall Plan in 1948 was to cut off all land and water approaches through their sprawling zone of Germany to the key city of Berlin. There the British, Americans, Russians, and French each held a sector. The Kremlin's strategy obviously was to starve out the three former Allies and then to turn over all Berlin to Communist stooges.

But "Battling Harry" Truman was not one to be bullied out of Berlin. Together with the British, the United States inaugurated the incredible Berlin airlift, which for about a year flew in 4,500 tons of food and fuel a day, including costly coal. Some on the intrepid aviators in this heroic airlift lost their lives in crashes, and there were some close encounters with Soviet planes, but the men in the Kremlin evidently did not want war or they would have let it come then. They finally ended their spectacular blockade after almost a year. Truman had called their bluff.

In the summer and autumn of 1948, fighting Harry Truman conducted an incredible lone-wolf "whistle stop" campaign for election in his own right against the Republican candidate, Thomas E. Dewey. Despite low finances, sinking popularity, and a splitting party, Truman toured the country giving the Republicans "hell"—only, he said, he was just telling the truth and "they think it is hell." Written off by the pundits, the prophets, the prognosticators—seemingly everybody except the ordinary people—Truman, this scrappy underdog, won election in his own right in what was regarded as the greatest political upset of the century.

The North Atlantic Treaty Organization of 1949 was another defensive roadblock against Soviet aggression in the Cold War. Revisionist historians have insisted since then that only Uncle Sam was seeing bogeys under the bed, but the stubborn fact remains that the dread menace of Moscow had already forced five nations of Western Europe into a five-year defensive pact at Brussels in 1948. The signatories were Britain, France, Belgium, the Netherlands, and Luxembourg.

Americans were hardly less concerned than Europeans with containing the westward surge of Moscow-directed Communism. Truman took full advantage of this opportunity to arrange for a meeting of the worried European nations in Washington in 1949. In vain Moscow protested that the United States was forming an aggressive bloc, but the Soviets had already used a network of treaties to line up their satellites. Under American guidance, twelve charter members of the North Atlantic Treaty Organization (NATO) affixed their signatures to the North Atlantic Treaty in Washington on April 4, 1949. Included with the United States were Canada, Britain, France, Italy, and seven smaller European nations, including Iceland.

Approval of the North Atlantic Pact by the United States Senate was relatively easy, so obvious was the Communist momentum westward. Tossed overboard was America's time-honored policy of no entangling alliances, for the new compact was an entanglement beyond compare. The twelve-power treaty stipulated that an attack on one nation would be regarded as an attack on all. In case of an assault on an individual member, each ally would take "such action as it deems necessary," including "armed force." The phrasing was obviously such as to make armed intervention a moral commitment rather than a binding shackle.

After this solid exhibition of a common purpose, eight of the West European nations signed agreements with Washington early in 1950. For starters, the beneficiaries would receive $1 billion worth of American arms. General Eisenhower took on the formidable task of creating a defensive army for NATO, obviously to restrain and contain Soviet communism. From then on the United States maintained a NATO force that ultimately numbered several hundred thousand American troops.

The Korean Confrontation

Intervention in the Korean War in 1950 was Truman's most memorable, costly, and unnecessary major act of military pugnacity. The irony is that the conflict was fought under the aegis of the United Nations, which was designed to preserve the peace, and in this sense the United States was enmeshed in a war to end a war. For his part, President Truman emerged as the most important defender of the United Nations Organization.

When Japan surrendered in 1945, invading Russian troops had taken over Korea north of the 38th parallel, while American forces had occupied the area to the south. Both the U.S.S.R. and the United States professed to want a united Korea, but the Soviets endeavored to make the country communist and the Americans labored to make it democratic. By 1949, when the two occupying rivals had withdrawn, North Korea and South Korea were both armed camps, each one fearing an invasion by the other.

The top military advisers of the United States had judged that South Korea was not vitally necessary for the protection of Japan or other American interests in East Asia. As a result, no formidable defenses were prepared in Korea by the United States, and the occupying force in nearby Japan was small, green, and not all ready for combat. Early in 1950 Secretary of State Acheson seemed to be washing his hands of the whole problem when he declared in a memorable speech that Korea, North and South, was outside the essential defense perimeter of the United States. He evidently meant that Korea was now a responsibility of the United Nations, not the United States. But the North Koreans needed no further encouragement, and, using Soviet military advisers and tanks, they burst across the 38th parallel in June 1950 with overwhelming force.

Captain Truman of Battery D was an old soldier, and he recognized at once that if he acted at all, he would have to act quickly. He could not count on that windy debating society known as Congress for a declaration of war. The only alternative to a shrug of his shoulders was to turn to the United Nations, which had nominal jurisdiction over this affair. He remembered that the League of Nations had driven a lethal nail into its own coffin when it declined to move against the Japanese on the spacious plains of Manchuria in 1931. History, which Truman had read avidly, should not be allowed to repeat itself, lest Soviet communism score another major gain.

The United Nations Organization, now stationed in the New York area at Lake Success, was in a position to act affirmatively because the Russian delegate to the Security Council was temporarily absenting himself in a huff and hence could not impose the customary crippling veto. Truman hastily secured from the Council a unanimous condemnation of North Korea as an aggressor, and a summons to all members (including the United States) "to render every assistance" to bring about peace.

Responding to the United Nations Council, rather than to slow-moving Congress, Truman promptly ordered American air and naval units into the fray, plus the few untested troops that General MacArthur had available in Japan. Officially the United States never declared war on North Korea or China but engaged in a United Nations "police action" under a U.N. flag, with relatively small support from fifteen other members. General MacArthur assumed command of the entire military operation, and he took his orders not from the U.N. Security Council, but from Washington.

Fighting doggedly on defense, MacArthur brilliantly seized the offensive when he landed at Inchon on September 15, 1950, in the rear of the North Koreans, thus forcing them into a hasty retreat north of the dividing parallel. To a military man like Truman it seemed foolish to permit the enemy to regroup behind a surveyor's line preparatory to a renewed assault. The United Nations tacitly authorized a crossing by General MacArthur, whom Truman ordered northward, provided that there was no intervention in force by the Chinese or the Soviets.

From here on MacArthur performed less brilliantly. Sensitive to their border, the Chinese had threatened to intervene if the invaders came too far north, but MacArthur brushed aside such fears. Unwisely, he divided his attacking force into two columns, which were crushed and driven back by Chinese "volunteers" in a panicky, frost-bitten retreat to an area south of the dividing 38th parallel.

A crestfallen MacArthur, eager to revive wilted laurels, urged a blockade of the Chinese coast and an aerial blasting of Chinese bases in Manchuria. But the military leaders in Washington vetoed "the wrong war, at the wrong place, at the wrong time, and with the wrong enemy." The major theater was in Europe, not Asia, and the major foe was expansionist Communist Russia, not war-torn China.

MacArthur knew perfectly well that overall military policy is and should be made in Washington, not by the commander in the field. But he sneered at the concept of a "limited war" and insisted that "there is no substitute for victory," although there obviously is one in a fair peace settlement. The proud general became so indiscreet as to publicize his disagreement with Washington's overall strategy, and when this happened he had to be removed. A long-suffering President finally dismissed him abruptly from his commands, and the imperious general came home to an overwhelming welcome. Truman was assailed as a "pig," an "imbecile," and an "appeaser of Communist Russia and Communist China."

The President rode out the storm in the consciousness that he had merely done his duty after having tolerated more insubordination than some less tolerant Presidents would have endured. Truman was technically right in sacking the defiant general, but out of deference to MacArthur's brilliant record theretofore, Captain Harry could better have shown the five-star general the door, rather than kicking him out the fifth-story window.

A Pugnacious President

Getting sucked into the Korean War was not only one of Truman's greatest blunders but also his most spectacular exhibition of pugnacity. Yet, if we can believe his own explanations, he intervened for peace, not war. He evidently wanted to save the United Nations from the fate of the League of Nations by fighting a small war to head off a bigger one. This thought probably entered Truman's mind when General MacArthur wanted real fireworks with China and possibly the Soviet Union. Actually, the Korean intervention did not "save" the United Nations, which merely demonstrated that in a crunch only a few nations are willing to put a limited number of lives on the line, and even those countries eventually weary of carrying the heavy end of the log.

The Korean War—"Truman's War"—was never officially declared or even ended. A stalemate armistice was agreed to in

1953, roughly along the 38th parallel, with neither side showing much in territorial loss or gain. The North Koreans continued to give every indication of preparing to come again, even through tunnels, and ever since the armistice there have been a few sporadic killings or other bloody incidents along the boundary line. At heavy expense tens of thousands of United States troops have been maintained in South Korea to support dictators at a cost of billions of dollars. This force is a grim reminder that the United States lost 54,000 dead and 103,000 wounded, while the North and South Koreans together suffered losses about ten times as high. And these gory statistics do not take into account the tens of thousands of invading Chinese "volunteers" who were killed.

On balance, Harry Truman's gamble for peace and the United Nations did not pay off. If he had bucked the decision up from his desk to a slow-motion Congress, rather than up to the United Nations, this militarily unnecessary war might have been avoided altogether.

Combative Harry Truman also gave the go-ahead for the hydrogen bomb in January 1950, but because the Soviets were probably working on one also, this step could be listed under the heading of legitimate self-defense. The President also made unusual use of federal troops to keep the economy moving. He threatened to seize the railroads to avert a strike in 1946. He took over the soft coal mines in 1946 and held them for about a week, pending a new labor contract. He also seized the steel mills in April 1952 in a vain attempt to avert a strike and keep supplies flowing to the Korean War. But the Supreme Court ruled, by a vote of 6 to 3, that the takeover was illegal. The Korean War (an undeclared war) was going full blast, but the President was judged to have no power under the Constitution to keep the steel furnaces going full blast.

"Give 'em Hell" Harry Truman was undoubtedly one of the most peppery of the Presidents, but much of his pugnacity was directed at what he regarded as the ultimate goals of peace and order. The same could be said of some of his predecessors and successors.

CHAPTER 34

DWIGHT DAVID EISENHOWER: THE WAR HERO PRESIDENT

I hate war as only a soldier who has lived it can, only as one who has seen its brutality, its futility, its stupidity.

General D. D. Eisenhower,
speech in Canada,
January 10, 1946

The Ike-Dulles Team

Five-star General Dwight D. ("Ike") Eisenhower was only the second West Pointer, after General U. S. Grant, to occupy the White House, and the only other Republican besides Grant to serve two full terms. Although a professional fighter, General "Ike" was not notably pugnacious. During his eight years as President, the so-called free world generally was on the defensive, particularly in the teeth of the expanding power of Soviet-directed Communism. The glamorous general was labeled a "dynamic conservative" who, as was his military habit, delegated the execution of orders to subordinates. In this way he saved an unusual amount of time for recreation, notably golfing.

Born in Texas in 1890, young Eisenhower was taken at age two to Abilene, Kansas, where he graduated from high school in 1909. Entering West Point in 1911, he graduated four years later, standing sixty-first in a class of 164. After advancing from post to post, in 1942 he finally assumed command of the United States forces in Great Britain. After leading the Allied forces to victory in the North African and Mediterranean campaigns, he became Supreme Commander of the Allied expeditionary forces in Western Europe and carried the war through the D-Day invasion of France to the final conquest of Germany. He showed great skill as a soldier-diplomat in persuading the clashing nationalities and egos under his command to pull together. In 1948 he was made president of Columbia University as a means of "civilianizing" him, but he took a leave of absence in 1951 to become Supreme Commander of the NATO forces in Europe. A captivating war hero, he was elevated to the White House by an overwhelming popular vote in 1952.

Keeping his fiery temper under a tight rein in public, Eisenhower was among the most likable of all the Presidents. A soldierly five feet, ten and one-half inches in height, weighing about 170 pounds, he was blessed with blue eyes, a ruddy complexion, and a captivating smile. The slogan "I Like Ike" not only took immediate hold but also testified to the general's enormous popularity.

Like most of his predecessors who had participated in armed combat, Eisenhower had no burning desire to lead his people into another bloodbath. Fortunately for his pacific intentions, he came into office during the aftershocks following the Great Depression, World War II, and the Korean War. Daring new initiatives in domestic reform and foreign affairs were not imperatively needed or wanted, and the country was reasonably content to rock along with General "Eisenhowever," whose most frequent command, critics charged, seemed to be "mark time" during the "Great Postponement."

A fiscal conservative, Eisenhower expressed grave concern about the unbalanced budgets of his predecessors, and in the interests of "fiscal responsibility" he refused to launch a frantic arms race with the Soviet Union. He limited the size of the army and navy and committed himself to special forces that would rely heavily on "massive retaliation" with nuclear bombs, at least when they were regarded as imperatively necessary. There would be, as was said, "more bang for the buck."

Eisenhower's Secretary of State, John Foster Dulles, enjoyed a relatively free hand and seemingly exercised more power than most of his predecessors. A part of the explanation for this activity is that Eisenhower suffered during his Presidency from three major illnesses, including one severe heart attack. Another problem was Dulles's bad case of "foot-in-mouth" disease. He spoke of the "liberation" of the Communist-dominated peoples of Central Europe as more desirable than mere "containment," with the result that the Hungarians were encouraged to stage their tragic revolt against their Soviet masters in 1956, all the while hoping vainly for American assistance. Dulles sparked considerable apprehension by threatening "instant" and "massive" retaliation against aggressors. He also spoke indiscreetly to the press of the "art" of going "to the brink" of war, but not over the edge. Journalists for their part branded this "art" as "brinkmanship," a word that had a hair-raising effect.

Dulles fought the advance of Communism in a number of specific ways. He helped to negotiate the Soviet withdrawal from Austria in 1955. He cooperated through the hush-hush Central Intelligence Agency in overthrowing in 1954 a Communist-oriented government in Guatemala; and he supported the Nationalist Chinese in Taiwan against the mainland Red Chinese.

During his heyday, Secretary Dulles added to America's defensive entanglement with foreign nations by increasing the number of defense pacts to forty-two ("pactomania"), among which was the Southeast Asia Treaty Organization, later used to draw the United States ever deeper into the jungles of Vietnam.

Explosive East Asia

During the presidential campaign of 1952 General Eisenhower had electrified the electorate by promising, if victorious, to fly to Korea and attempt to bring an end to the protracted no-win, no-end bloodshed. True to his word, after the election but before inauguration, he undertook, as a private citizen, the 22,000-mile air trip to Korea in December 1952. He achieved no immediate success during his three-day stay. But after he had hinted that nuclear bombs might have to be used, an armistice was finally agreed upon and the heavy fighting stopped on July 27, 1953, some seven months after Eisenhower's initial trip. To this day no peace treaty has been signed, and minor bloodshed has occurred intermittently along the embattled armistice line.

Following the uneasy Korean truce, the focus on Communist expansionism shifted to Indochina. There, since late 1946, the Communist Viet Minh rebels, aided by Communist China, had been fighting the French-led Vietnam loyalists. In the days of President Truman, the Washington government had contributed several billion dollars in military aid to the hard-pressed French, in line with the Truman doctrine of aiding foreign peoples then under the gun of communism.

In April 1954 a major conference of nineteen nations assembled at Geneva, Switzerland, to discuss the fate of Korea and Indochina. The tide of battle was running heavily against the French, and the key outpost of Dienbienphu fell to the North Vietnamese, after a fifty-six day siege, while the Geneva conference was in session. At one point some of the top advisers in Washington, including Vice-President Nixon and Admiral Radford, rather favored sending in carrier-based planes loaded with bombs to save Dienbienphu. Eisenhower evidently did not reject this recommendation out of hand but cooled off when he discovered that he could not count on the backing of the British.

In July 1954 the powers meeting at Geneva who were most intimately involved agreed to a "provisional" demarcation line along the 17th parallel of Vietnam. The North Vietnamese were to retain North Vietnam, and the fate of the South Vietnamese, whether to be Communist or non-Communist, was to be decided by a vote of the inhabitants in a general election to be held in 1956. General Eisenhower later wrote that if the election had been held as scheduled, the outcome would have been 80 percent pro-Communist. If so, and if Vietnam had been fully reunited at that time, there would have been no Vietnam war to suck in the United States.

The Eisenhower-Dulles team recognized the Geneva conference as a signal victory for the Communists, who had recently won in China and had fought to a stalemate in Korea. The Washington administration did not openly oppose the final settlement but seemed to acquiesce in it. Actually, the Eisenhower leadership sabotaged it by throwing its financial support to the regime of Ngo Dinh Diem in South Vietnam. The hope was that Prime Minister Diem could be persuaded to adopt needed reforms and thus undercut Communist pressures from North Vietnam. At the same time, Dulles induced the South Vietnamese to postpone the general election (forever, actually), thereby setting the stage for deeper enmeshment by Presidents Kennedy, Johnson, and Nixon.

Dulles also arranged for a significant eight-power conference in Manila in September 1954. It gave birth to the South East Asia Treaty Organization (SEATO), which was designed largely to halt a possible attack by the pushful Chinese Communists on Taiwan and by the North Vietnamese on South Vietnam. Although this paper pact was even less of an ironclad commitment than the North Atlantic Treaty Organization, it was later used to justify deeper involvement by the United States in the morass of Vietnam.

Back in 1949 the Chinese Communists had driven Chiang Kai-shek and his Nationalists out of China, and many of the survivors had found refuge on the offshore island of Formosa (Taiwan). The victorious regime in Peking repeatedly avowed its determination to storm this once-Chinese outpost and restore it to the People's Republic of China.

The Chinese Communists were evidently girding for an all-out assault on Formosa, and Eisenhower was deeply concerned. To act quickly, he would have to move without the consent of Congress, as the much-criticized Truman had done in Korea. Rather than be caught on the horns of this dilemma, Eisenhower formally asked for a signed blank check in January 1955. An anti-Communist Congress speedily and overwhelmingly obliged. It formally authorized the President to use the armed forces of the United States to protect Formosa and other outposts then in friendly hands—that is, non-Communist hands.

Eisenhower's Formosan doctrine received a severe test in the summer of 1958. Formosa (Taiwan) is situated about 120 miles off the coast of the Chinese mainland; two tiny island groups, Quemoy and Matsu, lie only a half-dozen or so miles distant. Chiang had foolishly committed some 90,000 troops, or about one-third of his effective force, to these minor outposts. The Chinese Communists, annoyed by such thorns in their side, subjected them to furious artillery bombardments. Chiang, who could ill afford to sacrifice these troops, stubbornly refused to pull back, though the U.S. Seventh Fleet stood ready to repel an invasion of Formosa. The American navy finally intervened to the extent of escorting Nationalist supply ships, though properly keeping outside of the three-mile limit.

Peking seems to have been held in check by the evident determination of the Americans to fight if this bombardment seemed about to escalate into a full-dress invasion. Secretary Dulles flew to Formosa to cool Chiang down, and after three days of negotiations a joint announcement proclaimed that Nationalist China had renounced military force as an instrument for regaining the mainland of China. Dulles regarded this whole venture as one of his most brilliant exhibitions of "brinkmanship," that is, going to the brink of war in a desperate attempt to prevent war. In any event, the big stick of the U.S. Seventh Fleet provided visible evidence that Eisenhower would use naval power to preserve the peace.

The Middle East Muddle

The most critical crisis during Eisenhower's eight years involved the Suez Canal in 1956. President Nasser of Egypt, an ardent Arab nationalist, was attempting to borrow money to finance the enormous Aswan High Dam on the upper Nile. The United States and Great Britain tentatively offered financial help, but Secretary Dulles cooled off when Nasser began to flirt openly with the Kremlin, evidently to improve his bargaining position in America. Dulles, acting in concert with London, responded by abruptly withdrawing the dam offer, with much loss of face for Nasser. Here Dulles fumbled the ball as a diplomat, although the result probably would have been about the same in any event. Prudence would have dictated dragging out the negotiations interminably until, if possible, they were lost in the desert sands of Egypt.

Egypt's Nasser, thus humiliated, responded by nationalizing the Suez Canal, then owned for the main part by British and French stockholders. This bold stroke placed a razor's edge at the jugular vein of Western Europe's Arab oil supply. Belatedly, Secretary Dulles tried desperately to avert an armed intervention by Britain and France—precisely the kind of intervention forbidden by the United Nations Organization.

After pulling wool over Washington's eyes, Britain and France coordinated a surprise attack on Egypt with one from Israel. President Eisenhower, forced to choose between errant NATO allies and the United Nations, finally honored the nonaggression commitment of the United Nations, as Truman had done in Korea, and supported a cease-fire resolution at the U.N. in New York. The Soviet Union, for once voting with the United States (strange bedfellows indeed), threatened to pour "volunteers" into Egypt, thus triggering World War III.

Reluctantly yielding to various pressures, Britain, France, and Israel abandoned their three-way invasions of Egypt, and for the first time in history a modest U.N. policing force was sent to a troubled area to maintain order. The NATO alliance received a body blow from which it was slow in recovering, but General-President Eisenhower emerged as a man of peace who forsook friends and allies to honor the nation's commitments under the United Nations Charter. Ironically, he was thrust into this disagreeable dilemma by the aggressive, rug-pulling diplomacy of Secretary Dulles. On the other hand, Nasser probably would have found some other excuse for seizing the Suez Canal, which remained clogged with sunken ships for five months.

In November 1956, almost simultaneously with Eisenhower's triumphant reelection, came the Suez Crisis and the brutal crushing of the Hungarian revolt under Soviet tanks. With World War III in scary prospect, many voters preferred an experienced war hero to a civilian in the top command. The Hungarians had been unduly encouraged by American radio propaganda featuring Dulles's "liberation" policy, and they wishfully expected American assistance. It never could have arrived there in force or in time to be effective; instead the Hungarians succumbed to the Soviet "Butchers of Budapest."

The Suez blowup in the Middle East impressed President Eisenhower with the importance of heading off trouble rather than waiting for it to explode. In January 1957, in line with the Formosa resolution for East Asia, he requested authority from Congress to provide American economic aid and military support to any Communist-menaced nation in the Near East that requested it.

After about two months of debate, Congress granted Eisenhower's request by passing a joint resolution. It authorized the President to extend $200 million for economic and military aid in the Middle East to any nation that requested such assistance, provided that it was threatened with "armed aggression from any country controlled by international communism."

In the spring of 1957 a pro-Soviet coup in Jordan threatened to wrap the Middle East in flames. The government in Washington ostentatiously dispatched the powerful Sixth Fleet, including the giant carrier *Forrestal*, to the eastern Mediterranean. Happily for Eisenhower, King Hussein of Jordan rode out the storm by accepting $10 million in financial aid from the United States. Technically the Eisenhower Doctrine was not invoked, although Eisenhower's use of the big stick was involved, for King Hussein had not requested the assistance of American armed forces.

America's Lebanon landing of July 1958 was far more spectacular and perhaps less necessary. Tiny Lebanon, fronting the eastern Mediterranean, was bedeviled by turmoil from within (partly Communist-fomented) and covetousness from without. President Nasser of Egypt, drawing ever closer to the Soviet Union, evidently had designs on troubled Lebanon. The explosion finally came on July 14, 1958, when the pro-Western King of Iraq was assassinated, and his country seemed about ready to fall prey to Nasser.

The panicky ruler of Lebanon, fearful that his country was about to be absorbed by enemies, appealed directly to Washington for help. This step was one of the two prerequisites laid down in the Eisenhower Doctrine. The second was that the applicant had to be threatened by a "country controlled by international communism." Nasser's Egypt was definitely not controlled by Soviet Communism, even though Nasser himself had recently formed intimate economic and political ties with the Kremlin.

Technically speaking, neither Eisenhower nor Dulles specifically invoked the Eisenhower Doctrine, although they both followed its spirit by acting defensively in what they conceived to be the national interest. The President had moved to protect American lives and forestall aggression, whether Communist or not, and he had acted with the decisiveness he had shown in launching the epochal invasion of France in 1944. The day after the assassination of the King of Iraq, Eisenhower ordered U.S. Marines to land in Lebanon, a force that eventually totaled some fourteen thousand troops. The operation was wholly unopposed, though condemned as barefaced aggression by the Soviets and by much of "neutralist" opinion.

Late the next month, August 1958, the Arab nations themselves backed and then secured passage of a resolution in the United Nations in which they pledged themselves not to interfere in one another's internal affairs. With calm thus restored, the

American troops left Lebanon. Hasty and unnecessary though the armed demonstration may have been, it generated increased respect for the decisiveness of Eisenhower. It also made clear that the Eisenhower Doctrine was not the proper tool with which to combat internal subversion by the Communists.

Spies in the Skies

For about four years prior to May 1, 1960, American aircraft had been gathering priceless photographic intelligence over the Soviet Union. The plane used was the specially constructed U-2, which had proved capable of flying infuriatingly above the maximum range of Soviet anti-aircraft guns. Eisenhower, as a five-star general, fully appreciated the value of military intelligence, and he not only knew all about these provocative flights but fully approved of them. He was also well aware that a small army of Soviet agents was busily at work in the United States gathering all kinds of valuable data.

The Soviets, long frustrated by these high-flying planes, finally managed to shoot one down in May 1960, capture the pilot alive, and then photograph the wreckage. The official spokesmen in Washington forthwith got themselves entangled in a series of lying denials, which left the impression that Eisenhower was a figurehead who did not know what was going on in his militarized administration. Sensitive to criticism that he was not in full command, he took the unprecedented step of accepting full responsibility for the U-2 flights. He could have said "regrettable if true" or "we are investigating"; in view of the Soviet record of fabricating evidence, such a statement would have mollified many people. Yet Eisenhower not only assumed full accountability for the flights but also defended them as necessary. The Russians had repeatedly threatened to "bury us" with city-busting nuclear weapons, and in self-defense the United States felt justified in peeking behind the Iron Curtain to head off another Pearl Harbor surprise party.

The Soviets, who had been heavily involved in stealing the "secrets" of the atomic bomb from the United States, did not come into court with completely clean hands, even though they had international law on their side. Flights over the soil of a sovereign nation in peacetime were obviously illegal, and Americans doubtless would have resented Soviet spy planes over Pittsburgh or Kansas City. But with the Cold War providing hot blasts, was this peacetime?

The hypocritical Soviets urged the Security Council of the United Nations to brand the United States the aggressor in this affair. But the charge of "aggressive acts" seemed so far-fetched that the Americans were exonerated by a vote of 7 to 2. Even so, the Washington spokesmen did not come away looking like Boy Scouts. They had stooped to snoop; they had lied, denied, and defied. All great powers have spies, only they rarely admit to spying.

A summit conference had been scheduled for mid-May in Paris, but in view of Soviet threats following the U-2 fiasco there seemed little point in Eisenhower's attending. Yet he dutifully arrived and, too late to do much good, announced that the U-2 flights had been suspended and would not be resumed. An angry Premier Khrushchev, speaking for the Soviet Union, showered Eisenhower with abuse. The red-faced general kept his legendary hot temper, but the conference got nowhere. Eisenhower returned with his dignity intact, but little else, only to be greeted with banners, "THANK YOU MR. PRESIDENT." Thanks for what? Time and again the country has rallied behind its leaders, and did so in this case, even after one of the most badly bungled diplomatic episodes in its history.

In the aftermath, Khrushchev canceled an invitation already extended to Eisenhower to visit the Soviet Union on a goodwill mission. Violent demonstrations erupted in Japan, where three spy planes had been based, and Eisenhower was forced to cancel his proposed visit there. His complete candor did not pay rich dividends, at least not in the short run.

The Eisenhower Legacy

Strategic Cuba, seemingly overnight, became a major piece on the chessboard of the Cold War in 1959. Dictator Fulgencio Batista, after having found favor for seven years with the United States and its capitalists, was overturned by the black-bearded Dr. Fidel Castro, the radical son of a wealthy Cuban family. At first hailed as an overdue reformer, Castro soon changed his stripes and assumed power as an openly Communist dictator. More than that, he tried to export his revolution to the rest of Latin America, including strategic Panama, where he abortively attempted to land some eighty men in April 1959. United States naval patrols helped to squelch such forays.

In retaliation for Castro's seizing of American properties—worthy nearly $2 billion—Washington cut off all of the formerly huge imports of sugar from Cuba and imposed a rigorous embargo. It included virtually all shipments from the United States except medicine and food. This falling out was made to order for the Soviets, who not only gave Castro generous financial support but threatened to rain nuclear rockets on the United States if it should intervene.

Soviet agents in Cuba thus established a dangerous base that was only ninety miles distant from the soft underbelly of the Yankees. The United States, having renounced armed intervention under Roosevelt's Good Neighbor policy, was powerless to clean house in Cuba except through the Organization of American States. This body was loath to take any effective steps to dislodge the Russians and bring Castro to book; in fact, many Latin Americans were delighted to see uppity Uncle Sam get his just desserts.

Castro finally gave the Yankees a stinging slap when, on two days' notice, he demanded that the American Embassy in Havana reduce its staff from some three hundred to eleven. President Eisenhower, whom Castro had branded a "gangster" and the "senile White House golfer," forthwith severed diplomatic relations. The date was January 3, 1961, only seventeen days before President John F. Kennedy fell heir to this prickly problem.

Kennedy inherited more than a perplexity; he was handed a recipe for disaster. In May of 1960, the Central Intelligence Agency, with the approval of the Eisenhower administration, had begun training in Central America some 1,500 Cuban exiles, equipped with arms from the United States, for an invasion of Cuba. The fatuous expectation was that the "freed" Cuban masses would rise and greet the right-wing invaders as deliverers. To a limited degree General Eisenhower, the five-star general, not Lieutenant John F. Kennedy, was the godfather of the Bay of Pigs debacle, with Vice-President Richard M. Nixon giving his chief a strong assist.

As he left the White House, Eisenhower's greatest disappointment was his failure to place the dove of peace more securely on its perch. Yet his proud boast was that he had not involved his nation in any foreign war and had, nominally at least, ended the Korean conflict. He had stood up to the Soviets, especially as

Eisenhower no lame duck in second term. Alexander in Philadelphia Bulletin.

regards Berlin; he had declined to recognize Red China; and he had held fast on Formosa, among other accomplishments. He was more than Eisenhower, "the mark-time general," although he did leave the beginnings of the shameful Bay of Pigs and Vietnam mess to his successor. On the whole, he was extremely lucky to have come off as well as he did.

As for internal affairs, "Ike" was not notably pugnacious, although he made liberal use of the veto with Congress. In 1960, when about to leave office, he wisely warned against the frightening power of the expanding "military-industrial [Congressional] complex," which, ironically, his own defense policies had helped to foster. He flatly refused to tangle with Senator Joseph McCarthy, even after this champion Red-baiter had libeled General Marshall and impugned the United States Army. Eisenhower, the professional fighter, reportedly declined "to get into the gutter with that guy." He could have had in mind the old American saying that in a hand-to-claw fight with a skunk there are no winners.

CHAPTER 35

JOHN F. KENNEDY: THE NEW FRONTIERSMAN

Mankind must put an end to war—or war will put an end to mankind.

John F. Kennedy, Address to
U.N. General Assembly,
September 25, 1961

A Fiery New Frontiersman

John F. Kennedy, child of a wealthy Irish-American family living in a suburb of Boston, was the first future President born in the twentieth century. He prepared for college at the exclusive Choate School in Connecticut, and although he graduated in the lower half of his class, his classmates voted him the member most likely to succeed. Entering Harvard University, he did not at first distinguish himself as a scholar but did manage to incur a long-lasting back injury while playing football.

Young Kennedy's millionaire father, Joseph P. Kennedy, was then (1937–1940) United States Ambassador in London, and the visiting John was admitted to high diplomatic circles. He was able to gather valuable information for his senior thesis at Harvard, which awarded it high honors. Rewritten and retitled *Why England Slept* (1940), it proved to be a best-selling book on why the British viewed the menacing rise of Adolph Hitler with almost suicidal complacency.

In October 1941, when clashes between American destroyers and German submarines were reaching a climax in the Atlantic, Kennedy dropped everything and qualified for a commission in the Navy as an officer. One night in the South Pacific in 1943 the fragile PT boat under his command was cut in two by a speeding Japanese destroyer. Lieutenant Kennedy's ailing back was seriously reinjured, but he shepherded the ten survivors to shore and towed an injured shipmate with his teeth for several hours through these dangerous waters. For his heroic efforts he received the Navy and Marine Corps Medal and the Purple Heart; he stands out as one of the few Presidents ever to have been seriously wounded in action.

One of the unsolved mysteries is how Kennedy, with a swift and agile craft, could have been run down. After he became President, a small boy on the West Coast asked him how he had become a war hero. Kennedy replied, with a modest touch of humor, "It was absolutely involuntary. They sank my boat."

In 1946 and again in 1948 Kennedy was elected to the national House of Representatives as a Democrat, and in 1952 he moved up to the Senate of the United States, to which he was reelected in 1958. In neither body did he particularly distinguish himself. In 1960 he defeated Richard M. Nixon, his Republican rival for the presidency, by an extremely narrow margin and became, at age forty-three, the first Catholic to enter the White House. A handsome six-footer, graceful, dark-haired, and with an ingratiating smile, Kennedy and his bewitching wife made as attractive a couple as Washington had yet seen in the White House.

Kennedy's inaugural address, although revealing some conciliatory overtones, was probably the most militant thus far in American experience. He took dead aim at the foes of freedom and democracy, obviously including dictators in general and the Soviet Communists in particular. In an early paragraph he avowed: "Let every nation know, whether it wishes us well or ill, the we shall pay any price, bear any burden, meet any hardship, support any friend, oppose any foe to assure the survival and the success of liberty." (This makes ironic reading in the light of the ignominious exit in 1975 from Vietnam, in which Kennedy had done much to involve American forces.)

A little later on in his inaugural address, obviously in reference to anticolonialism in Africa, Kennedy asserted, "To those new states whom we welcome to the ranks of the free, we pledge our word that one form of colonial control shall not have passed away merely to be replaced by a far more iron tyranny." (Yet Kennedy was unable to stop the emergence of bloodthirsty dictators in Africa.)

As for Latin America, the United States would offer "a new alliance for progress" so that these small republics would avoid becoming "the prey of hostile powers." "Let all our neighbors know," Kennedy continued, that we shall join with them to oppose aggression and subversion anywhere in the Americas. And let every other power know that this hemisphere intends to remain master of its own house." (This challenge also makes strange reading in view of the botched Bay of Pigs invasion in 1961, followed by the Cuban missile crisis and the Sovietizing of Cuba as a base for the Moscow brand of Communism. All these developments ran counter to the letter and spirit of the Monroe Doctrine.)

As for America's potential adversaries, the freshly inaugurated President went on to say, "We dare not tempt them with weakness. For only when our arms are sufficient beyond doubt can we be certain beyond doubt that they will never be employed." (Such arms came within a tragically narrow margin of being employed during the Cuban Missile Crisis of October 1962.)

With emphatically bellicose overtones, Kennedy finally asserted in this inaugural address that "only a few generations have been granted the role of defending freedom in its hour of maximum danger. I do not shrink from this responsibility—I welcome it." And so, "My fellow citizens of the world: ask not what America will do for you, but what together we can do for the freedom of man."

There can be little doubt that Kennedy's vision for the freedom of man in Africa, Laos, Vietnam, and Cuba did not turn out as he had hoped, either in his tragically truncated administration or in the turbulent days of his successors.

A Botched Bay of Pigs

Kennedy's new administration marked no sharp break with the past in the field of foreign affairs. Yet the new President did reverse the Dulles-Eisenhower doctrine of massive retaliation, which could mean either nuclear war or nothing. Embracing a "damn the deficits" philosophy, Kennedy attempted to build up conventional forces so that he could control "brushfire" wars without bringing on a nuclear holocaust. As a safeguard against war, he strongly backed the Peace Corps of down-to-earth experts sent to underprivileged nations, as well as an expensive "Alliance for Progress" program for the Latin Americans. The latter scheme, which provided no alliance and only little progress, proved inadequate for desperately needed economic, social, and political reform.

As for Cuba, Kennedy found on the White House steps an ugly inheritance that involved a Yankee-backed invasion of the island. In March 1960 President-General Eisenhower had given the go-ahead for training about 1,500 anti-Castro Cubans in Guatemala, where they were equipped with American arms under the guidance of America's Central Intelligence Agency. President Kennedy had not fathered this embarrassing baby but found it on his doorstep when he took office in January 1961. The pressures to adopt it were strong, largely because he had promised to do something about Cuba at a time when Castro's anti-Yankee insults were hard to bear. But Kennedy bluntly announced on April 12, 1961, that the armed forces of the United States would in no case be directly involved. In brief, he was willing to wound with American arms in the hands of Cuban rightwingers, but he was unwilling to strike hard enough with American strength to ensure the success of this presumably clandestine operation. So loyal and numerous were Castro's followers that, under the best of circumstances, failure was virtually certain.

A badly kept secret, the invasion finally came at the Bay of Pigs, April 17, 1961. But instead of being greeted, as hoped, by an uprising of anti-Castro elements, the invaders were crushed and then rounded up by the dictator's alerted militia in three days. President Kennedy came under severe pressure at the eleventh hour to rush in American aircraft for cover, but he stood firm on his pledge of no direct official involvement.

The Bay of Pigs fiasco was a staggering blow to America's prestige. This undercover foray ran counter to the nation's neutrality laws, to the spirit of the United Nations Charter, and to the specific obligations of the Organization of American States. The Soviets even threatened to intervene to check American "gangsterism." President Kennedy manfully assumed full responsibility for the setback, as was proper, although he might have blamed Eisenhower and the Central Intelligence Agency. "Victory has a hundred fathers," he wryly observed, "but defeat is an orphan."

The Bay of Pigs tragedy was clearly a hostile act against the bearded Castro by a clandestine branch of the United States government. Yet Kennedy's popularity shot up to 83 percent in the Gallup polls, evidently in the spirit of rallying behind the President. The youthful incumbent quipped that he was like Eisenhower after the U-2 affair; the worse he did the more popular he became. The 1,100 or so Cuban prisoners weighed so heavily on the Kennedy conscience and the nation's besmirched honor that something had to be done. A privately financed ransom of some $53 million in food and medical supplies was arranged, all of which helped implant Castro more firmly in power. More ominously, the Soviets seem to have concluded that the youthful and inexperienced President lacked the steely nerve with which to play the dangerous game of "brinkmanship."

Jolted by the Bay of Pigs fiasco, President Kennedy journeyed to Europe for talks with some of the leaders. In June 1961 he met with Premier Khrushchev at Vienna in what Kennedy found to be a nerve-racking conference. The millionaire President and the stocky former coal miner agreed on the neutralization of Laos but disagreed on what to do with Germany, on possible disarmament, and on polluting the atmosphere with nuclear testing.

A few days later Khrushchev deliberately poured oil on the Berlin embers. He went so far as to threaten to turn this four-sectored city over to Communist East Germany by the end of the year, in which case the Western powers in Berlin would be hopelessly trapped. But Kennedy did not shrink from this prospect of World War III—an unthinkable nuclear war. He dramatically called upon Congress to permit him to strengthen the national defenses and call up a quarter of a million reserves. The aroused legislators promptly obliged, and this evidence of Kennedy's determination not to be bullied out of Berlin presumably caused Khrushchev to draw back.

The next response of the Soviets came in August 1961, with the sudden completion of a forbidding wall of concrete and barbed wire between West Berlin and Soviet East Berlin. This drastic action was taken so quickly and secretly that little or nothing could be done, short of a hopeless war, to tear down the barrier. Mousetrapped in Berlin, the United States could respond only by adding some 1,500 men to its regular garrison of 5,000 troops.

Khrushchev's threatening deadline for abandoning Berlin expired quietly on December 31, 1961, whereupon the hastily called up American reservists were demobilized. It was clear that Kennedy had been willing to stand up resolutely for his nation's rights, but it is less clear that Khrushchev realized this sobering fact.

About a year and a half later, in the early summer of 1963, Kennedy visited Western Europe, in part to counter the undermining of NATO by the haughty lone wolf, President Charles de Gaulle of France. In West Germany Kennedy received enthusiastic acclaim when, standing near the Berlin Wall of Shame, he avowed the determination of the United States to "risk its cities to defend yours because we need your freedom to protect ours." He defiantly drove home his point before the cheering throng by shouting that since he also favored human freedom, "Ich bin ein Berliner" (I am a Berliner).

Southeast Asia Again

During Kennedy's truncated term, inherited problems loomed menacingly on the Far Eastern horizon. The Korean war, with China and North Korea on one side and with the South Koreans and the U.N. on the other, simmered along in the armistice stage. The United States continued to prop up the ruling South Korean regime, which, although dictatorial, at least had the merit of opposing the Moscow brand of Communism. About 50,000 American troops stood ready to help the South Koreans repel a renewed invasion from the north, and these imported warriors were destined to stay on the alert for many years to come.

Laos and South Vietnam were becoming increasingly worrisome trouble spots, and Laos appeared likely to succumb first to Communist jungle fighters. The collapse of Laos, despite inpouring American financial aid, was expected to have a falling-domino effect on neighbors to the south and west. At first President Kennedy seemed determined to stand firm in Laos, but within three months after his inauguration he decided to pull back to South Vietnam as a more defensible bastion.

In mid-May of 1962 Kennedy mounted a kind of counteroffensive. Disturbed by significant Communist gains in Laos, he hastily threw some five thousand American brushfire troops into adjoining Thailand. The Thais eagerly welcomed this evidence of support by powerful Uncle Sam, and the visiting Yankees had a steadying influence. They remained until December 1962, some seven months later. As usual, Communist elements raised the familiar cries of "imperialistic aggression."

President Kennedy's fateful decision to abandon Laos and fall back to South Vietnam was an almost certain formula for increasing America's military entanglement in undeclared war. South Vietnam harbored tens of thousands of Roman Catholics who had been driven southward fron North Vietnam. The new bastion of anti-Communism was headed by autocratic-aristocratic President Ngo Dinh Diem, also a Catholic. He was heavily involved in what amounted to a civil war with the disaffected guerrillas known as the Viet Cong. How much, if at all, Kennedy's Catholicism influenced the ultimate decision to intervene in force is a mystery. But there is no doubt as to the new President's determination, avowed eloquently in his inaugural address, to help subject peoples gain or preserve freedom, even under a temporarily dictatorial regime.

By early 1962 Kennedy had made the fateful decision to dispatch military assistance to South Vietnam in such force as to make voluntary withdrawal, without intolerable loss of face, a virtual impossibility. First he had sent in military advisers, then American helicopters, and then military personnel. By early 1962 some 10,000 American service men were reported to be in South Vietnam, involved in another undeclared war. By the summer of 1963 some seventy had been killed, the vanguard of about 55,000 American dead. Such were the ultimate fruits of Kennedy's defiant and politically popular anti-Communist efforts —at least popular at the time.

The Cuban Missile Crisis

After the Bay of Pigs catastrophe, Fidel Castro undertook to protect himself against a full-dress Yankee incursion by importing lavish quantities of high-grade Soviet arms. As further insurance, he rapidly developed the second largest standing army in the Western Hemisphere. Such was the setting when President Kennedy felt compelled to go to the brink of a defensively offensive invasion of Cuba, which could easily have touched off a nuclear holocaust involving the Soviet Union.

In mid-October 1962 official Washington was astounded by aerial photographs showing a small army of Russian technicians in Cuba hurriedly emplacing about forty nuclear missiles. These weapons were supposed to be capable of ranging as far as 2,000 miles, thus threatening many of the metropolitan centers of the United States, including Washington and New York. The Soviets, with this awesome blackmail at hand, presumably could force the Americans and their Allies out of Berlin and otherwise work their will.

President Kennedy reasoned that he would have to force the Soviets to back down in the few days that apparently remained before the Cuban missiles became operational. There was no time for long-winded debates in the United Nations or on the floor of Congress. Kennedy's grim response, as he presented it on nationwide television, October 22, 1962, was to impose a "quarantine," not a blockade, on all ships carrying offensive weapons to Castro's Cuba. "Quarantine" was used because a "blockade" in time of peace ran counter to America's traditional principle of freedom of the seas. If Soviet merchant ships refused to stop and submit to search for offensive weapons, American commanders were authorized to fire upon them—an almost certain prelude to war.

A fighting Kennedy minced no words in this electrifying television address. Declaring that nuclear weapons now for the first time were being stationed on non-Soviet soil, he deplored this deliberate attempt to upset the existing balance of power—a "change in the status quo which cannot be accepted by this country if our courage and our commitments are ever to be trusted again, by either friend or foe." Furthermore, he would regard "any nuclear missile launched from Cuba against any nation in the Western Hemisphere as an attack by the Soviet Union on the United States requiring a full retaliatory [nuclear] response upon the Soviet Union."

Fortunately for peace, armed hostilities were averted. The Soviet merchant ships turned back, and grim discussions and interchanges involved the Washington authorities and Moscow. In this eyeball-to-eyeball confrontation, the Soviets finally blinked. Khrushchev, having misjudged Kennedy's backbone, agreed to a last-minute compromise settlement, announced on October 28, 1962. The Soviets agreed to remove their offensive weapons from Cuba, under verification by U.N. representatives. For his part, Kennedy agreed to terminate the "quarantine" and not to invade controversial Cuba.

Critics of Kennedy claim that he overreacted. The Soviets already had some nuclear missiles zeroed in on the United States, and they also had missile-carrying submarines lurking offshore. The United States had already emplaced anti-Soviet nuclear missiles in Turkey and Italy, and Kennedy could presumably have saved Khrushchev's face before the world by offering to remove these offensive weapons in exchange for a withdrawal of the Russian missiles in Cuba. Indeed, Kennedy had already decided to pull the missiles out of Turkey and Italy, and had issued orders to that end. No President, critics complained, has the right to lead the nation so close to nuclear annihilation, when there is a quiet compromise conveniently at hand. As for the humiliated Soviets, they were determined not to have to knuckle under again, and they embarked upon a large-scale program that gave them nuclear superiority in certain categories—and a frantic new arms race.

There is an ancient Chinese curse, "May you live in interesting times." John F. Kennedy lived in extremely interesting times, when Soviet Communism was not only on the march but was making alarming gains—alarming to the free world. Kennedy not only announced but proclaimed in his inaugural address that he was prepared to stand up to the foes of freedom. All of his militant moves were aggressive but, as he analyzed the situation, defensively aggressive.

CHAPTER 36

LYNDON BAINES JOHNSON: THE TORMENTED TEXAN

I do not genuinely believe that there's any single person anywhere in the world that wants peace as much as I want it.

President Johnson,
Chicago speech,
May 17, 1966

A Tall and Talented Texan

Lyndon Johnson was born the son of a humble tenant farmer near Stonewall, deep in the heart of Texas. Educated in the local public schools, he finally earned his B.S. degree in 1930 from Southwest Texas State College. After teaching for about two years in a Houston high school, he entered political life by becoming secretary to a Texas Congressman in 1932. As a dedicated New Dealer, Johnson gained the friendship of an influential Texas Congressman, Sam Rayburn, who in 1935 persuaded President Roosevelt to appoint Johnson the director in Texas of the National Youth Administration (NYA). In later years the rising young politician would refer affectionately to Roosevelt as his political "daddy."

Johnson's star continued to rise. In 1937 the tall Texan won election to a vacated Congressional seat, and he was consistently reelected to the House of Representatives through 1946. After Pearl Harbor he patriotically entered the armed services as a Lieutenant Commander in the Naval Reserve and saw some extremely limited action in the Pacific theater. He returned to Washington when Commander-in-Chief Roosevelt recalled Congressmen from active duty, presumably because they could serve their country more usefully as legislators. Unlike many of his presidential predecessors, Johnson had observed the horrors of war at first hand.

In 1948, following an earlier rebuff at the polls, "Landslide Lyndon" Johnson was elected to the United States Senate after surviving the Democratic primaries by the paper-thin margin of eighty-seven disputed votes. As a Senator he gained prominence as an advocate of military preparedness, and became chairman of the Preparedness Investigating Subcommittee. Rising rapidly in the Senate hierarchy, he was made Democratic whip in 1951 and then Democratic floor leader in 1953. After the election of Eisenhower in 1952, Johnson, the Democrat, displayed great skill in cooperating with this Republican President in shepherding Republican legislation through a Democratic Congress. He proved to be a master of wheeling and dealing, and of pressuring Senators into voting the "right way."

At the Democratic national nominating convention of 1960 in Los Angeles, Lyndon Johnson, the towering Texan (six feet, three inches) ran second to John F. Kennedy. To appease the disappointed South, Kennedy persuaded his rival to accept the lowly vice-presidential place on the ticket. Many critics believed that Johnson was courting political oblivion, but he loyally supported Kennedy in the campaign of 1960, probably pulling with him enough votes to bring a breathlessly narrow victory to the Democratic ticket. As Vice-President the rangy Texan loyally backed the President's New Frontier program while serving usefully in other capacities. He was sworn in as President in November 1963, immediately after the assassination of Kennedy in Dallas, Texas.

Kennedy's tragic departure tended to obscure the fact that his ambitious legislative program was badly bogged down in

Congress at the time of his murder. But Johnson, using the shock of the assassination and his own legislative know-how, managed to breathe new life into the New Frontier. Among various achievements, Congress gave a boost to the economy by enacting an $11 billion tax cut (January 1964) and a sweeping Civil Rights Act (July 1964), a tremendous boon for blacks.

Franklin Roosevelt had proclaimed his New Deal, Truman his Fair Deal, and Kennedy his New Frontier. Not to be outdone, in May 1964 Johnson called for a nationwide War on Poverty (poverty won this conflict) and outlined an ambitious new program of economic and social welfare legislation to achieve what he hailed as the Great Society.

No American Boys for Vietnam

On August 26, 1964, Johnson the master wheeler-dealer, carefully ringmastered his nomination for the presidency in his own right in Atlantic City. The vote was confirmed by acclamation. The platform stressed peace and prudence abroad, and help for the impoverished and underprivileged at home. As for the no-end war in Vietnam, into which Kennedy had gingerly stepped, Johnson repeatedly stressed the theme that he was to present to an appreciative audience in Akron, Ohio: "But we are not about to send American boys nine or ten thousand miles away from home to do what Asian boys ought to be doing for themselves." These words came back to haunt him as he stepped up the tempo of the Vietnam War, which finally proved to be the longest major war in the history of the United States.

A nasty turn had come, on August 2–4, 1964, when North Vietnamese torpedo boats were reported to have attacked two American destroyers in international waters, apparently without damage. There is evidence that Johnson had been thinking of provoking some such incident several months before it occurred and that retaliatory targets had been tentatively earmarked. In any event, after the second attack of August 4, the President ordered American aircraft to destroy North Vietnamese vessels and naval installations along about 100 miles of the coast. The American public, with characteristic short-sightedness, widely applauded this two-fisted act of red-blooded Americanism.

Johnson may well have been hoping or planning for such a provocative incident so as to win votes in the presidential campaign. He may also have been scheming to use the affair to wring from a patriotic Congress a blank check to wage an unquestionably legal war against Communism in a strategic area where the French had failed. At all events, he asked Congress to pass the fateful Gulf of Tonkin Resolution. It specifically authorized the President "to take all necessary measures to repel any armed attack against the forces of the United States and to prevent further aggression." With alleged Communist aggression in view, the Tonkin Gulf Resolution stated that because the peace and security of Southeast Asia were "vital" to the "national interest," the President was authorized to take all necessary steps to assist those freedom-loving states of this area that sought assistance. Such language was made to cover Laos, South Vietnam, Cambodia, and Thailand.

The blank-check Gulf of Tonkin Resolution, so fateful for the United States, had a tranquil passage through Congress. The go-ahead thus given to Johnson passed the House on August 7, 1964 by a vote of 416 to 0 and the Senate 88 to 2. Many of those who so blindly voted in the affirmative later regretted their haste and shortsightedness.

All this occurred while Johnson's campaign for a four-year presidential term in his own right was gathering momentum. His Republican opponent, Senator Barry Goldwater, a Major General in the Air Force Reserve, took the high road to the right. Lambasting the Communists and Communism, he assailed the no-win war in Vietnam and indiscreetly proposed that American field commanders be permitted to use tactical nuclear weapons at their own discretion. But this nightmare of a nuclear war terrified many voters. One slogan ran, "He Will Barry Us." At all events, Johnson buried Barry with ballots in one of the nation's most overwhelming landslides. In later months, as Johnson sank ever deeper into the quicksands of Vietnam, the cynics quipped, "The people voted for Johnson but got Goldwater."

The Dominican Danger Spot

While Johnson was edging ever downward into the Vietnam War with his aggressively defensive tactics, his instinct to resort to arms against Communists got the better of him in the Dominican Republic, in April 1965. A revolt that ultimately cost about two thousand lives erupted against the rightist government, which had the sympathy of Washington. The fighting became so disruptive and dangerous that the American Ambassador in Santo Domingo urged President Johnson to send troops to protect hundreds of American lives. Countless past interventions by Uncle Sam in the republics of Latin America had been prompted by a determination to safeguard Yankee lives and property.

But gunboat diplomacy had disappeared with the enunciation of Roosevelt's Good Neighbor Policy in 1933, bolstered by Washington's later commitments to the Organization of American States and the United Nations. Yet haste was urgent to protect American lives, and President Johnson reasoned that legitimate self-defense would justify a temporary ignoring of existing pledges. Haste was imperative, so a reluctant Johnson helicoptered in several hundred American troops, whose numbers finally swelled to a substantial army of about 25,000.

Within four days after the first Marines landed, Johnson appeared on television to justify in solemn tones his aggressively defensive action. He made clear that his purpose was not only to save American lives but also to prevent the calamity of another Castro-like Cuba in the strategic Caribbean Sea. To many liberals, both at home and abroad, the Communist bogey seemed like a belated and an unjustified pretext, primarily because few known Communists were thought to be involved.

The intrusive Yankee troops were sporadically fired upon, and in the interchanges some men were killed on both sides. Outraged Latin Americans loudly claimed that they still had the right of revolution, and that Big Brother in the north was flouting the nonintervention pledges of Franklin Roosevelt's Good Neighbor policy as proclaimed in 1933. To them Uncle Sam was a heavy-handed aggressor, not an order-restoring policeman.

To some extent President Johnson was taken off the hot seat when the Organization of American States authorized an Inter-American Police Force by a vote of 14 nations to 5. Before the end, five Latin American nations had contributed some manpower, notably Brazil, the Portugese-speaking friend of the United States, whose general commanded the second largest contingent. As a gesture of courtesy and goodwill, he was put in official charge of the operation.

Under such impartial auspices, the Dominicans held new elections in June 1966, and a moderately right-wing candidate for President won by a comfortable margin over his left-wing opponent. American and other foreign troops gradually left for home, and Johnson's defensively aggressive maneuver took on a better odor. Latin Americans were thus encouraged to hope that this ugly departure from Good Neighborism was not to be established as a precedent for a return to the bad old days of "Marine diplomacy."

Renewed Vietnamese Vexations

Johnson's heavy bombing response against North Vietnam, following the Gulf of Tonkin episode in August 1964, proved to be only one more giant-boot step in his sinking deeper into the quicksands of Vietnam. On February 7, 1965, Viet Cong guerrillas, supported by the North Vietnamese, staged a punishing raid on the American barracks at Pleiku, in South Vietnam. Several United States aircraft were destroyed, while eight Americans were killed and more than one hundred wounded. Johnson reacted vengefully when he ordered severe bombing raids on military installations in North Vietnam. These aerial forays inflicted increasing damage on nonmilitary structures, as well as some loss of civilian life.

About a month after the Viet Cong attack at Pleiku, March 8, 1965, two battalions of U.S. Marines disembarked in South Vietnam. This, be it noted, was about three months after Johnson's presidential election campaign, during which he had emphatically declared that Asian boys should be used in fighting Asian wars. The U.S. Marines in question were evidently the first American combat troops of their kind to be brought ashore in large units, although considerable numbers of military advisers and others had filtered in earlier under Presidents Eisenhower and Kennedy. By mid-1968, when Johnson had "abdicated" by spurning possible renomination, the Vietnam War was costing the United States about $30 billion a year and engaging about a half-million American service men. Casualties were running into the tens of thousands.

Johnson regarded his entanglement in the Vietnam War as an act of defense or counteraggression rather than aggression itself. He felt deeply committed by his predecessors—Truman, Eisenhower, and Kennedy—to resist Communist aggression, and this course meant defense of people like the South Vietnamese seeking to be free. Each of these Presidents had gradually thrust the United States in deeper, in response to the myth of the "Communist monolith."

At one fell swoop, Communism had taken over China completely in 1949, with its one-fourth of the world's population. By 1951 the Communists had bulled their way into South Korea and had been repulsed after an enormous outpouring of blood. Now they were absorbing South Vietnam, and they presumably would have to be stopped or all Southeast Asia would collapse like a row of falling dominoes.

The Washington government was also promoting the fear that if the United States did not fight in Vietnam, embattled Americans would ultimately have to be fighting for their liberties on the shores of Hawaii or the Pacific coast of North America. In the 1940s and later, Republican partisans had hurt the Democrats with the cry, "Who lost China?" Now votes were to be garnered by crying, "Who lost Vietnam?" Many Republicans were critical of fighting a no-win, no-end war; they favored bombing the North Vietnamese, as General Curtis LeMay put it, back "into the Stone Age."

It finally dawned on many Americans that Communism was no monolith after all, but this realization did not strike home until it was too late to withdraw gracefully from Vietnam. Both Communist China and the Communist Soviet Union were providing their Vietnamese client state with vast quantities of military supplies, but these two sprawling supporters had undergone a violent ideological split in the 1960s and were now at daggers drawn. Moreover, Vietnam was itself a centuries-old foe of China, and although accepting military aid, the North Vietnamese were fully prepared to go their own way in Southeast Asia when the war ended—and they did precisely that. In 1979, only four years after the end of the Vietnam War, Communist China mounted a formidable punitive invasion of Vietnam.

Once Americans realized that Communism was no monolith, other reasons had to be found to avoid a highly embarrassing pullout from Vietnam. Promises had been made to the unreliable South Vietnamese regime in Saigon, and to abandon it in haste would be to dishonor American commitments. The North Vietnamese stubbornly maintained that they would fight—as they did—until the invading foreigners stopped their bombing and withdrew their troops. These jungle fighters claimed that this war was a civil war between North and South (as the American Civil War had been), and that the Americans had come some seven thousand miles to assail them at a time when they had no intention whatever of attacking the Americans. So the war ground bloodily on.

A major reason why the United States was unwilling to pull out of the Vietnam War without a face-saving victory was the durable American myth of invincibility. No President during this era wanted to assume responsibility for dishonoring the nation's supposed record of having gloriously won all of its wars. Actually, these Presidents—from Johnson to Nixon to Ford—should have known the nation's history better, or perhaps they did not want to acknowledge the truth. The War of 1812 was not won by the United States: At best it was a draw. The Korean War was not won by the United States, although it was nominally the responsibility of the United Nations.

Then there was the strange case of the *Pueblo*, an expensively prepared American ship equipped for gathering electronic intelligence. The North Koreans, on January 23, 1968, captured this vessel with superior force. It did not fire a single shot in its defense, although supposedly in international waters, some twenty-five miles off the coast. The eighty-three men of the crew were imprisoned, and one of them died in captivity.

The *Pueblo* was a United States warship flying the American flag in waters where it presumably had a right to be. In an earlier day, such an outrage would have been regarded as an act of war, and many red-blooded Americans did in fact demand drastic measures to rescue the ship and its imprisoned crew. But Johnson realized that he already had a no-win war on his hands in Vietnam, that the North Koreans had already fought the United States to a standstill, that nothing would be gained by bombing the North Korean capital, and that the belated rescue of the captured ship and its crew was a physical impossibility. The prisoners might be deliberately exposed to American bombing or even put to death in retaliation for it.

In these delicate circumstances, President Johnson showed restraint, despite American tradition to the contrary, although he called up sone fourteen thousand men in the air and naval reserve and the Air National Guard. After prolonged negotiations, the imprisoned men (but not the ship) were released after a detention of eleven months. But first the United States had to admit guilt and sign an apology for having penetrated North Korean waters. By odd prearrangement, this curious confession was openly repudiated by the Americans before and after the signing.

Johnson Bequeaths a War

The bombing and blasting of North Vietnamese positions, accompanied by the repeated repulse of Viet Cong guerrillas, had by March 1968 brought the enemy no nearer to accepting conditions for peace other than the complete withdrawal of all American forces. In the United States, the public was becoming completely disenchanted by the toll taken of American boys in this faraway jungle entrapment. Hundreds of thousands of marchers in America's big cities were chanting "Hell no, we won't go" and "Hey, hey, LBJ, how many kids did you kill today?" The United States commander in Vietnam was reportedly asking for some 200,000 more troops to add to some 535,000 already enmeshed there.

"We are Winning the War." The wasteland refrain of President Johnson and Ho Chi Minh. Courtesy Boston Globe. *Cartoonist Paul Szep.*

Such was the situation on March 31, 1968, when President Johnson took to the television in a sensational speech. Although presumably a candidate for reelection, he bluntly announced that he would not run again and that he would throttle down the war in Vietnam unilaterally. Future bombings by the United States would be limited to the scantily populated southern sector, and troop reinforcements would not be the rumored 200,000 but a mere 13,500. He earnestly hoped that these concessions would bring the North Vietnamese to the peace table ready for business. Why the increasingly unpopular Johnson "abdicated" at this time has caused much speculation, ranging from the state of his health to the prospect that he would be beaten at the polls in a rerun.

At all events, after weeks of haggling about a site for negotiation, the negotiators from North Vietnam and the United States met in Paris to talk about talks. Much valuable time was lost in argument about the shape of the conference table. The North Vietnamese stubbornly and tiresomely demanded that all bombing and other acts of war against North Vietnam be stopped before they would even consider any agreement. In view of the continuing North Vietnamese infiltration into South Vietnam, the United States found these conditions unacceptable. Yet President Johnson had decided on a unilateral de-escalation of the war pending the outcome of the presidential election of 1968.

For the ensuing presidential campaign of 1968 the Democrats nominated Hubert Humphrey, who as Vice-President was a prisoner of Johnson's policy of bombing the North Vietnamese into an "honorable" peace. The rival Republicans took essentially the same position, although their nominee, Richard M. Nixon, declared that he knew how to bring the war to a speedy and successful conclusion.

A week before the election in November 1968, Johnson announced that all bombing of North Vietnam would cease, pending the beginning of fruitful peace negotiations in Paris. This concession did not come soon enough to save Hubert Humphrey, who lost in a close finish. The victor, Richard M. Nixon, had promised an "honorable peace" and "no more Vietnams." Several weeks later, on January 16, 1969, the stalemated delegates in Paris from North Vietnam agreed to discuss substantive issues with the Americans. Johnson thus ended his administration on something of an upbeat, but few informed observers would say that the light at the end of the tunnel was discernible.

Lyndon Johnson was a perplexed and deeply frustrated President who had inherited a minor-league war and for reasons that seemed imperative to him and his advisers, deliberately expanded this entanglement into a major-league war. He was forced to back off substantially when he found that much public opinion had turned furiously against an all-out effort, and then passed the mess on to President Nixon. Johnson was probably the most unsuccessfully pugnacious of all the Presidents; he gained neither peace nor honor. Neither, critics say with much reason, did his successor, Richard M. Nixon.

CHAPTER 37

RICHARD M. NIXON: THE WARRIOR FOR PEACE

I pledge to you tonight that the first priority foreign policy objective of our next Administration will be to bring an honorable end to the war in Vietnam.... My fellow Americans, the dark long night for America is about to end.

Richard M. Nixon,
acceptance speech, Miami,
August 8, 1968, four years
before the formal end.

The Rise of "Tricky Dick"

Richard M. Nixon was born on January 9, 1913, at Yorba Linda, Southern California, a hamlet with a population of some two hundred souls and hitherto unknown to fame. He thus became the first native Californian to reach the White House. His father was a modest grower of citrus fruit, especially lemons, and young Richard, like Herbert Hoover, was brought up as a Quaker and a presumed devotee of peace.

After coming up through the local public schools, the future President enrolled in nearby Whittier College and graduated with a high standing in his class. As for extracurricular activities, he participated in football and debating, both of which brought out his ingrained pugnacity. In physical combat, he was not a first-stringer; five feet, eleven inches in his prime, he was never especially robust or well-coordinated, but he partially made up in determination what he lacked in brute strength. In debating, he was glib, clever, resourceful, and outstandingly successful. Later in political life he delighted in scoring verbal points, but often without scrupulous regard for fairness and truth.

Never affluent in early life, Nixon entered the Duke University law school on a scholarship, and by dint of assiduous study graduated second in a class of twenty-six. Failing to find a place with a New York law firm, he returned to Whittier, California, to practice law. In 1942, after war had broken out with Japan, he served as an attorney for about six months with the Office of Emergency Management in Washington. As a Quaker and a government official, he presumably could have escaped military service, but he volunteered for action as a Lieutenant Commander in the United States Navy from 1942 to 1946. As an aviation ground officer, he escaped heavy combat, but on occasion he was subjected to heavy aerial bombardment. He thus managed to see war at first hand and acquired a realistic conception of what it entailed. He was reputed to be an exceptionally successful poker player during off hours, and so admits in his memoirs.

Returning to California after the war, Nixon challenged the incumbent Congressman, Jerry Voorhis, and defeated him in 1946 for his seat in the House of Representatives. Nixon cleverly forced his rival into a series of public debates and made mincemeat of him with wild charges of Communist leanings. The brash young debater from Whittier was well on his way to becoming the nation's foremost Red-baiter.

Reelected to Congress in 1948, Nixon gained national fame by his service on the House Un-American Activities Committee. It was he who doggedly pursued and pinned Alger Hiss, a former State Department official, and finally had him convicted of perjury in connection with alleged pro-Communist activities.

Setting his sights on higher goals, Nixon ran for the United States Senate in 1950. His opponent was Helen Gahagan Douglas, an aggressive liberal but no Communist. Yet Nixon extravagantly painted her red, although delicately branding her the "Pink Lady." Nixon's foes, with considerable justification, responded by calling him "Tricky Dick"—a label that never wore off completely.

Aspiring to greater heights, Nixon was elected Vice-President in 1952 and 1956, both times as the running mate of "Ike" Eisenhower. In 1955, 1956, and 1957, he served efficiently and tactfully in the capacity of informal interim president during Eisenhower's three successive illnesses.

In 1958 Nixon embarked upon a goodwill tour of South America that turned out to be an ill will tour. Ugly demonstrations by mobs in Lima, Peru, should have brought about a cancellation of the trip, but Nixon, perhaps to show his fighting fiber, pressed on to Caracas, Venezuela. There a frenzied mob battered his car and evidently came close to tearing him limb from limb.

In 1960 the Republicans, seeking a successor to Eisenhower, nominated Nixon. The fighting Quaker narrowly lost to John F. Kennedy, the Democratic nominee. The outcome could have turned on any one of a number of incidents, but in retrospect "Tricky Dick" Nixon, who gloried in verbal combat, made the fatal mistake of agreeing to meet his challenger in four nationally televised encounters. Unfortunately for Nixon, a painful knee injury had kept him hospitalized for some time before the debates. He emerged pale and emaciated, with an ill-fitting collar, to clash with the robust and fact-crammed Kennedy, who met the challenger on about even terms. Yet a draw with the clever Nixon was equivalent to a victory.

Excluded from the White House by the two Democratic Presidents, Kennedy and Johnson, Nixon attempted to hit the comeback trail in 1962 by trying to wrest the governorship of California from the incumbent Edmund G. ("Pat") Brown. The challenger's sharpness on the platform availed him nothing, and he lost by a wide margin. The saying is that there are no good losers, only good actors, but Nixon ungraciously paid his disrespects to the assembled newsmen when he announced to them that they would not have Nixon "to kick around any more." He was not only buried by the voters but in this tart manner he seemingly sealed the tomb himself. Such was the combative Nixon at his worst. Six years later, in 1968, when he was narrowly elected President, one irreverent commentator hailed this achievement as the "greatest comeback since the resurrection of Jesus."

Vietnam Vexations

In assessing Nixon's role in nominally ending the shooting role of the United States in Vietnam early in 1973, we must keep in mind that he did not start America's large-scale involvement. That was begun under Kennedy and brought to a fruitless peak under Johnson. But Nixon, who inherited the war, took four years and one week to arrange for an unsatisfactory cease-fire—or a longer period than America's direct involvement in World War I or World War II. The major charge against Nixon is not that he started the Vietnam War but that he took so long to end it—even on illusory terms.

As the Republican nominee, Nixon had campaigned vigorously and successfully against the Democrat Hubert Humphrey in 1968. The clever Californian had promised "no more Vietnams," and he had declared emphatically on the stump that he knew how to "end the war and win the peace," if elected. But he refused to unveil what the press called his "secret plan" for fear, he explained, of interfering with the stalemated peace negotiations in Paris. Nixon's response seemed to many Democratic voters like an excuse for covering up some unworkable design.

The Vietnam imbroglio was further confused on April 15, 1969, when the defiant North Koreans shot down an American military aircraft (EC-121), which appears to have been well out over international waters, as reckoned by the United States. All thirty-one men aboard lost their lives, as compared with none in the earlier *Pueblo* seizure. The death toll was in itself a greater outrage, and in earlier days it could easily have resulted in massive retaliation.

President Nixon's first impulse, so he relates in his memoirs, was to meet force with force, perhaps by bombing a North Korean airfield. But such an explosive response might have triggered a renewed invasion of South Korea, where thousands of American troops were still stationed, and the United States already had its hands more than full in Vietnam. Instead, orders were issued to renew the reconnaissance flights with "combat escorts."

So it was that the new President Nixon, inaugurated in January 1969, had committed himself to ending the Vietnam War.

He would not only bring peace but he would bring it with "honor"—that is, he would not "bug out" and leave the South Vietnamese in the lurch. Such a cowardly course would, he believed, betray the anti-Communist government in Saigon, supported for so many years by his predecessors. A hasty pull-out would also tar his administration, he incorrectly believed, with the onus of having presided over the only "lost" war in the history of the United States.

The solution that Nixon proclaimed from the White House was "Vietnamization"—that is, gradually turning the fighting over to the South Vietnamese, while supplying them with essential money and military hardware. This proposed way out was hardly new, because Johnson had earlier proclaimed his determination to de-Americanize the fighting as soon as practicable. But Nixon gave this old policy a new twist by emphasizing the gradual withdrawal of American troops from this Asiatic death trap in such a way and in such numbers as to preserve America's "honor." Nixon declared that "the great silent majority" was behind this scheme, as indeed, according to the polls, it appeared to be. But gradually the great vocal minority began to engage in angry mass protests that shook the very foundations of the federal government.

Nixon did succeed in reducing the number of troops in Vietnam from about 536,000 in 1968 to 24,200 in 1972. Yet, at the same time, he widened the war by carrying it into Laos and Cambodia, chiefly by air. From a purely military standpoint, there were good reasons for his doing what he did in attempting to deny such staging areas to the North Vietnamese forces.

On April 30, 1970, Nixon sent American troops plunging into Cambodia to wipe out advanced North Vietnamese bases. Shock waves of outrage convulsed the United States, especially on college campuses where young men of draft age were registered. At Kent State University in Ohio, panicked National Guardsmen discharged their rifles into an angry crowd, killing four students and wounding nine others. The next day Nixon assured an outraged nation that the American troops would be withdrawn gradually from Cambodia during a two-month period. Also, they would not be permitted to penetrate more than twenty-one miles. Nixon kept these promises, although he did not announce that for more than a year previously he had been secretly bombing Communist positions in Cambodia.

In February 1971 the United States sponsored an invasion of Laos with South Vietnamese troops. Although supported by about a thousand American aircraft, the invaders were hurled back in panicky retreat. Thus ended one more vain attempt to Vietnamize the Vietnam War by counterattacking South Vietnam's neighbors to the west.

China, Russia, and India

Nixon also waged the Vietnam War on the diplomatic front, particularly by playing on the mutual fears of China and the Soviet Union. If Washington established better relations with both of these powers, they might be persuaded to reduce the massive influx of arms that they were pouring into North Vietnam. They might even induce the North Vietnamese negotiators in Paris to accept peace terms that would permit the United States to stage an honorable withdrawal from the jungles of Southeast Asia.

After preliminary feelers, Nixon, the veteran Red-baiter, accepted an invitation to visit China. The Chinese had fallen out with the Soviets in the early 1960s over the correct interpretation of Marxist-Leninism, and both were now bitter enemies. Nixon and the Chinese alike were fully aware of the effect that a closer association of the United States with China would have on the balance of power in East Asia. In any event, Nixon made the epochal trip and engaged in extended talks with the Chinese leaders in February 1972. The result was an inconclusive joint communiqué. It merely reaffirmed the controversial views held by both parties, rather than any sharp new shift of policy. Formal diplomatic relations did not result immediately, but at least an American foot was in the door. If Nixon hoped that his sidling up to China would arouse the Russians, his ploy evidently worked. In October 1971 the Soviets invited Nixon to Moscow, with conferences to be held in May 1972.

Meanwhile, in March 1972 the North Vietnamese had launched a smashing offensive. Employing foreign tanks, they burst southward through the Demilitarized Zone (DMZ) separating North and South Vietnam. The retreating South Vietnamese, although supported by heavy bombing from American aircraft, threatened the withdrawing American troops to the south with complete disaster. Nixon, his Vietnamization policy in grave peril, decided upon a dangerous response. He announced a heavy bombing of North Vietnamese cities, plus the aerial mining of the principal harbors of North Vietnam, through which Chinese and Soviet bloc merchant ships were bringing in massive quantities of war supplies.

Nixon, the expert poker player, was now gambling for high stakes. The danger loomed that Chinese and Russian vessels would be sunk or damaged and that China and the Soviet Union would intervene, thus precipitating World War III. Actually, both Peking and Moscow did protest—four Russian ships were allegedly damaged—but these remonstrances were unexpectedly mild. The vocal American public applauded Nixon's relentless bombing policy; in fact, many leading military men openly claimed that if such harsh measures had been employed from the beginning, the war would have been won long ago.

As for the Soviets, Nixon's visit to Moscow in May 1972 resulted in a memorable summit conference, which marked the beginning of the loudly heralded Nixonian policy of detente, or relaxation of tensions. Various accords of a secondary nature were reached, but overshadowing all others was a five-year Interim Agreement limiting the number of nuclear missiles on both sides. Such were the precarious gains for peace.

In at least two instances during these years President Nixon resorted to show-the-flag, gunboat diplomacy. In December 1971 war broke out between India and Pakistan, during which the Indians invaded Pakistan's Bangladesh and overran their objective in fifteen days. Pakistan happened to be an ally of the United States under the American-sponsored SEATO (Southeast Asia Treaty Organization). So Washington, with an obvious "tilt toward Pakistan," rushed a powerful naval task force to the Indian Ocean with carrier-based bombers. The transparent excuse given at the time was the need to rescue a handful of American citizens, most of whom had already left Bangladesh. Neither India nor Pakistan was pleased, as Uncle Sam emerged looking rather foolish.

"Peace" with Dishonor in Vietnam

How to end the war in Vietnam continued to be the burning issue in the presidential election of 1972, as it had been in 1968. This time Nixon ran for a second term against the Democratic candidate, Senator George McGovern. The challenger's clarion call was "Come Home America," meaning the turn-tail withdrawal of all American troops within ninety days, without regard for the commitments already made to President Thieu of South Vietnam.

The Republicans renominated President Nixon with high enthusiasm at Miami Beach, where they condemned the "New Isolationism" of the McGovernites. The Nixonites would continue their support of the dictatorial President Thieu by working for a "peace with honor" rather than a "peace with surrender." The Republicans demonstrated with graphic charts that Nixon had wound down "the Democratic war" of Kennedy and Johnson from some 550,000 troops to about 30,000, a number of whom were already scheduled to come home.

The McGovernite Democrats responded that Nixon, far from "winding down" the war, had spread the fighting into Laos and Cambodia; he had shifted to aerial bombing, actually some of the heaviest in all history. Far from securing the release of more than five hundred American prisoners of war (POWs), he was merely adding to their number. After "four long years of fighting," where was the peace that Nixon had promised with his alleged "secret plan" four years earlier?

Twelve days before the November election of 1972, the Democrats were essentially robbed of their peace issue. Secretary of State Kissinger came home from Paris, where he had been conducting prolonged negotiations with the Vietnamese, to say to the press, "We believe that peace is at hand." The McGovernites, suddenly deflated, responded that if peace had indeed arrived it should have come four years earlier.

But there were obvious loopholes in the agreement proposed by the North Vietnamese, and Nixon announced on November 2, 1972, five days before the polls opened, that he would sign no agreement until it was "right." He was reelected in a landslide, partly because of the ineptness of his rival and partly because of a general feeling that peace was indeed "at hand." To countless voters the two candidates presented a choice of evils.

The election safely in the bag, Nixon evidently decided that the only way out of the Vietnam morass "with honor" was to blast the North Vietnamese into accepting an agreement that would ensure an "honorable peace." On December 18, 1972, three days after the chief North Vietnamese negotiator in Paris left for home, Nixon unleashed a series of furious all-out bombing attacks on North Vietnamese cities and military installations. This "Christmas blitz" killed numerous Vietnamese, including civilians of all ages and both sexes, while the enemy shot down a disturbing number of America's aerial bombers. As a tactical maneuver, Nixon's assaults rivaled some of the heaviest attacks of World War II. After the devastating blastings had continued for eleven days (one day off in honor of the Christ Child), the North Vietnamese were forced to return to the Paris peace table.

This much must be said of Nixon's brutal tactics: They got results, at least temporarily and illusorily, when a cease-fire was signed in Paris on January 27, 1973. The terms were lengthy, complicated, and purposely ambiguous. The United States agreed to withdraw the remainder of its troops from South Vietnam, all told about 25,000 men. But the Americans would be permitted to provide South Vietnam with replacements for military equipment.

During these anxious weeks, Nixon used both the carrot and the stick. The stick was the "Christmas blitz"; the carrot was the vague promise that American dollars would be used to rehabilitate Vietnam, with North Vietnam receiving a talked-about $2.5 billion. This, in effect, was the ransom to be paid (but never paid) for the more than five hundred American prisoners of war. They came home naturally overflowing with gratitude to Nixon for having staged the Christmas assaults that had made possible their release.

Scant glory or honor was to be derived from this war. In 1968, at My Lai, U.S. troops had gunned down at least 450 unarmed South Vietnamese civilians—women, children, and old men. Nominally, the United States had fought North Vietnam to a draw, but actually a humiliating loss was incurred when South Vietnam finally surrendered in 1975, despite the continued inpouring of American supplies. The fanatical North Vietnamese Communists clearly had a will to fight that their South Vietnamese brothers could not match.

In the eyes of much of the civilized world, the United States had dishonored itself by intervening in a purely local civil war. By a so-called policy of gradualism, the Americans had spread the conflict; had added enormously to human misery and death; had napalmed men, women, and children; had defoliated the jungles and poisoned the soil—and then had run out on a hard-pressed "ally."

In this way President Nixon managed a face-saving retreat from a war designed to halt a nonexistent Communist monolith. But in the eyes of many observers there was no "peace with honor" but a continued war with dishonor. And Nixon had achieved this dubious triumph by a demonstration of sustained ferocity probably without parallel in America's presidential history. He actually maintained a savage aerial bombing of Communist positions in nearby Cambodia for more than six months after the cease-fire in Vietnam. Congress, which held the purse strings, literally forced Nixon to stop these assaults on August 15, 1973.

Post-Mortem on Peace

The Nixon-engineered "peace" was not kept, for shooting continued before, during, and after the armistice negotiations. In the first year of the "cease-fire" an estimated fifty thousand Vietnamese lost their lives. By the terms of the armistice a total of 145,000 North Vietnamese troops were left behind to strike again, as they ultimately did.

Nixon proudly boasted that he had achieved "peace with honor." Yet peace did not come—the peace of the graveyard—until April 1975, when the North Vietnamese captured Saigon, the capitol of South Vietnam, and ran out the American Embassy staff and the few remaining American officials.

As for honor, there was precious little of it to be derived from this bloody and frustrating jungle war. On paper, the United States had turned the struggle over to North Vietnam and President Thieu. He reluctantly accepted the American pull-out after receiving written assurances from Nixon that massive American aid, presumably aerial, would be forthcoming in a crunch. It never came, and Thieu, although a cruel and corrupt dictator, cried that he had been dishonorably treated.

More decisive was Nixon's reaction to the surprise attack by Egypt and Syria on the Israelis in October 1973. The desperately pressed Israelis were running short of weapons when Nixon ordered a gigantic airlift of some $2 billion worth of tanks, airplanes, and other material of war to offset the arms that were being supplied by the Soviets to the invaders. Fearful that the Russians would become more deeply involved in this strategic area, Nixon also ordered American military forces to go on a "precautionary alert." Finally a cease-fire was hastily arranged, and a buffer zone was established between the contending Egyptians and Israelis, with the United Nations providing the peacekeeping force.

It seems probable that if Nixon had not responded militantly and speedily during this crisis, Israel would have been wiped off the map. The NATO allies were generally opposed to permitting American weapons within their jurisdiction to be airlifted to Israel, and they were displeased to see the United States waste its strength in these desert sands. Actually American military stocks were seriously depleted. Insofar as America had moral commitments to Israel, Nixon's intervention was more honorable than his forsaking South Vietnam earlier in 1973. His stock rose sharply with Jewish-American voters at a time when the Watergate scandals were threatening his impeachment. He resigned in August 1974 to escape formal removal from office.

A prisoner of circumstances, like his embattled predecessors, Nixon turned out to be one of the most persistently pugnacious of the Presidents. He was fully supported in his iron-handed moves by Secretary of State Kissinger. There was considerable talk of Nixon's eligibility for the Nobel Peace Prize in 1973, but it was awarded jointly to Kissinger and Le Duc Tho, the two principal negotiators at Paris. The North Vietnamese recipient refused his share of the prize on the ground that peace had not come to Vietnam, and in fact it had not.

"The Ancient Mariner." Nixon troubled by Watergate albatross. Courtesy Scrawls and the Palm Beach Post.

CHAPTER 38

GERALD R. FORD: THE HEALING PRESIDENT

I do believe that the buck stops here, that I cannot rely upon public opinion polls to tell me what is right.

President Ford, televised
address on Nixon's pardon,
September 8, 1974.

From Football to Forensics

Gerald Ford, though born in Nebraska in 1913, was taken by his divorced mother at age two to her family's home in Grand Rapids, Michigan, near the rapids of the Grand River. Here she married again, and "Junior" was legally adopted by the new father. At the local high school young Ford became a standout player on the football team and managed to win an "athletic scholarship" at the University of Michigan, where he starred as an All-Conference center while earning his A.B. degree. He wisely turned down offers to sign with professional football teams so that he could continue with his education.

Next came Ford's acceptance of a job as assistant to the football coach at Yale University, while also coaching freshman boxing. In due season he requested permission to take some courses in the prestigious Yale law school, which admitted him on a trial basis. He was forced to register for a light load because of preoccupation with his coaching duties, and he did not graduate with his LL.B. (Bachelor of Laws) degree until 1941, when he was twenty-seven years of age. He then returned to Grand Rapids, where he began the practice of law.

Up to this point the picture emerges of an athlete, gifted enough physically to be a professional, who gloried in physical contact, whether with shoulder pads or boxing gloves. There is a common tendency, not altogether ill founded, to equate brute strength with brutish stupidity, and Ford himself was prompted to insist while President that he was not just another "dumb" football player. Quips going the rounds were President Johnson's sneers that Jerry Ford had played football too long without a helmet, and that he was not well enough coordinated to chew gum and walk at the same time.

The truth is that while an undergraduate football player at Michigan, young Ford had enough energy left to accumulate a respectable record in his course work. At the Yale law school, in part-time competition with many Phi Beta Kappas, he consistently earned grades of "B" and ranked in the top 25 percent of his class. Although not a brilliant political philosopher like John Adams and James Madison, Ford was no blockhead, and besides was one of the finest physical specimens ever to occupy the White House. Better than six feet tall, he kept his weight at about 203 pounds, only four pounds above his college prime.

When young Ford returned to Michigan to practice law early in 1941, he could not foresee that the Japanese would attack Pearl Harbor in December of that year. Yielding to the call of duty and country, he enlisted in the navy, served from 1942 to 1946, and emerged with the rank of lieutenant commander. Not illogically, he was first assigned to a physical training program, in which he was charged with whipping new recruits into shape. But he craved action, and his superiors granted his wish by sending him to a carrier in the South Pacific, where he found himself in the thick of the fighting, and where he received commendation as a dependable "team player."

When the shooting stopped, Ford returned to his law practice in Michigan, but finally became involved in politics as a Republican "internationalist" who supported the United Nations and the Marshall Plan. He defeated an isolationist Republican mossback in the Republican primaries of 1948 for the local seat in Congress, snowed under his Democratic opponent, and was then returned to the House of Representatives for twelve consecutive times, from 1948 to 1972. In 1965 he was chosen House minority (Republican) leader.

As for pugnacity, Congressman Ford was conspicuous in urging the Johnson administration to escalate the war in Vietnam. Like a former boxing instructor, he asked, "Why are we pulling our punches?" He further urged the administration to "unleash devastating air and sea power." Like Teddy Roosevelt, he believed in not hitting soft, if any hitting was to be done. Many American military men argued, then and later, that if the United States had struck with devastating blows at the outset, the enemy would not have had time to build up adequate defenses.

A Hawk in the White House

In October 1973 Vice-President Spiro Agnew was forced to resign, following an exposé of corrupt payoffs dating back to his governorship of Maryland. With Nixon in grave danger of being ejected by the impeachment route, an impeccably honest Vice-President was urgently needed. The President appointed Gerald Ford, subject to approval by Congress, in conformity with the new (1967) Twenty-fifth Amendment. After an incredibly exhaustive investigation of the appointee's private affairs, he emerged as Mr. Clean at a time when impeccably sterling characters were in short supply. In August 1974 Ford became President after Nixon resigned to escape certain impeachment for Watergate-related offenses.

At the outset "nice guy" Gerald Ford got off on the right foot with Congress when he asked not for a prolonged "honeymoon" but a "good marriage." But the new "era of good feelings" had lasted only about a month when, out of a clear sky, the newly "appointed" President issued a blanket pardon to Nixon for any crimes he may have committed while in the White House. Ford's avowed purpose was to calm the country, but the result was a protracted uproar. He had not secured an admission of guilt, only an implicit admission; he had not pardoned the subordinates of Nixon who were in jail for carrying out their chief's orders; and he had aroused suspicions of a "buddy deal" prior to his being awarded the presidency. This charge was never proved, although Ford, as a compassionate man, evidently believed that a desperately ill Nixon had suffered enough for his sins.

In domestic affairs, Ford's chief problems related to "stagflation"—a stagnant economy (with much unemployment) combined with an inflated currency that was driving prices skyward. In foreign affairs, the principal concern was the Nixonian détente with Russia, a give-and-take arrangement that seemed to be a one-way street, with the United States selling advanced technology and other wares, while the Soviets were responding with seemingly little in return. At the same time the Russians were sending immense shipments of arms (plus technicians) to pro-Communist forces in Asia (conspicuously Vietnam) and to Africa. There, in addition, tens of thousands of Cuban soldiers, at the behest of Moscow, were fighting in "wars of national liberation" for Communist ends.

With the hard-nosed Secretary of State Kissinger at his side, Ford continued the established policy of supporting NATO in Europe, obviously against the Soviets but on a purely defensive basis. The United States was also continuing to ship replacement military supplies to South Vietnam, as agreed, even though Congress had cut back substantially on the projected appropriations. President Ford greatly resented this reduction as an improper interference, though technically it was not, in the President's conduct of foreign affairs.

In January 1975 the North Vietnamese unleashed their long-expected southward drive. South Vietnamese morale, never as high as Washington had hoped, collapsed, and the fleeing troops abandoned to the attackers a vast amount of expensive military equipment direct from the United States. President Ford, long a "hawk" on the Vietnam War, urged Congress, in an address on April 10, 1975, to send millions of dollars in war supplies at once, all the while deploring the perfectly constitutional interference of the Congress in the President's conduct of foreign affairs. But by this time, as many observers could see, more military supplies in significant quantities could not have been sent before the complete collapse of South Vietnam. Nineteen days later the invaders took over billions of dollars' worth of American tanks, aircraft, and other weapons of war—perhaps the greatest haul of its kind in history.

The panicky finale came on April 30, 1975, when helicopters of the U.S. Seventh Fleet airlifted to safety the remnants of the American Embassy. During these anxious days the United States snatched away from a possible bloodbath about 130,000 refugees, most of whom were in some way tainted by association with the American presence. As a compassionate man, Ford exercised his presidential authority to succor these displaced persons and to welcome them to the United States—traditional home of the "huddled masses."

As a "hawk" regarding the Vietnamese War, Ford had favored supporting the faithful "ally" in South Vietnam. His motives were probably mixed, but to his credit he was much concerned about the honor and credibility of his own country. It is true that President Thieu of South Vietnam was a cruel and corrupt dictator, the very negation of democracy, and that the South Vietnamese had not shown the requisite backbone if they hoped to defeat their brothers from the north.

We recall that the United States had persuaded President Thieu to consent to a cease-fire in 1973 by promises of continued support. President Nixon had privately promised Thieu in writing that he would respond with heavy force to a violation of the cease-fire agreement, evidently meaning heavy aerial bombardment. Of course Nixon's assurances did not bind Ford legally, only morally, but the new Chief Executive was much concerned about the credibility of America's defense treaties with many other nations, including Japan and the Philippines. So Ford remained loyal to an unworthy "ally" until Thieu had fled the country, reputedly with wealth siphoned off from open-handed Uncle Sam.

Upholding National Honor

In mid-May 1975, about two weeks after the fall of South Vietnam, the compassionate President Ford engaged in his most spectacular act of belligerency. Involved were the honor of the flag and the lives of thirty-nine seamen.

A U.S. merchant ship, the *Mayaguez*, was seized in the international waters of the Gulf of Siam by forces of the new hardline Communist regime of Cambodia. If the captives were brought to the Cambodian mainland, the chances were that they would never again be seen alive. This prognosis takes on greater reality when we note that subsequently the ruling regime deliberately killed off hundreds of thousands of fellow Cambodians in a colossal holocaust. Washington was powerless to establish direct communications with Cambodia, for diplomatic relations with it had not yet been established. Efforts to deal through the government of China drew a flat refusal.

Under such pressures, President Ford mounted a far-flung, strongarm rescue of the thirty-nine men manning the *Mayaguez*. In the process, United States naval and aerial units sank three Cambodian gunboats, invaded an island, and then bombed the Cambodian mainland. The elaborate rescue operation cost the lives of forty-one Americans, to say nothing of fifty wounded, to rescue the thirty-nine seamen.

The use of a sledgehammer to combat the Cambodian mosquito evoked enthusiastic applause for Ford. There can be little doubt that the public, disheartened by the recent failure in Vietnam, was weary of being pushed around by "pipsqueak nations." From early days the President had used the armed forces in foreign lands to protect American lives and property. We recall that a warship of the U.S. Navy, the *Pueblo*, was seized in 1968 by the North Koreans, and that this intolerable offense drew no armed response, largely because a war with Korea was no guarantee that the ship and crew would be retrieved, even if the war should be won.

In fairness to Ford, we must hesitate to charge him with undue pugnacity in the *Mayaguez* affair. The trouble-seeking Cambodians had provoked the response. Ford had consulted the National Security Council, and in addition Secretary of State Kissinger had strongly favored direct and speedy action. What we have since learned about the Cambodian Communists suggests that the President acted more wisely than he then knew.

In another dangerous area, President Ford and his "hawkish" Secretary Kissinger also made a determined effort to involve the United States in formerly Portuguese Angola in 1975. There the natives were warring for control among themselves, while the Soviets backed the chief pro-Communist element with military supplies. To outsiders the Soviet Union was evidently attempting to secure strategic naval bases from a victorious Marxist regime oriented toward Moscow.

At first Washington undertook to offset Soviet support in Angola by using the Central Intelligence Agency to funnel in arms and supplies. When this scanty inflow proved woefully inadequate, the aggressive Ford–Kissinger combination urged Congress to provide a more abundant inflow of material aid, but not military manpower. Congress balked, for it remembered that in bottomless Vietnam money, supplies, and men proved to be merely the vanguard of an army of more than half a million fighting men. Congressmen reasoned that if the United States let nature take its course, the Soviet-backed regime (with Cuban soldiers) would win. Then the main defeated faction or factions would take to the bush in guerrilla warfare. This is precisely what happened, and the Cubans, not the Americans, then had a Vietnam of sorts on their hands.

Secretary Kissinger, strongly seconded by President Ford, roundly scolded Congress for having interfered harmfully in the conduct of foreign affairs. Ford bluntly accused the members, many of whom he knew well, of "having lost their guts" in rejecting his recommendations for assistance to the anti-Communists in Angola. But this time Congress was responsive to public opinion and not to the tongue-lashings of Kissinger and Ford. Both leaders seemed to forget that under the Constitution, the Congress is clothed with the power to have a large hand, though often a negative one, in the shaping of foreign policy. Treaties are approved or disapproved by the Senate, and all appropriations of money, for domestic or foreign purposes, must be supported by a majority of both houses of Congress.

But to concentrate on Ford's pugnacity or lack of it is to obscure the main point. He dragged the nation into no war. He also restored respectability to the post-Watergate Republican party and integrity to the presidency of the United States. These were no mean achievements. His successor, Jimmy Carter, began his inaugural address with these words: "For myself and for our nation I want to thank my predecessor for all he has done to heal our land." The crowd applauded, and Gerald Ford, so he writes in his memoirs, felt deeply touched.

CHAPTER 39

JIMMY CARTER: THE BORN AGAIN PRESIDENT

We are a strong nation, and we will maintain strength so sufficient that it need not be proven in combat—a quiet strength based not solely on the size of an arsenal but on the nobility of ideas.

President Carter,
Inaugural Address,
January 20, 1977

A Peanut Man for President

President "Jimmy" Carter (as he insisted on calling himself), was born in 1924 near the hitherto unknown village of Plains, Georgia, population about 600. At age eleven he was baptized at the local First Baptist Church, and as a "born again" Christian he ultimately became a deacon and a Sunday school teacher. After attending the local schools, Carter registered for several years at the Georgia Southwestern University and the Georgia Institute of Technology. He was next appointed to the Naval Academy at Annapolis, from which he graduated in 1946 with a Bachelor of

Science degree, standing 59th in a class of 820, or about the top 7 percent. This record would have entitled him to Phi Beta Kappa honors in many civilian universities.

After about seven years in the Navy, during which the future President worked on nuclear submarines, Carter's father died and Jimmy, as the oldest son, resigned his commission in the Navy to take over the family farming (mostly peanuts) and warehousing business. He served in the Georgia State Senate from 1962 to 1966 and then ran unsuccessfully for the governorship of Georgia in 1966. But he triumphed in his next try, following which he served as Governor of the state from 1971 to 1974. Not long thereafter "Jimmy Who" launched his prolonged campaign to work his way up from political obscurity—Deep South obscurity—to the presidency of the United States. His winning smile, his folksy manner, his promises of wholesome change, and his sympathy for blacks and women, plus the Nixonian scandals, worked to his advantage. As a Democrat, Carter defeated the Republican Jerry Ford in what this former football star rightly called "a close one."

Carter had obviously seen enough of the Naval Academy and nuclear submarines—about a decade of experience—to know what war, especially nuclear war, was all about. With his soft Southern accent, his ever-smiling teeth, and his record as a dedicated follower of the gentle Jesus, he could be expected to be a man of the olive branch rather than a man of the sword.

Humanitarianism in High Places

Preeminently a man of peace, Carter at the outset embarked upon an aggressive program of humanitarian diplomacy. Although a former naval officer, he forthwith pardoned outright some ten thousand draft evaders from the era of the Vietnam War, and he did so on terms far more Christlike than those offered by President Ford. At about the same time Carter verbally lashed the dictatorial regimes in nearby Cuba and far off Uganda as contravening basic human rights. He also cut off foreign aid from Uruguay, Argentina, and Ethiopia for essentially the same reason. Yet he did not extend the same harsh treatment to the iron-handed governments of Korea and the Philippines, obviously because they were presumably helping the United States to hold back the tide of Communism in critical areas. In short, there was a double standard: Bad dictators become good dictators if they are on the right side.

In line with human rights (and the black vote at home), the Carter administration at the outset championed the cause of the black element in the white-dominated nations of Rhodesia and South Africa. Also in line with human rights (and the Jewish vote at home) Carter urged the Soviet regime to cease the persecution of dissidents (many of them Jews) and permit the large-scale exodus of emigrants from the Soviet Union. Most of the unfortunates were Jews, and many of them preferred to come to the United States rather than emigrate to war-cursed Israel.

The Kremlin, for its part, took the stubborn position that what it did with its own nationals, whether Jewish or not, was nobody else's business. Russian spokesmen were prone to remind the holier-than-thou United States that it had treated blacks and Indians as purely domestic problems, and consequently they were no proper concern of the U.S.S.R. These skeletons rattling in the closet of the Americans were so numerous and horrendous that the United States was in a poor position to be hurling stones at the towers of the Kremlin.

As Commander-in-Chief, Carter was naturally concerned about the continuing pressures of the Soviets in Africa, where in various places they were using tens of thousands of Cuban troops as proxies on a large scale. Strategic naval bases for the U.S.S.R. were an obvious goal. At the same time Carter attempted to put some kind of a cap on the arms race by completing the negotiations with the Soviets for the SALT II pact. As anticipated, this signing touched off a prolonged debate in the Senate, with the outcome much in doubt.

In what was hailed as another signal victory for peace in 1978, Carter barely rammed through the Senate by the narrowest of margins two treaties with Panama. Under them Uncle Sam would relinquish ownership and control of the Panama Canal by the year 2000 A.D. The President thus did penance for Teddy Roosevelt's precipitate "taking" of Panama in 1903. The heated opposition in the United States to this act of generosity, actually conceded under threat of terroristic blackmail, was essentially nonpartisan. The dissent came chiefly from conservatives of all stripes, whether Democratic or Republican. Actually, the "giveaway" of the canal had also been supported by the previous Republican administrations of Nixon and Ford.

Carter's most spectacular achievement as a peacemaker reached fruition in 1979. After strenuous efforts, he succeeded in persuading Egypt and Israel to sign and ratify a peace treaty nominally ending their long years of warfare. Against enormous odds, he revealed extraordinary skill and persistence as a negotiator, and for a brief time his popularity shot up spectacularly in the polls. Yet the peace treaty, though a significant step forward, was no guarantee of permanent peace in the explosive Middle East. The problem of the displaced Palestinians still loomed large.

Multi-Front Crisis Diplomacy

Much of Carter's rather limited pugnacity related to his dealings with Congress, where he had a divided Democratic majority that contained combative conservative and liberal elements. He fought hard to get the Panama treaties approved; he issued an earnest call to the Congress to adopt an energy program ("the moral equivalent of war") to deal with the emerging crisis. But the Congress dillydallied and failed to produce satisfactory solutions, although one watered down energy measure was finally passed. Meanwhile Carter's domestic battles against inflation and rising unemployment were losing ground.

Many citizens blamed the nation's troubles on Carter's alleged lack of leadership. The President responded in July 1979 by spectacularly announcing an astronomically costly program to harness energy. He followed this effort by ruthlessly purging his official family of a large number of its most distinguished members. This new-found aggressiveness was obviously designed, with the presidential election coming up the next year, to project the image of a decisive, two-fisted leader. But Carter certainly did not give the impression that he would resort to the hoary trick of provoking a foreign war to divert public attention from domestic troubles.

Carter's precarious policy in the Middle East suffered a devastating setback beginning late in 1978, when a popular uprising forced the despotic Shah of Iran to flee his country. Washington's strategy had been to sell enormous supplies of modern arms to him in hope that he would help to restrain the neighboring Soviets form barging in and taking over the enormous oil reserves of the Middle East. The new revolutionary regime in Iran brought dismay by sharply reducing the oil outflow to the United States, and also eliminating the American listening posts located near the Soviet border and used to monitor Soviet arms activity.

During this uproar in Iran, Soviet-backed communist elements in South Yemen attempted to penetrate North Yemen. A worried Carter resorted to the old gunboat policy of earlier days when he ordered a naval force, then in the Indian Ocean, to head for the troubled Arabian waters. Then having second thoughts, he ordered the ships to hold back.

Obviously to strengthen China against the Soviet Union, Carter also extended formal recognition to Peking (The People's Republic of China) on January 1, 1979. At the same time he terminated America's defense treaty of 1954 with independent Taiwan, once a part of China and insistently claimed by China. This was the price that Carter had to pay for closer relations with Peking, but right-wingers in the United States raised a noisy outcry. The credibility of the United States as an ally was undermined, and an anti-Communist ally, which America had sponsored since about 1949, was being turned adrift in dangerous waters. Yet this betrayal of a trust seemed necessary to bolster mainland China against its powerful and unfriendly Soviet neighbor.

In August 1979 American intelligence operatives revealed that the Soviets for some time had been stationing in Cuba a complete combat brigade of from two thousand to three thousand soldiers. Probably the force was there in part to help defend Cuba while tens of thousands of surrogate Cuban soldiers were fighting for Soviet objectives in Africa. President Carter responded with a low-key statement of his displeasure, leaving the impression that he would put some kind of quiet pressure on the Russians to withdraw, as he did. The prospects were that although the Soviet brigade might interfere with Senate approval of the pending SALT II treaty with Moscow, no eyeball-to-eyeball confrontation, like President Kennedy's in 1962, seemed likely. A single Soviet brigade posed no real offensive threat to the United States, although it did raise disquieting questions.

As for American and Russian arms limitation under the proposed SALT II pact in 1979, Carter was willing to make concessions to the Soviets that many military men and conservative politicians thought would be dangerous signs of weakness. In any event, despite a few slight slips from grace, Carter could by no means be regarded as one of the more pugnacious of the Presidents as his bid for reelection loomed in 1980. In fact, bringing formal peace between Israel and Egypt caused him to become mentioned prominently as a candidate for the Nobel Peace Prize.

Iranian Blackmail

During the Nixon-Kissinger era (1969-1974) the United States had sold the pro-Western Shah of Iran billions of dollars worth of sophisticated weapons, including the most advanced aircraft. The obvious purpose, aside from profits for American manufacturers, was to strengthen this vulnerable but oil-rich area against a possible Soviet intrusion. The Shah, a ruthless despot, was finally forced to flee the country in January 1979, after an uprising that temporarily reduced critical oil shipments to the United States.

The fugitive Shah finally took up temporary residence in Mexico, and then was permitted by President Carter, as a humanitarian gesture, to enter the United States for treatment of cancer in New York City in November 1979. Taking advantage of this opportunity, a mob of Iranian "students" seized the American Embassy in Teheran on November 4 and captured some fifty Americans found therein. The captors then proclaimed that the captives would not be released until the Shah was returned for trial—and almost certain execution.

President Carter, who had been warned privately of some such eventuality, was immediately confronted with the most explosive problem thus far in his administration. Should he yield to barefaced blackmail or undertake iron-fisted reprisals? The Shah had no doubt committed crimes, but to surrender a ruler who had loyally supported American policies would be a stain on the nation's honor and credibility. In addition, the Iranians were attempting to blackmail the United States by invading an embassy, which in all civilized countries was regarded as an inviolable part of the nation whose flag it flew.

At the outset, countless American citizens clamored for the rescue of the prisoners by helicopter, but Teheran was too far inland, and besides, the hostages would almost certainly be killed immediately. Partly because such strongarm alternatives could only worsen the crisis, Carter moved with conspicuous caution and restraint. He embargoed the importation of Iranian oil (thus beating the Iranians to the punch) and then "froze" the billions of dollars of Iranian assets in the United Sates. He also undertook to retaliate by deporting the large number of Iranian students illegally in the United States. On the military front, Carter ordered two American naval task forces to the area within striking distance of Iranian outlets to the ocean. This was obviously a return to gunboat diplomacy, followed by talk of a blockade of all shipping serving Iran.

The Shah was finally allowed to leave the United States for Panama, but the attempted blackmail dragged on into 1980. President Carter managed to secure an overwhelming condemnation of the Embassy seizure from the International Court of Justice at the Hague in the Netherlands and from the Security Council of the United Nations in New York. Carter's obvious reluctance to resort to force evidently redounded to his political credit at home, for his prospects for renomination rose sharply in the polls. Strongarm measures would neither rescue the hostages nor avoid antagonizing the Soviets. Force might even arouse the entire Muslim world against the United States. At all events, President Carter pursued a course of restraint, at least militarily, but experts wondered how long such relatively mild responses would be acceptable to American public opinion.

The Carter Doctrine

An already tense international situation became highly explosive early in January 1980, when thousands of massively equipped Soviet troops poured into neighboring Afghanistan. Their obvious purpose was to prop up the puppet pro-Soviet government of this backward country, but the Western World, particularly the United States, feared that the Soviets planned to keep on moving farther south, even through Iran, until they reached their centuries-old goal of a warm water port on the open sea. At the same time the Russians might conceivably undertake to gain control over all exports from the oil-rich nations bordering on the strategic Persian Gulf.

Hitherto President Carter had been one of the most pacific of presidents in his dealings with foreign governments, particularly the Soviets, but the invasion of Afghanistan turned him into one of the most bellicose. Among his most vigorous responses were his announcements of a cancellation of huge shipments of grain to the Soviet Union; an embargo on the sale of high-technology equipment to the Soviet Union; a call for a boycott of the scheduled summer Olympic games in Moscow; and a proposal to grant Pakistan, which adjoined Afghanistan, $400 million in economic and military aid.

On January 23, 1980, President Carter appeared before a joint session of Congress to present what was probably the most bellicose State of the Union addresses ever delivered. His high point was what commentators called "The Carter Doctrine." He declared, "Any attempt by an outside force to gain control of the Persian Gulf region will be regarded as an assault on the vital interests of the United States. It will be repelled by the use of any means necessary including military force." This, of course, meant war, possibly nuclear. Carter further declared that if existing volunteer troops should not prove adequate, the draft would have to be revitalized.

Some critics charged that the "Carter doctrine," like the original Monroe Doctrine, was a bluff. The United States simply did not have enough conventional forces in being or available to drive the Soviets out of the Persian Gulf region if the invaders should elect to seize this crucial oil center. In any event, Carter won political popularity at home by thus standing up to the Soviets, as military and naval preparations went forward aimed at defensive operations in southwest Asia. Détente was dead, at least temporarily, as was the Salt II arms limitation treaty.

On April 25, 1980, a saddened Carter shocked the nation by announcing on television that an airborne team of some ninety American commandos, because of engine trouble, had been forced to abandon in an Iranian desert a long-rehearsed plan to rescue the fifty or so American hostages in Teheran. Eight American volunteers had lost their lives. Yet this abortive raid was not so much an act of aggression by Carter as an effort, in response to repeated demands in the United States, that something be done to free the imprisoned Americans, unlawfully seized. At least President Carter had shown that he was prepared to risk failure while attempting to release his fellow countrymen languishing in captivity. Many citizens denounced the fiasco while others patriotically rallied behind the President.

CHAPTER 40

PUGNACITY IN PERSPECTIVE

After subjecting each of the Presidents to the microscope, one may safely conclude that there was little or no demonstrable connection between the incumbent's party and his involvement in war, major or minor. Most of the scores of inconsequential incursions into foreign lands by the United States have come in response to the obligation resting squarely on the Chief Executive, regardless of party, to protect American lives and property in places—from the Greek islands to the shores of China—where such intervention was feasible.

The United States, regardless of the President's party, got involved in all of its major foreign wars primarily because a larger war already existed to suck in the Americans. This observation is obviously valid for the War of 1812 (the Napoleonic wars were raging); and the Mexican War (annexed Texas had not yet ended its quarrel with Mexico); the Spanish-American War (the Cuban insurrection was dragging drearily on); World War I of 1917-1918 (begun in 1914); the World War II of 1941-1945 (begun in 1939); the Korean War (a U.N. intervention in an ongoing civil war); and the Vietnam War (intervention in another civil war).

In all these instances the President, regardless of party, appears to have led the nation into hostilities for what he regarded, rightly or wrongly, as the national honor or interest, either or both. Most of the Presidents, including Polk and Lincoln, preferred peace to war, but they let the shooting come when they judged that the welfare of the United States would not be as well served by the quiet ways of peace. In some instances, notably after Eisenhower and Dulles had undermined the Geneva Accord of 1954 and laid the foundations for American intervention in Vietnam, the incumbent of the Republican party, Eisenhower, bequeathed a war to the luckless Presidents of the incoming Democratic party, in this case Kennedy and Johnson.

The hoary game, traditionally played by emperors and kings, of stirring up a foreign war to divert attention from domestic discontent has been generally avoided by American Presidents. One basic reason was that the major foreign war was already there, and America was caught in the middle. Madison, Polk, Lincoln, McKinley, Wilson, Franklin Roosevelt, Truman, and Johnson all tried first the quiet channels of diplomacy without success. In all these instances Congress formally declared the war, except in the case of Truman, who felt obligated to act directly under the U.N. aegis, and Johnson, who cleverly contrived to extract the ambiguous Tonkin Gulf resolution from Congress. The unanswerable question remains whether or not Johnson's Republican opponent, the so-called trigger-happy Barry Goldwater, would have used the iron fist, if elected, or even the nuclear bomb.

No President or group of Presidents and no political party can be stigmatized as hell-bent for war. The party out of power normally blasts the President for having got into war (as the Federalists did Madison) or for not fighting it with both fists (as right-wing Republicans did for the Democratic Johnson in the 1960s). But at the beginning of every major clash the President has had substantial public support, narrowly so with the War of 1812, but overwhelmingly so with the Mexican War, the Spanish-American War, World War I, World War II, the Korean War, and the Vietnam War (Gulf of Tonkin resolution). Opposition normally becomes more vocal and partisan as the going gets tougher and the victories, if any, grow fewer.

Much incidental evidence was found in this investigation to support the controversial view that the United States became a world power considerably before the Spanish-American War of

1898. In their official messages to Congress, several Presidents well before that date referred to the American republic as a great power, ranking with the mightiest of Europe. Naturally, these leaders were also much concerned with the nation's honor. Nearly a century before 1898 the United States engaged in scores of landings of Marines. Gunboat diplomacy and rescues in foreign lands were thus pursued, ranging from North Africa and Turkey, through much of Latin America, to the Islands of the Pacific and the teeming shores of East Asia. Except for Britain, France, and Spain, especially in pre-1812 days, what other power in the world, major or minor, was throwing its weight around in the Americas on land, at least on this scale? Or, for that matter, in the world? Where were the Chinese marines and warships protecting Chinese lives and property in California in the 1870s?

One glaring oddity is that the two Presidents who were probably the most pugnacious personally, Andrew Jackson (Democrat) and Theodore Roosevelt (Republican), were discreet enough or lucky enough to stay out of all major foreign wars. Ironically, Roosevelt (Republican) received the Nobel Peace Prize, as did Woodrow Wilson (Democrat), who led the nation with his eyes open into World War I. The two West Pointers, Grant and Eisenhower, both Republicans, were fortunate enough to stay out of all foreign wars, although both had several close calls. In such cases happenstance, combined with the pressures of public opinion, is obviously more significant than the political coloration of the occupant of the White House.

BIBLIOGRAPHY

Footnotes have been dispensed with in this volume primarily because the major episodes in United States history that relate to wars are matters of general knowledge. The present book is designed to pull together the material relating to recurrent conflict in United States history and to arrive at some conclusions regarding the pugnacity level of each of the Presidents.

Most of the general information included herein was gathered during a lifetime of studying and teaching American history, and from the preparation of about twenty other books, twenty additional revisions, and more than a score of footnoted articles. For this particular study, the author has worked anew through James D. Richardson's *Messages and Papers of the Presidents*, in the present case the twenty-volume edition. Important statements by Presidents are usually referred to herein by giving the date and nature of the message, which can readily be located by such designations.

One of the major contributions of this study is that it weaves into the story more than 160 armed interventions of the United States from 1798 to 1970. These occurred all over the world, mostly without a declaration of war, and have ranged from the eastern Mediterranean Sea to the China Sea. This lengthy listing was printed for the Committee on Foreign Affairs, 91st Congress, 2d session, and specially prepared by the Foreign Affairs Division, Legislative Reference Service, Library of Congress.

The list of books printed herewith, mostly biographies, contains much of the material that has been worked into the present volume.

These selections are listed without derogation of older but meritorious works. A much fuller but older listing appears in Thomas A. Bailey, *Presidential Greatness* (1966).

Chapter 1. George Washington (1789-1797)
James T. Flexner, *George Washington* (4 vols., 1965-72); D. S. Freeman, *George Washington* (7 vols., 1948-57); Forrest McDonald, *The Presidency of George Washington* (1974).

Chapter 2. John Adams (1797-1801)
Gilbert Chinard, *Honest John Adams* (1933); S. G. Kurtz, *The Presidency of John Adams* (1957); Page Smith, *John Adams* (2 vols., 1962).

Chapter 3. Thomas Jefferson (1801-1809)
Dumas Malone, *Jefferson and His Times* (5 vols., 1948-1974); M. D. Peterson, *Thomas Jefferson and the New Nation: A Biography* (1970).

Chapter 4. James Madison (1809-1817)
Irving Brent, *The Life of James Madison* (6 vols., 1948-1961) and *The Fourth President* (1970).

Chapter 5. James Monroe (1817-1825)
William P. Cresson, *James Monroe* (1946); Arthur Styron, *The Last of the Cocked Hats* (1945).

Chapter 6. John Quincy Adams (1825-1829)
Samuel F. Bemis, *John Quincy Adams and the Foundations of American Foreign Policy* (1949) and *John Quincy Adams and the Union* (1956).

Chapter 7. Andrew Jackson (1829-1837)
John S. Bassett, *The Life of Andrew Jackson* (2 vols., 1928); Marquis James, *The Life of Andrew Jackson* (2 vols., 1938).

Chapter 8. Martin Van Buren (1837-1841)
J. C. Curtis, *The Fox at Bay* (1970); R. V. Remini, *Martin Van Buren and the Making of the Democratic Party* (1959).

Chapter 9. William Henry Harrison (1841)
Freeman Cleaves, *Old Tippecanoe* (1939); Dorothy Goebel, *William Henry Harrison* (1926).

Chapter 10. John Tyler (1841-1845)
Oliver P. Chitwood, *John Tyler* (1939); R. J. Morgan, *A Whig Embattled: The Presidency Under John Tyler* (1954); Robert Seager, *And Tyler Too* (1963).

Chapter 11. James Knox Polk (1845-1849)
E. I. McCormac, *James K. Polk: A Political Biography* (1922); Charles A. McCoy, *Polk and the Presidency* (1960); Charles G. Sellers, *James K. Polk* (2 vols., 1957-1966).

Chapter 12. Zachary Taylor (1849-1850)
Brainerd Dyer, *Zachary Taylor* (1946); Holman Hamilton, *Zachary Taylor* (1966).

Chapter 13. Millard Fillmore (1850-1853)
W. E. Griffis, *Millard Fillmore* (1915); Robert J. Rayback, *Millard Fillmore* (1959).

Chapter 14. Franklin Pierce (1853-1857)
Roy F. Nichols, *Franklin Pierce: Young Hickory of the Granite Hills* (1958).

Chapter 15. James Buchanan (1857-1861)
Philip S. Klein, *President James Buchanan* (1962).

Chapter 16. Abraham Lincoln (1861-1865)
Richard N. Current, *The Lincoln Nobody Knows* (1958); J. C. Randall, *Lincoln the President* (4 vols., 1945-1955); Benjamin P. Thomas, *Abraham Lincoln* (1952).

Chapter 17. Andrew Johnson (1865-1869)
E. L. McKitrick, *Andrew Johnson and Reconstruction* (1960) and *Andrew Johnson, A Profile* (1969).

Chapter 18. Ulysses S. Grant (1869-1877)
Bruce Catton, *U. S. Grant and the American Military Tradition* (1954); W. B. Hesseltine, *Ulysses S. Grant, Politician* (1935).

Chapter 19. Rutherford B. Hayes (1877-1881)
Harry Barnard, *Rutherford B. Hayes and His America* (1954); H. J. Eckenrode, *Rutherford B. Hayes: Statesman of Reunion* (1930).

Chapter 20. James A. Garfield (1881)
R. G. Caldwell, *James A. Garfield, Party Chieftain* (1931); Allan Peskin, *Garfield* (1978); T. C. Smith, *The Life and Letters of James Abram Garfield* (2 vols., 1925).

Chapter 21. Chester A. Arthur (1881-1885)
G. F. Howe, *Chester A. Arthur* (1934); T. C. Reeves, *Gentleman Boss* (1975).

Chapter 22. Grover Cleveland (1885-1889)
H. S. Merrill, *Bourbon Leader: Grover Cleveland and*

the Democratic Party (1957); Allan Nevins, *Grover Cleveland: A Study in Courage* (1932).

Chapter 23. Benjamin Harrison (1889-1893)
Harry J. Sievers, *Benjamin Harrison* (3 vols., 1952-1968).

Chapter 24. Grover Cleveland (1893-1897)
See Chapter 22.

Chapter 25. William McKinley (1897-1901)
Margaret Leech, *In the Days of McKinley* (1959); H. W. Morgan, *William McKinley and His America* (1963).

Chapter 26. Theodore Roosevelt (1901-1909)
W. H. Harbaugh, *The Life and Times of Theodore Roosevelt* (1961); Edmund Morris, *The Rise of Theodore Roosevelt* (1979); Henry F. Pringle, *Theodore Roosevelt: A Biography* (1931).

Chapter 27. William Howard Taft (1909-1913)
P. E. Colletta, *The Presidency of William Howard Taft* (1973); Henry F. Pringle, *The Life and Times of William Howard Taft* (2 vols., 1939).

Chapter 28. Woodrow Wilson (1913-1921)
R. S. Baker, *Woodrow Wilson: Life and Letters* (8 vols., 1927-1939); Arthur Link, *Wilson* (5 vols., 1947-1965).

Chapter 29. Warren G. Harding (1921-1923)
R. K. Murray, *The Harding Era* (1969); Andrew Sinclair, *The Available Man* (1969).

Chapter 30. Calvin Coolidge (1923-1929)
Claude M. Fuess, *Calvin Coolidge* (1940); Donald R. McCoy, *Calvin Coolidge* (1967).

Chapter 31. Herbert Hoover (1929-1933)
E. E. Robinson and V. D. Bornet, *Herbert Hoover* (1975); Herbert Hoover, *Memoirs* (3 vols., 1951-1952).

Chapter 32. Franklin D. Roosevelt (1933-1945)
J. M. Burns, *Roosevelt: The Lion and the Fox* (1956) and *Roosevelt the Soldier of Freedom* (1970); Frank Freidel, *Franklin D. Roosevelt* (4 vols., 1952-1973); A. M. Schlesinger, Jr., *The Age of Roosevelt* (3 vols., 1957-1960).

Chapter 33. Harry S. Truman (1945-1953)
R. J. Donovan, *Conflict and Crisis: The Presidency of Harry S. Truman* (1977); Harry S. Truman, *Year of Decisions* (1955) and *Years of Trial and Hope* (1956).

Chapter 34. Dwight D. Eisenhower (1953–1961)
D. D. Eisenhower, *Mandate for Change, 1953–1956* (1963) and *Waging Peace, 1956–1961* (1965).

Chapter 35. John F. Kennedy (1961–1963)
Arthur M. Schlesinger, Jr., *A Thousand Days* (1965); R. J. Watton, *Cold War and Counter-Revolution: The Foreign Policy of John F. Kennedy* (1972).

Chapter 36. Lyndon B. Johnson (1963–1969)
Eric Goldman, *The Tragedy of Lyndon Johnson* (1969); L. B. Johnson, *The Vantage Point* (1971).

Chapter 37. Richard M. Nixon (1969–1974)
R. M. Nixon, *RN: The Memoirs of Richard Nixon* (1978); Gary Wills, *Nixon Agonistes: The Crisis of the Self-Made Man* (1970).

Chapter 38. Gerald R. Ford (1974–1977)
G. R. Ford, *A Time to Heal* (1979); Clark Mollenhoff, *The Man Who Pardoned Nixon* (1976).

Chapter 39. James Earl Carter, Jr. (1977–)
J. E. Carter, *Why Not the Best?* (1975); David Kucharsky, *The Man from Plains* (1976).

INDEX

Chester A. Arthur
1881-1885

Grover Cleveland
1885-1889
1893-1897

Benjamin Harrison
1889-1893

William McKinley
1897-1901

Theodore Roosevelt
1901-1909

William H. Taft
1909-1913

Woodrow Wilson
1913-1921

Warren G. Harding
1921-1923

Calvin Cooledge
1923-1929